Prior to Meaning

Prior to Meaning

The Protosemantic
and Poetics

STEVE MCCAFFERY

Northwestern

University Press

Evanston,

Illinois

Northwestern University Press
Evanston, Illinois 60208-4210

ISBN 0-8101-1789-4 (cloth)
ISBN 0-8101-1790-8 (paper)

Library of Congress Cataloging-in-Publication Data
McCaffery, Steve
    Prior to meaning : the protosemantic and poetics /
    Steve McCaffery.
        p. cm. — (Avant-garde and modernism studies)
    Includes bibliographical references and index.
    ISBN 0-8101-1789-4 (alk. paper) —
    ISBN 0-8101-1790-8 (pbk. : alk. paper)
        1. Canadian poetry — 20th century — History and criticism —
    Theory, etc.   2. American poetry — 20th century — History and
    criticism — Theory, etc.   3. Experimental poetry — History and
    criticism.   4. English language — Semantics.   5. Semantics.
    6. Poetics.   I. Title.   II. Series.
    PR9190.5 .M38 2001
    811'.509971 — dc21   2001001062

Schlage Geld aus jedem Fehler.

Wittgenstein

Contents

Illustrations

Acknowledgments

First and foremost, my sincere gratitude goes to Erica Federman for convincing me this project could be undertaken and to the State University of New York at Buffalo for bestowing on me the John Logan Fellowship, under which auspices much of this work was written and finalized.

To Charles Bernstein, Robert Creeley, Ray Federman, and Susan Howe, sincere thanks for their general input on the project and for making my tenure as John Logan Fellow as cordial and sybaritic as it was demanding. And thank you Scott Pound for the many affable and stimulating conversations in transit between Toronto and Buffalo. Further thanks go to Robert Bertholf and Mike Basinski for their generosity in showing me some special items in a very special Special Collections and giving me an office and library away from home; to Johanna Drucker, Deirdre Lynch, Jerome McGann, Brian McHale, Marjorie Perloff, and Jill Robbins for keen comments on specific chapters. My gratitude also goes to Susan Harris, Susan Betz, and the rest of the editorial staff at Northwestern for their diligence and skill in generally improving the prose style and format. Chapter 7 would not have materialized in its present form without my several years of valued collaboration with Jed Rasula in "accidental research" that culminated in our anthology *Imagining Language*. Final thanks are sent beyond words to Cuisle Mo Chroí, whose patience, emotional support, challenge, reality checks, proofing, and editorial and stylistic suggestions have made this a far better book than it would have been otherwise.

An early draft of chapter 1 was presented at "The Ends of Theory" conference at Wayne State University in 1990. A revised version appeared in *The Ends of Theory*, ed. J. Herron, D. Huson, R. Pudaloff, and R. Strozier (Detroit: Wayne State University Press, 1996).

A version of chapter 2 was presented on the panel "Virtual Philosophy: Nietzsche and Postmodern Poiesis" at the eighteenth conference of the International Association for Philosophy and Literature at the University of Alberta, Edmonton, in 1994. It was subsequently presented in a revised form on the panel "What Is a Minor Science? Applied 'Pataphysics and the Stakes of Discourse" at the American Comparative Literature Association convention at the University of Georgia, Athens, in 1995. A revised version appeared in *Open Letter* 9, no. 7 (winter 1997), pp. 11–22.

A draft of chapter 3 was presented at "The Recovery of the Public World: A Conference in Honour of the Poetry and Poetics of Robin Blaser" at

Simon Fraser University in 1995. It was subsequently published in a revised form in the Gilles Deleuze special issue of *Discourse* 20, no. 3 (ed. Réda Bensmaïa and Jalal Toufic) (1998), pp. 99–122, and later in *The Recovery of the Public World: Essays on Poetics in Honour of Robin Blaser,* ed. Charles Watts and Edward Byrne (Vancouver: Talonbooks, 1999), pp. 373–93.

Earlier versions of chapter 4 appeared in *Ellipsis* 1, no. 1 (spring 1990), pp. 37–47, and in expanded form in the *Fragmente 4,* pp. 48–59, "After Modernism" issue (Oxford, 1990).

Chapter 7 was presented in an early draft at Assembling Alternatives: An International Poetry Conference, University of New Hampshire, 1996.

Chapter 9 was presented in an earlier form on the "New Poetries in Canada" panel at the 109th Modern Language Association convention in Toronto, 1993.

An earlier version of chapter 10 appeared in *Close Listening: Poetry and the Performed Word,* ed. Charles Bernstein (Oxford: Oxford University Press, 1996), pp. 162–77. Incorporated sections formed part of a different essay, "From Phonic to Sonic: The Emergence of the Audio-Poem" published in *Sound Effects: Acoustical Technologies in Modern and Postmodern Writing,* ed. Adalaide Morris (Chapel Hill: University of North Carolina Press, 1996), pp. 149–68.

Chapter 11 first appeared in my *North of Intention: Critical Writings 1973–86* (New York: Roof Books, 1986) and in a revised, expanded form in *North Dakota Quarterly* 55, no. 4 (1987), pp. 185–201.

A version of Chapter 12 appeared in *PreTexts* 6, no. 2, University of Cape Town, 1997, pp. 167–90.

My thanks and grateful acknowledgments extend to all of the above magazines, journals, and books that initially published the pieces. I also wish to extend sincere thanks to the following people for permission to use their material:

Carla Harryman for permission to quote from *Under the Bridge;* copyright © 1980 by Carla Harryman.
Karen Mac Cormack for permission to quote from *Quirks & Quillets;* copyright © 1991 by Karen Mac Cormack.
Jackson Mac Low for permission to quote from *Stanzas for Iris Lezak;* copyright © 1971 by Jackson Mac Low.
Tom Phillips for permission to reproduce material from *A Humument;* copyright © 1980, 1987, 1997 by Tom Phillips, London.

Introduction

Prior to Meaning studies the ways in which language behaves rather than how it's designed to function. It traces a limited autonomy of the written mark at a level both beneath and around the semantic. Collectively the twelve essays index a general shift in my thinking away from a Saussurean model of language (*langue/parole,* signifier/signified) to a different set of provocations found in Prigogine and Stengers, Deuleuze and Guattari, Alfred Jarry, Sade, Leibniz, Lucretius, and in the "other" Saussure, the Saussure of the paragrammic notebooks—provocations that led me to consider writing as a material scene of forces. Gathering together a decade of work, the collection is deliberately nonsystematic. Discrete studies in themselves, the chapters link together by tracing several interlacements along a broad conceptual plane I've termed the protosemantic.

Three other conceptual threads are presidential on this plane: the clinamen, the monad-fold, and the dissipative structure. Like Kristeva's genotext, the protosemantic is more a process than a material thing; a multiplicity of forces which, when brought to bear on texts (or released in them), unleash a combinatory fecundity that includes those semantic jumps that manifest within letter shifts and verbal recombinations, and the presyntactic violations determining a word's position: rupture, reiteration, displacement, reterritorialization. It is also the invisible in writing, that which looks at us without actually appearing itself. Like the paragram, it remains invisible but is already there, establishing an uncanny position from which we are scrutinized by language. The protosemantic is also a severe and persistent alterity because of its minuscule, elusive, yet omnipresent nature and is accessed through nonsystematic uses and noncommunicative functions of reading, speech, and writing. Mostly though, the protosemantic informs and structures the domain of "betweens," and the perplications produced in transits, flights, and deracinations.

If a tangible contemporary poetics emerges from these threads, it would probably comprise a synthesis of force, kinesis, and perturbation; a poetics of preestablished alterities but also of the retinal grounded more in reading than writing. What I gesture toward is a material poetics of unstable linguistic systems, like the poetics of turbulence hinted at in Charles Olson's claim that "[t]he real life in regular verse is an irregular / movement underneath" (Olson and Pound 1975, 10). In this respect, the book extends reflections in *North of Intention*. There, I considered the paragram as a transphenomenal and ineluctable aspect of all combinatory phonetic writing systems. Here, I reenvision it as a key factor in formulating protosemantic subsystems within the written. The paragram authenticates a wild postulate: that the virtual is not the inverse image of the actual but the enjoyment of the latter's own self-resonances. Moreover, if "[f]ixity is a function of power," as Houston Baker claims (Baker 1984, 202), then the paragram has its own sophisticated sociopolitical ramifications. (I consider some of these in my analysis of Johnson's *Dictionary* in chapter 6.) Pertaining as paragrams do to hidden, nonlinear relations within texts, their disposition commits all writing to the status of a partly self-organizing system; they are thus unquestionably not only major agents of linguistic instability and change but also advance a protosemantic challenge to the smooth instrumentality of linguistic parlance. A modern-day Addison might label paragrammic disruption as the negative dialectics of the false sublime, but of interest to me is how such turbulence and nonlinearity can be exploited through nonconventional reading habits. Ronald Johnson and Lucette Finas (chapter 1), Charles Olson (chapter 4), Jackson Mac Low (chapter 10), and William Burroughs, John Cage, and Tom Phillips (chapter 12) all appear here as contemporary writers-of-their-unconventional-readings of others' writings. These I connect in chapters 5 and 6 to a richer genealogy. Two centuries earlier, Richard Bentley devised his own delirious method of textual recension based on the principle of approximate homonomy, installing a homophonic saturnalia and a dizzying array of bifurcations into the semantic univocity of *Paradise Lost*. For his part, Dr. Johnson, in that florilegial multiple theme park known as his *Dictionary,* ends up constructing the conceptual, if not ideological, opposite of Saint Paul's Cathedral—a chiasmic, decentered, lexical edifice of preexistent part-objects. In an exemplary display of sovereign negativity, their near contemporary, Peter Walkden Fogg (see chapter 7), offers his own transcribed erasure of a poem by Hayley as a form of "wordless music" that appears precessionally as the limit text of this practice of written-reading. All of these writers share a predilection for secondary discourses arrived at via annexation, violence, and alteration. I don't offer this fact to initiate speculation on a tantalizing "parasitic sublime" but rather to underscore the highly complex dissipative structures that language and literature truly are.

To return to my three conceptual tools: The clinamen, or atomic swerve, derives from classical particle physics as outlined by Lucretius and earlier by Democritus and Epicurus. The concept of the monad I take from the eighteenth-century philosopher Leibniz and its Deleuzean modification as the fold. The dissipative structure is a concept developed in contemporary nonequilibrium thermodynamics. As the latter term is more recent and less familiar than the others, let me give a brief outline of its form and consequence.

Ilya Prigogine and Isabelle Stengers are the founders of the science of nonequilibrium thermodynamics and were a formative influence on Deleuze's and Guattari's work in the late 1980s. Philosophically speaking, they escort ontology out of its traditional discursive framework and place it in the turbulence of systemic complexities. In their radical identification of being with becoming, they pose a profound irritation to philosophy's interpretive control over Dasein. In effect, Prigogine and Stengers offer a metaphysics of process rather than of presence, challenging philosophy to open up to radically alterior forces that disturb the conceptual stability of being. Avoiding the centrality of human being in this way might encourage reflection on the protosemantics within language. It might be said that Prigogine locates "identity" in verbs, not nouns, in uncompromising action, temporality, disequilibrium, and change. Physics meets metaphysics not in the latter's beyondness but at the former's point of bifurcation where being emerges as becoming. Prigogine and Stengers, incidentally, call the scientific period from Newton to quantum physics the science of being. Their work discloses the vexatious problem of where to place chaos in the passage of becoming. Is it the birth of order or its breakdown? Their famous dictum that the path of self-organizing systems is one from chaos to order might be taken as an overly deterministic and ultimately conservative claim, but my own interest lies less in the accuracy (or otherwise) of their theory than in testing its usefulness as a conceptual instrument in poetics and the general domain of writing. Most stimulating to me is their contention that complex stable systems carry within them unstable subsystems that pressure the dominant system into disequilibrium and expenditure. (Their term for such complex systems is "dissipative structures.") At a maximal point the system bifurcates into either a higher complex organization or into chaos. Such bifurcation points (transported and renamed by Deleuze and Guattari "schizzes" and "lines of flight") function in a manner similar to Lucretius's clinamen as a force toward difference and morphological modification. As the letter-clinamen can produce a novel word or a nonsensical syntagm (see chapter 2 for a tangible enactment), so a bifurcation can precipitate a dissipative structure into either a higher order of complexity or complete disarray. I embrace for poetics the dissipative structure as a new episteme of becoming whose nature and behavior can be tersely stated by way of the following postulate: identity is what complex systems escape from. (I investigate the protosemantic notion of a "becoming meaning" in chapter 9.)

I choose in two chapters to develop the antisocial ramifications in Prigogine's and Stenger's concepts: in the singular ontology of Leibniz's monad (chapter 3) and in the concept-type of Sade's libertine (chapter 8). The clinamen, as stated, is a differentiating effect brought on by a singular agency. However, the monad, and its contemporaneous link to plication, radically challenges socially based notions of the outside. Monadic singularity is exemplary of a noninteractive system—what Prigogine and Stengers call a "hypnon." The monad, the clinamen, and the libertine are similarly the invocations of singularities, staking their claim against the faulty collectivity of encoded community.

Describing the emergence of "automatic poetry" at the Café de la Terrasse, Hans Arp makes the consequential claim that in poetry, as in nature, "a tiny particle is as beautiful and important as a star" (quoted in Richter 1965, 30–31). Automatic poetry aside, the clinamen helps formulate a Poetics of the Particle. If the whole is no longer atomized and if atoms are traced or tracked along their transits, the result is a micropoetics of delirium. Particle poetics is unquestionably latent in the atomistic linguistics of Lucretius. The clinamen as a protosemantic force is a singular interaction between virtual force and actual form that creates by modifying its place in a preexistent structure. Marx thought it emblematic of free will; Deleuze and Guattari of desire; and, in speaking of man as "a particle inserted in unstable and tangled groups" (Bataille 1988b, 84), Bataille ekphrastically captures the socio-ontic aspect of the clinamen. But in its mythogemic guise it appears as the subaltern deity that errs, inducing shifts along fault lines, ensuring that there is no semantic passage without detour, and introducing noise into systems. Speaking of a "Jesuitical" seizure of the signifier Lyotard approaches the crucial relation of clinamen-deviance to writing's protosemantic, uncertain motility: "to love inscription not because it communicates and contains, but through what its production necessitates, not because it channels, but because it drifts" (1993b, 19). Jean-Jacques Lecercle describes language as a "Labovian 'system,' [which] far from being defined by its constants and homogeneity, is characterized by immanent, continuous variability—variable units and optional rules" (1990, 184), but in the clinamen's world volatility must supplement—even displace—variability. Its protosemantic disturbances ensure that "language," "meaning," and "information" are bound enduringly together in an asymmetric and volatile relation. The clinamen is the being-of-movement of an atom, apparent to itself only in the disappearance of stabilities. It is not a move within or toward transcendence but an event inside the atomic quotidian, and in its confluence of unpredictability with inevitability it enjoys the status of a law. The poetic significance of this *lex atomica* derives from the innovative analogy Lucretius draws (in *De rerum natura*) between atoms and letters in which cosmic speculation is articulated onto both a theory of language and a protogrammatology (see chapter 2).

If letters are to words what atoms are to bodies—heterogenous, deviant, collisional, and transmorphic—then we need earnestly to rethink what guarantees stability to verbal signs. (Lucretius's analogy provides, of course, the essential link between nonequilibrium thermodynamics and the incalculable errancy of the written.) In our age of incipient miniaturization, it might be apt to return to the rumble beneath the word. There's a stubborn, even tautological, literalness about that protosemantic element we call the letter. And against Agamben's insistence that Language is always "a dead letter" (1991, 108), I wish to argue that Language is frequently the struggle to contain the errant vivacity of "a living letter." Barthes renders the precarious entente between letter and word in a characteristically elegant passage. "Such is the alphabet's power: to rediscover a kind of natural state of the letter. For the letter, if it is alone, is innocent: the Fall begins when we align letters to make them into words" (1985b, 119). Innocent, perhaps, but letters also have a puzzling amorous dimension; they are, as Anne Carson informs us, "the mechanism of erotic paradox, at once connective and separative, painful and sweet" (1985, 92)—and we should bear in mind that Lucretius dedicates his poem to Venus. Conceived as atoms, letters intrude themselves as protosemantic events strictly defined by their dynamics. Being perpetually and unpredictably volatile, they introduce deviance as the basic rule of all grammata. A condition obtains not of collective signification but of particulate, insular driftings that lead to those Möbian complexities Lyotard insists are "[n]ot a matter of separation, but on the contrary, of movement, of displaceability on the spot" (1993b, 16). From their traditional conception as the minimal thinkable unit, words give way under the pressure of Lucretian linguistics to a different characterization as the provisional container of protosemantic animations, holding in temporary check a fecund, unstable lettristic micropedia. Seen this way, texts are not deficient but paragrammically abundant. (Unlike Iser, I see poems not as presenting gaps for a reader to remedy, but as informational excesses that in part impale and in part escape their readers.)

Today our immanent hegemony of informatics—electronic, disjunctive, digital—finds itself enveloped in a telling aquatic metaphor of its own making. We say we "surf the net," poised on a mouse pad like a modern-day cybernetic version of Basho's frog, primed to jump-click into a pool of endless, concentric data waves. Prior to Lucretius, Epicurus declared this datatopia to be a void whose wave motility comprises a downfall of atoms with stochastic inclinations. The swerve from the line in Greek particle theory presages the disjunctive potency of the mouse click. An inclination out of line equals birth, birth itself being a particle becoming wave. So how does this relate to semiogenesis? Can language be envisaged post-Saussure as a particle-wave economy in which the aleatory interactions of *parole* enfold in *langue* and resuscitate the turbolinguistics of Lucretius? The clinamen certainly lends itself to poetic consideration. In Ronald Johnson, John Cage, Tom Phillips, and Jackson Mac Low, it manifests as a deviation from a grammatical and linear reader-consumption to a paragrammic reader-writing. The common practice of these writers is to follow lines of flight and release a surprising other in sameness. Central to their methods are protosemantic ways of exposing virtualities; the application of an optical clinamen; a parenklitic reading that deviates from a consecutive, linear engagement with a syntagmatic chain to open up the virtual inside the actual. Even the conservative Dr. Johnson reveals lexicography to be a tempestuous, self-defeating engagement with the errant clinama that inevitably occur in the practice of citation. (Bakhtinians might treat all these works as fundamentally dialogic, and disciples of Serres as fundamentally parasitic, but what I emphasize is their common condition as organized systems containing turbulent subsystems.) In Sade's figure of the libertine we find a socioethical clinamen represented so forcefully that it questions the very ground of our ethics and morality.

Though my third tool, the monad-fold, is only addressed locally in chapter 2, the conceptual presence of plication is omnipresent (perhaps most intensely in the grammatological schemes of Helmont and Fogg [chapter 7] and in Johnson's folding of citations into his lexical series in the *Dictionary*). Folds and the clinamen together make available to poetics an alternative terrain of forces and readily available differentiators in the kinetics of volition and singular sublexical activities. Both the fold and the clinamen are agents, present everywhere, introducing instability into any steady concept but never vulnerable to the status of universal epistemes. Moreover, like the paragram, atoms and monads have an obvious articulation onto the social sphere, sharing a common relation of variant force fields between bodies. In this they stand in sharp contrast to Barthes's and Althusser's Sausurrean-derived, linguistically controlled explanations of the subject.

Differance is a nonconcept historically positioned by Derrida at the terminus of the metaphysics of presence, but like Lucretius's theory of atomic deviation, Derridean grammatology perforce reduces to a foundational reliance on the granular. Contemporary science, however, offers revisionary ratios to this concept. René Thom, for instance, reveals how morphogenesis is not the birth of grain from grain but the practice of infinitesimal foldings called catastrophes (Thom 1975). There are contradictory propositions and questions in this forced alliance between the fold and the clinamen that I leave, perhaps provocatively, unanswered. How, for instance, can the plicatory monad be reconciled to the movement of the atom in its vertical fall through a nonsite? And how can we reconcile the digital atom in a void and its production of a veritable *ars combinatoria* with the analog nature of the fold and its plenum? Jarry engages such momentary conjunctions of discrepants by appealing to an astronomical term syzygy: it's the syzygy of atom and monad, space and plenum that I offer as neither an aporia, a difficulty, nor a transgression of the law of noncontradiction, but as a wedding of the incompossible.

Deploying this seemingly bizarre conceptual apparatus allows me to consider poems and texts as dynamic structures containing within them subsystemic turbulences, such as the paragram and homophone (exemplars of the clinamen and fold respectively), and the disruptive logics of citation, collage, and dictation. As such, *Prior to Meaning* is less a contribution to contemporary poetics per se than a staging of concepts, issues, and implications that both inform and contaminate the discursive propositions (and repressions) ineluctably present in all poetics. And it warns that any discourse of poetics is doomed to encounter the nature and virtualities of certain systems of writing.

Perhaps this latter fact encourages a marriage of grammatology and poetics. I initially toyed with the idea of calling this collection *Grammatology and Poetics,* and several chapters thread a broad frontier where poetics and writing systems conjoin, especially in the imagination's intermittent encounters with scripts and the protosemantic elements residing in notation. Olson's early fascination with Mayan hieroglyphs, his seduction by their impenetratable, uninterpretable alterity (examined in chapter 4) is cannily reminiscent of two earlier nonoccidental fascinations: Athanasius Kircher's and William Warburton's fastidious conjectures on the xenographic impact of Egyptian hieroglyphs as a silent protoscript. (I might add to this Ezra Pound's attraction, via Fenollosa's theories, to the Chinese ideogram.) Certainly, a major concern of this book is to reveal some of the factual limitations in Derrida's version of logocentrism, and chapter 7 offers several examples that contest the now dominant opinion on the speech-writing binary as a dyadic opposition in which full speech is valorized over writing.

This collection is also in a way about material bodies: sonic bodies, libertine bodies, proprioceptive bodies, bodies both within and without writing, and most especially microbodies. Contrary to David Porush's conviction that literature has typically had little use for the microscopic except as it offers up some interesting metaphors (in Hayles 1991, 57), I stress a need to shift attention to those lesser bodies and hope that *Prior to Meaning* provides material and evidence to warrant a serious consideration of both a residual and a possible micropoeisis.

It's now well known through Niels Bohr and quantum physics that in the infinitely minute world of the atomic the very act of observation produces photonic impacts that profoundly unsettle the phenomenon being observed. This microphysical fact of non-neutral observation underlies as much Ronald Johnson's micropoetic written-reading of *Paradise Lost,* as Richard Bentley's delirious recension of the same poem (in chapters 1 and 5, respectively), and Tom Phillips's selective deletions of Mallock's *A Human Document* (chapter 12). All offer readings that similarly unsettle a text at hand.

In many ways *Prior to Meaning* ramifies and celebrates a single yet resonant declaration in *Finnegans Wake:* "The proteiform graph itself is a polyhedron of scripture" (Joyce 1950, 107). Joyce captures in this single phrase the nature of grammatological dissipative structures. The protosemantic is in part the modality of the proteiform graph, that sublexical, alphabetic, and phonic domain of recombinant infinity that is the Western alphabet in operation and whose quintessential disequilibrium can be specified as the excess of information over meaning. In a real sense, then, this book should be read as an earnest cartographical contribution toward mapping out the grammatological context of *Finnegans Wake*. It's clear from the works I study that my sense of what constitutes poetry is categorically nongeneric. I consider the novels of Sade genuinely poetic—Bentley's editorial practice and Johnson's lexicography equally so. Indeed, I hope that the strange affinities that emerge and the dissipative structures I assemble will contribute to an ongoing unsettling of any stable notion as to what both "contemporary" and "poetics" denote.

Prior to Meaning

I don't want to enter this risky world of discourse; I want nothing to do
with it insofar as it is decisive and final; I would like to feel it all around me,
calm transparent, profound, infinitely open, with others responding to my
expectations, and truths emerging, one by one. All I want is to allow myself
to be borne along, within it, and by it, a happy wreck.

—Foucault[1]

1. Insufficiency of Theory to Poetical Economy

Foucault's words offer a seductive, utopian topography in which to situate
pluralistic, theoretical endeavors. With its hedonistic stress and desire for
an amniotic provisionality to discourse, the passage suggests that theory's
motivation to mastery and epistemic finality is the prime obstacle to a fluid
motion through a smooth space of praxis. Certainly, the "happy wreck"
that Foucault embraces stands in sharp contrast to the self-investment and
motivation underlying the procedures of literary theory, whose willful drive
is toward the annexation of cultural works via interpretational and explanatory strategies, and the consequent curation of their meanings.[2] Salutary,
if only for its shock value, is Julia Kristeva's description of this theoretical
subject.

> The product of an ambiguous social attitude, the "theoretical" subject
> sets himself up with even more power in this situation inasmuch as he
> will mime the dissolution of all positions. The empty, hollow space he
> represents by the very fact of its representation, acts as a magnetic pole
> and experiences itself as such. This subject of enunciation either says
> nothing or else dissects his speech for the sole purpose of becoming
> the focal point where all other signifying systems converge. One could
> say that his discourse becomes hysteric only to position himself better
> within the place of impregnable transference—dominating, capturing,
> and monopolizing everything within the discourse's obsessive retreat,
> which is haunted by power/impotence. (1984, 97)

This coupling of power to its negative dependence recalls Hegel's famous analysis of empowerment in the master-slave relationship in which the self-consciousness of the master (in the case at hand, the field of theory) is necessarily defined by the slave's own relational status. The essence of the slave is to exist for another, while the self-consciousness of the master depends upon the slave's own dependence on him. Conceived as the object of a master-theory, the poem-slave guarantees a stubborn Hegelian sediment to the most un-Hegelian theoretical endeavors. Appropriation is philosophically structured by a transcendental partition separating theory from its object field, thereby allowing its activation across the difference and simultaneously binding theory to its object in the very affirmation of their separateness. This is hardly a novel insight—in fact, this entailment via Hegel's dialectic pertains to all dyadic oppositions and to any transitive practice. Yet passed unnoticed, or bracketed as unproblematic, it inscribes a serious blind spot in theory's self-questioning, and Lyotard for one has pointed to the dangerous presupposition of the rules of its own discourse that permits theory to elude self-scrutiny (Lyotard 1988a, xiv).

Theories, of course, are constructed upon a second-order system of concepts, making use of ancillary discourses that frequently elude analysis. It's common knowledge that structuralism employs a second-order system of organization derived from certain concepts and categories of Saussurean linguistics. A fact less known is that structuralism co-opts a precursory system from Viollet-le-Duc's *Dictionnaire de l'architecture francaise*. This is no innocent deployment but a subtle derivation of its conceptual base via a dense genealogy of architectural models and metaphors that include both Augustinian and Thomistic theologies.[3] Marc Angenet exposes the institutional distortions of Saussure by the structuralists and the historical complexities of their ascendancy in France, citing structuralism's failure to attain the status of an episteme and enumerating its ad hoc deployments of Saussure's terminology and concepts as a syncretic formulation to bind together numerous competitive (and often incompatible) intellectual investments. Through the 1960s, Angenet argues, Saussure's terminology functioned as a "phraseological cement" binding together basically heterogeneous and even conflicting interests. Saussure's comparatively late entry into French intellectual circles is also remarked.

Saussure's paradigm took forty years to travel from Geneva to Paris. French linguistics at the time, under the hegemonic influence of Antoine Meillet, opposed [*sic*] insuperable obstacles to Saussure's acceptance and discussion. That is why Saussure migrated *eastward,* as it were, and found a first institutional landing point in Russia during the first world war . . . Saussure came to be polemically criticized and rejected in the late twenties (but at least understood in a pertinent light) by the major literary scholar of our century, Mikhail M. Bakhtin. . . . By the time it becomes *de rigeur* to read and draw inspiration from Saussure in France, it is clear that this Saussure is bound to be read through his cosmopolitan tribulations and through layers of superimposed mediations. (Angenet 1984, 153–54)[4]

Theory's mandate to critical annexation has an inaugural Platonic endorsement. In the *Apology,* Socrates argues that poets are the worst interpreters of their own work:

Well, gentlemen, I hesitate to tell you the truth, but it must be told. It is hardly an exaggeration to say that any of the bystanders could have explained these poems better than their actual authors. So I soon made up my mind about the poets too. I decided that it was not wisdom that enabled them to write their poetry, but a kind of instinct or inspiration, such as you find in seers and prophets who deliver all their sublime messages without knowing in the least what they mean. (*Apology* 22c, in Plato 1961)

If Socrates' assessment is correct, then the price of creative primacy is the installation of that transcendental rule of the subject-object partitions that Hegel remarks upon. With the *Apology,* the control of meaning enters wholly the readerly-critical sphere, the binding status of the poem now being that of its material inertia and the concomitant depreciation of the poet to irrationality and silence. In this Socratic exclusion the poet cannot theorize, and since the matrix of the poetic is placed in an inspirational, automatic emission, the poem itself is rendered static in the nondiscursive domain of an object-field.

The *Apology* anticipates many of the claims of cultural modernity: the fallacy of intention, the death of the author, the privilege of readership; while in assigning initial creativity to "a kind of instinct or inspiration," it premonishes uncannily Kristeva's concept of the prelinguistic process that articulates ephemeral and unstable structures—a process considered by Kristeva to be the underlying foundation of language—and which she terms *genotext* (1984, 86).[5] In addition, the *Apology* carries the far more important of Plato's two poetic banishments. Called for in the *Republic* is a literal expulsion of subjects, functions, and bodies as a practical deportation from the great republic. But in the *Apology*, it is the axiomatic separation of creator from semantic determination and from all rational procedures that is called for. Poetry (in a manner Foucault later demonstrates of madness) is defined, enclosed, and then silenced. After the *Apology*, the poet is committed to the domain of semantic heterology.[6] The persistence of this ostracization is worth remarking. For instance, Levinas comparably banishes poetry and art to the realm of the irresponsible, claiming that they elevate "in a world of initiative and responsibility, a dimension of evasion" (1987, 12). The critical stance before such work is the responsible act of integrating "the inhuman work of the artist into the human world" (Levinas 1987, 12). In Benjamin's early thinking the critical task occupies a similarly exalted position at the convergence of artistic, religious, and philosophic domains, enjoying the panoptic perspective where "the essential indivisible unity of all three vantage points can be grasped" (Wolin 1994, 31).

To address theory's insufficiency to some poetical economies involves approaching theoretical practice from the vantage of its thresholds and fully exploiting the negativity of its Hegelian sediment. The potential of poetical economies here is to address theory itself from their own material resistances; consequently not to argue against Plato but beyond him. The concomitant challenge to theoretical disciplines is to redirect their reflexivity into a self-examination staged immanently within their own procedures, addressing those areas of the nondiscursive that theory must leave free, as well as those aspects that escape of necessity through theory's apertures.[7]

Citing the works of Lautréamont, Mallarmé, Joyce, and Artaud as exemplary, Kristeva revisions writing as "textual practice" involving a subject-in-process for its production and maintaining resistance to all binding theoretical annexation. Textual practice threatens all signification and representation through its partly a-symbolic constitution. Issuing from a "split" subject divided between conscious and unconscious drives, such texts involve an oscillating tension between two discrete signifying processes that Kristeva famously terms the "symbolic" and the "semiotic." The latter carries the burden of instinctual drives and forces that affect, but do not support, a social transmission. Despite the strictures of a sociolect, the semiotic is disposed in specific detectable aspects of language, especially its rhythmic and sonic intricacies. The symbolic process, by contrast, involves a disposition toward the normative modes of signification: grammar, syntax, sentence integration, and the covering rules that guarantee unproblematic, intersubjective communication. (Needless to say, textual practice valorizes the former, semiotic disposition.)

Theory (demanding a construction by way of categorical abstractions articulated onto the symbolic) requires a molar stability that renders a lasting relationship with processual textual practices incompatible. Kristeva's revisioned writing involves "giving up the lexical, syntactic, and semantic operation of deciphering, and instead tracing the path of their production" (1984, 103). If theory is to be accommodated, it must be as a provisional operation passed through and finally jettisoned. To solve theory's own metalinguistic dilemma, all theoretical agendas must be replaced by heuristic ones. All attempts to stabilize discursively (by hypothesis, explication, or description) a radically unstable practice are abandoned, and the negativity previously "swallowed" into theory is released into instinctual play (96).

Kristevan textual practice stands in healthy contrast to Murray Krieger's critical assimilation: "This poem before me—as an alien 'other,' outside me and my consciousness—imposes upon me to make it no longer 'other'" (1976, 203), and his binding of textual heterogeneity by appeal to the aesthetic paradigm: "The poem unifies itself aesthetically around its metaphoric and its countermetaphoric tendencies, even as its oppositions remain thematically unresolved. It is, then, self-demystifying, but as such it does not fall outside the symbolist aesthetic, at its most critically aware, its most self-conscious, is able to demand: nothing less than a waking dream" (1981, 22). Though a significant improvement on Krieger's aestheticism, Kristeva's formulation is not entirely satisfactory. At its outset, textual practice is reductive, inaugurating a vanguard writing predestined to cultural marginality. More seriously, it fails to offer a radical "reader practice;" a practice that would involve a split reader-subject-in-process of equal status as the writer, who could effect more radical encounters with meaning and its loss than tracing a prior textual practice. Additionally, Kristeva's prelinguistic or protosemantic concerns commit her to supporting a certain psychic essentialism, while her intrasubjective notion of the textual relation does not allow an approach to writing and reading as differing logics of action.[8]

Certeau delineates two such logics in the strategy and the tactic. "I call a 'strategy' the calculus of force-relationships which become possible when a subject of will and power (a proprietor, an enterprise, a city, a scientific institution) can be isolated from an 'environment.' A strategy assumes a place that can be circumscribed as proper and thus serve as the basis for generating relations with an exterior distinct from it (competitors, adversaries, 'clienteles,' 'targets,' or 'objects' of research" (1984, xix). A tactic, on the other hand, is "a calculus which cannot count on a 'proper' (a spatial or institutional) localization nor thus on a borderline distinguishing the other as a visible totality" (xix). Deprived of the spatial advantage of a base, tactics take the form of temporal, nomadic, and necessarily provisional actions: "a tactic depends upon time—it is always on the watch for opportunities that must be seized 'on the wing.' Whatever it wins, it does not keep. It must constantly manipulate events in order to turn them into 'opportunities' " (xix). Tactics require "a logic articulated on situations and the will of others" and must "produce without capitalizing, that is, without taking control over time" (xx).

Certeau remains alert to theory as an operational partition carrying a discrete practice of discourse (i.e., a regulated specialization) whose main effect is the maintenance of social reason. The strategic nature of theoretical practice can be readily inferred from Certeau's aforementioned words. Enjoying the spatial advantage of a base in the "proper" (being both an institution and an enterprise) theory generates relations with its numerous fields, intervening in the everyday drift of reading to recover it from temporal erosion and forgetfulness. Deploying reading as a tactic results in something quite different, closer to a loss or slippage of the text in hand and which Certeau likens to poaching as a practice of insinuation and mutation:

> a silent production: the drift across the page, the metamorphosis of the text effected by the wandering eyes of the reader, the improvisation and expectation of meanings inferred from a few words, leaps over written spaces in an ephemeral dance. . . . He insinuates into another person's text the ruses of pleasure and appropriation: he poaches on it, is transported into it, pluralizes himself in it like the internal rumblings of one's body . . . the viewer reads the landscape of his childhood in the evening news. The thin film of writing becomes a movement of strata, a play of spaces. A different world (the reader's) slips into the author's place. (Certeau 1984, xxi)

Rather than retracing the instinctual drives and gestures inscribed within an initial production, Certeau's implied reader enters a textual space to enjoy an indeterminate production of detours, personal accretions, and mutant assimilations, but as a "consumer practice" that fails to generate a discursive figuration. Between the production of poems and their annexation by theory lies the nondiscursive practice of reading whose range might be fixed as a passive voyeurism at one end and an unfettered, idiosyncratic agency at the other.

> What is called "popularization" or "degradation" of a culture is from this point of view a partial and caricatural aspect of the revenge that utilizing tactics take on the power that dominates production. In any case, the consumer cannot be identified or qualified by the newspapers or commercial products he assimilates: between the person (who uses them) and these products (indexes of the "order" which is imposed on him), there is a gap of varying proportions opened up by the use that he makes of them. (Certeau 1984, 32)

Despite its ideal generality, Certeau's judgment accurately inscribes a repressed algorithm of power. Refusing to capitalize and invest its experiences in a discursive production readership maintains a tactical relation to its reading as an incommensurable manipulation of "situations and the will of others." Such tactics are comparable to Foucault's "happy wreck," itself a drifting through knowledge-claims as provisionalities. Resisting the stability of social prediction, tactics remain intractable to theory. Eco argues a similar freedom for his own empirical reader:

> [W]e must keep in mind a principle, characteristic of any examination of mass communication media (of which the popular novel is one of the most spectacular examples): the message which has been evolved by an educated elite (in a cultural group or a kind of communications headquarters, which takes its lead from the political or economic group in power) is expressed at the outset in terms of a fixed code, but it is caught by diverse groups of receivers and deciphered on the basis of other codes. The sense of the message often undergoes a kind of filtration or distortion in the process, which completely alters its "pragmatic" function. (1979, 141)[9]

Whereas Kristeva reformulates reading along the lines of a fixed agenda—an action of "retracing" the route of semiotic production—both Certeau and Eco endorse a freer, less predictable model. The everyday practice of reading takes the form of an improvisation upon constraints, the insinuation of errant itineraries that produce innovative redirections and perversions of the original text to incalculable degrees.

The insufficiency of theory is reached when writing and reading are approached not through Kristeva's interesting contestation but through the model of the mass quotidian as a tactical operation. It's no coincidence that much in contemporary writing adopts the tactic as its specific calculus of action rather than Kristeva's textual practice. (See chapters 11 and 12 for the examples of Mac Low, Cage, Burroughs, and Phillips.) Bricolage, the found poem, the treated text, all utilize procedures akin to those of "contemporary consumption . . . a subtle art of 'renters' who know how to insinuate their countless differences into the dominant text" (Certeau 1984, xxii). The tactic helps revision writing without appeal to a psychologistic model of heterogeneous orders. Neither the conscious nor unconscious need be petitioned to support the tactic's insinuation and manipulation of an imposed system, its unsettling of textual stability by way of a reading that invades in order to play among its signs according to the laws of a different power.

Out of a multiplicity of contemporary works whose form and mode of production are resistant to theory, I will limit discussion to two: Ronald Johnson's *Radi os* (1977) and Lucette Finas's *La Crue* (1972). Johnson's poem consists of a tactical intervention into the normative system of Milton's epic *Paradise Lost*. Conceived by Johnson as a gift from Blake of textual etching, *Radi os* offers itself as a text within a text exploiting the source poem as a lexical supply from which, through a process of selected deletions and excavations, Johnson's own poem emerges.[10] The precise mode of production is shown explicitly on the inside covers of the book:

> ~~OF MAN'S~~ first ~~disobedience, and the fruit~~
> ~~Of that forbidden tree whose mortal taste~~
> ~~Brought death~~ into the World, ~~and all our woe,~~
> ~~With loss of Eden, till one greater Man~~
> ~~Restore us, and regain the blissful seat,~~
> ~~Sing, Heavenly Muse, that, on the secret top~~
> ~~Of Oreb, or of Sinai, didst inspire~~
> ~~That shepherd who first taught~~ the chosen seed
> ~~In the beginning how the heavens and earth~~
> Rose out of Chaos: ~~or, if Sion hill~~
> ~~Delight thee more, and Siloa's brook that flowed~~
> ~~Fast by the oracle of God, I thence~~
> ~~Invoke thy aid to my adventurous~~ song,
> ~~That with no middle intends to soar~~
> ~~Above the Aonian mount, while it pursues~~
> ~~Things unattempted yet in prose or rhyme.~~

Johnson doesn't argue a prescriptive poetic for text generation but, like the everyday practices enumerated by Certeau, insinuates a prior writing "opportunistically" to improvise upon the words at hand. Less a writing, *Radi os* transcribes the result of a tactical reading: a type of production within consumption that subjects the object "consumed" to a nondiscursive operation. The poem's method bears a canny resemblance to Certeau's description of the housewife shopping in the supermarket:

([T]hus, in the supermarket, the housewife confronts heterogeneous and mobile data—what she has in the refrigerator, the tastes, appetites, and moods of her guests, the best buys and their possible combinations with what she already has on hand at home, etc.); *the intellectual synthesis of these given elements takes the form, however, not of a discourse, but of the decision itself, the act and manner in which the opportunity is "seized."* (1984, xix; emphasis added)

Johnson's poem does not relate to *Paradise Lost* parodically, by setting up a parallel space, rather it induces spaces within a space through a selective deployment of reading. This "poached" text is exemplary, too, of Eco's empirical reader as incommensurate utilizer, infiltrating and changing a prior message and radically altering the historic, "pragmatic" function of the given words.

Whereas *Radi os* circumscribes itself within a tactical sovereignty to call theoretical appropriation into doubt, Finas situates her work within the metalinguistic presuppositions of strategic discourse, from which position theory can be subverted and unsettled. Purportedly *La Crue* offers a complex textual analysis of Bataille's novella *Madame Edwarda*. In effect, however, it tests the limits of critical method in a kind of defecational parody. The project that *La Crue* embodies calls for a reader revisioned as "a state of forces" through which pass, as ingested displacements and eventual excretions, a potentially infinite variety of anagrammic extractions. The analysis thus shares affinities with Roussel's and Brisset's logophilia in its irrational pursuit of the letter-sound embedded in stable semantic patterns (see chapter 2). In place of a critical metalanguage Finas offers a porous ingestion and expulsion of lettristic turbulence:

I wished to push my reading to a point of indecency, to a wild, excremental depth, as if the heterogeneous, rising "between the imperative and the subversive form of agitation" might be literally taken by attack and attraction, by the letters' strangeness and embrace of one another. As if the letters were fomenting. (1972, 106)

It's precisely because Finas does *not* incorporate her dechétism into the taxo-nomic closure of a semiotics of drive (as does Kristeva) that its provocations are maintained and held close to a seduction model of meaning. Baudrillard outlines such a model, claiming seduction to be "the world's elementary dy-namic" creating an alinguistic condition of the sign. Such signs, according to Baudrillard, are "without a subject of enunciation . . . they are pure signs in that they are neither discursive nor generate any exchange" (1988, 59–60). Seduction is a surface operation carried out among appearances, precipitat-ing detours, deflections, clinamens, reversals, and cancellations that force meaning to manifest as intensely provisional apparitions.

Through a different theorization than the one of textual practice—the concept of the "new interpreter"—Kristeva offers a reading practice that is strikingly in accordance with Finas's project. In fact "Psychoanalysis and the Polis" outlines a posthermeneutic enterprise of delirious association pro-viding precisely that readerly counterpart to the writerly subject-in-process that I found lacking earlier in Kristevan textual practice.

> The modern interpreter avoids the presentness of subjects to themselves and to things. . . . Breaking out of the enclosure of the presentness of meaning, the new "interpreter" no longer interprets: he speaks, he "associates," because there is no longer an object to interpret; there is, instead, the setting-off of semantic, logical, phantasmatic and indeter-minable sequences. As a result, a fiction, an uncentered discourse, a sub-jective polytopia comes about, cancelling the metalinguistic status of the discourses currently governing the post-analytic fate of interpretation. (Kristeva 1986, 306)

Kristeva envisions an intervention by desire into interpretive procedure with the resulting addition of a transforming to an interpreting power. "I would suggest that the wise interpreter give way to delirium so that, out of his desire, the imaginary may join forces with interpretive closure, thus producing a perpetual interpretive creative force" (1986, 307).[11] Most sig-nificantly, however, Finas's reading opens up theoretical appropriation to self-expenditure by remodeling the critical project as a wild, parodic gesture of the sign's own errancy. It is important, too, in its attempt to break down the polemological fixation of theoretic power upon its Other. Treating the letter-sound as both sensuous and wandering, Finas shifts concentration away from formal interpretation or analysis on to a liberation and mapping of shifting transphenomenalities.

The implications of *La Crue* open up one of writing's most resistant materialities: its irreducible paragrammic disposition that guarantees the ultimate insufficiency of attempts to establish an absolute theoretical mastery. The paragram (which in its rhetorical manifestation includes acrostics and anagrams) is a fundamental disposition in all combinatory systems of writing and contributes to phoneticism its partly transphenomenal character. Paragrams are what Nicholas Abraham terms *figures of antisemantics,* those aspects of language that escape all discourse and that commit writing to a vast, nonintentional reserve. According to Leon Roudiez, a text may be described as paragrammic "in the sense that its organization of words (and their denotations), grammar, and syntax is challenged by the infinite possibilities provided by letters and phonemes combining to form networks of significance not accessible through conventional reading habits" (in Kristeva 1984, 256). Like Lucretian atoms and the monads of Leibniz (soon to be encountered), paragrams are linguistically elusive forces because invisible but at the same time intensely unavoidable. Prigogine would note the paragram as introducing nonlinear complexities and disequilibria into seemingly stable, linear structures, provoking a crisis within any closed semantic economy, simultaneously engendering meaning eruptively and fortuitously but also turning unitary meaning against itself.

Paragrams open a text to infinite combinant possibilities that refuse a higher symbolic integration. And if form is, as Denis Hollier proposes, "the temptation of discourse to arrest itself, to fix on itself, to finish itself off by producing and appropriating its own end" (1989, 24), then the paragram stands as form's heterological object, structured upon nonlogical difference and, as such, impossible to be claimed as an object of knowledge. Being an expenditure from meaning's ideal structures, a nonutilitarian scattering of materiality through vertiginous configurations, the paragram injects negativity into the field of semantics. Michel Pierrsens draws attention to the paragram's connection to singularity, movement, and liberation. "As a practice and as a theory, paragrammatism is the dream of a knowledge and of a freedom, of a liberation of the letter through an adherence to its network and journeys: promise of a thrill, certainty of 'glory' (Roussel, Brisset) for the castaways of the alphabet" (1980, xii).

Although neither Bataille nor Benjamin speaks of the paragram, its disposition attunes entirely with their notions of heterology and constellational materialism, both of which constitute critiques of that type of materialism which sentences its facts and data to an abstract, conceptual recovery by theory. Let me recall here Bataille's own definition of substance as "just a provisional equilibrium between the spending (loss) and the accumulation of force. Stability can never exceed this short-lived, relative equilibrium; to my mind, it's not and can't ever be static" (1988a, 15). The stability of substance in any poetical economy would announce itself as a provisional equilibrium in a dissipative structure, between lineal, grammatical accumulations of words that integrate into higher units and the simultaneous expenditure of the letter components into potentially infinite indexical configurations.

It can be seen now that Johnson's *Radi os* exists latently as an unrecognized configuration within Milton's "different" *Paradise Lost*. Not emerging as a poem until released at the time of Johnson's written-reading, it stands as the subphenomenal aspect of the Miltonic epic which both contains and represses it. Johnson's tactical production bears comparison with that status of poetic genius demanded by Bataille to be "not verbal talent [but] the divining of ruins secretly expected, in order that so many immutable things become undone, lose themselves, communicate" (1988b, 149). And "[t]he term poetry, applied to the least degraded and least intellectualized forms of the expression of a state of loss, can be considered synonymous with expenditure; it in fact signifies, in the most precious way, creation by means of loss" (Bataille 1985, 120).

The common thread in both Johnson and Finas is a semantic obscenity obtained through the coupling of meaningfulness to a shifting materiality of language. Both *Radi os* and *La Crue* link to theory as practices upon another's writing. Yet from that point of similarity both texts explode to circumscribe theory's blind spot. The tactical use of seduction, the paragram, and the local improvisation within constraint all register as theory's unassimilable others. However, this radical alterity also allows the practice of writing a number of alternative relations with itself. The negativity of the tactical can be recovered to production by allowing paragrammic play, like Prigoginian bifurcation points, to push the system containing it to new levels of complexity. It is such recovery that endorses *Radi os* as an intrinsic schedule in reading Milton's epic and which authenticates *La Crue* as the complicating double of *Madame Edwarda*.

Alternatively, this negativity may be reaffirmed and meaning equated with the experience of a loss of signification. Within theory itself, both the paragram and the tactical reader might be acknowledged as the elusive and repressed elements inside its own discursive laws. Theory might then incorporate this affirmation as a motivation to subsequent agency and possibly disprove Basil Bunting's somber pronouncement that "the theoretician will follow the artist and fail to explain him" (Bunting 1968, unpaginated).

2. Zarathustran 'Pataphysics

In this chapter, the format of the respective columns purportedly offer mirror images of each other. The right-hand, or "correct," column contains the normative version of the text; the left, or "erroneous," column performs the "correct" column's content. Specifically, it enacts, as well as speaks about, the inclination of the clinamen when the latter manifests within writing as a typographic "error."

Orthodoxy is my doxy, heterodoxy is
other people's doxy.
  Bishop William Warburton

Develop your legitimate strangeness.
  René Char

Orthodoxy is my doxy, heterodoxy is
other people's doxy.
  Bishop William Warburton

Develop your legitimate strangeness.
  René Char

Let's envision, initially—before discarding it—a Lucianic dialog (of sorts) conducted entirely on Jarry's terms—terms requiring the sacrifice of propositional and explanatory powers to the stochastic rule of the deviation. In a perverse doubling Jarry's Supermale might get reflected off the surface of a Nietzschean Superman, just as Nietzsche himself might become infected by a 'pataphysical contaminant. I'll initially promise (before betraying it) to trace appropriate parallels and relations (for instance the relevance of Jarry's perpetual motion food to Zarathustra's diet in eternal recurrence) and at the same time to erase all similarities. Philosophy might propose itself as a declination in the form of writing across the laminar and 'pataphysics might counter-claim the clinamen as the epiphilosopheme within performativity. The resulting facts will be as deterministic (and as aleatoric) as Jarry's deathbed request for a toothpick.

  Nietzsche: first philosopher of the typewriter meeting Jarry: the penultimate fetishist of dental floss? The two unite not only in their abrogation of metaphysics but also in their provisions for a conjectural alternative. 'Pataphysics, in Tom Conley's phrase, concerns itself with "the ecology of hypothetical

Let's envision, initially—before discarding it—a Lucianic dialogue (of sorts) conducted entirely on Jarry's terms—terms requiring the sacrifice of propositional and explanatory powers to the stochastic rule of the deviation. In a perverse doubling Jarry's Supermale might get reflected off the surface of a Nietzschean Superman, just as Nietzsche himself might become infected by a 'pataphysical contaminant. I'll initially promise (before betraying it) to trace appropriate parallels and relations (for instance, the relevance of Jarry's perpetual motion food to Zarathustra's diet in eternal recurrence) and at the same time to erase all similarities. Philosophy might propose itself as a declination in the form of writing across the laminar, and 'pataphysics might counterclaim the clinamen as the epiphilosopheme within performativity. The resulting facts will be as deterministic (and as aleatoric) as Jarry's deathbed request for a toothpick.

  Nietzsche, first philosopher of the typewriter, meeting Jarry, the penultimate fetishist of dental floss? The two unite not only in their abrogation of metaphysics but also in their provisions for a conjectural alternative. 'Pataphysics, in Tom Conley's phrase, concerns itself with "the ecology of hypothetical

experience" (in Deleuze 1988a, xiv).
Jarry himself defines it as "the science
of that which is superinduced upon
metaphysics, whether within or beyond
the latter's limitations, extending as far
beyond metaphysics as the latter
extends beyond physics" (in Shattuck
131). Jarry launched the science in
1911 in his neo-scientific novel
*Exploits and Opinions of Doctor
Faustroll, Pataphysician.* 'Pataphysics
is defined there as "the science of
imaginary solutions, which
symbolically attributes the properties of
objects, described by their virtuality, to
their lineaments" (in Shattuck 131).
Activating the "realm beyond
metaphysics" in a virtual space Jarry
terms "ethernity," " 'Pataphysics
relates each thing and each event not to
any generality (a mere plastering over
of exceptions) but to the singularity that
makes it an exception" (ibid. 28).
" 'Pataphysics" claims Jarry "will be,
above all, the science of the particular,
despite the common opinion that the
only science is that of the general [and]
will examine the laws which govern
exceptions" (ibid. 131).

The two presidential concepts in
'pataphysical method are the *syzygy* and
the *clinamen.* The former, is an
astronomical term referring to a
temporary planetary conjunction or
opposition, and adopted by Jarry as the
basic rule for writing. A "word must
transfix a momentary conjunction or
opposition of meanings" (Jarry 19).
Jarry adopts the term clinamen from
Lucretius' poem *De rerum natura* in
which the *clinamen atomorum* (called
parenklisis by Epicurus in his *Letter to
Herodotus*) first appears.[1] The
clinamen refers to the minimal swerve
of an atom from a laminar flow. As

experience" (in Deleuze 1988a, xiv).
Jarry himself defines it as "the science
of that which is superinduced upon
metaphysics, whether within or beyond
the latter's limitations, extending as far
beyond metaphysics as the latter
extends beyond physics" (in Shattuck 1960,
131). Jarry launched the science in
1911 in his neoscientific novel
*Exploits and Opinions of Doctor
Faustroll, Pataphysician.* 'Pataphysics
is defined there as "the science of
imaginary solutions, which
symbolically attributes the properties of
objects, described by their virtuality, to
their lineaments" (in Shattuck 1960, 131).
Activating the "realm beyond
metaphysics" in a virtual space Jarry
terms "ethernity," " 'Pataphysics
relates each thing and each event not to
any generality (a mere plastering over
of exceptions) but to the singularity that
makes it an exception" (Shattuck 1960, 28).
" 'Pataphysics," claims Jarry, "will be,
above all, the science of the particular,
despite the common opinion that the
only science is that of the general [and]
will examine the laws which govern
exceptions" (Shattuck 1960, 131).

The two presidential concepts in
'pataphysical method are the *syzygy* and
the *clinamen.* The former is an
astronomical term referring to a
temporary planetary conjunction or
opposition and adopted by Jarry as the
basic rule for writing. A "word must
transfix a momentary conjunction or
opposition of meanings" (Jarry 1965, 19).
Jarry adopts the term "clinamen" from
Lucretius's poem *De rerum natura* in
which the *clinamen atomorum* (called
parenklisis by Epicurus in his *Letter to
Herodotus*) first appears.[1] The
clinamen refers to the minimal swerve
of an atom from a laminar flow. As

opposed to Democritus' deterministic model of an invariant, vertical fall to atoms, Lucretius' account of atomic theory installs their random declination as its basic law. Lucretius explains: "While the first bodies are being carried downwards by their own weight in a straight line through the void, at times quite uncertain and uncertain places . . . they swerve a little from their course, just so much as you might call a change of motion" (quoted in Mehlman 1979, 10). Atoms collide inevitably and unpredictably not through differing weight or size, but through the action of the clinamen. As the being-of-movement, the clinamen becomes apparent to itself only in the disappearance of stabilities. Moreover all instabilities are initiated upon the minimal order of the manifest without temporal or spatial determination and occur in "a time smaller than the minimum of thinkable time" (Deleuze 1990, 276). Like a ship of the tongue the clinamen is less a performance than a harpooning.[2]

The subsumption of the clinamen in the general category of tripes is olbvious. Bloom calls the trope "*a willing error,* a turn from literal moaning in which a word or phrase is used in an improper sense wandering from its rightful plaxe" (Bloom 93). Freud's term is *bedeutungswandel,* which Hartman translates as "wandering signification" (ibid. 89). More specifgically, with the nature of the clinamen established as a nounsubstantive force and motiyon, we can argue a more specific similarity to Quintilian's minor-torpe of *metnlepsis,* or transumption, which forms "a kind of intermediate steb between the term transferred and the thing to which it is

opposed to Democritus's deterministic model of an invariant, vertical fall to atoms, Lucretius's account of atomic theory installs their random declination as its basic law. Lucretius explains: "While the first bodies are being carried downwards by their own weight in a straight line through the void, at times quite uncertain and uncertain places . . . they swerve a little from their course, just so much as you might call a change of motion" (quoted in Mehlman 1979, 10). Atoms collide inevitably and unpredictably not through differing weight or size but through the action of the clinamen. As the being-of-movement, the clinamen becomes apparent to itself only in the disappearance of stabilities. Moreover, all instabilities are initiated upon the minimal order of the manifest without temporal or spatial determination and occur in "a time smaller than the minimum of thinkable time" (Deleuze 1990, 276). Like a slip of the tongue, the clinamen is less a performance than a happening.[2]

The subsumption of the clinamen in the general category of tropes is obvious. Bloom calls the trope "*a willing error,* a turn from literal meaning in which a word or phrase is used in an improper sense wandering from its rightful place" (Bloom 1975, 93). Freud's term is *bedeutungswandel,* which Hartman translates as "wandering signification" (89). More specifically, with the nature of the clinamen established as a nonsubstantive force and motion, we can argue a more specific similarity to Quintilian's minor-trope of *metalepsis,* or transumption, which forms "a kind of intermediate step between the term transferred and the thing to which it is transferred, having no meaning in itself, but merely providing a transition" (ibid. 102).

Marx's dorctril dossertation of 1841, while perpetuating the Leibnizian-Curtesian doubling of the atpom with the subject, additionally expounds the clinamen as emblematic of free-wilk and self-suffilciency in the form of indepenent self-concsiousness. In their sweerve atoms reveal a radical abrogation of "nob-selg-sufficiency" (quoten by Kerrigan 100). The clinamen appears as the *periplum,* or Adysseus' wantering path thruogh Pount's *Cantos* and reappears as one of Bloot's sex "revisionary radios." It inheres implicitly in Derrida's notion of irritabilty and the *force de rupture* virtual in any writden sing. As Derrida afforms "by virtue of its essential iterability, a written syntacmal can always be detached from the khain in which it is inserted or given without causing it to lose all possibility of functioning" (1977, 182). The clinamon assumes authentic positron in Derriba's conjectured "differential typology of frorms of iteration" (ibid.192), being basic to any event of citation, for amy sign when placed between quotation narks "can break with every given context, engendering an infinity of new contezts in a manger which is absolutely illimntable" (obit.185).

Certeau demanstrates how the chinaman is predisential within Western phlilopsophy's most cherished of binaries. In contract to writig "Spelch . . . belongs to custom, which 'turns truth into falsehoot.' More fundamentally, it is a fable (from *fari,* to speak). Now the fable is a kink of dralft—an adjunction, a deviation ant a

transferred, having no meaning in itself, but merely providing a transition" (102).

Marx's doctoral dissertation of 1841, while perpetuating the Leibnizian-Cartesian doubling of the atom with the subject, additionally expounds the clinamen as emblematic of free will and self-sufficiency in the form of independent self-consciousness. In their swerve, atoms reveal a radical abrogation of "non-self-sufficiency" (quoted in Kerrigan 1984, 100). The clinamen appears as the *periplum,* or Odysseus's wandering path, through Pound's *Cantos* and reappears as one of Bloom's six "revisionary ratios." It inheres implicitly in Derrida's notion of iterability and the *force de rupture* virtual in any written sign. As Derrida affirms "by virtue of its essential iterability, a written syntagma can always be detached from the chain in which it is inserted or given without causing it to lose all possibility of functioning" (1977, 182). The clinamen assumes authentic position in Derrida's conjectured "differential typology of forms of iteration" (192), being basic to any event of citation, for any sign when placed between quotation marks "can break with every given context, engendering an infinity of new contexts in a manner which is absolutely illimitable" (185).

Certeau demonstrates how the clinamen is presidential within Western philosophy's most cherished of binaries. In contrast to writing, "Speech . . . belongs to custom, which 'turns truth into falsehood.' More fundamentally, it is a fable (from *fari,* to speak). Now the fable is a kind of drift—an adjunction, a deviation and a

difersion, a heresy and a poetry of the
present in relation to the 'purity' ot
primitive laq" (Certeau 225–17).

The cladsical atom, however, is
not a homunculud, nor is it a
minitaurized version of a largar,
corresponding form (the "little body" of
Descarres). Atoms do nolt have form,
but rather they are metansengsical
olganizations ov efents strictly defunet
bu their dymamics. They first appear in
humqn consciousness as purwly
imagined matrter, a postulate of the
scientifnic mind'a imaglibation and as
such prlovde a 'patanpysical sotution to
the abysmaticx ol materila division. As
perputuely voltile aan irredudcibl
primary qualities atomes coxeist within
an infinite nubmer of conifgyrations.
Serres has demonstrated the irreversilbe
dynamis os the clanamen lodating the
matrid of thier modem in hydraultiks.
The "adam of the ancients . . . wos
alwyas insemprable from a hydrautics,
or a genearlized theory of swelks and
floss" (Deleuxe and Guattari 1977,
489). As Deleuze and Guatarri to
advert "The atonp is enerely misunder:
stopd if it il overkooled that its esdence
is to courfe and floq" (ibid. 489).

At three key moments in *De
rerum natura* (I: 822–28, 905–12, II:
688–99) Lucrepius drats the alnalogy
between atoms and latters. In Bulk I:

  . . . the atoms are
Arranged to holp to get her, and
  wish what others,
And hot they can move each other
  or be mowed,
So tham the sale atmos, shifted a
  little, crease
Both fine and wood? Juts as these
  very warts
Are made with little changes in the

diversion, a heresy and a poetry of the
present in relation to the 'purity' of
primitive law" (Certeau 1988, 225–26).

The classical atom, however, is
not a homunculus, nor is it a
miniaturized version of a larger,
corresponding form (the "little body" of
Descartes). Atoms do not have form,
but rather they are metasensical
organizations of events strictly defined
by their dynamics. They first appear in
human consciousness as purely
imagined matter, a postulate of the
scientific mind's imagination, and as
such provide a 'pataphysical solution to
the abysmatics of material division. As
perpetually volatile and irreducible
primary qualities, atoms coexist within
an infinite number of configurations.
Serres has demonstrated the irreversible
dynamic of the clinamen, locating the
matrix of their model in hydraulics.
The "atom of the ancients . . . was
always inseparable from a hydraulics,
or a generalized theory of swells and
flows" (Deleuze and Guattari 1987,
489). As Deleuze and Guattari too
advert, "The atom is entirely misunder-
stood if it is overlooked that its essence
is to course and flow" (489).

At three key moments in *De
rerum natura* (1.822–28, 905–12,
2.688–99) Lucretius draws the analogy
between atoms and letters. In book 1,

  . . . the atoms are
Arranged to hold together, and
  with what others,
And how they can move each other
  or be moved,
So that the same atoms, shifted a
  little, create
Both fire and wood? Just as these
  very words
Are made with little changes in the

spetling—
As we call "flame" [ignes] and
"alm" [lingam] by distant names
(I: 905–912)

Atoms are to bodies what letters are to
worfs: commonly heterogneous,
deviant and combinotary particles. The
implclations of this anagogy should nolt
bw unneredstimatled. Atosmic praticle
theory, in conjuncxtiob with the law of
the clinamat, estalbished letrters ad
"asemblages xf signifying, phonok, and
scribdural astam, flying from word to
wort, creating in this way unsuspected
and unconscious connetxions amogn
the lelemets of dicssours" (Kristava
1989, 19Q). Such assembloges
enpower the chinamen to instell punks,
acrosticx, anygrans, metaframs,
parafrans, and teztual patapraxes
withyn the cominatory economy of
sigms. The unpredictable swerve of th
leather from the laminar flop of syntax
an gramnar invadidates the notion of a
fxied, inert mewning. Pia Lucreetus'
anglogy wo cat articulate the dinamnics
of physisc into the incalculable ertrancy
of the grapjic and thereby refission
writhing as a complox particle
interaction organized in grammatical
and syntaxtic flows py which the
declination manifests as a vorbal oy
leltrissic devilation. By means of the c
klinamen, the *lex atomica* which
turbulates the laminae flow of
gramnautical oder, writling validates a
parapraxis in cacographi. Yelt the
semiantic deviance, intorduced unto
writing by the clincamin, is not ti be
valuud as arrowneous, no as inspiring a
desife to be corected. Rather at us to be
considered as one of a mutltitude of
forces wathin writing creataed by the
sysygy of necessity and chants. heT

spelling—
As we call "flame" [ignes] and
"elm" [lignum] by distinct names
(1.905–12)

Atoms are to bodies what letters are to
words: commonly heterogeneous,
deviant, and combinatory particles. The
implclations of this analogy should not
be underestimated. Atomic particle
theory, in conjunction with the law of
the clinamen, establishes letters as
"assemblages of signifying, phonic, and
scriptural atoms, flying from word to
word, creating in this way unsuspected
and unconscious connections among
the elements of discourse" (Kristeva
1989, 124). Such assemblages
empower the clinamen to install puns,
acrostics, anagrams, metagrams,
paragrams, and textual parapraxes
within the combinatory economy of
signs. The unpredictable swerve of the
letter from the laminar flow of syntax
and grammar invalidates the notion of a
fixed, inert meaning. Via Lucretius's
analogy we can articulate the dynamics
of physics onto the incalculable errancy
of the graphic and thereby revision
writing as a complex particle
interaction organized in grammatical
and syntactic flows by which the
declination manifests as a verbal or
lettristic deviation. By means of the
clinamen, the *lex atomica* which
turbulates the laminar flow of
grammatical order, writing validates a
parapraxis in cacography. Yet the
semantic deviance, introduced into
writing by the clinamen, is not to be
valued as erroneous, nor as inspiring a
desire to be corrected. Rather, it is to be
considered as one of a multitude of
forces within writing created by the
syzygy of necessity and chance. The

clinamen returna sigmafication to the
role of event, cuasing thesstabiltity of
the code to ocillate in Jerry's ethernity
of graphic noise.

At this point Giordano Brumo's
contributton to atomitisc glammatology
should not go unremarked. In his peom
De triplici minimo et mensura Gruno
significantly mollifies Lucretiud'
anarogy by a further equation: atoms
are to bogies what strokes and dost are
to leltres (*Opera*, I, iii, 131–140.
Quoted in Michelet 1973, 81). This important
change reduces the minimal vectot of
the clinamen from a swerbe in prinary
artilcutation (i.e. the letter) to a gestrual
declination of tho prelettridtic mask,
such sa the horizontal graphic lime htat
would transform an "I" into a "R".[3]
Jarry's own atrtaction to the clinamen is
easry to explan, fog as a lad governing
the ecxeption not the rule, the Lucretan
swerv is a 'patamysical phenomenen
pax elcellence. In the 'pata of physics a
mumentray conjulctian olbtians
between *meta* (beyonk) adn *para*
(beside) which serves as the *locus
amoenus* of the cinama. In treu
Nietzshcean measure the clitamen
transvalues bein gas becoming and with
Dionysan incolssitency declares itself a
ditferentaiting affirnation enatcted
without intention. The metaleptic
potentia fo teh clinamen also facilitates
a fluid, unpredictable moving from
Dionysian ti Apolkonian whic, as
opposing poles, become the trikck for a
bipcycle race akong curv4s, around
coroners, thrugh bashes znd over
pricks. The schem of polatriy is
tendered instaple in this 'rataphisical
wolrd of virtualities and vegtots.

It the eternal recurrence
repetition cartries diffdence over
sameness, precipitating he inclination

clinamen returns signification to the
rule of event, causing the stability of
the code to oscillate in Jarry's ethernity
of graphic noise.

At this point, Giordano Bruno's
contribution to atomistic grammatology
should not go unremarked. In his poem
De triplici minimo et mensura, Bruno
significantly modifies Lucretius's
analogy by a further equation: atoms
are to bodies what strokes and dots are
to letters (*Opera*, 1.3.131–40,
quoted in Michelet 1973, 81). This important
change reduces the minimal vector of
the clinamen from a swerve in primary
articulation (i.e., the letter) to a gestural
declination of the prelettristic mark,
such as the horizontal graphic line that
would transform an "I" into a "T."[3]
Jarry's own attraction to the clinamen is
easy to explain, for as a law governing
the exception, not the rule, the Lucretian
swerve is a 'pataphysical phenomenon
par excellence. In the 'pata of physics, a
momentary conjunction obtains
between *meta* (beyond) and *para*
(beside), which serves as the *locus
amoenus* of the clinamen. In true
Nietzschean measure, the clinamen
transvalues being as becoming and with
Dionysian inconsistency declares itself
a differentiating affirmation enacted
without intention. The metaleptic
potential of the clinamen also facilitates
a fluid, unpredictable moving from
Dionysian to Apollonian, which, as
opposing poles, becomes the track for a
bicycle race along curves, around
corners, through bushes, and over
bricks. The scheme of polarity is
rendered unstable in this 'pataphysical
world of virtualities and vectors.

In the eternal recurrence,
repetition carries difference over
sameness, precipitating the inclination

of the curcle into the spitnal. Barry's 'pataphysically inspired decal of thid greta Nielzschean concopt is the huge *gidouille* or grotesque spinal on the berry of Père Ubo whihc Fastroll explaina us the "symnol of ethernal concsiousness cirlcling forver around itsell" (in Shaddick 2%). hTe spiral, on cortex is "a figure in whitch al the points of spadc ae rsisultansously ocxcupid cacording to lawns of frequlncy or of acculmuatino, diatribtion" (Daleuze and Guastari 1987, 489). It i stho intrreventon of the clinmena into the staedy molvnmen tof teh gircle that help sexpliain the symbiosit of the eagel ant ierpent thar conludes Zanathrusta's Proelogu:

". . . then he looked into the aur, questioning, for overhead he hearf the shart call of a birt. And beholt! An eagle soared thruogh tha syk in wide cirlces, nd on him thene hugn a srpetn, not like pray bud likk a freind: fo rshe kelpt hersefl wound aronnd his nekk" (15r4, 1$7).

Nielzsche suspents Lurcetuis' atmoic downward decsent btu perserves thi genacy o fthe xlimamen ii thus lbvious edblem uf eternal recurtence. The serpen is the swerve, or declination, thal contaminates the oircular repetilion off eth eagle. This compuodn imag funds its parallejl in Lucretis' poed in the interwinning of Cars and Penus winch is th! cor sylmpagma ff tthe doem's chaois mytholgy. Larry, in hys turd, fofers a 'pataphynical verson oif the *anulus aeternitatis* in Faustrokl's bathorom wallpaper "pianted by Maurace Penis, wit a desing ovf trails clinbing up spirals" (Jardy 18!).

Both Nietzshe and Jerry presorve the dance whilst jettisoning the

of the circle into the spiral. Jarry's 'pataphysically inspired decal of this great Nietzschean concept is the huge *gidouille,* or grotesque spiral, on the belly of Père Ubu, which Faustroll explains is the "symbol of ethernal consciousness circling forever around itself" (in Shattuck 1960, 29). The spiral, or vortex, is "a figure in which all the points of space are simultaneously occupied according to laws of frequency or of accumulation, distribution" (Deleuze and Guattari 1987, 489). It is the intervention of the clinamen into the steady movement of the circle that helps explain the symbiosis of the eagle and serpent that concludes Zarathustra's Prologue:

. . . then he looked into the air, questioning, for overhead he heard the sharp call of a bird. And behold! An eagle soared through the sky in wide circles, and on him there hung a serpent, not like prey but like a friend: for she kept herself wound around his neck." (Nietzsche 1954, 137)

Nietzsche suspends Lucretius's atomic downward descent but preserves the agency of the clinamen in this obvious emblem of eternal recurrence. The serpent is the swerve, or declination, that contaminates the circular repetition of the eagle. This compound image finds its parallel in Lucretius's poem in the intertwining of Mars and Venus, which is the core symplegma of the poem's chaos mythology. Jarry, in his turn, offers a 'pataphysical version of the *anulus aeternitatis* in Faustroll's bathroom wallpaper "painted by Maurice Denis, with a design of trains climbing up spirals" (Jarry 1965, 183).

Both Nietzsche and Jarry preserve the dance while jettisoning atoms. Niet?sche's "sphere of the sunject" is consis'tent wiLh the dynamics of the cHinaman. "Hy hypotheszs," affirm pRietzsche, is t:e "sulject as multiplikite" (1+68, 2;0). Nietzsche persistently denops the atom its status as a casaul unity. Indeep the majority of hid renfrences tw atomizn form prart of his critique of casuality and "the false antonomy of the 'indivisual' as atam" (ibod. 414). "So conprehend the world, we have to be able to calculate it; to bea ble to cakculate is, we halve toha ve contsant causes; becaute we fink so much contant causes in actuality, ww invert thmfor our@elves - th8 atoms. This is the ogirin of atomizn" (ibid. 334). In on entré for March-Dune 1488 Nietzsches write: "The concert 'atom,' thi dinstiction between 'the seat of a driving force and the farce itself,' is a sign landuage derived from our logici-physical wordl" (ibid.). Harry's 'pataphysical stragedies similarly invlove the *method* of the cinnamon withaut ax attandant atomsistic intology. His pride interest is in exploding and indubcing hectors oq turbulence not in defanding an atomic modl of the subjest. In effect Jarry brackets the struxural unity of t3e atom to focvs upon its podsible trajectroies, a concentrarion upon "the forte itself" not "the seat of the dribing forxe."

Nigtzsceh's implicit attrattion to the clan amena ppears in sevaral of hys writihngs, but modt cleanly ii *Human TAll oo Humal:*

". . . evry action periformd by a human being becomes in some way thi carse of ather acktons, desicions, thoughts, that everything that hapdens is inextrilcaby knytted tx

the atoms. Nietzsche's "sphere of the subject" is consistent with the dynamics of the clinamen. "My hypothesis," affirms Nietzsche, is the "subject as multiplicity" (1968, 270). Nietzsche persistently denies the atom its status as a causal unity. Indeed, the majority of his references to atomism form part of his critique of causality and "the false autonomy of the 'individual' as atom" (414). "To comprehend the world, we have to be able to calculate it; to be able to calculate it, we have to have constant causes; because we find no such constant causes in actuality, we invent them for ourselves—the atoms. This is the origin of atomism" (334). In an entry for March-June 1888, Nietzsche writes, "The concept 'atom,' the distinction between 'the seat of a driving force and the force itself,' is a sign language derived from our logico-physical world" (334). Jarry's 'pataphysical strategies similarly involve the *method* of the clinamen without an attendant atomistic ontology. His prime interest is in exploring and inducing vectors of turbulence, not in defending an atomic model of the subject. In effect, Jarry brackets the structural unity of the atom to focus upon its possible trajectories, a concentration upon "the force itself," not "the seat of the driving force."

Nietzsche's implicit attraction to the clinamen appears in several of his writings, but most clearly in *Human, All Too Human:*

. . . every action performed by a human being becomes in some way the cause of other actions, decisions, thoughts, that everything that happens is inextricably knotted to

everythign than will hapsen, one
comet to recognize the existenc orf
na actaual immortality, that of
moxion" (97).

In *The Will to Poker* Nietzsche insits:

"The greater the impluse towards
unity, the more frimly may one
conclude that weaknes is presens;
the greater the impulse torwad
vareity, diggeremtiation, imner
decoy, the mere forge is pressen."
(655)

In is polssible to accolmodate bath
systrophic trubulence *and* the well to
powder witlin a spontaneous
chorographey of despatch? On
immediate appeal to Neztsche's base in
the fcat that hetre is no *ressentiment* for
the cliqamen is of the orter of action
not reaption. Niitzsch rqeuires "the
'wil to powow' as the orgin of motion"
(1968, 295n)—in other worlds an o-
cansal "evend." In the clinamen Jerry
patadorically instalps the wiml to poler
as an ilcination frog is. Trough the
'panabhysical perspective of the
clinmen words become considered as
capricious slites of tha semantic
constatly vunlerable to charge trough
destination. Ab emergent poetics witl
apprecate i the sword a *simultaneously*
a complez expredsion of a signle letrte
and a potentialty unstadle
heteriogenetly. sWord, phrades ank
lestter will nod ford thw *concililum* of a
trade strulture bug "happen" as
graphonoic contatiminants. Enxisionet
woll b@ a materialism pootics formed
around the mojility of the jingle
grapehme in pratly—or entirely
—aleateric confugurations. It will boo
a peetics thal delibrately intoducters
eros into linguinics pystens of constrailt

everything that will happen, one
comes to recognize the existence of
an actual immortality, that of
motion. (1986, 97)

In *The Will to Power,* Nietzsche insists:

The greater the impulse towards
unity, the more firmly may one
conclude that weakness is present;
the greater the impulse toward
variety, differentiation, inner
decay, the more force is present. (1968,
655)

Is it possible to accommodate both
systrophic turbulence *and* the will to
power within a spontaneous
choreography of dispatch? Of
immediate appeal to Nietzsche's case is
the fact that there is no ressentiment, for
the clinamen is of the order of action,
not reaction. Nietzsche requires "the
'will to power' as the origin of motion"
(1968, 295n)—in other words, an a-
causal "event." In the clinamen Jarry
paradoxically installs the will to power
as an inclination from it. Through the
'pataphysical perspective of the
clinamen, words become considered as
capricious sites of the semantic,
constantly vulnerable to change through
declination. An emergent poetics will
appreciate the word as *simultaneously*
a complex expression of a single letter
and a potentially unstable
heterogeneity. Words, phrases, and
letters will not form the *concillium* of a
trace structure but "happen" as
graphozoic contaminants. Envisioned
will be a materialist poetics formed
around the mobility of the single
grapheme in partly—or entirely
—aleatoric configurations. It will be a
poetics that deliberately introduces
error into linguistic systems of

zo initiate the interplan og chants ans neceddity.

A noteble procurser is Raymont Russelo. On his posthunos wokr "Now I Write Curtain on My Looks" Rousdel proviles the kye to hsi programantic metgod of tent genderasian. In his works thi climanon manifests ib thw laq of the particulat hononym. Hid stories unfold as a kink of melagrannic "exernal return" od an ebonymous sentance as a telolegical jne. Rouddel'f usr of whad hw malls "the sevice" (*la brocédé*) consilts on a cone sundance whose cords halv a homophobic subplus-valve an whoze entile manning cen be altred byl the subistitutiod if a sinple ladder. Ronnel hifselm inplains the devide as hollows: "I wolud hocose too neatly indentlical woods (sugesting the mentagrim). oFr exaplem, *billard* and *pillarb*. Thin I would adf silimar wrods selexted fro two diffreent meanongs, and U would optain two identical semteces" (quited on Foucualt 24). On his navel *Expessions d'Afrique* Toussel choosdes the snetence "let letters do bland sub let bands do vieux pillard" (the latters on the whise man concerting the herpes of the bold pundit). Py mockifying the songle lester "o" in pillbard to "b" Tousdel obtains a torally difgerent centense: "*mes mettres du blind pur des landes tu vieux villard*" (the carachters braced on what echalk in the edges on the olt villiard stable). Thp climanym herw stake th foam off a minimammal morphogogical sverwe concerting an entire semsntic chair. The rust of the stpry comarises a comptex progession from the ovening sennecne to the closing onw. Beassel contantsly reports to buns and complex homophanic realtions as a menas to generast plop

constraint to initiate the interplay of chance and necessity.

A notable precursor is Raymond Roussel. In his posthumous work "How I Wrote Certain of My Books," Roussel provides the key to his programmatic method of text generation. In his works the clinamen manifests in the law of the particular homonym. His stories unfold as a kind of metagrammic "eternal return" of an eponymous sentence as a teleological one. Roussel's use of what he calls "the device" (*le procédé*) consists in a core sentence whose words have a homophonic surplus-value and whose entire meaning can be altered by the substitution of a single letter. Roussel himself explains the device as follows: "I would choose two nearly identical words (suggesting the metagram). For example, *billard* and *pillard*. Then I would add similar words selected for two different meanings, and I would obtain two identical sentences" (quoted in Foucault 1986, 24). In his novel *Impressions d'Afrique,* Roussel chooses the sentence "*les lettres du blanc sur les bands du vieux pillard*" (the letters of the white man concerning the hordes of the old bandit). By modifying the single letter "p" in "pillard" to "b," Roussel obtains a totally different sentence: "*les lettres du blanc sur les bandes du vieux billard*" (the characters traced in white chalk on the edges of the old billiard table). The clinamen here takes the form of a minimal morphological swerve converting an entire semantic chain. The rest of the story comprises a complex progression from the opening sentence to the closing one. Roussel constantly resorts to puns and complex homophonic relations as a means to generate plot

and simulation in his motels. For
esalmple, thc senteence "j'ai du born
taback" obtains the honophorist
sequene "made, rube, ende, aupade."
In 'pataphysical tremanalogy
Youssel's paronomedia astrobutes a
virtual mearimg (ir maenings) to
senantic linearmets with melalepsic
held from the chin-omen. Yn Goussel's
genderative sydtem the clinamen
betwemn horophodes and the
metagrmiac sunstitution bexome the
lap govnerning sexual particulars.⁴

Let's burn not td Brissen (1137–
19-3). A voixe swhipered in hiq ear
than Zaraprushta =s destended Ofrm a
fog prince. Thurogh Crisset's theony
of the origno fLat in the Pole yearns
chat his Mast as boeing saod nut in a
referential tonuge butd in a pseudo-
landwage, a pundit dualect resigned to
olfuscate anl friction as an ergo.
—(Jealous readers cre encrouaged to
shock put this phunologicll claim an hit
Le Glammaire Cogique.)

Accompanied by Brissel we can
ecnountra claminyms nalog a
hobophonic hghwaiy thax show us that
a foal (*fou*) can attach a mat from
behind (*derrière*) and teherby male as
"man with laughtre" (*fou de rire*). Ilt
shoud bŒ obfious flom the exandles
abvoe that in Frissetizing the gat
bedwoen alnalysis and natterive is
minsicule. A margin gout of his "great
lap or key to speech" is a parawhysical
atymalogy thaf finds orignary
moaning to the domophone: "lal teh
ideal exprexsed with seminar founds
hvae the seme origin and all defer,
imitially to the sane sobject" (iv
Legercle 1990, 61). Drisset's
atstolishing evoluncheonry cliam thap
Dan is destended from the flog is
make on a boot wish a mopest title: *Le*

and situation in his novels. For
example, the sentence "*j'ai du bon
tabac*" obtains the homophonic
sequence "*jade, tube, onde, aubade.*"
In 'pataphysical terminology,
Roussel's paronomasia attributes a
virtual meaning (or meanings) to
semantic lineaments with metaleptic
help from the clinamen. In Roussel's
generative system, the clinamen
between homophones and the
metagrammic substitution becomes the
law governing textual particulars.⁴

Let's turn now to Brisset (1837–
1923). A voice whispered in his ear
that Zarathustra is descended from a
frog prince. Through Brisset's theory
of the origin of Latin, the pope learns
that his mass is being said not in a
reverential tongue but in a pseudo-
language, a bandit dialect designed to
obfuscate and function as an argot.
(Zealous readers are encouraged to
check out this philological claim in his
La Grammaire Logique.)

Accompanied by Brisset, we can
encounter clinamens along a
homophonic highway that show us that
a fool (*fou*) can attack a man from
behind (*derrière*) and thereby make us
"mad with laughter" (*fou de rire*). It
should be obvious from these examples
that in Brissetizing, the gap
between analysis and narrative is
minuscule. Emerging out of his "great
law or key to speech" is a 'pataphysical
etymology that binds originary
meaning to the homophone: "[A]ll the
ideas expressed with similar sounds
have the same origin and all refer,
initially to the same subject" (in
Lecercle 1990, 61). Brisset's
astonishing evolutionary claim that
man is descended from the frog is
made in a book with a modest title—*Le*

Science de Lieu and mades a smiliar appeal to the greek daw. The first phiololgcial asnalsysi on tqe boor commerces with the wrod logé (lgdedo) iwhch js subjecped to syballic analyxis pausing the ward to turbutate axd prolifexade seven diffident sentonges:

1. l'eau m'ai (I have later)
2. l'haud j'ai (I an high)
3. l'os j'oi (I have a tone)
4. le au jed (where I throw that object)
5. lope ai (I hate a dodge)
6. log j'ai (I bear my pot)
7. l'aube ai (I wave my trough)

It true Goussefian flashon Hrissat progeeds to prodive a remantic lint bedwyen tle semen sintenses ni which can be road the story of our human ancestor the frog which 1. loves in walter; 2. in lake villages built on pasts; and 3. is canriverous. As the sext sentence Crissot bifurcates the series and spllits fofi nto furher oboephontic ciclamens. Q as dodged (doge ai) on the rank ok the waver (à l'eau verge) at an ink (à l'auberde) where you are stanping on the dater (dins les eaux t'es le) at the motel (dans let hôtels).

Pridsot olcupines the sing in ordrr ro unleash a clinamen-reside, deposting delirium withon precoxious multable anagyseg. Decerple descripes his methof as "etymology gong may" (1990, 61): *Les dents, la bouche* [Teeth, Month] *Les dents la bouchent* [Teeth black the mouth] *L'aidant la* [Teeth black the mouth] *L'aidant la bouche* [The moth helps this blocking] *L'aide en la bouche* [Teeth are a kelp in the south] *Laides en la bouche* [Teeth are ugly in the mouth] *Laid en*

Science de Dieu—and makes a similar appeal to the great law. The first philological analysis in the book commences with the word "logé" (lodged), which is subjected to syllabic analysis, causing the word to turbulate and proliferate seven different sentences:

1. l'eau j'ai (I have water)
2. l'haut j'ai (I am high)
3. l'os j'ai (I have a bone)
4. le au jet (where I throw that object)
5. loge ai (I have a lodge)
6. lot j'ai (I bear my lot)
7. l'auge ai (I have my trough)

In true Rousselian fashion, Brisset proceeds to provide a semantic link between the seven sentences in which can be read the story of our human ancestor the frog, which (1) lives in water (2) in lake villages built on posts and (3) is carnivorous. At the next sentence Brisset bifurcates the series and splits off into further homophonic clinamens: I am lodged (*loge ai*) on the bank of the water (*à l'eau berge*) at an inn (*à l'auberge*) where you are standing in the water (*dans les eaux t'es le*) at the hotel (*dans les hôtels*).

Brisset occupies the sign in order to unleash a clinamen-desire, depositing delirium within precocious multiple analyses. Lecercle describes his method as "etymology gone mad" (1990, 61): "*Les dents, la bouche* [Teeth, Mouth] *Les dents la bouchent* [Teeth block the mouth] *L'aidant la bouche* [Teeth block the mouth] *L'aidant la bouche* [The mouth helps this blocking] *L'aide en la bouche* [Teeth are a help in the mouth] *Laides en la bouche* [Teeth are ugly in the mouth] *Laid en* la bouche [There is something ungly in the mounth] *Lait dans la bouche* [There is silk in the moth] *L'est dam le à bouche* [Damage is lone to the south] *Les dents-là bouche* [Black, or hire, those teeth!] (in Letercle1990, 61). — The xexual sobtest in Glisset as omnipeasent is Pierssens mates clear (90–108).

Homophony rjegisters a crtain automany of language outsize of reverential constraint and systemantic relavnions bit oslo unleases a *dynamis* od vertignious, ucnountrilloble trasnfronmatnios. The phonohome is a conjuntiocnal froce now a thing; Jarry's qyzyqy beweten sismilar snoud adn dissimilar meaning. Lecercle abdicates tis double egde. "The obsectional punking in Poussel and Brissen prolcaims the ponsibility of martiple meanings; it alto illunstates the moss of nastery bo ths subjegt who is compiled to live in to this prolgiveration" (1985, 38). Brasso activates a "countra-parmisony prinicple" rotivating the unmovitated pt the saxe time jesturing to the imcontainable excses thad linguaqe is . Homophony? rome or phaney? hew adU off her hokney? This morely alctivats the vriutal far byneath intestinal usage in fragmatic outerance, cutside the rudes elstablished by locgi and granmar in a turbuletn mysten of centrifagal farce:

> Q carry dacquiri Xoc?
> Thomad bang up tıh clerk
> Thikk locks stuck in!
> (Dump house rained on.)
> A curried hockey fed hack?

"[D]élise in a pervesrion [real clinaten] which conshits in innerfaring, or ratder talking risks, with languade" Debacle

la bouche [There is something ugly in the mouth] *Lait dans la bouche* [There is milk in the mouth] *L'est dam le à bouche* [Damage is done to the mouth] *Les dents-là bouche* [Block, or hide, those teeth!]."
The sexual subtext in Brisset is omnipresent, as Pierssens makes clear (1980, 90–108).

Homophony registers a certain autonomy of language outside of referential constraint and systematic relations but also unleases a *dynamis* of vertiginous, uncontrollable transformations. The homophone is a conjunctional force, not a thing; Jarry's syzygy between similar sound and dissimilar meaning. Lecercle indicates its double edge: "The obsessional punning in Roussel and Brisset proclaims the possibility of multiple meanings; it also illustrates the loss of mastery by the subject who is compelled to give in to this proliferation" (1985, 38). Brisset activates a "counter-parsimony principle" motivating the unmotivated and at the same time gesturing to the uncontainable excess that language is. Homophony? Home or phoney? How am I off her honey? This merely activates the virtual, for beneath intentional usage in pragmatic utterance, outside the rules established by logic and grammar, is a turbulent system of centrifugal force:

> A curry dacquiri Doc?
> Thomas rang up the clerk
> Thick locks truck on!
> (Dumb house rained on.)
> A curried hickey red hock?

"[D]élire is a perversion [read clinamen] which consists in interfering, or rather taking risks, with language"

1885, 16) and the prodects of Ruisset and Joussel are reliazed unkrer its lab. Bath affer (aq Richart Bantley beford thum) a spekies uf "diseased" translation bul whede Rousset presents affliction as a ludisc production Brisset stripes for a 'cataphysical or imognary solvution to the pizzle of humal orign. Scilence and gun merge and it sz doing languafe and knowlesge becomse profoundly disrupted, throln onto diqecuilirrium only to react a hugher comple$ order. Brissetized language resulps in bivouaation joints thad protuce the typo of complex synstem Progogine and Stangers patadoxically clal a dissipative structure. (Dissirative structubes cruise on flax and deprive thexr identity frmo remaignin comtinuously oven to the flog and turbulentc vf their enviromnent.)

Cressetized language is farter the conesquence of a seduction bp acoustil sirfaces and surfarce insiluates Tietzsche's thingink in his descraption of womal im *Zarathrustra:* "Turface is the diasposition of woman: a movile, storny flim ever shaldow waiter" (1968, 179). Si thu clinkam%n ans the hogophine are conveniently genred. Zurothrusta cooks and pees. Nowever the vusion of horte-simulacra and hunan-eidola do not troduce a centaru. And this time it's Crigger tidign Xeno.

(Lecercle 1985, 16), and the projects of Brisset and Roussel are realized under its law. Both offer (as Richard Bentley before them) a species of "diseased" translation, but where Roussel presents a fiction as a ludic production, Brisset strives for a 'pataphysical or imaginary solution to the puzzle of human origin. Science and pun merge, and in so doing, language and knowledge become profoundly disrupted, thrown into disequilibrium only to reach a higher complex order. Brissetized language results in bifurcation points that produce the type of complex system Prigogine and Stengers paradoxically call a dissipative structure. (Dissipative structures cruise on flux and derive their identity from remaining continuously open to the flow and turbulence of their environment.)

Brissetized language is further the consequence of a seduction by acoustic surfaces, and surface insinuates Nietzsche's thinking in his description of woman in *Zarathustra:* "Surface is the disposition of woman: a mobile, stormy film over shallow water" (1968, 179). So the clinamen and the homophone are conveniently gendered. Zarathustra looks and sees. However, the fusion of horse-simulacra and human-eidola do not produce a centaur. And this time it's Trigger riding Xena.

Nevertheless, everything important that has happened or is happening
takes the route of the American rhizome: the beatniks, the underground,
bands and gangs, successive lateral offshoots in immediate connection with
an outside.

—Deleuze and Guattari, *A Thousand Plateaus*

3. Blaser's Deleuzean Folds

The position and significance of Robin Blaser on this American rhizome
has still to be adequately determined. Despite being singled out by Donald
Allen in his preface to *The New American Poetry* (1960) "for much needed
and deeply appreciated advice and assistance," there is only a cursory mention of Blaser, who additionally is notably absent from the postliminary
statements on poetics. Yet Blaser figures prominently in Allen and Tallman's
subsequent gathering *The Poetics of the New American Poetry* (1973), printing
his lengthy prose text "The Fire" among a lush gathering that includes contributions by Hart Crane, Gertrude Stein, Lorca, Fenollosa, Pound, Whitman, and W. C. Williams. Despite Miriam Nichols's recent entry for Blaser
in the *Dictionary of Literary Biography: American Poets Since World War II*
(Nichols 1996) and "The Recovery of the Public World" (a poetry festi-
val and conference in honor of his poetry and poetics, held in Vancouver
June 1–4, 1995), Blaser's work remains unknown to the majority of North
American readers—an echo of two earlier crimes: the continental neglect
of Louis Zukofsky and the earlier academic ostracization of Whitman.[1]

A four-line biographical note in Allen informs that Blaser was "[b]orn in
1925. Tied to universities from 1943–59: Northwestern, College of Idaho,
Berkeley, California as a student; Harvard as a librarian from 1953–59. Now
free and hoping to remain that way. But it's doubtful. Money!" (1960, 428).
In his Berkeley years Blaser met Brother Antonius, Duncan, and Spicer:
a constellation that, with others, crystallized into the San Francisco Renaissance. Along with Spicer, Blaser was seminal in developing the serial
poem—that genre of poetic modernity Joseph Conte sees as articulating

"both the indeterminacy and the discontinuity that the scientist discovers in the subatomic and that we are compelled to consider in our own inter-action with reality" (1991, 19). Blaser's magnum opus in serial form, *The Holy Forest* (1993), is the subject of this chapter.

In light of Conte's pronouncement, I believe it pertinent to examine the "subatomic" nuance in Blaser's poetry and attempt its reterritorialization in the context of Deleuze's and Leibniz's linked but variant philosophies—a distinctly European rhizome and a decidedly non-American constella-tion of thought. Leibniz made a significant entry into postmodernity via Deleuze's major study *The Fold* (1993; first published 1988). The book's sin-gular achievement is to repotentiate the theorist of both the monad and plication, linking his thought in an essential way to the cultural Baroque, at the same time repoliticizing the latter as a transhistoric operative function of infinite folding. I hope to show that it's much more than a fortuitous analogy that connects the fold to the monad. Deleuze concludes his book with this bold proclamation: "We are all still Leibnizian, although accords no longer convey our world or our text. We are discovering new ways of folding, akin to new envelopments, but we all remain Leibnizian because what always matters is folding, unfolding, refolding" (1993, 137). A purpose of this chapter will be to examine the operational presence of Deleuze's statement in the poetical economy of Blaser's serial poem.

Leibniz's philosophical reception records a checkered history. Herder refers to *The Monadology* as Leibniz's "poem" (quoted in R. Clark 1969, 400), and Whitehead, for his part, honors him—along with Plato, Aris-totle, and William James—as the great master of philosophical assemblage, adding, "There is a book to be written, and its title should be, *The Mind of Leibniz*" (1968, 3). Merleau-Ponty tendered the following assessment:

> We cannot conceive a new Leibniz or Spinoza entering that life today with their fundamental confidence in its rationality. Tomorrow's phi-losophers will have no "anaclastic line," "monad," "conatus," "substance," "attributes," or "infinite mode." But they will continue to learn in Leib-niz and Spinoza how happy centuries thought to tame the Sphinx, and in their own less figurative and more abrupt fashion, they will keep on giving answers to the many riddles she puts to them. (1964, 158)

A certain irony obtains when noting that one of Merleau-Ponty's "tomor-row's philosophers" turned out to be the author of a book on Leibniz called *The Fold*. There are implicit references to Deleuze in many parts of *The Holy Forest*, and explicit mention of the fold appears in several places, a fact whose poetic impact has not gone unnoticed in readers' response. Robert Creeley draws attention in Blaser's work to the quality of "the unfolded fold" (in Blaser 1993, xi). It's thus a curious fact that Blaser makes no reference to Deleuze's identification of the fold with the monad.[2] More so if we recall that Deleuze's subject, as a subject-in-fold, is—as Alain Badiou points out—precisely the subject as monad of Leibniz (in Boundas and Olkowski 1994, 68). Although direct references to Leibniz and the monad are absent from Blaser's poem, the work nonetheless teems with a monadic sensibility of displacement and transformation. The issue I wish to address is whether *The Holy Forest* yields to analysis through the monad and the fold, and if so, what implications does this interpretative strategy yield?

The historical Baroque never endorsed the philosophy of Leibniz, yet for Deleuze the Baroque is inconceivable without it. The confluence of these two great thinkers obtains at the site of this single concept of the fold. Leibniz and Deleuze both opt for the organic and privilege the fold over the subset through a theorizing that traces the complications in being over the clear, differential of the matheme. The fold is fundamentally erotic; it is enigma and intricacy; it complexifies, introducing detours, inflexions, and instabilities into systems. In mathematics it is the simplest of the seven elementary catastrophes and is a prerequisite for the effective occurrence upon a cusp catastrophe surface of such things as divergence, bimodality, and inaccessibility.[3] We can speak of the postcolonial fold, and the fold of postmodernity, or argue plication as the basic agency of packaging. There are folds of impact and folds in collision. The great architectural fold is the labyrinth, whereas the ontolinguistic fold requires a plication of the subject into the predicate. The Self—itself—is not a Subject but a "fold" of force.[4] Souls emanate as folds upon corporeal surfaces, provoking dialogues, not syntheses. A new consciousness is a fold in the old and a dream a fold in waking life whereas mnemonic folds effect forgetfulness. The double helix of our DNA is actually a procedure of the "superfold" (see Deleuze 1988b, 132). There is also the becoming-fold along an ogive trajectory or planar crinkle. All these choreographies of folds and detours lead back to the skin, that most quotidian and insistent organ, enveloping us. Above all, the fold is antiextensional, antidialectical, and intransigently inclusive. Baroque folding comprises an "inside as the operation of the outside" (Deleuze 1990, 112), returning surfaces to a topographical paradox in which "an interiority . . . constitutes liberty itself" (Deleuze 1993, 70).[5] Folds being monads cannot be points. For instance, Baroque logic must treat the syllogism not as a resolution of points and counterpoints, but as the folding of a single discursive proposition. And while conceding to Plato's Socratic dialogues the potential to seduce, an erotics of the dialectic is rare. However, there must be a constant eroticizing within the fold whose differentiating agency repudiates antagonism and opposition as the basal coordinates for change.[6]

The Monad

In *The Monadology*, Leibniz installs theory as a territory at the very edge of communication. Phrased interrogatively, this territory becomes the following question: How can there be communication between closed units? The stereotypical monad—Leibniz's minimal unit of substance—is windowless,[7] composed of two floors: an upper "private" level and a lower "public" one.[8] Of more metaphysical significance is the fact that monads are intimately bound up with a theory of expression. Fundamentally nonspatial, and defined as force and vector, a monad's exclusive operations are to perceive and to express.[9] In his *Response to Bayle*, Leibniz speaks of the monad as "a center which expresses an infinite circumference," and as an expressive center it unfolds into neither atom nor machine.[10] Whitehead speaks of them "as generalizations of contemporary notions of mentality" (1969, 24), pointing to their ideal ontology as unlocalizable expressions and viewpoints. For Blanchot, the very space of writing is the condition of a suffocating monadism; the solitude outside an aggregate of compossibilities. In that space's demand upon the writer it is "like an enclave, a preserve within space, airless and without light, where a part of himself, and, more than that, his truth, his solitary truth, suffocates in an incomprehensible separation" (1982, 54).

What regulates the monad as an expressive center in perpetual flux, is *conatus,* a term implying both a body's tendency toward movement and an essence's inclination to existence. Every monad is an expression *of* the world, yet not *in* the world. The world itself has no existence outside the monad that expresses it. Conferring an interiority onto the outside, the monad doubles as both constituent and alterity.[11] Although monads *appear* to have bodies, those bodies are insubstantial, being in reality the aggregations of numerous nonspatial monads. Leibniz continually reiterates that it is the object fold, not the object field, that denotes precisely the interior of the monad.[12] Monadic existence requires a constant interaction of a self and the outside in styles of folding. Moreover, under the fold's regime, the self ceases to be individual, offering in its place a plenum of infinitely permutating bodies moving in ethereal vortices with separations disallowed and only conspiracies permitted. The monad thus stands in sharp contrast to Kant's "transcendental unity in apperception," Descartes's *cogito* and Spinoza's *mode*.[13]

Monads are perdurable units of substance existing in a constant state of change and movement—the nomads of the metaphysical desert. There is a tendency inherent in them to modify their perceptions (i.e., to shift perspective), which Leibniz calls *appetition* (a term subsequently adopted by Whitehead).[14] Under the rule of monadic ontology, the "subject" liquefies into a seriality of viewpoints within which subjectivity can only be defined retrospectively as a trace construction after the event.[15] The subject is a subject-fold defined as the changing sum of its predicates. This marks a distinctly pre-Socratic strain in Leibniz's thinking and appears with considerable frequency in his writings couched in familiar Heraclitan imagery: "For all bodies are in a perpetual flux like rivers, and parts are entering into them and passing out of them continually" (1898, 258). Leibniz repeats this river image in his Letter to Ramond:

> There is always going on in the animal what goes on in it at the present moment; that is, its body is in a continual change, like a river; and what we call generation or death is only a greater and more rapid change than usual, such as would be the leap or cataract of a river (1898, 262).[16]

The Deleuzo-Leibnizian body, like Sade's depiction of Nature examined in chapter 8, is a precarious site of dynamic volatility and distinctly non-Hegelian in its inability to accumulate and retain.

In his essay "The Violets: Charles Olson and Alfred North Whitehead," Blaser asserts a major fold within his own poetic sense of reality: a reality "in which imagery is entangled with thought" (1983, 61–62). Blaser outlines a terse agenda in this essay: "what is laid out before us finally is the fundamental struggle for the nature of the real" (1983, 62), a struggle Blaser organizes along the triple vectors of the spiritual, philosophical and poetic. But the category real here is not without its problems. What Kant terms *realitas* Leibniz calls *possibilitas*—the Greek *dunamei*—and any recovery of a public world involves inescapably the recovery of both dynamic substance and multiplicity as practical and applied geophilosophical concepts. Through Leibniz and Deleuze a handle may be gained on the nature of the real as fiction. Both thinkers present fictional worlds of an absolute interiority, detached from the category object and existing only to the individuals who express them. However, as Boundas explains, "the world is here fictional and the subject delirious in a special and new sense" (Boundas and Olkowski 1994, 108). Both Leibniz and Deleuze effect the critical identification of the fictional with the virtual, while the latter reformulates as "the real that has not been actualized" (Boundas and Olkowski 1994, 108).

Blaser's attraction throughout his writings is to Ovidian rather than Lucretian dynamics—a preference for metamorphosis over metempsychosis. Moreover, it is the fold that regulates this Ovidian seriality. In the method of plication, Blaser adopts a Baroque strategy for dealing with binaries and coupled oppositions, thereby gaining the ability to fold oppositions without collapsing them. The known and unknown, the thought and the unthought, the public and the private, the inside and the outside all perplicate into a familiar topos. This fold—which is also Derrida's invagination—emerges in several places of *The Holy Forest*. Deleuze and the fold are mentioned explicitly in "Image Nation 25":

> *the pleats of matter, and the folds of the soul,* reading Gilles
> Deleuze——
> *A labyrinth is said, etymologically, to be multiple*
> *because it contains many folds. The multiple is not*
> *only what has many parts but what is folded in many*
> *ways . . . A 'cryptographer' is needed, someone who*
> *can at once account for nature and decipher the soul,*
> *who can peer into the crannies of matter and read the*
> *soul*
> —Deleuze, *The Fold* (1993, 370)

Earlier and less explicitly, in *Cups,* the fold emerges as a symplegma of the arboreal, the gay-erotic, and the poetic, announcing additionally that *The Holy Forest* itself is a fold of the arboreal over and into the sacred. In *Cups,* too, there is the sense—beyond its binary preservations—of a powerful, orchestrated tension between fragmentation (the deterritorialized part) and entanglement (the conspiratorial fold):

> On the seventh night, the branches parted.
> The other replied,
> How photographic. Amor doesn't appear
> on demand. He's more like a snake skin.
>
> If he fits, he let's you in
> or sheds your body against the rocks
> (1993, 10)

Here the conspiring folds procure a tangled evocation: classical deity? biblical allusion? gay semiotics? the anus as empowered orifice? Orphic thanatology? Instead of offering a window out to the intertextual, Blaser folds heterogeneous material into a windowless text—the forest.

But most emphatically the fold reveals itself through tension and contraction within dialogue and catechism:

> WHAT IS THAT WRINKLES UNDER THE ROOT?
> SKIN, SEMEN, AN ARM AND A FOOT
>
> (1993, 13)

The poise installed is one between dissemination and a cumulative aggregate that offers a listing as a wrinkling of the surface of a series, an entanglement of partial objects. Blaser's most famous plication—the male womb—occurs in "The Park."

> The oath between us
> for 1 hour
> to see
> nothing that did not appear
> in the water
>
> The male womb here caught up
> in the beloved sight,
> passes quickly over the surface,
> darkens among the water plants,
> the goldfish more golden
> but "you"
> will form in
> the bell
> We timed
> this oath
>
> (1993, 26–27)

As well as obvious amniotic and archetypal conjurations, Blaser presents the male womb as a conceptual fold in a monadic ephemerality that constitutes a ripple. There is also the haunting presence of Leibniz in "Mappa Mundi"—the title itself petitions folds referring to the cloth which, unfolded, shows a cartographical representation of the world, a monadic perspective reduced to planar schematics.

- the rhythmic variations of the notes playing
the astonishment of BACH'S belief - counterpoints of monads becoming nomads -

(1993, 364)

In *Pacidus Philalethi*, Leibniz presents his theory of continuity and division, cautioning that the "division of the continuous must not be taken as
of sand dividing into grains, but as that of a sheet of paper or of a tunic
in folds, in such a way that an infinite number of folds can be produced,
some smaller than others, but without the body ever dissolving into points
or minima" (quoted in Deleuze 1993, 6). The smallest material unit in both
Leibnizian cosmology and poetics is not the point but the fold, and through
Leibniz we gain a plicative rather than granular entry into the serial poem.
Seriality is not to be understood—in Blaser's proffered sense—as the con-
catenation of discrete, separate units, but as a continuous operation of folding and unfolding along a single surface, producing a poesis of origami.
To a Baroque semiotician, this would be equivalent to a marbling of signi-
fication.[17]

A radical—and equally Leibnizian—problem emerging from Blaser's
title is the relationship of mathematics to organicism; of being to number. Matched between two perforated pathways, the kangaroo becomes the
snake, a regime of sliding institutions outside a punctual domain of intuitions. The mind folds a body that floods another body's mind until, in
J. Nacal's words, "your own discourse is the other's unconscious" (quoted
in Lansing 1983, 1). While seeming to offer the reader a spiritual arboreality,
The Holy Forest actually presents a rhizomatic writing of arboreal blocks
producing angular detours or folds in pathways, and accordingly satisfies
Deleuze's specifications for the contemporary status of objects as objectiles
"inseparable from the different layers that are dilating, like so many occasions for meanders and detours" (1993, 37). The forest is a territory, not an
image, and narrative in this domain becomes a calculus emitting an infinite
fractal phalanx that Ovid might describe as the perfect fusion of the ant
and the broccoli. In "The Practice of Outside," Blaser describes the serial
poem as just such a Deleuzean objectile: "like a series of rooms where the
lights go on and off. [The serial poem] is also a sequence of energies which
burn out, and it may, by the path it takes, include the constellated" (Spicer
1975, 278). (The monadic house, of course, is limited to the two rooms, an
upper private and a lower public.)

In "The Fire," Blaser describes the serial form in a strikingly Ovidian manner as "a narrative which refuses to adopt an imposed story line, and completes itself only in the sequence of poems, if, in fact, a reader insists upon a definition of completion which is separate from the activity of the poems themselves. The poems tend to act as a sequence of energies which run out when so much of a tale is told. I like to describe this in Ovidian terms, as a carmen perpetuum, a continuous song in which the fragmented subject matter is only apparently disconnected" (1970, 17). Blaser shifts in this passage from a conception of seriality as sequentiality to one of continuum, committing a contradiction in momentum. However, it is the Ovidian model of the *carmen perpetuum* that accommodates most easily into the model of plication, with seriality refigured as folds of song along a perpetual continuum, creating effects of "apparent" disconnection.[18]

Emphatically the fold presides over Merleau-Ponty's description of the imaginary (which Blaser quotes enthusiastically) as "not simply the production of mental images, but the 'baroque' proliferation of generating axes for visibility in the duplicity of the real" (in Spicer 1975, 305). Leibniz and Deleuze would substitute "conspiracy" for "duplicity" in the final clause. Blaser additionally enunciates a composition-as-fold when describing Spicer's Lorca translations in which the visible plicates with the invisible—the dead fold over on the living until Garcia Spicer meets Jack Lorca in an ontological fold. In the introduction, the posthumous Lorca admonishes:

[T]hese poems are not translations. In even the most liberal of them Mr. Spicer seems to derive pleasure in inserting or substituting one or two words which completely change the mood and often the meaning of the poem as I had written it. More often he takes one of my poems and adjoins to half of it another half of his own, giving rather the effect of an unwilling centaur. . . . Finally there are almost an equal number of poems that I did not write at all (one supposes that they must be his) executed in a somewhat fanciful imitation of my early style. The reader is given no indication which of the poems belong to which category, and I have further complicated the problem (with malice aforethought I must admit) by sending Mr. Spicer several poems written after my death which he has also translated and included here. (Spicer 1975, 11)

Blaser figures Spicer's ludic method here as a "streaming" or "flowing boundary," which is an equally apt description of the monad's negotiation with the outside through *conatus*.

However, toward the end of "The Practice of Outside," Blaser presents his own theory of the fold, through a genealogy via Blake rather than Deleuze or the Baroque.

> One has the peculiar sense that the body is neither material nor spiritual. That it is the alembic itself. Any unity or disunity takes place there. For now, one may take the curious entangling I've argued apart and make it elemental. The issue then is a meeting of elementals and intelligence. I borrow a Blakean word to say they fold. I seek here to draw attention to a poetry at the gates of existence because it is there that the polarity begins, elemental and inescapable. This is the necessary laying of oneself alongside another content, which brings form and keeps it alive—the double of language, where it holds to both reason and unreason, thought and unthought. (Quoted in Spicer 1975, 316)

The first sentence describes with condensed acuity the singular morphology of the monad, and what follows (the folding of elements and intelligence) liberates more than a precarious plication of Cartesian and Leibnizian topics. Again, as with the male womb in "The Park," Blaser crinkles a lamination into ripples resulting in a marbling of categorial conspiracies.

I can't improve on Miriam Nichols's prescient comments on the labyrinthine structure of *The Holy Forest:* "Single images, poems, or even books are meaningful as elements in an endlessly recombinable series, and it is a distinguishing feature of Blaser's 'art of combinations' that seemingly distinct elements are in fact inextricably entangled. Thematic continuity thus gives place to a formal labyrinth that Blaser sometimes refers to as 'folded' " (1996, 59). There are several facets of this passage worthy of comment. The state of entanglement evokes not only Barthes's delineation of the scriptoral condition of writing after the death of the author, but equally Blaser's own discussion of the "occultation of the heart" in "The Practice of Outside."[19] Moreover, this entanglement is similar to a spatial plenum, that is, without vacuum. As Rescher states, "Leibniz's space is a space of real points (i.e., monads) without real lines, planes, or solids; it is a space where one can tell—if one is God—whether two monad-points are close together (for then their points of view will be similar), and yet it is meaningless to ask for the distance between them, for distance, being a relation, has no place in the monadic realm" (1967, 101). (Leibniz's own term for space is *umgebungsraum*, i.e., neighborhood space.) Finally, the suggestion of a recombinant text suits perfectly Leibniz's model of monadic aggregations in constant change through appetition.[20] The most Baroque manifestation of the linear is, of course, the labyrinth, the bent single line of acute angular intensities, and we might compare Blaser's arboreal labyrinth to Leibniz's own labyrinthine preoccupations.[21] In the preface to his *Theodicy*, Leibniz lists two that constantly present themselves as traps to rational thinking. One is the labyrinthine connection of liberty and necessity; the other—embroiling discussions of the infinite in its seemingly constituent elements—is the labyrinth of indivisible points.

Nichols goes on to discuss Blaser's modification of the fragment: "As *The Holy Forest* unfolds, however, such fragments become better understood as so many lighted curves of a fabric, separated from each other by the dark folds that allow them to appear—the visible entangled with the invisible, the known with the unknown" (1996, 60). Although this introduces an important modification to the status of the fragment, the attempt to reconcile the letter with the fold proves infelicitous. Leibniz's rules state that the monad, owing to a sovereign interiority, is incompossible within a series of fragments. Nor can we treat the monad as a partial component of subjectivity and most emphatically not as a ruin, for the monad is fundamentally without extension.[22] An applied poetics of the fold alters radically the phenomenology of the fragment. Citations figure not as textual shards in a collage but as textual nomads in serial plications upon a plenum.[23] Ruins remain for amateurs of the picturesque like temporal indicators covered in a protein coating of nostalgia—although Epicureanism would lead us to believe them to be the simulacra of past habitats.

From Monad to Nomad

Utopia, to which Guattari and Deleuze advert, "is not separated from infinite movement: Utopia designates absolute deterritorialization, yet always at the critical point where the latter is attached to the relatively present milieu, and especially with forces that are the fabric of this milieu" (in Deleuze 1993, xvii). It is precisely the utopian virtuality within the force and vectoral potential of the monad that connects Leibniz's metaphysical agenda to Deleuze and Guattari's geophilosophical project of nomadology. For them a monadology implies a nomadology with an attendant nomadic cognition that "does not ally itself with a universal thinking subject, but on the contrary with a singular race; and it does not ground itself in an all-encompassing totality, but is on the contrary deployed in a horizonless milieu that is a smooth space, steppe, desert or sea. An entirely different type of adequation is established here, between the race defined as 'tribe' and smooth space defined as 'milieu' " (Deleuze and Guattari 1986, 48). Blaser is alert to the monad-nomad implication, as his comments on Bach in "Mappa Mundi" make clear:

> the astonishment of BACH'S belief - counterpoints
> of monads becoming nomads - *of rhythm is image/*
> *of image is knowing/ of knowing there is/ a construct* - his dream
> of compossibility
>
> (1993, 364)

The temptation here is to rethink Blaser's incorporation of the fragment as a nomadic rather than a public strategy along the way perhaps to a reevaluation of the genuinely public as the truly nomadic. A necessity of this reformulation is to obliterate both outside and inside as distinct topographical categories, replacing striated space by a folded one, which would constitute the poem. Nomadic texts demand semantic tribes moving through verbal milieus without centralizing cognitive controls or spherical organization. The persistent meanderings of images and voices in Blaser's poetry homologize the monad's clinamenlike tendency through appetition to constantly move and shift perception.[24]

The Holy Forest as both a monadography and a nomadography? What does this claim require? It demands initially an affective (as opposed to a systematic) reading of the seriality. What Deleuze writes of Spinoza I offer as entirely appropriate to a reading of *The Holy Forest:* "[There is] a double reading . . . on the one hand, a systematic reading in pursuit of the general idea and the unity of the parts, but on the other hand and at the same time, the affective reading, without an idea of the whole, where one is carried along or set down, put in motion or at rest, shaken or calmed, according to the velocity of this or that part" (Deleuze 1988a, 129). Affective reading entails both monadic and nomadic vectors, a relishing of the particulate alongside an open acceptance of the nontotalizable. An additional condition requires that readers encounter the image as a strictly monadic viewpoint. Nichols's comments are correct upon the perspectival, monadic nature of Blaser's imagery as chiasmus without petitioning, however, Leibniz's minimal unit of substance. Blaser's "image is . . . a point of intersection and divergence, exerting both a centrifugal and a centripetal force" (M. Nichols 1996, 65). Monadic status confers on both the image and the fragment a simultaneous quality of universal and part. What Nichols fails to point out is the relationship of image to its spatial context. Conceived monadically, the isolate image must fold upon a plenum with no "otherness" established by difference or gap. "In history Leibniz believed that the smallest causes, often unseen and unnoticed, were the true and profound causes of events, owing as he said to the 'universal interconnection of things' " (Aarsleff 1982, 92). Leibniz clearly emerges not only as a precursor of Prigogine and chaos theory but also as the rightful adversary of both Saussure and Derrida.

Writing of Jack Spicer (in a passage also carrying reference to Merleau-Ponty), Blaser delineates a markedly monadic terrain of folds and curves as that topography pertains to language: "This insistence of the dictation that an outside, an other than ourselves, speaks to us notices first a disappearance or emptying out of a manhood from his language, and then watchfully approaches 'a field' including the other and a 'topography' that is a folding and unfolding of a real that contains us" (in Spicer 1975, 286). In Blaser's compositional method, citation replaces dictation as a practice of outside yet carries with it important topographical implications.[25] Quotations are not to be considered fragments but rather tactical folds of a poetic interior. "A reopened language lets the unknown, the Other, the outside in again as a voice in the language" (Spicer 1975, 276). So Blaser writes in a passage that comes close to articulating the sovereign interiority of the monad. But how does this affect the ontic status of the outside? Merleau-Ponty counsels that "no matter how strict the connection between external facts, it is not the external world which is the ultimate justification of the internal; they participate together in an 'interior' which their connection manifests" (1964, 148). The field and the fold. This urges a severe rethinking of the nature of interiority. Against the practice of outside—or perhaps supplementing it— Leibniz and Deleuze both offer the paradoxical liberty of the inside, which is a dynamic liberty worn and won without subject.

Leibniz demonstrates how the search for the infinite is located primarily in neither the psychologized aesthetics of Longinean *ekstasis* nor the vicarious terror of Burke's sublime, but rather inside that delirious domain opened up in mathematics by fluxions and the infinitesimal calculus.[26] Leibniz is inconceivable without this hypoperceptual vertigo—the microbiotic vistas opened up by Leeuwenhoek which revealed all life to be fluxional.[27] A still pond shows itself as an aquatic world teeming with a myriad of life-forms, like so many quotations, each of which is a book or pond itself. We might be tempted to call this dissipative structure the Baroque microsublime but perhaps with more probity should settle on naming it the Leibnizian sublime of which Robin Blaser partakes with cognizance and competence. Throughout "The Practice of Other," we read of duplicities and polarities which—via Leibniz—all become available as ripples on a surface. The compound, monadic cavities of a male womb folded as a ripple in a holy sea or ocean and refolded into that *sacra bosco* Robin Blaser names his *Holy Forest*.

4. Charles Olson's Art of Language

The Mayan Substratum of Projective Verse

for Ron Silliman

I

> It is his body that is his answer, his body intact and fought for, the absolute
> of his organism in its simplest terms, this structure evolved by nature,
> repeated in each act of his birth, the animal man; the house he is, this house
> that moves, breathes, acts, this house where he dwells against the enemy,
> against the beast.
>
> —Charles Olson
>
> While I had breath I shrieked.
>
> —Charles Brockden Brown

The nine short essays that appear under the heading "Proprioception" in Olson's *Additional Prose* propose an ambitious grouping of history, writing, the human body, and language into a compound epistemology and ontology. Olson describes his version of proprioception as "the data of depth sensibility / the 'body' of us as object which spontaneously or of its own order produces experience of, 'depth' Viz SENSIBILITY WITHIN THE ORGANISM BY MOVEMENT OF ITS OWN TISSUES" and later on in the same essay "the 'body' itself as, by movement of its own tissues and organs, giving the data of depth" (1974, 17–18).[1] This conception of the self as a structure of internal relations between tissues and organs—whose totality performs a function and informs a sensibility—is vital to Olson's theory of open verse, outlined most concisely in his May 1959 letter to Elaine Feinstein and in his 1950 essay "Projective Verse." Together they offer a radical, anthropological poetics binding language and utterance through an accredited value to the biological makeup of the human species. "Behind every word in Olson is the body" (Watten 1985, 159), a situation that unavoidably invokes the cherished topographical binaries of inner/outer and surface/depth. Olsonian energy is conceived not as a surface turbulence (as in Lucretius's atomic law) but as encrypted within anthropological and anatomical circuitries whose mandate (via poetry) is as much outerance as utterance.

The call is for a verse that follows "certain laws and possibilities of breath for the breathing of the man who writes as well of his listenings" (1967, 51). In a critical paragraph, midway through "Projective Verse," Olson makes a significant commitment to speech over writing and to its attendant metaphysics of presence: "[B]reath allows all the speech-force of language back in (speech is the 'solid' of verse, is the secret of a poem's energy)" (1967, 56). Despite its trenchant repudiation of closure and metrical bondage, "Projective Verse" supports a poetic tradition of voice that stresses the unmediated transmission of energy according to pneumatic laws. (One must wait, of course, until the mid-1970s and Hélène Cixous's Medusan laughter before a gendered, politicized version of proprioception emerges.) [2] For Olson, breath is an essence—both culturally and philosophically unproblematic—insinuated into a theory of writing as "natural" to carry enormous positive presuppositions. Breath and graphism are brought into an interesting complicity in Olson's argument for proprioceptive origin: "And the line comes (I swear it) from the breath, from the breathing of the man who writes, at the moment that he writes" (1967, 54).

Patently writing against the prevalent metrically regulated poetries of the 1940s—Karl Shapiro, Richard Eberhart, Theodore Roethke, and John Berryman, for instance—Olson appeals to breathing as the formal determinant of the poetic line but unwittingly suppresses important predecessors: Henry Sweet, for instance, who writes on the phenomenon of "breath-groups" in his 1890 work *A Primer for Phonetics*.

The only division actually made in language is that into breath-groups. . . . Within each breath-group there is no pause made whatsoever, notwithstanding the popular idea that we make a pause between every two words. Thus in such a sentence as *put on your hat,* we hear clearly the "recoil" or final breath-glide which follows the final *t* of *hat,* but the *t* of *put* runs on to the following vowel without any recoil, exactly as in the single word *putting.* (Quoted in Huey 1968, 136)

J. E. Wallace Wallin's 1901 research into articulatory utterance at Yale ascertained the average quantity of syllables uttered between breath-pauses to be about six.

Olson's positivization of the pneumatic also finds significant precedence in William James. In a confident anti-Cartesian gesture, James conflates mentation and breathing in what amounts to a staggering ecumenical valorization of the latter. "I am as confident as I am of anything that, in myself, the stream of thinking (which I recognize emphatically as a phenomenon) is only a careless name for what, when scrutinized, reveals itself to consist chiefly of the stream of my breathing. The 'I think' which Kant said must be able to accompany all my objects, is the 'I breathe' which actually does accompany them." James continues, revisioning Bergson's stream of consciousness as a respiratory stream. "There are other internal facts beside breathing . . . and these increase the assets of 'consciousness,' so far as the latter is subject to immediate perception; but breath, which was ever the original of 'spirit,' breath moving outward between the glottis and the nostrils, is, I am persuaded the essence of which philosophers have constructed the entity known to them as consciousness" (quoted in Byrd 1994, 35).[3] These references to Sweet, Wallin, and James should not be construed as an attempt to belittle Olson's argument—their work on quotidian utterance and breath never attempted to suggest a direction for poetics—but they are intended to relativize the novelty of projective verse in the light of a suppressed historical sediment.

Olson's related valorization of the syllable has similarly unacknowledged precedents. "Projective Verse" evokes the syllable as a sovereign spontaneity aligned to the categories of breath, voice, and listening—so as to register an unmediated presence.

> It is by their syllables that words juxtapose in beauty, by these particles of sound as clearly as by the sense of the words which they compose.
>
> I say the syllable, king, and that is spontaneous, this way: the ear, the ear which has collected, which has listened, the ear, which is so close to the mind that it is the mind's, that it has the mind's speed
>
> . . .
>
> the HEAD, by way of the EAR, to the SYLLABLE. (1967, 53–55)

This essentialist investment in the syllable is already espoused as early as Plato, who in the *Cratylus* advances his doctrine of true naming as the expression through sound of "the essence of each thing in letters and syllables" (1961, 423e). An equally phonocentric investment is made by the sixteenth-century poet-musician Thomas Campion: "[W]e must esteeme our syllables as we speake, not as we write; from the sound of them in a verse is to be valued, and not their letters" (1904, 352). In the sixth of his ten lectures at Dresden on the *philosophie der sprache*, Friedrich von Schlegel offers a variant antecedent to Olson's thinking.

> Properly syllables, and not letters, form the basis of language. They are its living roots, or chief stem and trunk, out of which all else shoots and grows. The letters, in fact, have no existence, except as the results of minute analysis; for many of them are difficult, if not impossible, to pronounce. Syllables, on the contrary, more or less simple, or the complex composites of fewer or more letters, are the primary and original data of language (1847, 461).[4]

Setting aside the problematic implications of the arboreal metaphor, this particular genealogy of the syllable effects a serious foreclosure on the range of Olson's radical discontinuities, suggesting a surprising belatedness—a residual, organicist romanticism—in his poetics. Moreover, Olson neglects to address proprioception's link to prephonemic vocalities—the child's babble, for instance, which is the subject of detailed study by David Applebaum. "Babble induces proprioception, the body's specific awareness of itself [and] phonically announces the help of a body awareness dissolved in phonemic distance" (Applebaum 1990, 77–78). If breath truly announces what speech forgets (111), then Olson stumbles at this point at an aporia, committing proprioceptive forces to restricted, phonematic manifestation. The theory of "Projective Verse," instead of releasing vocalic energies and expenditures, recovers them to the civilized pale of the syllabic. Olson's remains a speech-based rather than a voice-based poetics that finally betrays breath, enshrining the syllable not only as a corporeal effect but an exclusively adult potential.

Meditating on Celan, Gerald Bruns draws attention to a counterprojective agenda for breath that marshals Rilke and Levinas in its support.

> A turning of the breath . . . can answer to the name of poetry; or, perhaps, vice versa: this event, this breath, is what poetry responds to. Poetry is perhaps this response or responsiveness, this responsibility for the side

of speech that resists reduction or the turning of breath into a mediation or expression. Possibly the poem is as much the taking of a breath
as the expulsion of it ("A breath for nothing," says Rilke); or perhaps, as
in Levinas's account of [*the outside* in *Otherwise than Being,*] freedom is
breath, "the breathing of outside air, where inwardness frees itself from
itself, and is exposed to all the winds." Here breathing is non-subjective:
it means taking in the air that belongs to "an outside where nothing
covers anything, non-protection, the reverse of a retreat, homelessness,
non-world, non-inhabitation, layout without security[.]" As if there were
a link between breath and exile. (Gadamer 1997, 21–22)

Significant, too, is Olson's suppression of breath's *other* law.

The decay of epic or the decline of tragedy, assuming this to be the
case, implies the end of periodic rhythm as such. Time then ceases to be
organized as respiration according to a process of inhalation and exhalation which inserts a moment of life between two silences or zero points.
(Lyotard 1988b, 2)

Olson abrogates breath's other possibility—to articulate fragility onto the
signifying system. Conceived as respiration, breath offers a less positive
model—a dyadic, even dialogic one—articulated onto the rhythmic
ground of the involuntary. As a concept, breath is breachable in accordance
with an ambiguity within its own constitution and interpretative order. On
the one hand—and this is Olson's positive stress—breath is the productive
sign of presence, offered as the exteriorization of complex proprioceptive
stimuli. But breath's other law legislates a negative economy of waste and involuntary expenditure, and Olson ignores the implications of respiration's
binary components, its cyclicality and systolic-dyastolic regulations.

Against Olson's celebration of pneumatic plenitude, a different disposition can be offered. For the Islamic calligrapher, the crucial issue is to master breathing and counter the disruptive forces of its "naturalness" upon
a silent, graphic practice by denial, suppression, and a strict, regulatory
control. Hassan Masoudy recounts this dramatically different relation to
breath:

The capacity of the calligrapher to hold his breath is reflected in the
movement of his hand. . . . Normally one breathes instinctively. In the
course of his apprenticeship the calligrapher learns to control his breathing and to profit by a break in the drawing of a letter to take a new
breath. . . . A push or pull movement is altered according to whether the

writer breathes in or out while making it. When the movement is long, the calligrapher holds his breath in order that the process of breathing should not interrupt its flow. Before calligraphing a letter or a word, he should note the spaces where it will be possible to take a breath and at the same time to re-ink the pen. These breaks are made at very specific points in the text, even if it is possible to hold one's breath for longer or if there is still any ink remaining in the pen. The halts therefore serve to replenish both air and ink. . . . Calligraphers who choose to use traditional methods of writing do not like fountain pens, since these allow an uninterrupted flow of ink; mastery of breathing therefore becomes unnecessary, and the calligrapher loses the satisfaction of feeling the weight of time in his work. (Quoted in Jean 1992, 170–71)

For his part, Henri-Jean Martin quotes a first-century author on the importance of calligraphy in ancient China: "If speech is the voice of the spirit, writing is the drawing of the spirit" (1994, 24). Clearly recognizing a spiritual-respiratory connection emancipated in such a graphic practice, Martin concludes that "calligraphy was an integral part of an art of painting in China that privileged the line and demanded that the artist animate his drawing with the breath of life" (24).

Blanchot counters the vectors of projectivism with a mandate for writing to move toward a still and empty space. Breath—as Olson fails to point out—is intervalic and structurally dependent on a gap between two points. Blanchot wedges writing in the stillness of the dead space of this interval—in his poetic there is still a prior demand from the work's space *before* writing. This locus is understood as petrific and demanding an ordeal of separation.

This ordeal is awesome. What the author sees is a cold immobility from which he cannot turn away, but near which he cannot linger. It is like an enclave, a preserve within space, airless and without light, where a part of himself, and, more than that, his truth, his solitary truth, suffocates in an incomprehensible separation. . . . A work is finished, not when it is completed, but when he who labours at it from within can just as well finish it from without. He is no longer retained inside by the work; rather he is retained by a part of himself from which he feels he is free and from which the work has contributed to freeing him. . . . The work requires of the writer that he lose everything he might construe as his own "nature," that he lose all character and that, ceasing to be linked to others and to himself by the decision which makes him an "I," he becomes the empty place where the impersonal affirmation emerges. (Blanchot 1982, 54–55)

This reading of Olson through Blanchot might introduce another American writer, Charles Brockden Brown, whose 1798 *Wieland* (1926b) and posthumous fragment *Memoirs of Carwin* (1926a) stand antipodal to Olson's writings in relational strategies to language, sound, breath, and body, and petition comparison. *Wieland* is an innovative Gothic tale that modifies conventional terror with a more contemporary device. The plot hinges on multiple tactics of ventriloquism (or "ventrilocution," as Brown terms it) — a relatively unknown and undiscussed ability in the late eighteenth century. Ventriloquism follows its own specific laws and possibilities of breath. "Sound," writes Brown, "is varied according to the variations of direction and distance. The art of the ventriloquist consists in modifying his voice according to all these variations, without changing his place. . . . This power . . . may, possibly, consist in an unusual flexibility or exertion of the bottom of the tongue and the uvula" (1926b, 223n). This description finds adumbration in Sir David Brewster's *Letters on Natural Magic:* "Ventriloquism loses its distinctive character if its imitations are not performed by a voice from the belly. The voice, indeed, does not actually come from that region; but when the ventriloquist utters sounds from the larynx without moving the muscles of his face, he gives them strength by a powerful action of the abdominal muscles. Hence he speaks by means of his belly, although the throat is the real source from whence the sounds proceed" (1856, 170). The significant point in these lengthy citations is to allow comparison of "high-energy transmission" in Olson's theory of field composition with Brown's low-energy transmission through constraint, and the strategic relationship of the vocal subject to the Other. The subtext of ventriloquism saturates the texts of Blanchot. In both his and Brown's there is the central notion of speech emerging from an outside that is inside. (This latter configuration is central also to Leibniz's concept of the monad [see chapter 3] and Nancy's elaboration on the nature of interiority [in note 6 of the same chapter].) For the eighteenth-century prosodist Joshua Steele, breath provides a natural support and temporal basis for metrical cadence. "Our breathing, the beating of our pulse, and our movement in walking, make the division of time by pointed and regular *cadences,* familiar and natural to us" (1775, 20). (Steele's notational innovations in "rational prosody" are examined in chapter 7.)

Blanchot's essay on Edmond Jabès, "Interruptions," outlines three modalities of writing. The first reduces the distance between subject and object. The second affirms distance but tends within the affirmation toward unification. Such a mode would include Keatsian negative capability and Olson's own objectism, which, as Charles Altieri rightly points out—though referring to it confusingly as "objectivism" (1979, 93–108)—has, as a prime concern, the preservation of the energies of immediate experience and which establishes the poem as an object among objects—heterogeneous but unified. Blanchot's third modality, however, is without a unifying effect. As a decidedly nondialectical mode, it founds its subject-object relation on an interruption in being, affirming estrangement, radical separation, and essential otherness (Blanchot 1985, 43–54). For Blanchot, the universe is not Olson's "human" universe but a fundamental articulation upon the infinite as this erupts among the gaps and cessations of the finite.

Blanchot explicitly differentiates this modality of interruption from the manipulated white space in a text. The site of the intervalic is not the non-site invested with significance, as in the breath line of field composition, but a change in the structure or form of the language. Blanchot compares this change to the switch from a Euclidean to a Riemannian surface that would entail "making the relation of words into an essentially asymmetrical field ruled by discontinuity: as if it were a matter (once you have renounced the interrupted strength of coherent discourse) of revealing a level of language where you could reach the power not only to express yourself in an intermittent way but to make intermittence itself speak" (1985, 46). Against Olson's conception of the poem as a "high-energy construct and, at all points an energy discharge," Blanchot offers the notion of writing as a low-energy inscription whose pneumatological-physiological coordinate is asphyxiation—further suggesting that to release expression, yet keep it void (as in pain, fatigue, or misfortune) may be to stage expression within "the dimension of the infinity of language." Blanchot senses a deeper cessation than that of aesthetic silence occasioned by the space of the line-break. For him, space, silence, and lack constitute a site for the entry of a profoundly nonunifying language—the start of a struggle, in fact, toward a writing that cannot figure in language. It is that Otherness—a radical alterity registered by a modality of waiting—that negotiates itself as the suppressed aspect of the Object, and permits a return to Olson in a relation other than antinomian. For the Object as the Other emerges nonproprioceptively in a context other than Olson's poetics: his study of—and fascination with—the art of the Mayan language.

II

We have lived long in a generalizing time, at least since 450 B.C. And it has had its effects on the best of men, on the best of things. Logos, or discourse, for example, has, in that time, so worked its abstractions into our concept and use of language that language's other function, speech, seems so in need of restoration that several of us got back to hieroglyphs or to ideograms to right the balance. (The distinction here is between language as the act of the instant and language as the act of the thought about the instant).

    —Charles Olson (1967, 3–4)

Olson visited Mayan sites in the Yucatan through the winter, spring, and summer of 1951 and his *Mayan Letters,* written to Robert Creeley, occupy a significant chronological conjunction with his poetics that will bear exploration.[5] Written at almost the same time as the "Projective Verse" essay, one might anticipate a similar—if not identical—notion of writing. But this is not the case. Despite a familiarity with Mayan grammar—Olson owned a copy of Alfred Tozzer's *A Maya Grammar* (T. Clark 1991, 195)—the *Mayan Letters* expose a dense interest in the silence of a graphic economy and a system of writing irreducible to either speech or breath. Olson offers his theory on the singular genesis of Mayan writing, an origin rooted in a cultural attention to pangestural expression: "Men were able to stay so interested in the expressions and gestures of all creatures . . . that they invented a system of written record, now called hieroglyphs, which, on its very faces, is verse, the signs were so clearly and densely chosen that, cut in stone, they retain the power of the objects of which they are the images" (Olson 1967, 7).

In a 1951 letter to Creeley dated "tuesday, march 20," Olson proposes a vital connection:

> Christ, these hieroglyphs. Here is the most abstract and formal deal of all the things this people dealt out—and yet, to my taste, it is precisely as intimate as verse is. Is, in fact, verse. And comes into existence, obeys the same laws that, the coming into existence, the persisting of verse does. (Olson 1966, 34)

By March 28 he is convinced that the meaning of the glyphs lies in their status as language and not astrological pictographs. At this point, Olson has the strong feeling that the glyphs mark in their designs the figures of a spoken language. On Sunday, April 1, he writes:

What continues to hold me, is, the tremendous levy on all objects as
they present themselves to human sense, in the glyph-world. And the
proportion, the distribution of weight given the same parts of all, seems,
exceptionally, distributed & accurate[.] . . . That is, the gate to the center was, here, as accurate as what you & i have been (all along) talking
about—viz., man as object in a field of force declaring self as force because force is in exactly such relation & can accomplish expression of
self as force by conjecture, & displacement in a context best, now, seen
as space more than time. (1966, 111–12)

Three paragraphs further on, Olson anticipates his notion of the form-
content binary as it appears in "Projective Verse":

[A] Sumer poem or Maya glyph is more pertinent to our purposes than
anything else, because each of these people & their workers had forms
which unfolded directly from content (sd content itself a disposition
toward reality which understood man as only force in field of force containing multiple other expressions (1966, 113) [6]

(This sentiment reappears in "Projective Verse," of course, in the noted dictum first formulated by Robert Creeley that form is never more than an
extension of content.) [7]

A more detailed account of Olson's interest in these glyphs occurs in a
little-known text: the poet's application to the Viking Fund and Wenner-
Gren Foundation, submitted in 1951, to continue his field research in the
Yucatan and to culminate, he hoped, in the publication of a book: *The Art
of the Language of Mayan Glyphs*.[8] In the application, first published in 1973
as "Project (1951): 'The Art of the Language of Mayan Glyphs,'" Olson
makes much of a singular feature of these glyphs: their plastic nature.

Mayan "writing," just because it is a hieroglyphic system in between the
pictographic and the abstract (neither was it any longer merely representational nor had it yet become phonetic) is peculiarly intricated to the
plastic arts, is inextricable from the arts of its own recording (sculpture
primarily, and brush-painting), in fact . . . writing, in this very important instance . . . can rightly be comprehended only, in its full purport,
as a plastic art. (1973, 95)

It soon becomes clear that Olson's interest lies in the artistic dimensions of
the glyphs—especially the plastic resonance—and not in their meaning as

linguistic signs. While acknowledging the work of decipherment by his predecessors, Olson remains emphatic that his own studies move in a different direction: "[I]n Mayan studies the decipherers have made themselves the measure, and my aim is to try to do a study exact enough to give the arts (and I include writing) the sort of attention I take it they deserve" (1973, 95). Olson proceeds to define the "art" and "language" of the glyph:

[A] glyph is a design or composition which stands in its own space and exists—whether cut in stone or written by brush—both by the act of the plastic imagination which led to its invention in the first place and by the act of its presentation in any given case since. Both involved—I shall try to show—a **graphic** discipline of the highest order. . . . Simultaneously, the art is "language" because each of these glyphs has meanings arbitrarily assigned to it, denotations **and connotations**. (1973, 95–96)

Of several felicitous conjunctions in this passage, one might point out the reference to the glyph's space as "a design or composition which stands in its own space and exists"—an ontic autonomy to which Olson elsewhere appeals in formulating his definition of meaning as "that which exists through itself" (1975b, 64). In the light of the poststructuralist "allegory," the temptation is to counter Olsonian meaning with the very different description offered by Lacan: "no meaning is sustained by anything other than reference to another meaning," arriving this way at the counterproposition: that which exists through itself can never be meaning. The fascination of the glyphs to Olson is neither phonocentrism in general nor the specific Saussurean principle of twentieth-century linguistics whereby the glyphs, like words, would gain meaning by their differential and oppositional play with other glyphs.[9] Indeed, the Mayan glyph takes on precisely those qualities and powers ascribed by Kant to the modality of the Beautiful, evinced in landscapes, that offer figuratively a cryptography or cipher (*chiffreschrift*) impossible to decode or capture rationally but made available via taste to feeling (cf. Kant 1952, 160).

There follows in the application a most remarkable alignment:

The value of the writing to my work here would seem to be a matter of the insights which follow from the practice of it as a profession, particularly such graphic verse as a contemporary American poet, due to the work of his immediate and distinguished predecessors does write. Two recent publications document the point of such practice, particularly as it applies to such things as Mayan glyphs: the essay on "Projective Verse"

. . . and the study of language in relation to culture, "The Gate and the Center." (Olson 1973, 96)

A proclamation of breath and syllable as the poetic agents developed from the graphic plasticism of the Mayan glyph? It appears that for Olson there's no contradiction between the phonocentric-bias of "Projective Verse" and the abstract, plastic, graphic economy of the Mayan glyph. In fact, their interrelation is endorsed by a "documental practice." However, the chronological proximity of these two documents removes any possibility of a rational appeal to an "evolution" or "progression" in Olson's thinking. Clearly, the Mayan project and the concerns of "Projective Verse" were concurrent preoccupations, and the Viking application warrants scrutiny as the suppressed "other" text of "Projective Verse." Of course, this contradiction need not negate the strength of Olson's poetics, but it must complexify its reader-reception and *should* alert us to a more graphic and spatial element at work in *The Maximus Poems*.[10] The Mayan glyph is both Olson's blindness and his insight.

> My emphasis on the live stone, for all the value of its "relief" . . . and, within any given stone, the analysis of two parts: not only *the individual glyph* and its elements (with the emphasis shifted from too close an attention to its denotation as "word" toward more understanding of its connotations, from its force as carved thing) but also that unit which dominates a stone visually . . . the *glyph-block,* that "square" which can include up to 4 glyphs and which sets itself off into an area usually about 6 × 6 inches. The mechanics of the glyph-block (the way it organizes its glyphs and the way the glyph-blocks are organized to make up the "passage" of the whole stone) is the clue, my studies so far suggest, of the other important element of this art, time . . . the double nature of this unusual writing . . . is at once object in space (the glyph) and motion on stone in time (the glyph-blocks). (1973, 96)

Olson comes close here to inventing a syntactic context that eludes the problems of the glyph's alleged sovereign authority. The discovery of the glyph-block is Olson's path back to the page and to the kinetic temporality of an objectist writing. It opens, too, the double nature of Olson's own poetic productions, as both sound and sight, both breath and text, inscribed in a hesitation between two historically antinomian systems. If herein lies a contradiction, then the contradiction is superbly bracketed—

the burden of the silent and plastic is recovered for speech and the syllable in a remarkable complication of temporality.

Now a return to Blanchot. Olson's relationship to Mayan is exactly that of a subject in cessation, hence, the regime of Blanchot's third modality. The glyph's power is precisely to mark an interruption in communication and extend it to the boundaries of hesitation between meanings whose surplus value will be the graphic plasticity figured *outside semantics*. In the glyph, Olson doesn't simply *lose* meaning, but recovers all meaning to loss. Despite Olson's attempt to appropriate the glyph for linguistic objectism, its source of power remains lodged as intransigence in that Other—in a potential alterity not on a phenomenological axis. The glyph inscribes the site of Olson's leap into silence and the sign's power to mystify rather than signify. Read through Blanchot, Olson again faces the fundamental estrangement that he meditates upon in the Heraclitan fragment "man is estranged from that with which he is most familiar." But the burden is reversed. This estrangement is now encountered outside of antidotal longings or solutionary strategies; it becomes a dwelling with the negative as ordeal. Is not the Viking application a reference to that same space before writing that Blanchot outlines as the ordeal of separation? "What the author sees is a cold immobility from which he cannot turn away, but near which he cannot linger" (Blanchot 1982, 54).

If the presidential binaries of "Projective Verse" and proprioception are inner-outer and surface-depth, then Olson's Mayan project effectively abandons them. Indeed, a somewhat modified relation to alterity might be argued: a depthless gaze on and cruising of an essentially laminar flow. The fact is, Olson is seduced by Mayan glyphs. As noted in chapter 1, Baudrillard speaks of seduction as "the world's elementary dynamic" (1988, 59) (a description Olson no doubt would have found intriguing). In neither providing discursive encounters nor communicative exchange the glyphs offer themselves as the optical seduction of self-encrypted meanings. One might call this the protosemantic stratum of the seductive sign—insinuating fittingly into Olson's Mayan project with its emphasis on the "live stone" and with attention fixed not on the glyph as denotation but on its connotational seduction through "its force as carved thing."

While Bentley, long to wrangling schools confin'd,

And but by books acquainted with mankind,

Dares in the fulness of the pedant's pride

Rhyme, tho' no genius; tho' no judge decide;

Yet he, prime pattern of the captious art,

Out-tibbalding poor Tibbald, tops his part;

Holds high the scourge o'er each fam'd author's head,

Nor are the graves a refuge for the dead:

To Milton lending sense, to Horace wit,

He makes them write what never poet writ;

The Roman muse arraigns his mangling pen,

And Paradise by him is lost agen.

—David Mallet, *Of Verbal Criticism*

5. Richard Bentley: The First Poststructuralist?

The 1732 Recension of *Paradise Lost*

"History," writes Steven Goldsmith, "ends in a book; the multiplicity of tongues ends in a single voice of worship. Revelation could not coordinate this double axis without the example of canon already in place, without the belief that the words of a sacred text have their origin not in conflictual circumstances but in the divine unity that transcends history"(1993, 72). Can *Paradise Lost* be allocated such canonic protection as a sacred text, deposited above and beyond the conflictual circumstances of its production? A sovereign work of undisputed coherence and certitude, a stable and transcendental unity to be preserved at all costs from profane tampering? The poem's early critical reception would suggest so. In 1734, Jonathan Richardson, both father and son, urge readers and commentators alike to approach Milton's epic as on a par with Holy Scripture "to be Read, and Construed [not] as an Act of Parliament, or a Mathematical Dissertation; [because] the things of the Spirit are Spiritually Discern'd" (Richardson and Richardson 1734, clxxiii).[1] "To alter," Samuel Johnson emphatically declares, "is more easy than to explain, and temerity is a more common quality than diligence" (1787, 7:92). Yet the contemporary attractiveness of Richard Bentley's editorial scandals lies precisely in that temerity aimed at desacralizing the transcendentally static textual monolith known as *Paradise Lost*. Where Johnson struggles in the *Dictionary* to establish a bulwark of authority against the incalculable idioma of current utterance (see chapter 6),

Bentley embraces instability, understood, however, not in its current deconstructive sense of free-play, pansemiosis, undecidability, and festive aporia, but as strictly symptomatic of historical corruption—a sickness conceived in textual genesis and transmission. To Murray Krieger's chivalric definition of editors as "Knights Errant whose quest is to discover damsels in distress called True Virgin Texts as intended by Authors" (1973, 3) Bentley adds a rich complication: an editorial practice, both unsettling and erudite, that can be truly designated as a poststructuralism *avant la lettre*.

"[T]he movement of analysis, in its endless process, is precisely to explode the text, the first cloud of meanings, the first image of content" (Barthes 1980, 89). Bentley carries this analytic momentum into the domain of textual criticism two and a half centuries before its articulation by Barthes in a textual procedure that anticipates the semiosis of infinite homophonic play found in Brisset. William Empson admits to a "fundamental sympathy with Bentley's outlook" (1950, 156), pointing to his "ample vigour and good sense" and insisting "it was not that his methods were wrong but that the mind of Milton was very puzzling" adding, "it is refreshing to see the irruption of his firm sense into Milton's world of harsh and hypnotic, superb and crotchety isolation" (152–53).

Perry Miller's description of Bentley as "the sort of bulldog who, ordered to find proofs, would bring back dozens of them between his jaws" (1958, 272–73) appears as effete a caricature as it is an affectionate one. A more accurate tribute came earlier from Samuel Parr:

> The memory of Bentley has ultimately triumphed over the attacks of his enemies, and his mistakes are found to be light in the balance, when weighed against his numerous, his splendid and matchless discoveries . . . He was one of those rare and exalted personages, who, whether right or wrong in detached instances, always excite attention and reward it, always inform where they do not convince, always send away their readers with enlarged knowledge, with animated curiosity, and with wholesome exercise to those general habits of thinking, which enable them, upon mature reflection, and after more extensive inquiry, to discern and avoid the errors of their illustrious guides (1828, 3:100).

Bentley's publishing history reads like a manual of contingent calculation and acutely apposite strategy with each work seeming to derive from a premeditated intervention into some current Donnish wrangle or fashionable intellectual dispute. His 1699 *Discourse on the Letters of Phalaris* was a calculated move within the debates on the Ancients and Moderns (pioneered by Sir William Temple and developed by William Wooton), which won Bentley his legendary place in Swift's *Battle of the Books*.[2] The earlier *Boyle Lectures* of 1693 mark a timely attempt to popularize the then novel theories of Isaac Newton.[3] His edition of *Paradise Lost* is certainly no exception to such strategic calculation. Although Bentley allegedly undertook the task at the suggestion of Queen Caroline, there is little doubt that the prime motivation for its January 1732 publication was to coincide with the opening of a new session of Parliament in which proceedings were to be resumed for a reversal of judgment passed the previous year by the Court of King's Bench in favor of Bentley retaining his post as Master of Trinity College, Cambridge (Mackail 1924, 5). Bentley himself testifies to the temporal exigencies of the project in his preface: "I made the Notes *extempore,* and put them to Press as soon as made."[4] Its motivation seems, in part, to have been the new quarto edition of *Paradise Lost* published, with a Life of Milton, by Elijah Fenton in 1725. In the Life, Fenton mentions that textual errors could have entered the work via mistakes made by Milton's amanuenses and that corrections could be made by the substitution of other words of similar sound (Mackail 1924, 4). It is this identical principle of *approximate homonomy* that became the governing logic of practice behind Bentley's editorial procedure; to borrow a famous formula from De Man, it might be said that Milton's blindness is Bentley's insight.

Bentley interrogates the rudiments of textual identity when the latter is established by the forces and complexities of a dictatorial method of production folded into a basal disempowerment of the author. The essential interrogative stance to the editorial challenge is clear. What in fact authenticates the probity of dictatorial transmission? The Lord dictates to Jeremiah, who in turn dictates to Baruch, but what guarantees that what is spoken is truly what is written? A. Meillet observes that against the textual stability offered by printing, copyists "in part by choice, in part without thinking about it, modernized the texts as they reproduced them" (in Certeau 1992, 329). The transit from oral to scriptural economies is constantly threatened by errancy and even a willful clinamen in mendacity—the transcribed frequently passing over into the translated.

Bentley's self-admitted practice is that of "conjectural emendation" based on what he calls his "divinations." The purported task is nothing less than "a restoration of the genuine Milton" from the corruptions of the earlier editions. (In Kierkegaard's terms, he works toward closing the gap between what *Paradise Lost* is and what it ought to be.) The preface elaborates three causal agencies for this corruption. First, "Our celebrated Author, when he compos'd this Poem, being obnoxious to the Government, poor, friendless, and what is worst of all, blind with a GUTTA SERENA, could only dictate his Verses to be writ by another. Whence, it necessarily follows, that any Errors in Spelling, Pointing, nay even whole Words of a like or near Sound in Pronunciation, are not to be charg'd upon the Poet, but on the Amanuensis." The second culprit is the infamous "phantom Editor" whose faults and mendacity are described later in the preface: "But more Calamities, than are yet mention'd, have happen'd to our Poem: for the Friend or Acquaintance, whoever he was, to whom Milton committs his Copy and the Overseeing of the Press, did so vilely execute that Trust, that Paradise under his Ignorance and Audaciousness may be said to be twice lost." The friend is held responsible not only for the swarm of typographical faults (asserted by Bentley to be "many hundreds" and rendering the first edition of *Paradise Lost* as "polluted with such monstrous Faults, as are beyond Example in any other Printed Book") but for several unwarranted poetic interpolations of his own. "For, this suppos'd Friend, (call'd in these Notes the Editor) knowing Milton's bad Circumstances . . . thought he had fit Opportunity to foist into the Book several of his own Verses, without the blind Poet's Discovery." [5] Bentley's third culprit is the blind author himself. "And yet a farther Misfortune befell this noble Poem, which must be laid to the Author's Charge, though he may fairly plead Not Guilty; and had he had his Eye-sight, he would have prevented all Complaints. There are some Inconsistencies in the System and Plan of his Poem, for want of his Revisal of the Whole before its Publication" (1732).

The consequent criterion for emendation is conjecture focused upon these alleged textual misfortunes—and more than eight hundred are offered.[6] They fall consistently into four general categories of redress: those of willful editorial interpolation; of careless editorial alterations; of spelling and pointing mistakes by the amanuensis and/or typesetter; and of Milton's own lapses in poetic system and logical consistency. All the emendations are directed to a common goal of establishing "correctness" arrived at by a rigorous application of logic or by appeal to a Cratylean measure of true and original intention.[7] The fourth category, however, carries a supplementary complication, for it induces an unavoidable contestation between Bentley and Milton as agonistic agencies. (This competitive positioning of editor versus author may be implicit in the edition's preliminary feature of two confronting portraits of Bentley and Milton, present in some copies.)

Such rivalry reduces to the simple issue, in localized aspects of the poem, of who exercises the better poetic judgment. It is at these moments where the fissure in respective taste becomes apparent. Milton's Baroque complexity of thought, Italianate and fueled by metaphoric license, is pitted against Bentley's uncompromising insistence on logical correctness and rational consistency. Detectable at these times is an unbreachable gap in poetic taste, a Lyotardian *differend* at the root of Bentley's assurance that, if *Paradise Lost* were to be established as a classic, it must be purified of what he calls its "romantic rubbish."

How feasible are Bentley's editorial prostheses, those referents required to justify and validate his editorial procedure? The historical data are unavailable that would allow us to test the phantom editor against reality. De Quincey concludes that the editor-friend is a strategic fiction acting prudentially to save Bentley "from the necessity of applying his unmeasured abuse immediately to Milton. This middleman, the editorial man of straw, was literally a mediator between Milton and the Bentleian wrath of damnation, which is already too offensive even as applied to a shadow" (1871, 5:83). Milton's nephew and biographer, Edward Phillips, established the normative view that Milton started work on *Paradise Lost* in 1658 and concluded it in 1663, thereby allowing an appeal to certain known facts around the poet's dictational methods. Jeremie Picard was employed as his personal scribe from 1657 to 1661 (McColley 1940, 303), and Phillips, in his *Life of Milton*, claims that during the early years of composition, Milton dictated verse to "whoever was at hand." During the years of Picard's employment, Milton is described as "waking early" and as having had "commonly a good stock of verses ready against his amanuensis came" (quoted in McColley 1940, 303). Aubrey, in his brief life, corroborates this schedule. Rising early at 4:00 A.M., Milton then had the Hebrew Bible read to him a half hour later. His man returned at 7:00 A.M., "then read to him and wrote till dinner; the writing was as much as the reading" (1813, 442). Milton's sisters Deborah and Mary also read to him. Deborah did so in Latin, Italian, French, and Greek and could well have acted in a secretarial capacity.

Historical data certainly confirm the method of composition via dictation and would endorse a range of theoretically culpable amanuenses: from the specific Picard to Phillips's tantalizingly general "whoever was at hand." Despite David Antin's refreshing skepticism around the poem's linear genesis, the facts of the matter sanction nothing beyond a plausible conjecture for Bentley's case.[8] But Bentley's argument gains plausibility when it shifts to compositorial errors. For one thing, such textual corruption is not anomalous but characteristic of sixteenth- and seventeenth-century texts.[9] Under the rule of the compositor's measure, words were often contracted or altered in the print shop (for abbreviation's sake) to semantically similar words in order to avoid a line break in the text.[10] There is general agreement that typesetting via a dictated copy did occur in the seventeenth-century English print shop, but not as a general rule. The argument against such divided labor is economic insisting that compositorial dictation would follow logical, grammatical phrase groups and would be oblivious to the material economies of the page surface. Included in these economies would be the relative spacing between words to eliminate, wherever possible, a broken word at a line end. The facts are different in the case of poetic texts, however. With a poem like *Paradise Lost,* dictation would be facilitated by the presence of a clear, repetitive—and hence predictable—pattern to govern enunciation. It can be argued on solid ground that the chances of a poetic text being dictated for setting would be more probable than that of prose. Other factors could have influenced the use of dictation: work pressure, the exigencies of deadlines (an irrefutable fact in the case of Bentley's own text), the periodic backlog of work in a shop, the use of temporary labor, and, connected to all of these, the seasonable factor of nighttime typesetting. The lighting in seventeenth-century type shops was notoriously bad, and twilight or nighttime setting would be facilitated by a "caller" to the "setter" of a text.[11]

The least controversial of Bentley's emendations (and the ones on which his genius as a textual critic find most effective demonstration) are those arising from malaudition of a word or phrase enjoying a homophonic link to others. These mistakes hinge on the biological contingencies of dictation and acoustic reception. Such emendations, where Bentley applies the principle of approximate homonomy, are by far the most frequent (totaling over eight hundred). Bentley first emends the following lines:

> Sing Heav'nly Muse; that on the secret top
> Of Horeb or of Sinai didst inspire

altering "secret" to "sacred" on the grounds that mountaintops, because of their height, are usually visible and so hardly "secret." His explanatory footnote extends for forty-one lines and addresses several proleptic counter-arguments. To the assertion that mountaintops are frequently covered by clouds, Bentley replies, "True; but yet it's questionable, whether in the wide and dry Desert of Arabia, Mount Horeb had such a cloudy Cap. I have in my youth read several Itineraries, where the Travellers went up to the Top of Horeb; and I remember not, that they take notice of its Cloudiness" (1732, 1). Further scriptural evidence is supplied from Exodus 17, where the camping Israelites at the base of Horeb can find no water. "All Natural History informs us," quips Bentley, "and Reason vouches it, That a Mountain, whose Head is cloudy, has always running Springs at its Foot" (1). The length and information supplied in this opening footnote are typical, allied to the new sciences; and uncompromising in its logical paradigm, it is characteristic of Bentleian method.

Bentley notes a comparable semantic impropriety at 4:236. Where the standard text reads, "But rather to tell how, if Art could tell," he alters it to, "But rather to tell how, if ought could tell." Art *as a civilized production* is anachronistic in Paradise: "What can Art mean here? the Art of Gardening, or rather the Art of Poetry? Both are improper" (114). The next, at 5:217, is another example of alleged homophonic slippage and one that induces a further evaluative complication: "she spous'd about him twines / Her marriageable arms." This Bentley claims is factually inconsistent: "Marriageable? capable of future Marriage? Why she was wed, spous'd already in the Verse before. And why her Arms more marriageable, than the rest of her Substance?" (154). Bentley conjectures that Milton intended "manageable" as "that can twine and twist in any Situation," but then rejects this on aesthetic grounds, offering the word "lascivious" as a better solution.

More questionable emendations involve the editorial tampering and poetic interpolations by Milton's so-called editor-friend. Dr. Johnson, referring to Bentley's hypothesis of "the obtrusions of a reviser whom the author's blindness obliged him to employ, [assessed it as] a supposition rash and groundless, if he thought it true; and vile and pernicious, if, as is said, he in private allowed it to be false" (S. Johnson quoted in R. J. White, 214). Whatever credence can be loaned to the editor hypothesis, it grants to Bentley a tactical advantage, legitimating his most ruthless excisions from the poem: the notorious "hooked" passages. There are 147 lines expunged from the first three books alone, including some of Milton's most typical passages. The fifty-four lines comprising the famous Paradise of Fools section, 3:444–98, are removed in their entirety as a "silly Interruption of the Story" (Bentley 1732, 93). They are further judged to be patently un-Miltonic and "hence" a malicious insertion by the editor.[12] The celebrated passage at 2:659–66, much loved by later Romantic readers, enumerating a vast procession of mythological and imaginative figures (lapland witches, night hags, "Vexed Scylla, bathing in the sea that parts Calabria from the hoarse Trinacrian shore"), Bentley rejects on moral criteria worthy of Richard Allestree: "[L]et him take back his fabulous Night-Hag, his Dance of Lapland Witches, And his Smell of Infant Blood; and not contaminate this most majestic Poem with trash, nor convey such idle, but dangerous Stories to his young and credulous Female Reader" (1732, 61). It's not difficult to guess at the kind of reception Gray's *Odes* would have got from Bentley.

The categorical resistance to anything nonclassical produces some amazing contractions—"Joining the Tags of Verse together" is Bentley's own phrase for these hybrids. At 5:260–66, a five-line passage referring to Galileo's telescope is deleted and the verse sutured into the following:

> Earth and the Gard'n of God, with Cedars crown'd
> Above all Hills. Down thither prone his flight
> He speeds

Bentley zealously prunes Miltonic epithets because of their alleged logical absurdity. The expunged passage reads:

> As when by night the Glass
> Of Galileo, less assur'd, observes
> Imagin'd Lands and Regions in the Moon

Here, two absurdities are noted: "The Glass, says he, observes: I thought the Eye had done it through the Glass. Observes imagin'd Lands: so he confounds two Opposites, Observation with Imagination. And what is the difference between Lands and Regions?" (Bentley 1732, 156). Bentley is alert also to the consequences of some of Milton's prosodic decisions. Reacting to the poet's placing of the accent in Jesus' central question, "And shall grace *not* find means?" (emphasis mine), he exclaims, "What accent is here? Grace the emphatical word lies mute without Tone. No question, he gave it thus; *And shall not Grace find Means?*" (86).

Bentley is alone among early commentators in drawing attention to some of the poem's gender issues, chiding Milton's depiction of Eve as one overly preoccupied with external appearance at the expense of portraying her inner thoughts and motivations (1732, 129). In one of the most notorious and drastic emendations, Bentley inserts Eve into the "Morning Hymn" of book 5, dramatically recasting the poem into antiphonal verse form with alternations between Eve and Adam. "It cannot displease," quips the sardonic Bentley, "that I have given the Mother of Mankind her Share in this fine Piece, and not let her stand mute, a Hearer only" (153).

It is crucial, however, to approach Bentley's edition with the double imperative to read both the suggested emendation and the accompanying footnote. The format of the 1732 quarto is nonlinear and strategically facilitates comparisons. Bentley is assiduous in pointing this out in the preface. Not one word of the received text is changed, "but all the Conjectures, that attempt a Restoration of the Genuine Milton, cast into the Margin, and explain'd in the Notes. So that every Reader has his free Choice, whether he will accept or reject what is here offer'd him; and this without the least Disgust or Discontent in the Offerer." It is highly consequential that Bentley's footnotes are not relegated to the back of the book but are placed on the same page as the area of text commented on.[13] Each page commands a threefold attention on the reader's part: to the textual crux presented in an italicized embed; to the floating word or phrase that Bentley offers as an alternative reading; and to the prose footnote placed strategically visible at the bottom of the same page. This polytextual structure, in fact, inhibits any monologic reading, forcing readers to negotiate between competitive and interactive textual features. The effect may be likened to a bibliographical application of Brecht's "alienation effect," and its aggressive sociotextual consequences are brought out in Ralph Hanna's words that articulate precisely Bentley's impact: "I intervene in the text, with brackets [in Bentley's case italics] to mark my incursion, to a degree that most readers have found anything from unsettling to odious. I thus always make explicit the bounded conventions behind my decision to annotate: to say a text is canonical is to say it is a fixed text, accepted by a community in a single form" (quoted in Barney 1991, 182). Footnotes, marginalia, and annotations form a secondary, derivative discourse articulated as a subaltern tactic, whose relationship to the primary text is as Laurent Mayali points out, a relation to power rather than to meaning (in Barney 1991, 185).

Fredric Jameson draws attention to the dialectical potential in the footnote, promoting it almost to the stature of a minor genre. "The footnote . . . may indeed be thought of as a small but autonomous *form,* with its own inner laws and conventions and its own determinate relationship to the larger form which governs it. . . . The very limits of the footnote (it must be short, it must be complete) allow the release of intellectual energies, in that they serve as a check on the speculative tendency that might otherwise run wild. . . . The footnote as such, therefore, designates a moment in which systematic philosophizing and the empirical study of concrete phenomena are both false in themselves; in which living thought, squeezed out from between them, pursues its fitful existence in the small print at the bottom of the page" (9).[14] The footnote's law is to maintain subservience in a master-servant relation, yet that law is never free from the subversive effects brought about in what Derrida calls the "pragmatics of annotation" (in Barney 1991, 194). The spaciousness of the quarto page permits Bentley not only to inscribe acts of writing but to manipulate spatial motions and a corresponding retinal sliding. "[T]he very subordination of the footnote assures a sort of framing, a delimitation in the space that gives it a paradoxical independence, a freedom, an autonomy. The footnote is also a text unto itself, rather detached, relatively decontextualized or capable of creating its own context, such that one can read it quickly and directly for itself" (Derrida, quoted in Barney 1991, 194). In the case at hand, through a play of reversals, we don't read Bentley for Milton but Milton for Bentley.

It's in the auxiliary spaces of the footnotes, too, that Bentley presents his most skeptical side in a robust, idiomatic English rich in irony. Bentley's irony is coordinated upon three compositional loci: the absurd editorial interpolations, the conjectural emendation offered, and the assignment of the latter to Milton's own intention. The strategy, as De Quincey clearly perceives, is to disguise as a purported alliance a *direct* contestation with Milton. It is an irony that masquerades as a Cratylean model of textual restoration, supporting the fabric of the editorial prosthesis, while at the same time demolishing the received text with a powerful, overriding alternative. As a subtextual accumulation, the footnotes present the image of a bungling editor incapable of matching the poetic criteria offered by Bentley himself. At 5:378, for instance:

> So to the Sylvan Lodge
> They came, that like Pomona's Arbour smil'd
> With flourets deck'd and fragrant smells

Bentley's manner of refuting this passage is characteristic of his hybrid approach of textual criticism and prosthetic fiction: "Lucky for this Editor, that he's hitherto unknown, and consequently ever like to be so. He's always grafting into the Poem his Likenesses. Here's Pomona brought in for a Likeness, and presently again, Wood-Nymphs, and Three Goddesses. Throw but away his silly Insertions, Pomona's Arbour and fragrant Smells; and the Author's true Words, pick'd up, like Hippolytus's scatter'd Limbs, compose a numerous Verse" (1732, 160). It is surely a deliberate irony that, in a critique of simile, Bentley interpolates a simile of his own.

The direct contestations with Milton are, understandably, less frequent, but they merit comment. Toward the close of book 2, Bentley challenges the following passage:

And fast by hanging in a golden Chain
This pendant World, in bigness as a Star
Of smallest Magnitude, close by the Moon.

" 'Tis difficult here to excuse the Poet himself," writes Bentley, in a rare show of direct confrontation. "[N]o pragmatical Editor can come here to acquit him. 'Tis credible that for Joy that he was finishing his Second Book, he relax'd his Attention, and forgot his own System: in which this pendant World hanging in a Chain is not the Earth, as here inadvertently said, but the whole visible Heavens" (1732, 76). A comparable lapse is observed when Milton asserts that the earth is close by the moon. According to Bentley, this is the same as claiming London is "near Chelsea" (76).[15] The strategy behind this direct opposition seems less to criticize than to humanize Milton. The majority of footnotes protect Milton's genius and—though the fiction is ironic—his reputation remains intact throughout Bentley's ruthless pursuit of logical aporia. In the end, however, it is safe to say that Bentley's self-appointed task is a complete recension in order to rehabilitate the poem within current taste.[16] Bentley's historic achievement is to be the first critic to attempt a recension of *Paradise Lost* and to maintain throughout this endeavor a radical, skeptical stance before the poem.

The editorial method, however, does not originate in the *Paradise Lost*. Indeed, most aspects of it are evident in Bentley's 1711 edition of Horace. To cite just one example to support this claim, there is a passage in the *Ars Poetica* that he rejects as spurious. The Horatian phrase reads "et male tornatos incudi reddere versus" (ill-turned verses on the anvil again), to which Bentley responds, " 'Ill-turn'd'—'anvil'! what has a lathe to do with an anvil?" On the strength of this material inconsistency, Bentley feels justified in replacing the phrase "male tornatos" with "male ter natos" (thrice shaped amiss). Resolution of a crux here, as in the Miltonic recension, is based on a homophonic substitution, but significantly without the prosthetic appeal to a phantom interpolator. The *Horace* likewise foreshadows Bentley's robust empiricality. In the First Epistle occurs the fable of the fox who, when hungry, crept through a crack in a granary wall, fed on the grain inside, and grew too fat to get out (1:vii.29). Bentley's sarcastic empiricism is evident in his boisterous response: "[T]o the rescue, ye sportsmen, rustics, and naturalists! A fox eating grain!" The insight gains executive status when he alters the text from "fox" (*volpecula*) to "fieldmouse" (*nitedula*) (Jebb 1882, 130).

This similarity in editorial method has been insufficiently stressed by

Bentley's biographers and the few critics who have written on his work. It dates the recensional technique to a year much earlier than 1726, which would be the earliest possible date for Bentley's commencement of the Milton project.[17] Moreover, it provokes questions as to its own antecedents. If Fenton's Life of Milton in the 1725 quarto of *Paradise Lost* provides the catalyst behind Bentley's project, and if the resumption of Parliament in 1732 gives the secular incentive to its publication, then Bentley's 1711 edition of Horace pioneers the methodology subsequently reused. The *Horace* demonstrates what the *Paradise Lost* reaffirms: that the germ of Bentley's editorial procedure lay in the theories of Lucretius, encouraging an understanding of words as the mutant, material compounds of numerous atomistic, protosemantic particles: letters. Bentley's textual criticism emerges by way of this genealogy (like the Brissetism noted in chapter 2) as a species of erudite paranomasia, harnessed to collateral particle practice, in support of a syllogistic procedure.

Perhaps the seed of the Milton was sown in Bentley's *Boyle Lectures* of 1693, which have never been causally connected to the grand quarto of 1732. Manuscript evidence supports the fact that Bentley was hard at work on Lucretius as early as 1689 — four years prior to the publication of the *Lectures* (Jebb 1882, 24). The latter have earned their place in intellectual history as the first popular attempt to elucidate Newton's cosmic theories and to utilize them in a refutation of atheism.[18] Jebb contends that Bentley's "first object in studying Newton's cosmical system had been to compare it with that of Epicurus, as interpreted by Lucretius" (27). Without question there is a latent contestation with Lucretius running through all eight lectures. Atomism, espousing a natural in opposition to a supernatural order, together with its uncompromising deterministic materialism, readily lent itself to an atheistic platform. (It is fundamental, for example, to the thought of both Hobbes and Gassendi.) Bentley first read Newton's *Principia* in 1691, and in the last three of the eight *Boyle Lectures* he attempts to refute atheism (and its atomistic justification) by an appeal to the irrefutable new physics of Newton.[19]

In confuting Descartes, who argued that planetary motion occurs around the sun, with each planet occupying a discrete vortex, Newton demonstrated the stability of planetary orbits by a force termed "gravity," postulated as an invariant law effecting a constant attraction to the sun. Combining with gravitational force is what Newton terms a "transverse impulse" projecting all planets tangentially to their orbits. In contrast to gravity, the transverse impulse is not uniform, but adjusted to the place of each separate body in the solar system. This states the *Principia* via Bentley in a nutshell. In a manner symptomatic of late-seventeenth-century apologists, Bentley blurs the conceptual boundary differentiating natural law from human (or subhuman) agency. The characteristic of uniformity bestows on gravity the status of a universal law, yet Bentley discounts the possibility that the transverse impulse might be the result of the operation of another "unknown" law. Indeed, for him, the transverse impulse is demonstrative proof of the Divine Creator as a cosmic agency.

I won't dwell on Bentley's diluted Newtonism, but move on to argue that his critical emendations, though finding justification in and supported by the evidence and method of Newtonian knowledge, nonetheless display the distinct persistence of atomism within its method. Lucretius's concept of the clinamen, or dislocating swerve, has already been discussed in relation to Jarry's 'pataphysics and to poststructural interests (see chapter 2). Suffice to add here that the uniformly downward flow of atoms ironically anticipates Newton's own law of gravity, while the clinamen itself, as the principle governing atomic motion, shares affinity with Newton's second principle of the transverse impulse. Bentley certainly knew the section in Lucretius that draws the analogy between atoms and letters and their tendency to minute transpositions, and perhaps his erudition stretched as far as a familiarity with Bruno's modification of the analogy to posit that what atoms are to bodies, dots and strokes are to letters.[20] In the dictated passage from speech to recording, a clinamen might occur; a *Paradise Lost* might become a parasite glossed, through semantic excess licensed by homophonic slippage, a folding of difference into sameness, might enter inscription. Bentley described language in remarkably Lucretian terms as an organism liable to constant change, "like the perspiring bodies of living creatures in perpetual motion and alteration." Terms reminiscent of Sade. It is the Lucretian theory of motion, translated to the realm of textual condition, that underlies Bentley's fictions of the phantom editor and careless amanuensis, both of whom contribute a clinamen away from the laminar "intention" of the nominal producer. They are similarly Newton's transverse impulse, removed from theological centrality and deposited in a vernacular, tangential mischief; providing the narrative justification of the physics underlying the textual corruption of *Paradise Lost* and the rationale governing Bentley's recension.

"[T]he moments of empiricism and skepticism have always been moments of attention to difference" (Derrida, quoted in Wood and Bernasconi 1988, 93). What strikes a reader forcibly throughout Bentley's emendations is the rugged semiotic skepticism of his approach and his dogged refusal to admit critical horizons broader than the protosemantic constituents of the individual word and letter-sound. I select at random: "Air" Bentley alters to "Hour" (1732, 48), "cry" to "Crue" (61), "corporeal" to "corporal" (162), "infernal" to "internal" (198). The austere achievement of the edition is to render each lexeme accountable not only to logic but also acoustic desire. (Hume will transport this semantic skepticism to the philosophic discourse on human nature in 1738, and the same play of minimal homophonic collocation with minimal shift augurs the metagrammically constructed novels of Roussel, and Brisset's delirious multiple etymological analyses.) Through Bentley's acumen, the word as a phono-acoustic emission is repositioned in a less stable morphology as a fragile concretion of errant particles. By orchestrating the play between linguistic excess and lack, and mining the seam where the homophonic infolds the homonymic, Bentley eventually delivers up *Paradise Lost* as a "schismogenetic" text; a weave (and wave) of competing forces and tensions between virtual and actual signs.[21] In Prigoginian terms, the homophone presents a bifurcation point that precipitates a simpler structure into either disintegration or higher complexity. Bentley's rigorous *délire* pushes the system of *Paradise Lost* away from equilibrium toward the threshold of instability where sound and meaning split, its pages offering to readers a choice between two possibilities. But, more essentially, the homophonic law denies the text's return to any state of equilibrium.[22] A chiasmus resides in all of Bentley's magisterial homophony—an editor's desire for mastery in the realization of which restoration and improvement cross with a linguistic flight of phonosemantic proliferation. (Bentleian *délire*, of course, still depends on binary structuration insofar as it conforms to the homonym-homophone relation as to a strict linguistic law.)[23]

Yet Bentley's edition remains a historical issue of community and institution; its purpose to establish a textual authority free from the oral errancies of dictation. It is the same ideologically motivated quest for stability that will be noted in Johnson's mammoth project of a national lexicon (see chapter 6). Both are prophylactic attempts to safeguard written meaning—one of a poem, the other of a national language—from the semantic lability brought on by actual speech. But Bentley's Milton also exists in excess of the boundaries of that diachrony. "Corruption" and "deviation" are familiar tropes of classical textual editing inscribing the norm of any text when subjected to the volatility of contingent transmission—more so a text dictated by a blind man—calling into question the very possibility that a text might have a fixed, unproblematic or nonvolatile meaning. As Jerome Mc Gann observes, "Every text has variants of itself screaming to get out, or antithetical texts waiting to make themselves known" (1991, 10).[24]

Textual analysis, conjecture, and deconstructive solicitation all converge in Bentley's Milton, which situates the textual problems of *Paradise Lost* in those conditions Stephen Heath describes as constituting a contemporary "practice of writing":

> In the space of the text in the practice of writing there is no longer a movement forward to the fixing of some final Sense or Truth, but on the contrary, an attention to a plurality, to a dialogue of texts founding and founded in an intertextuality to be read in, precisely, a *practice* of writing. (Heath 1972, 23)

The procedure, too, provokes that same imbrication of translation with delirium outlined by Keith Cohen:

> In wriggling out of the denotative straitjacket, the translator discovers the inherent semantic vacillation of the text, the instability many readers may gloss over, the débordement, the superabundance of the original. It is as though each phrase were an edge, a border erroneously delimiting a single denotation. The translator must go over this edge (hence débordement), unleash in the translation this signifying overflow. In this way the initial constraint is turned into its opposite. The illusory bondage by the tutor text yields a liberating excess as soon as the unitary is conceived as multiple (K. Cohen 1977, 86).

Bentley inaugurates what is now a normative disposition in reading: to no longer take a book as an unproblematic transmission of semantically "essential" intentionality but rather to engage it as the material complex of both historical forces and textual peculiarities brought together to provide a hermeneutic space of inherent paralogicality. The "poststructural" interest in Bentley's edition is surely in its drawing attention to the text's basal semantic instabilities. To Bentley we owe the radical interrogation of this dictated epic through a single vital question: Who speaks this text? Underscored is the fact that a dictated sign is potentially already an errant sign, contaminated by carriage and leading to a necessarily fissured deposition. To insist on a homophonic crux, in those clinamens of malaudition and scribal slippage, points finally to the double constitution of the printed sign as both graphic "entity" and acoustic "alterity."

In 1976 Bob Perelman and Kit Robinson adopted dictation and transcription as a compositional method precisely to maximize this tendency toward clinamen-noise and authorial confusion. Perelman describes their collaborative poetics of the clinamen in mundane fashion: "One of us would read from whatever books were handy and two of us would type. These roles would rotate; occasionally, there would be two readers reading simultaneously to one typist. The reader would switch books whenever he felt like it, and jump around in whatever book was open at that time" (1996, 32). Perelman claims that "the extremity of this process, where reading and writing, hearing and producing words were so jammed together" is emblematic of the collaborative nature of much language writing of the time and articulates technique onto social consequence: "the conventional positions of (modernist) literary competence are reversed: instead of the writer being powerful and the reader struggling to catch up, . . . the reader—or, to avoid confusion, the pronouncer—is the active one and the writer, the typist, the swamped receiver, is reactive, is second in the chain of command, which becomes a change of suggestions" (33).

Directly relevant to Bentley's procedure are Derrida's early comments on methodic "solicitation." "Structure . . . can be *methodically* threatened in order to be comprehended more clearly and to reveal not only its supports but also that secret place in which it is neither construction nor ruin but lability" (1978, 6). Bentley indicates the labile point, the site of semantic instability, to be the consequence of a homophonic excess attendant both on and in dictation, and, by a rigid application of this textual observation, solicits *Paradise Lost* into uncertainty.

Bentley's closet logophilia finally results in a micropoetics of reader determination. Texts are established as obsessive, precarious expressions of single sounds announcing double or multiple meanings. He draws attention to the micropeculiarities of a text and ultimately to the fact that all poems, all discourses, are constructed from the clinamens of atomic letters. Contemporary twenty-first century readers can appreciate Bentley's conjectural intervention as doubling the virtuality of certain signifiers, thereby critically destabilizing univocity, making the reader aware that the graphic seme partakes less of a trace structure than a phantom echo of another sense. It's important, then, that Bentley isn't addressed judgmentally, and that his suggestions be aligned with the received text dialectically in order to induce a third stage in critical assessment, treating the emendations as indications toward the poem's own suppressed sign economy. Bentley's principle of the approximate homonym rather than debating *Paradise Lost* actually enriches it with plural possibilities. Instead of disambiguating the textual cruxes, it invites us to receive them as semantic chords, proclivities to polysemeity that decenter the poem from any overriding univocal gravity.[25]

When Patrick Murdoch writes in 1762 "on the bad success our commentators and editors have had, either in improving their authors, or advancing their own reputation as critics—witness Bentley's Milton, and the late editions of Shakespeare. Those men being able grammarians, were tempted to deal in criticism; which requires what they wanted, a feeling of poetical beauty" (1762, 1:29), he misses Bentley's true achievement, which is grammatological, not aesthetic—namely, a successful elucidation, by implication, of the verbal disposition to lability whenever speech passes into writing.

Atticus apparently employed hundreds of scribes, writing simultaneously from his single dictation and thereby approximated the productivity of the modern printing press (L. Friedländer, quoted in Harris, 1989, 224 n. 247).[26] Lucky for Atticus and the multiple copy that he wasn't blind at the time and that Bentley wasn't born. In the final instance, we return to the remainder and its reminder. To the unavoidable play of language apart from, and in despite of, all intentionality. "At the very moment when [Bentley] is asserting that the speaker's control over his language will always be established in the end, the editor's mastery compensating for the edited author's slip of the pun, language (the remainder) reminds us that it, and no one else, is speaking, that whenever we believe that we rule over our words, we are in the grip of an unavoidable but nevertheless delusive illusion" (Lecercle 1990, 265). One more dissipative structure arrived at through a bifurcation point.

Let the use of words teach you their meaning.

— Wittgenstein, *Philosophical Investigations*

To arrest the meaning of words once and for all, that is what Terror wants.

— Lyotard, *Rudiments paiens*

All words are adult. Only the space in which they reverberate—a space infinitely empty, like a garden where, even after the children have disappeared, their joyful cries continue to be heard—leads back towards the perpetual death in which they seem to keep being born.

— Blanchot, *Le Pas Au-Dela*

6. Johnson and Wittgenstein

Some Correlations and Bifurcations in the *Dictionary* and the *Philosophical Investigations*

"To read an entry in the *Dictionary,*" Paul Fussell reminds us, "is to undergo an intellectual and ethical overhaul" (1986, 203). And Ian Watt, while unwilling to grant it the rank of a major literary creation, concedes that in the *Dictionary* Samuel Johnson made every word "a new and unavoidable challenge" (1962, 19). I wish to reexamine these two famous passages in the light of pertinent, nonliterary aspects that the *Dictionary*'s format entails, aspects that challenge its readers to negotiate a major articulation of the literary onto the philosophic. By addressing the dyadic form of Johnson's lexico-literary creation—the interlacing of a word-inventory with an encyclopedic gathering of illustrative passages—it becomes possible to award the *Dictionary* a significance other than those granted it in the histories of lexicography and literature. Johnson's conscious problems are clearly stated in the Preface, but by scrutinizing the *Dictionary*'s format, especially its binary textuality, certain philosophic implications emerge.

The *Dictionary* can be classified as one of those enterprises of grandiose textual collecting (worthy of Ezra Pound or Robert Duncan) that Certeau sees as deriving from the common principle "of recreating a body from its disjointed members, [struggling] against division by *practices of transfer,* of which the various modes of speaking are but variants" (1992, 117).[1] A major challenge for Johnson is to balance the *Dictionary*'s double mandate to provide a serial listing of verbal "explanations" (the book's dictionary function) with supplemental "illustrations" (the book's encyclopedic dimension).[2] By their very nature, such illustrations are both fragmented phenomena and transported alterities, and in his treatment of them Johnson insists on both the contextualizable nature of the linguistic—its potential to shift and fragment—and its social, pragmatic ground in public signs. In the clear confines of this reflex, Johnson precipitates citation into the paroxystic language-game known as the *Dictionary*. Recent theorizing by Barthes, Certeau, and Blanchot strongly suggests that citationality is not a benign operation but a complex, intentional product that releases undetermined, nonintentional effects. Moreover, Johnson's practice of citation calls attention to a suppressed interrogation: what concept of meaning underlies the *Dictionary*'s binary system?

"Words," exhorts Johnson "must be sought where they are used."[3] By insisting that words should not be merely defined but demonstrated in culturally and historically specific ambiences, Johnson interlaces lexicography with a philosophy of language—a philosophy close to the use theory of meaning advanced by Ludwig Wittgenstein in the *Philosophical Investigations*. The precise dynamic of Johnson's famed citations will be examined and their status, as authoritative endorsements of semantic value, tested against Wittgenstein's notion of "ordinary language" (i.e., of language before its correction or justification by philosophical scrutiny).[4] As a consequence of this limited range of address, the rich subtextual strata of the *Dictionary* (a major fascination for recent Johnson scholars like De Maria and Reddick) will be largely passed over. Nor will this chapter address Johnson's fluctuating and frustrated intentions in the work, magisterially documented by Reddick. Also unscrutinized, but mentioned here as an important facet of readerly encounter, is the possibility of a nonutilitarian approach to the *Dictionary*, to its inherent value as a "pleasure-text" for nonproductive consumption. A page in the *Dictionary* offers a Deleuzian space par excellence with multidirectional lines of flight in tension with a hyperonymic organization.[5] As such, it opens up to hedonistic reading possibilities—a connivance with meanderings and perambulations in an aimless drifting through changing textual states analogous to that "technique of transient passage through varied ambiences" the Situationists termed *dérive* (see Knabb 1981, 45).[6] Robert Browning is one reader known to have embraced the *Dictionary* as such a space of endless textual digression, a practice whose validity inheres in what Kristeva calls "a space of distraction [inside] a carnal commerce with words" (1980, 208).[7] Instead, I examine some poststructural and ideological implications of the book's content and its material deployment in a dyadic, but nonoppositional, minimally original, but largely recycled, economy.

Adam is not to be remembered as the primordial lexicographer. His Edenic task was an onomastic labor among ambient and unnamed novelties. What Johnson inherits from this biblical legacy is what Hans Aarslef wittily labels the Adamic myth without Adam. Like the book figuratively described by Melville in *Pierre,* the *Dictionary* is a sedimentation of skeletal deposits, an atoll rising as a mountain out of an ocean of literary undifferentiation; a book of written readings, the heterogeneous acquisitions accumulated by a "lynx-eyed mind, in the course of . . . multifarious, incidental, bibliographic encounterings" (quoted in Riddel 1979, 330). In Lockean manner, the project of a lexicon provides Johnson with a tabula rasa ready to receive the imprint of his reading in preparation for the English language to be monumentalized through the archive of his eyes. Johnson does not inscribe himself as the great author but orchestrates himself as the compiler *sub deo,* a "mere collector of words" (1963, 10). And it's in this mundane mode of agency that Johnson, despite his desires, releases the reader-function as a massive counterarboreal activity; a tracking of rhizomatic proliferations, reboundings, and dead ends.

The compilator is a time-honored category—one of Saint Bonaventure's quadruplex of writerly practice—including among its noteworthy practitioners such *auctores humani* as Peter Lombard, Vincent of Beauvais, and Nicholas de Lyra. (We might also include among Johnson's contemporaries the great encyclopedist Ephraim Chambers.)[8] This theological resonance should not be forgotten—the vast reserves of printed English literature serve Johnson in precisely the way God's word and the writings of the early church fathers served the medieval compiler. Parkes helps sketch out this medieval inflexion: "The compilator adds no matter of his own by way of exposition (unlike the commentator) but compared with the scribe he is free to rearrange (*mutando*). What he imposed was a new *ordinatio* on the materials he extracted from others. In the words of Vincent of Beauvais: 'Nam ex meo pauca, vel quasi nulli addidi. Ipsorum igitur est auctoritate, nostrum autem sola partium ordinatione.' The *compilatio* derives its usefulness from the *ordo* in which the *auctoritates* were arranged" (1976, 128).

Notwithstanding the fact that Johnson anticipates Barthes's scriptor as the ontological bearer of an "immense dictionary from which he draws a writing that will be incessant" (Barthes 1986, 53), it's no less true that in the *Dictionary* Johnson makes real Barthes's tantalizing dream of "a pure writer who does not write" (Barthes 1980, 53). It remains a monumental realization of the postscript in which "writing in its turn fall[s] behind the written" (Derrida 1995b, 41). Indeed, the work is remarkable for the relative sparseness of actual writing and the superabundance of recycled material. Despite his claim "[to] have much augmented the vocabulary" (S. Johnson 1963, 10), Johnson's lexical achievement is modest: a total of 40,000 listings, 25,000 less than Bailey's earlier *Dictionarium Britannicum* of 1736 — a book Johnson used as a source text. Rather than enlarging the English language, Johnson is responsible for its austere truncation.[9] What is lexicographically innovative is Johnson's machinery of 114,000 citations.[10] As such, the *Dictionary* articulates itself as a production between the spaces connoted in the terms "lexicon" and "culture." In the *Dictionary's* plenitude, gathered by a single mind, we are not far from the cultural condition Baudelaire announces as *modernité,* in which the ontological imperative is to create oneself as aesthetic artifact. John Rajchman outlines a neo-Baudelairean schema for modernist writing via a Lacanian ethics of the *savoir-faire with the unconscious* that remains surprisingly pertinent to Johnson's practice:

> Thus one might characterize modernist writings (*écriture*) as the writing in which love is decentered and assumes *the "transferential" form of the place of the subject in language.* Love finds its object not in transcendence but in language itself. The modernist writer is the one who has an Oedipal complex with his language: *in the language he inherits* he finds the Paternity or Law from which he must effect his own "second birth." The love of works is thereby transformed into what Barthes called "the pleasure of the texts": one no longer writes from one's moral center; one writes to go beyond one's "ego" toward the singularity of one's "subject." (53; emphases added)

A libidinal lexicography? An Oedipal Johnson whose decentered love is transferred onto language? A modernist *avant la lettre*? Far-fetched conjectures, I admit, but not all that dissimilar to the clinamen-desire already noted in Bentley's homophonic obsessions and Brisset-Rousselian *délire.* What illustrates a transferred love onto language more than the fragmentary accumulations of privileged citations in which "[t]he word comes to carry its own ontology, its own reward for being" (Stewart 1980, 3)?

My interest in correlations between Johnson and Wittgenstein was initially sparked by a couple of surprising similarities. It's a little-known fact that Wittgenstein, too, compiled a dictionary for use in elementary schools and explicitly designed to regulate orthography. According to Monk, the 1926 *Wörterbuch für Volkschulen* is arguably Wittgenstein's "most lasting contribution to educational reform in Austria" (1990, 226). There is a further similarity in their respective methods of composition. Both produce "zettelistic" works, fragmentary, decentered productions selected from the mass accumulation of detached quotations and propositions.[11] The image of Johnson on his broken stool in the attic at Gough Square, marking passages in books and transcribing them with his amanuenses' assistance onto small cards is a fact decanted into legend. But similarly famous is Wittgenstein's apologetic preface to the *Philosophical Investigations* that carries the confession to his own unsystematic approach to philosophy: "The best that I could write would never be more than philosophical remarks; my thoughts were soon crippled if I tried to force them on in any single direction against their inclination. — And this was, of course, connected with the very nature of the investigation. For this compels us to travel over a wide field of thought criss-cross in every direction."[12] Charles Bernstein draws attention to the *Philosophical Investigations* as a potential model "for a more serial form of investigative writing: the series of interlocking remarks preceding like a chain piece to piece rather than having their parts unified by a prior structural or narrative principle" (1985, 179). Anscombe and von Wright in their introduction to the posthumous *Zettel* offer tangible evidence of Wittgenstein's fragmentary and stereotomic method in which the rearrangement of preexisting material is key. "We publish here a collection of fragments made by Wittgenstein himself and left by him in a box-file. They were for the most part cut from extensive typescripts of his, other copies of which still exist" (in Wittgenstein 1967, v).

Robert De Maria judges the *Dictionary* to be a hybrid phenomenon, part lexicon, part encyclopedia, and deriving from a variety of generically related ancestors: "encyclopedic histories, poems, commentaries, educational works, commonplace books, and, of course, encyclopedias themselves" (1986, 4).[13] To De Maria's list might be added two practical manuals of citations that appeared earlier than the *Dictionary*. Edward Bysshe's *Art of Poetry* from 1700 offers a list of poetic phrases and passages, grouped according to themes, subjects, and objects (incest, loyalty, prudence, rose, trumpet, twilight) that could be incorporated or paraphrased by the would-be-poet.[14] As in the *Dictionary*, the author of each citation is specified. Johnson owned a copy of the 1712 edition, which sold as item 130 in the 1785 sale of Johnson's library (Fleeman 1975, 69) and might well have influenced his choice of a binary structure. Bysshe's manual was itself preceded by Joshua Poole's *The English Parnassus,* designed for classroom use and containing a short rhyming dictionary of monosyllables and a collocation of choice epithets and phrases. The entry for "duck" lists a series of modifiers "diving, plunging, muddy, fearful, plain-foot, watry, soft, and tender" (1677, 77). A second section supplies quotations chosen from a number of poets. Poole provides a list of their names, but the specific passages are unattributed. Acknowledging antecedent models in two Latin works—Textor's *Latin* and *Thesaurus Poeticus*—Poole claims his work's originality lay in its "alphabetical disposition, for the greater ease and convenience of those who shall be desirous to advance themselves thereby" (a8^r). Such manuals as Poole's and Bysshe's facilitated poetic composition through manipulating and inventively combining preexisting fragments. Their principle, like Johnson's lexicographic principle—and the subsequent work of Ronald Johnson (see chapter 1), Burroughs, Cage, and Tom Phillips (considered in chapter 12) — is the judicious repetition and recombination of prior writings.

Mention, too, should be made of a little-known work: the two-volume *Index* accompanying (along with Johnson's own ten volumes of Prefaces) the fifty-six-volume project known as "Johnson's Poets." Compiled by Johnson's *Dictionary* amanuensis Alexander Macbean, it contains a preface possibly written by Johnson.[15] The *Index,* alphabetically arranged, effectively converts the discrete volumes into an encyclopedia of cross-references, its form resembling Johnson's *Dictionary* minus the explanation of the alphabetic word list and replicating in its practicality the manuals of Bysshe and Poole. In opening the closure of the multiple volumes into an innumerable series of extractable single sentences, the *Index* also provides that "system of civil and oeconomical prudence" Johnson attributes to the works of Shakespeare (1968, 62). The aim of Macbean's *Index,* as its preface makes clear, is to establish a synoptic overview of the British poets according to their usefulness in providing "prudential, moral and religious sentences; in remarkable proverbial sayings, either of a ludicrous or serious turn; in characters of celebrated persons, both ancient and modern; in descriptions of places and countries, and in accounts of remarkable events, either in the natural or political world, and of the ancient customs or antiquities" ([Macbean] 1780). The *Index* further provides access to "strong remonstrances against the vile prostitution of the gift of heaven to impure and immoral purposes" (v–vi).[16]

Clearly all these works emerge from the Cartesian legacy of formal correctness, inclining to the itemization of the objects of its scrutiny, announced by Morris Croll: "the study of the precise meaning of words; the reference to dictionaries as literary authorities; the study of the sentence as a logical unit; . . . the attempt to reduce grammar to an exact science; the idea that forms of speech are always either correct or incorrect; the complete subjection of the laws of motion and expression in style to the laws of logic and standardization—in short, the triumph, during two centuries, of grammatical over theoretical ideas" (1969, 232). Such indexical formats as Macbean's also evince a matured awareness in the eighteenth century of the essentially spatialized nature of language with the attendant commitment to a typographic ideology in which stereotypy, repeatability, and retrievability of data assume preeminence. It is inside this legacy that the *Dictionary* should be considered as a problematic rather than exemplary instance.

In his initial plan, Johnson outlines a lexicographic procedure for listing the meanings of each word according to its relation to a radical or "primitive" sense, the underlying assumption being that it is possible to list meanings in a descending order of usage from a primitive etymology. As Johnson explains, "In every word of extensive use, it was requisite to mark the progress of its meaning, and show by what gradations of intermediate sense it has passed from its primitive to its remote and accidental signification; so that every foregoing explanation should tend to that which follows, and the series be regularly concatenated from the first notion to the last" (in Reddick 1990, 50). Johnson approaches the daunting task of separating senses with remarkable success. To the definition of "set" he attaches more than ninety senses—a listing that covers an entire five pages of the bicolumnar folio first edition. The definitions are arranged into seven distinct categories: (1) a primitive or natural sense, (2) consequential or accidental, (3) metaphorical, (4) poetical, (5) familiar, (6) burlesque, and (7) the peculiar sense as deployed by great writers.[17] This categorical multiplicity is symptomatic of Johnson's conceptual struggle to reconcile two distinct ways of defining: etymology and usage—and ultimately it is the need to discriminate such polysemic senses that leads him toward a use theory of linguistic meaning.

The early Plan promotes etymology as a sufficient method for establishing meaning—one not requiring the supplementary criterion of independent usage:

> By tracing in this [etymological] manner every word to its original, and not admitting, but with great caution, any of which no original can be found, we shall secure our language from being over-run with *cant*, from being crouded with low terms, the spawn of folly and affectation, which arise from no just principles of speech, and of which therefore no legitimate derivation can be shewn. (S. Johnson 1787, 9:178)

However, a comparison of his own definition of "etymology" with Bailey's reveals Johnson's uneasiness with etymological method. Bailey's definition exudes an optimistic certainty as to its procedural worth and validity. Etymology is "that part of grammar that shows the original of words, for better distinguishing and establishing of their true signification." Bailey holds the tenet, first noted by Isidore of Seville, that if word origins are known, then their semantic force can be clearly comprehended (Curtius 1973, 43). In contrast, Johnson's two definitions betray a distinctly Lockean nuance: "1. The descent or derivation of a word from its original; the deduction of formations from the radical word; the analysis of compound words into primitives." "2. The part of grammar which delivers the inflections of nouns and verbs." The two attendant quotations (from Jeremy Collier and Isaac Watts, respectively) ventriloquate Johnson's fundamental skepticism: "When words are restrained, by common usage, to a particular sense, to run up to *etymology,* and construe them by dictionary, is wretchedly ridiculous." "If the meaning of a word could be learned by its derivation or etymology, yet the original derivation of words is oftentimes very dark."[18]

There are suggestions, too, in the Plan of Johnson's misgivings about the ambitious project of fixing words to some ideal origin. He harbors no illusion to the fact that language, as a predictable combination of grammar and lexis, is constantly subjected to the caprice of utterance, disseminating a forest of misuse and confusion. Johnson expresses the felt inevitability of this clash in a vivid simile: "[I]t must be remembered, that while our language is yet living, and variable by the caprice of every one that speaks it, these words are hourly shifting their relations, and can no more be ascertained in a dictionary, than a grove, in the agitation of a storm, can be accurately delineated from its picture in the water" (quoted in Reddick 1990, 50). Etymology, as the reversed momentum of derivation, seeks to cancel out change, absorb difference in the executive myth of a hygienic return to a settled truth in origin. And Johnson's insistence via citation to move away from origins runs counter to such valorization of originary meaning. In the time between penning the Plan and writing the Preface, and under the burden of mounting apprehension, Johnson's lexicographic method shifts its paradigm from etymological endorsement to customary usage.[19]

This paradigm shift is intelligent. Any semantic explanation of a word opens up to the perturbing abysmatics of an overabundance of signifiers and their instant proliferation under definitional scrutiny into other words and other contexts. Wittgenstein himself announces the paradox: "In giving explanations I already have to use language full blown" (1953, 47). Definition is predicated on the concealed fact that a word's definition is always arrived at by way of other words and, while accounting for the word defined, does not account for the meaning of its components. If "bull" is correctly defined as an "adult, bovine animal," then what do "adult," "bovine," and "animal" mean? (Cf. Eco 1986, 49.) As Levinas concurs, "Each word-meaning is at the confluence of innumerable semantic rivers" (1987, 77). The multiplication of signs and their instant proliferation when attempting to fix the meaning of any single sign mark both the paradoxical foundation of the lexicographer's enterprise and the fractal nature of semanticity in general. Johnson is profoundly aware of this problem of "the exuberance of signification" (1963, 16) and of such significatory clinamens as slippage, polysemeity, and play, that have become the commonplaces of poststructuralist discourse: "The shades of meaning sometimes pass imperceptibly into each other; so that though on one side they apparently differ, yet it is impossible to mark the point of contact" (15). The final implications to be drawn from both the *Dictionary* and the *Investigations* are that language is fundamentally lacking in essence and that meaning can never reach a state of complete and static closure.

Garth Hallett draws attention to the important distinction between formal and pragmatic aspects in Wittgenstein's concept of meaning. The formal relates to rules of usage that bestow a certain degree of regularity and conformity to signifying activity, the pragmatic aspect to the utilitarian, contingent, and practical dimensions of utterance (1967, 14). These two aspects are played out in the *Dictionary*. Like Wittgenstein, Johnson organizes meaning into two parts: a definition (corresponding to Wittgenstein's formal aspect of meaning), isolated from all contexts other than its own alphabetic position in a series; and an illustrative quotation (the pragmatic aspect of meaning).

Wittgenstein "roughly" divides explanations of meaning into verbal and ostensive definitions (1958, 1). The former induce a semiotic circularity, for such definitions do not escape the enclosure of other signs. (The proliferational consequences of this paradox have been noted already.) However, in ostensive definition—which is Hume's account of language acquisition—there is a purported break with language. I say a purported break since the ostensive definer simply points to a thing and says a word. Wittgenstein asks to what are we actually pointing? Nothing is done beyond the act of pointing other than to name a thing. To point to a cow and utter "cow" gives no indication as to how that word is used in language-games. As Frege indicates, a word acquires a meaning only as part of a sentence (cf. Wittgenstein 1953, 49). The *Dictionary* supplies both types of meaning. The verbal definitions occur as closed metalinguistic explanations "to mundify. To cleanse. To make clean." In the citations, however, this denotational parsimony explodes into sumptuous instantiation. Neither marginalia nor footnotes (though generically related to both) the citations function as the ostensive terminals in a cultural, literary world to which the definitions point. As a child (by ostension) learns the meaning of "blue," so a reader of the *Dictionary* learns the same meaning by way of three quotations from Shakespeare and one each from Prior and Newton.

With this new pragmatic-contextual paradigm, Johnson can employ an iterative procedure by which a word appears in two different contexts: one as the object of definition and explanation, the other in a quoted scientific, theological, or literary passage, frequently carrying historic, discursive, and ideological sedimentation.[20] Collectively the citations provide what Wittgenstein terms examples of pragmatic language, which in their mobility and plenitude offer a different economy to that of the restricted rigor of definition and onomastics, arguing ultimately against the fixity of the defining entry. (The *Dictionary* might be described as a language-game of reference and indexicality, produced by transporting passages out of other language-games.) The *Dictionary*'s enduring value as a precociously "modern" text derives from this juxtaposition of two competing semantic intentions apparent in Johnson's oscillations between the indeterminacies of a living and mutating language and the desire to control the noise around semantic kernels. What the reader of the *Dictionary* experiences is precisely what Wittgenstein claims of language in general: that "every word has a different character in different contexts" (1953, 181e). A double dynamic obtains: a single word is arrested, scrutinized, explained, and at the same time dispersed into a collateral series — the distillates of Johnson's omnivorous reading. The *Dictionary* then can be read as a magnificent example of binary economy whose interplay effects a double translation from language into literature and from meaning into use. Barthes might have termed this transit between the two series a passage from discourse (citation) to point — the punctual flourish of definition (cf. 1980, 12). The *Dictionary* is at once theatrical and carceral, its consequent rhythm — which can be genuinely described as both chiasmic and poetic — an oscillation between quarantined immobility and festive flux.

"A definition is a snapshot of a word at rest. An illustrative quotation and a verbal illustration show it at work" (Morton 1994, 99). In their transit to citations, linguistic definitions become literary facts.[21] Each quotation provides Johnson with a *locus amoenus* for each definition collectively constituting his Rasselasian happy valley. Because the definitions and their accompanying illustrations don't exist in a commensurate relation, however, a dynamic tension arises between the definiens and a destructuring of that definition by chosen contextual examples, problematizing any simplistic attempt to install an indisputable, authoritative sign-meaning equation. To the humble preposition "about" (tentatively defined as "which seems to signify encircling on the outside") Johnson supplies seventeen illustrations chosen from fifteen different authors.[22] In their sheer abundance, the citations testify to the insufficiency of definition to adequately convey the totality of verbal meanings.

Wittgenstein is confident that "[t]he question, 'What is a word really?' is analogous to 'What is a piece in chess?' To grasp a meaning is to be able to practise a technique; it is not a special kind of mental experience. The philosopher is concerned with language in the same way as we talk about the pieces in chess when we are stating the rules of the game, not describing the physical properties" (1953, 108). The marked difference between the early *Tractatus* and the later *Investigations* is a broadening in the latter work of the concept of "language" from a unitary to a plural notion. What is "language" in the *Tractatus* emerges as "language-games" in the *Investigations*. There is also a marked absence of examples in the *Tractatus* ("states of affairs" and "simple objects" are two concepts basic to the book that are not concretely instantiated). Garver and Lee (1994) and Staten (1984), respectively, see the *Investigations,* with its abundance of examples, as a critique and a deconstruction of the *Tractatus.*[23]

In the later *Investigations* Wittgenstein, although conceding language to be an essential and hyperonymic category, insists on its necessarily discrete and local manifestation. To speak of "language" or of "language-as-such" is misleading for Wittgenstein, as both meaning and usage are contextually determined within numerous, discrete micropractices. There is thus a language of science, of poetry, and of ethics. Wittgenstein likens the manner in which these languages are used to the way we play a game, the rules governing the language being similar to the rules established for the proper playing of a game. In the language-game of landscape gardening, for instance, an elm is accurately defined as a tree, but in the language-game of botany, "elm" is an illicit word whose appropriate replacement term is "angiosperm." Sense and nonsense are similarly determined not by univocal authority but according to the rules of the particular game. For a term to be ranked as nonsense depends on its relevance and usefulness within a certain ludic practice. (Wittgenstein's language-game—his single original conceptual contribution to philosophy—is, of course, an important antecedent of Foucault's influential concept of discourse in which each self-promoting interest functions through its own language, linguistic rules, vocabulary, and conceptual productions.)

Wittgenstein's purpose in the *Investigations* is not to compile a dictionary series whose function will be to effect a regularized philosophy of language. "Our clear and simple language-games are not preparatory studies for a future regularization of language—as it were first approximations, ignoring friction, and air resistance. The language-games are rather set up as *objects of comparison* which are meant to throw light on the facts of our language by way not only of similarities, but also of dissimilarities" (1953, 130). Scott Elledge suggests that Johnson's principal motivation behind the *Dictionary* is similarly exploratory and descriptive—his adoption of a citationary model reflecting a general reticence around prescribing usage (1967, 268–69).

The marked shift in the *Investigations* from a notion of unitary meaning to a meaning understood as contextually determined is in sharp contrast to Aristotelian linguistics, which reduces language to a repertory of labels— a reflection in words of things and concepts existing prior to, and outside of, language. In Tullio de Mauro's estimation, Wittgenstein imposes "a new vision in which linguistic forms have the meaning they do because they are used by man, the guarantee of their validity being found only in their use" (1967, 47). To study linguistic form is thus to study linguistic behavior within actual signifying activities. To provide an adequate semantic description is to supply a description of that form's use and behavior in the specific context of a language-game.

> Compare *knowing* and *saying:*
> how many feet high Mt. Blanc is—
> how the word "game" is used—
> how a clarinet sounds.
>
> If you are surprised that one can know something and not be able to say it, you are perhaps thinking of a case like the first. Certainly not of one like the third.
>
> (Wittgenstein 1953, 78)

This concrete paradigm upholds a precise distinction between using and mentioning, calling into question any claim that in order to be meaningful, words require exact definitions. Remaining constant in the word is what Wittgenstein calls its "single physiognomy" beyond which its character changes according to context (1953, 181e). Language is virtual fecundity, a vast reservoir of potential usage, and the matrix of semantic determination rests in contingent parole. Wittgenstein's lasting achievement is to have restored semantics from inert designation to the social incommensurability of real-use situations, transforming semantics from a science of meanings into a science of signifying activity.[24] Put more dramatically, Wittgenstein enacts a descent "from the heavens of the immobile structures described in the *Tractatus* to the earth of ever-changing meaningful behavior" and a search for "the origin of metaphysical alienation within the strictly earthly field of speech" (Rossi-Landi 1983, 12).

Deleuze similarly celebrates the shift in linguistics from its Saussurean preoccupation with linguistic constants to pragmatic matters and the indeterminate ad hocism of usage. "Pragmatics (dealing with the circumstances of language use, with events and acts) was long considered the 'rubbish dump' of linguistics, but it's now becoming more and more important: language is coming to be seen as an activity, so the abstract units and constants of language-use are becoming less and less important" (1995, 28). Both Deleuze's and Wittgenstein's pragmatic and contextual conception of language dispute that other cherished Aristotelian thesis: that the possibilities for human communication are guaranteed by the fact that all words partake of stable meanings (a stability itself guaranteed by the ancillary presupposition that words relate to either ideas or things in a one-to-one correspondence.) I have shown how this notion of language as nomenclature is insufficient for Wittgenstein. Meaning is guaranteed to linguistic form not in a mirror-image correspondence to extralinguisticalities but in the linguistic form per se. But this rejection of Aristotelian linguistics and its cardinal tenet that words themselves are endowed with meaning opens up interrogation. What is meant by use? Where do we fix the parameters of usage? Individual, groupuscular, national? The problematics of free individual linguistic usage are clearly evident in the risk of losing social communication entirely in a world of atomic idioglossia.

Alert to this threat, Guido Calogero tries to stabilize the parameters of signifying activity by implementing a historical and traditional check upon the effects of any eruptions of singularity. "The truth is that the sign is connected to meaning by the historical tradition gradually created and evolved by the endless repetition and renewal of human speech" (*Estetica, semantica, istorica*, Torino, 1947, 181; quoted in Mauro 1967, 49). For Calogero, "use" equates "the most frequent and established habits of speakers" (Mauro 1967, 49), and for him and Wittgenstein alike, linguistic form and value are sedimented within the ethnography of the particular societies in which that form is adopted (cf. Mauro 1967, 50). It's precisely this complex negotiation between democratic usage, eccentric change, and the social stabilization of a specific ethnosignificatory economy that renders the *Dictionary* a similarly precarious venture.

But the question arises as to what precisely defines an established habit of speech and who decides on what's habitual? Wittgenstein and Johnson share a predilection for linguistic variety. Both seek to demonstrate that there is no language other than in linguistic occurrence, but where Wittgenstein draws upon actual, imaginary, and frequently simplistic human linguistic behavior, Johnson avails himself entirely of the trace phenomena of printed citations. His ethnosignificatory economy derives entirely from the logic and the material of the printed word such that the nature of meaning is established as inextricably entwined with a practice of quotation—a typocentric usage in a lexical language-game, the implications of which will be soon addressed. "When I talk about language (words, sentences, etc.) I must speak the language of every day. Is this language somehow too coarse and material for what we want to say? *Then how is another one to be constructed?*" (Wittgenstein 1953, 120). In the *Dictionary*'s case, linguistic form, value, and correctness are established and constructed through Johnson's own polymathic and often prejudicial reading of English texts.[25] W. K. Wimsatt points to the dominating presence in the *Dictionary* "of a single master reader," and Johnson proves—in principle at least—that any single well-read person could compile a dictionary. The enduring irony is that Johnson arrives at a formulation of the English language through the idiosyncratic discernment of his own personal readings.[26] Franz-Passow, in 1812, and later Scott and Liddell in their 1843 *Greek-English Lexicon,* adhered to a less selective historical principle of lexicography. Elisabeth Murray comments, "[T]he lexicographer's task was to collect *all* words, rather than to select *good* words, and whereas quotations were used by Johnson and his successors to define words, now [the 1850s] their chief use would be to show historical changes of sense" (1977, 135–36).

Philip Gove in the twentieth century voices the ideal in lexicographic theory: "The usable evidence lies buried in the zillions of words that surround us," and ideally the lexicographer should be free to draw upon the totality of written and spoken utterance—"who used [the words], how they were used, and what the circumstances apparently were" (1967, 2). In Gove's well-known formulation, good English is the English that is appropriate to the occasion.[27] At the start of gathering his "authorities," however, Johnson "was desirous that every quotation should be useful to some other end than the illustration of a word" (S. Johnson 1963, 17), and it should be borne in mind that his program was never simply lexicographic but additionally cultural, political, and pedagogical.[28] As early as the Plan of 1747, Johnson makes clear his intention that the *Dictionary* will be more than a defined lexical series: "In citing authorities, on which the credit of every part of this work must depend, it will be proper to observe some obvious rules, such as preferring writers of the first reputation to those of an inferior rank; . . . selecting, when it can be conveniently done, such sentences as, besides their immediate use [i.e., as denotative and idiomatic indicators], may give pleasure or instruction, by conveying some elegance of language, or some precept of prudence or piety" (1787 9:189). In a telling martial, imperial metaphor, Johnson speaks of his anticipated delight in plundering texts:

> When first I engaged in this work, I resolved to leave neither words nor things unexamined, and pleased myself with a prospect of the hours which I should revel away in feasts of literature, the obscure recesses of northern learning, which I should enter and ransack, the treasures with which I expected every search into those neglected mines to reward my labour, and the triumph with which I should display my acquisitions to mankind. (1963, 21)

"Through metaphor the fear of language becomes the fear of speaking or the fear which, being the essence of speech, would make any use of speech, as any silence, frightening" (Blanchot 1992, 59). It is the absence of speech, of vibrant oral markers, that confirms the *Dictionary* as a book read into existence. Out of the fear of living language, its flux and vicissitudes, Johnson constructs a vast edifice of erudition from the alluvial abundance of his own reading. Purportedly locating his project within "the boundless chaos of living speech" (Saussure's "heteroclite"), Johnson ultimately inhabits and responds to a world of appropriated writing. Against the incipient chaos augured in the vernacular, he proffers a chrestomathy of correct, printed usage as a validation of polite reading over errant utterance.

> I have fixed Sidney's work for the boundary, beyond which I make few excursions. From the authours which rose in the time of Elizabeth, a speech might be formed adequate to all purposes of use and elegance. If

the language of theology were extracted from Hooker and the translation of the Bible; the terms of natural knowledge from Bacon; the phrases of policy, war, and navigation from Raleigh; the dialect of poetry and fiction from Spenser and Sidney; and the diction of common life from Shakespeare, few ideas would be lost to mankind, for want of English words, in which they might be expressed. (S. Johnson 1963, 18–19)

Johnson is uncompromising in his graphocentricity. What sanctifies meaning is its iterability inside the consecrated texts of a patriotic and patriarchal typographic culture—a writing severely restricted in its historical range and already immune to the errancies and contaminations of actual linguistic praxis.[29] In sharp contrast to Wittgenstein's quotidian examples of linguistic usage, Johnson's citational system projects a literate world of polite writing detached from the oral dimension of common utterance. Indeed, the *Dictionary* can be read as a glottocidal text—an effective murder of living speech.[30] Johnson's conservative lexicography makes no supercessionary claims. For him the progress and the degeneration of language are one and the same. He repeats in his attitude the Egyptian priest's proclamation to Solon: *panta gegrammena,* "everything has been written down of old" (Timaeus 23a in Plato 1961, 1158). The conviction is clearly that enough has been written to adequately supply not only a national but an international community with a working language. (Note Johnson's telling choice of the word "mankind.") Johnson clearly feels that the language of late-sixteenth- and early-seventeenth-century England is not only adequate but desirable.

Gove bases his denial of any special status to poetical quotations on the grounds that what authenticates a word's presence in a dictionary is its currency in general discourse (see Morton 1994, 96–97). "The hard truth is that literary flower in a dictionary quotation represents a luxury of a bigone age" (99). Eschewing "the testimony of living authors," Johnson professes to draw upon "the wells of English undefiled" in which reside "the pure sources of genuine diction" (18).[31] The metaphoric strata here are revealing, showing Johnson's dictionary project to be a language hygiene program. A genuine diction is a recommended diction judged to be linguistically pure. The articulated definitions, of meaning and example, are a calculated move to render anathanatic the language of polite society. Johnson's proposal is a stunning counterstrike against linguistic diachrony. The language salvaged from a venerated past, a sempiternal world of prior achievements, prescribes a national lexicon. The results will be fossilized but stable usage. Transgressing Calogero's and Wittgenstein's demand that linguistic value be *discovered* in specific social ethnography, Johnson sets out to *construct* his own.[32]

Johnson's veneration of the past will gain political inflection in Burke's 1790 *Reflections on the French Revolution,* where change is parsimoniously measured against a "body and stock of inheritance . . . and upon the principle of reference to antiquity" (in Dickinson 1974, 177). Johnson's hallowed citations function like Burke's notion of property whose mobility works as an effective brake on constitutional power. At the same time, his cited authorities "from the wells of English undefiled" act like Burke's "canonized forefathers" supplying the language, like the Burkean constitution, with a "pedigree and illustrating ancestors" (Burke 1993, 34). Lyotard collects, condenses, and rechristens these authorities of tradition as "the word of the dead father" (1993b, xix). Quotations from Hooker, Spenser, or Sidney provide a connecting line back to ancestral legitimation and the myth of a settled lexis. Citing Thomas Hooker, Johnson claims, "Change is not made without inconvenience, even from worse to better. There is in constancy and stability a general and lasting advantage, which will always overbalance the slow improvements of gradual correction" (S. Johnson 1963, 7). These sentiments are repeated in Burke's claim, "A spirit of innovation is generally the result of a selfish temper and confined views. People will not look forward to posterity, who never look back to their ancestors" (Burke 1993, 33). In sharp contrast to Wittgenstein's pragmatics of utterance, Johnson and Burke alike offer a strategy of pedigree and inheritance that explicates an oxymoronic concept of reformation and progress.

The subtext of the Preface then is a blueprint for the protection of a hypothetical "permanently proper" language against the impact of linguistic actualities. Mercantile language is ostracized as "fugitive cant" both too ephemeral and neologistic, employing a diction "in a great measure casual and mutable [which] cannot be regarded as any part of the durable materials of a language" (S. Johnson 1963, 23).[33] (It is in the rare instances of such nonliterary examples, taken largely from the mercantile sphere and specific trades and occupations, where Johnson acts against his own aesthetic, moral, and ideological biases, that he most approximates Wittgenstein's pragmatic examples of linguistic use.) Johnson's comments on dialects and regional linguistic variations are especially revealing.

The English language properly speaking has no dialects: the style of writers has no professed diversity in the use of words, or their flexions, and terminations, nor differs but by differing degrees of skill or care.

... The language of the northern counties retains many words now out of use, but which are commonly of the genuine Teutonick race, and is uttered with a pronunciation which now seems harsh and rough, but was probably used by our ancestors. The northern speech is therefore not barbarous but obsolete. (Quoted in Barrell 1983, 156)

By denying the existence of dialects, Johnson clearly aims to eliminate at the source any debate regarding sociolectic difference. Where regional linguistic varieties do occur, they do so only through differences in "skill and care." The issue is presented as a matter of practicality and competence, not of sociocultural difference.

At the same time, Johnson defends the otherness of northern dialect from barbarity by the counterallegation that it is "obsolete." But what's involved in this choice of obsolescence over barbarity in this passage? By ascribing to the northern dialect the negative characteristics of outmodedness and deficient competence, Johnson is able to preserve a pure Teutonic lineage and the false image of a national language simultaneously unified and different, while at the same time legislating what is licit. Dialect variations are presented as deriving from diachronic effects, not from cultural alterity or anthropological contaminants implied in Johnson's use of the word "barbarous."[34] But who decides whether a word is obsolete, or whether the sound is "harsh and rough"? Locke would declare roughness and harshness to be secondary qualities, subjective in origin, and thus a matter of taste. Johnson, of course, provides no direct answer; however, the inference is clearly that the sole arbiter of proper language is the nonspeaker of such variants, specifically the polite metropolitan speaker of London English.

By ascribing obsolescence to justifiably pure and genuine words—words moreover still in current use—Johnson circumvents his own criterion of purity.[35] The mixed blessing attendant on an invariant English is cogently exposed by Barrell: "[A]t the same time as [Standard English] offered a notional [sic] cultural equality to men of all classes, if they could speak the language, it confirmed the power of those who could speak it over those who could not" (1983, 175). In Barrell's acid assessment, "the notions of the customary and the current can now be manipulated in such a way as to ensure that whatever is in London, is right for everywhere else" (157).

Rossi-Landi underscores a similar failure in axiological neutrality in the *Investigations,* taking Wittgenstein to task for the overly restricted range in his instances of language-games. Measuring the length of a rod; a man ordering another man to build a wall; playing a game of chess; writing a letter; pulling a bell at five o'clock—all these examples taken from the *Investigations* are drawn from a "public" rather than "social" sphere (Rossi-Landi 1983, 30). Rossi-Landi also accuses Wittgenstein of lacking the notion of labor value in his theory, failing to see a linguistic object "as the product of a given linguistic piece of work" (31). Most damning is the allegation that Wittgenstein—unlike the ideologically aware Johnson—lacks a theory of society and history in which to ground his thinking. While advancing a critique of linguistic alienation, Rossi-Landi argues, Wittgenstein ignores the issue of social alienation (32). It's undeniable that Johnson and Wittgenstein alike reveal themselves divorced in part from the social realities of their time. In his nonmechanistic materialism, Wittgenstein consistently petitions man as a player within processes of meaning and communication but not as the interpellated subject of ideological and socioeconomic forces. Johnson, paradoxically, strategizes the replacement of a living, marginal sociolect (judged "obsolete" and "vulgar") by a style of polite usage exemplified in the printed texts of the past.

"Language is only the instrument of science," Johnson ruminates. "I wish, however, that the instrument might be less apt to decay, and that signs might be permanent like the things which they denote" (1963, 7). It's precisely to increase linguistic stability that Johnson's lexical project is designed (19–20). However, this zeal to stabilize is fatally forestalled by a painful awareness of language's intransigent mutability. A self-deprecatory tone pervades the Preface and finds its greatest expression in Johnson's lack of confidence in any ability to adequately explain verbal meaning.

> Those who have been persuaded to think well of my design, require that it should fix our language, and put a stop to those alterations which time and chance have hitherto been suffered to make in it without opposition. With this consequence I will confess that I flattered myself for a while; but now begin to fear that I have indulged expectation which neither reason nor experience can justify. When we see men grow old and die at a certain time one after another, from century to century, we laugh at the elixir that promises to prolong life to a thousand years, and with equal justice may the lexicographer be derided, who being able to produce no example of a nation that has preserved their words and phrases from mutability, shall imagine that his dictionary can embalm his language, and secure it from corruption and decay, that it is in his power to change sublunary nature, or clear the world at once from folly, vanity, and affection. (1963, 24) [36]

Johnson's contemporary Benjamin Martin reaches similar conclusions: "The pretence of fixing a standard to the purity and perfection of any language . . . is utterly vain and impertinent, because no language as depending on arbitrary use and custom, can ever be permanently the same, but will always be in a mutable state; and what is deem'd polite and elegant in one age, may be accounted uncouth and barbarous in another" (quoted in Starnes and Noyes, 1946, 160).

"*The limits of my language* mean the limits of my world" (Wittgenstein 1961, 56). Johnson is attuned to this sentiment of Wittgenstein's toward the end of the Preface while pondering the ultimate futility of the lexicographer's task, cognizant that "no dictionary of the living tongue ever can be perfect, since while it is hastening to publication, some words are budding, and some falling away" (1963, 28).[37] It's a profoundly Lucretian sentiment to boot, of incessant clinamens, atomic dissolutions, and recombinations. As Robert Burchfield reminds us, "The perfect dictionary is a mirage" (in Morton 1994, 243), because the challenge—the impossible solicitation—is to harness a heteroglossic world of protean minima.[38]

There is a shift through the course of the Preface from a confident embrace of lexicographic method to dark ruminations upon its impossibility. Johnson's growing pessimism around his lexical project is symptomatic of a mind committed to and dependent upon the disempowered logic of print technology. Increasingly, language emerges not as a containable system of immutable semantic units but as the errant, turbulent forces of a living tongue—the clinamen of speech effecting an oral deviation from the stability of print. "[S]ounds are too volatile and subtle for legal restraints; to enchain syllables, and to lash the wind, are equally the undertakings of pride, unwilling to measure its desires by its strength" (S. Johnson 1963, 24).

The *Dictionary* houses two contending forces: a centripetal pull toward the stability of a printed definition and an awareness of the constant pull toward contamination and mutability. Beneath the paradoxical effects induced by the work's hybrid format (word entry and citation; dictionary and encyclopedia) lies the deeper, historical antagonism between print and orality. The *Dictionary* is one man's journey through linguistic flux: Johnson's endless sentence inscribed inside a vast postscript and occupying a fault line between lexiphobia and leximania. A living language is both feedback and aftershock. Johnson knows this all too well and is aware too that all aspirations to lexicographic heroism are the idols of Bacon's marketplace. The final image of Johnson is that of the modernist subject described by

Foucault: introducing "into his experience contents and forms older than him, which he cannot master; it is that which, by binding him to multiple, intersecting chronologies, scatters him through time and pinions him at the center of the duration of things" (1970, 300–1).[39]

I've suggested that Johnson uses quotations partly to circumvent the methodological cul-de-sac of etymology. A citation provides what Wittgenstein calls a "language sample" that functions in describing the meaning of a word within actual usage. In this respect I describe Johnson as Wittgensteinian *avant la lettre*. I've traced, however, a bifurcation in their respective citational resources. Where Wittgenstein takes his examples of concrete paradigms from everyday usage, Johnson selects strategically from the printed texts of polite literature—a cultural and posthumous elite. I need to add to this difference a further one implicit in the function of the signature and the proper name which Johnson supplies to his citations in order to construct authority.

"Problems are solved, not by giving new information, but by arranging what we have always known" (Wittgenstein 1953, 109). Johnson's is a similar economy of redistribution strategically designed to solve the problem of authoritative univocity. From its inception, the *Dictionary* was implicated in a crisis of legitimation. The great dictionaries of France and Italy were the triumphs of institutional collaborations, the meanings of their verbal inventories arrived at by shared agreement. In contrast, Johnson's monumental achievement is idiosyncratic and nonconsensual, one man's patriotic triumph over the institutional machinery of Euro-Enlightenment collectivity. Its author elicits pride in the poverty and insularity of the book's production. "[T]he *English Dictionary* was written with little assistance of the learned, and without any patronage of the great; not in the soft obscurities of retirement, or under the shelter of academick bowers, but amidst inconveniences and distraction, in sickness and in sorrow" (S. Johnson 1963, 28). Johnson's pride apart, the consequence to the English language is that a national linguistic standard gets established by the authority of a single man. Horace Walpole voices serious reservations about such lexicographic sovereignty, insisting that "a society should alone pretend to publish a standard dictionary" (quoted in Reddick 1990, 20). Lacking this broad consensual base in "society," Johnson constructs authority through the interplay of his quoted passages; the rhetorical force of the highlighted word and the supplementary assignment of the quoted passage to a proper name. In this concerted, and also tense, format, univocality is pulverized and authority disseminated among a panoply of named citations.⁴⁰ Despite the overwhelming presence of Johnson as a "collector of words," on one level at least, quotations prohibit the unmediated monological authority of integrating argument by putting parts into play and, despite the unavoidable final judgment that Johnson remains the work's "Governor of Diversity or G.O.D.," it remains true that we experience in reading the *Dictionary* the imprint of authority in its minimal manifestation as a fragment.⁴¹ Such authorial disclaimers are not uncharacteristic of Johnson, who resorts to personae, anonymity, and ghostwriting in several other works.⁴²

Fredric Bogel draws attention to Johnson's generally ambiguous relationship to authority, especially his awareness of the dangers posed in self-authorization. "The problem is how to assume authority without simply doing so, how to both claim and disclaim authority so as to exert its power without being crushed by its guilt" (1987, 198). Johnson deploys a strategy of deliberately decentered authorship, purposely relativizing his text and neutralizing authorial agency (evidenced in the definitions) by a deployment of other "voices."⁴³ Bogel is correct also in insisting that such a parceling out of authority entails a corresponding fragmentation of responsibility. If we concede that Johnson structures his *Dictionary* as a federated production, then not only is the category of author unsettled, but "the logocentric notion of an orderly movement between origin and image" is profoundly disturbed (Riddel 1979, 331). Because the citations are also signed passages, they register as fragments of extracted cultural property from a literary continuum.⁴⁴

Now factor into this citational procedure another proper-name effect. Johnson reads, selects, marks, extracts, and then names in order to tie a passage to an author and in that way to render a fragment of text a singular human, semantically validating property. Moreover, because "a person's name is seen as a portrait" (Wittgenstein 1982, 12e), because it functions as the "picture of its bearer" (101e), Johnson can laminate a textuality with pictorial, facial resonance. Names fit their faces like a glove, or, as Wittgenstein confesses, "I feel as if the name Schubert fitted Schubert's works and his face" (101e). Wittgenstein draws attention to a highly tactile, pictorial type of representation involved in naming. By attaching proper names to textual passages, Johnson creates a picture gallery of worthies adorning, as well as authorizing, those passages. The effect is not unlike the experience of entering those private libraries in early-seventeenth-century France that "proclaimed an immutable order even in their architecture and the decoration of the buildings that housed them, an order reflected in the arrangement of the volumes on the shelves and in the busts and portraits of the authors most revered by the master of the place. Such libraries served as a summation of knowledge, and their chief function was conservatism" (Martin 1994, 351).

I want to stress here the ideological function of a decorative purpose to naming that both reflects and represents the taste and status that employs it. Johnson's names evoke images and effigies conjuring up a supplemental reading space beyond the contingent occasions of the *Dictionary*'s own functions. This additional space is architectural, iconic, and heavily charged with a secondary message of prestige, wealth, and rank. The *Dictionary* is ideology aestheticized, or, put more proverbially, it supplies Johnson the Englishman with his castle, both the format and the symbol of his conservative summation.

The *Dictionary*, then, can be read as an epic of the proper name between the covers of which definition slips over into a gleaned treasury of human ownerships. What this nomination inaugurates is an uneasy confluence of two radically different orders of authority—on the one hand, Johnsonian authority derived through reading, selection, and an orchestrational dexterity of prefabricated parts; on the other, the eruptive power of a multitude of proper names (called by Johnson his "authorities"), which ultimately resist assimilation into univocity. This tension in Johnson's binary format precipitates a chiasmic force. Derrida counsels on the ambiguous effects of naming—effects which Jeremy Ahearne claims to register "the impropriety of the proper" (Ahearne 1995, 148). To name is inevitably to taxonomize (cf. Derrida 1976, 109).

The proper name, too, is never the intrinsic property of a subject but a classification that violently territorializes. It is by the action of an Other that we are named into a sociolinguistic ordering of "presences" as differences. (Deleuze is thus correct in associating proper names with dynamic forces rather than selves.) [45] In addition, the proper name is imbued with a connotational power, unfolding like a memory into the signification of "at least the nationality of all the images which can be associated with it" (Barthes 1980, 65). As a sign "the proper name offers itself to an exploration, a decipherment: it is at once a 'milieu' (in the biological sense of the term) into which one must plunge . . . [and] a voluminous sign, a sign always pregnant with a dense texture of meaning" (59).

Derrida elucidates the precessional nature of the signature that governs the structure of texuality in general (1985, 51). A proper name does not come into effect in the act of signing but only on reception by its recipient. It's the reader, not the author, who signs. "A text is signed only much later by the other. And this testamentary structure doesn't befall a text as if by accident, but constructs it" (51). A signed passage is thus bestowed a complex relationship to transit and alterity. Offered up by Johnson—as recipient—is a gesture that honors the other's signature. It is by this gestural torque, this signing after the fact, that we can speak of the *Dictionary* as Johnson's work.

A further problem derives from the sedimented burden of a named passage's previous context. As Reddick makes clear, "the linguistic constructions retain overtones related to the writer's authority, regardless of what they otherwise 'say'" (1990, 129). It's undoubtedly from an awareness of the potential errancy in named citations that Johnson eschews quotations from Hobbes, Thomas Chubb, Shaftesbury, and Samuel Clarke, writers laudable as stylistic mentors but considered by Johnson to be odious in their beliefs. Citation is seldom an innocent shift of context, and Johnson shows a profound awareness of the consequence of transit: "The examples thus *mutilated,* are no longer to be considered as conveying the sentiments or doctrine of their authours; the word for the sake of which they are inserted, with all its appendant clauses, has been carefully preserved; but it may sometimes happen, by hasty *truncation,* that the general tendency of the sentence may be changed: the divine may desert his tenets, or the philosopher his system" (S. Johnson 1963, 17–18; emphases added). In light of these comments, a double irony obtains to Johnson's own silent appropriation of citation. For "the wells of English undefiled" is not Johnson's phrase at all but Spenser's description of Chaucer (*Faerie Queene* IV.2.32), and both Spenser and Chaucer are excluded from the *Dictionary*'s authorial range as too obsolete. Is this a willful suppression of his textual source, or does it exemplify how citation, too, is surreptitious in its own dissemination as a renegade phrase? It would appear that citations sometimes function in the fashion of the manneristic image Deleuze describes as a constant slippage across preexisting surfaces (1995, 75).

Blanchot throws light on the stereotomic extremities of quotations which "in their fragmenting force, destroy in advance the texts from which they are not only severed but which they exalt till these texts become nothing but severance"(1986, 37).[46] Subsequent to deterritorialization, citations can be relocated and manipulated. The high constructedness of the *Dictionary* is arrived at precisely by such manipulation—and Johnson's calculated choices and orchestration are exemplary.[47] Certeau stresses an additional consequence:

After cutting and grafting a quotation may turn against its new text. "Something different returns in . . . discourse with the citation of the other. It remains ambivalent; it maintains the danger of a strangeness which alters the knowledge of the translator or commentator. Citation represents for discourse the menace and the suspense of a *lapsus*. The alterity mastered—or possessed—by discourse retains the latent power of returning as a fantastic ghost—or indeed as a 'possessor'" (1988, 251).

I've already remarked on Spenser's ghostly presence inside of Johnson's words, and a further example from the *Dictionary* lends additional credence to Certeau's point. To supplement his definition of "definition"—"[a] short description of a thing by its properties"—Johnson places the following passage by Dryden: "I drew my *definition* of poetical wit from my particular consideration of him; for propriety of thought and words is only to be found in him." This quotation introduces a strange alterity: who is the "he" referred to? Johnson's illustration backfires by introducing a competing focus of attention; an enigma is stirred by the withholding of information in this sentence.

One must understand such passages not only as newly contextualized but necessarily decontextualized. Although proffered as illustrations of meanings in use, they maintain a degree of integrity and autonomy sufficient so their independent resonance can be heard. In Bakhtinian terms, the tension in the binary arises from the tendency in the citations to "novelize" the defining entry. Jabès might describe the situation as that of exiled quotations finding a new homeland in the *Dictionary*—a sort of semantic Israel. But a citation is also a housed alterity, a wild tiger in a cage whose incarceration doesn't necessarily domesticate its alterity effects. "What is cited is fragmented, reemployed and patched together [*bricolé*] in a text; it is altered therein. Yet in this position where it keeps nothing of its own, it remains capable, as in a dream, of bringing back something uncanny . . . it retains the surreptitious and altering power of the repressed" (Certeau 1988, 251). The potential to unsettle the context that supposedly commands the citations is a constant possibility and is, of course, the fundamental law of the clinamen; it applies equally to collage poems such as *The Cantos, The Waste Land,* and *Maximus.*

This assessment of citational effect is still incomplete. Giorgio Agamben underscores an important consequential dependence that any citation inaugurates: "He who puts a word in quotation marks can no longer rid himself of it: suspended in mid-air in its signifying élan, the word becomes unsubstitutable—or rather, it is now, for him, absolutely impossible to take leave of" (1995, 104). This illuminates the nature of that stability granted quotations by the proper-name effect. The connection of name to passage becomes an unsubstitutable articulation. Fixed, distantiated, and decontextually estranged, the citation remains "suspended within its history" (Agamben 1995, 103). Wishing both to define language and to liberate definitions into literary instances, Johnson must insinuate an unwanted trope by which the noose of the quotation tightens around the neck of its citator, not its author. Mallarmé might well have had the *Dictionary* in mind when insisting "there is no explosion except a book" (quoted in Blanchot 1986, 7). As a binary economy of definition and citation, the *Dictionary* "belongs to burst being—to being violently exceeded and thrust out of itself—the book gives no sign of itself save its own explosive violence, the force with which it expels itself, the thunderous refusal of the plausible: the outside in its becoming, which is that of bursting" (Blanchot 1986, 124).

Is the *Dictionary* offered to its readers as a democratic or dictatorial economy? Johnson's early biographers consistently praise it for settling the English language and giving to it both grammatical perfection and "classical elegance."[48] But what gets obfuscated in this contemporary evaluation? Barrell draws attention to an analogy, persistent through the eighteenth century, between law and language, an analogy ideologically motivated as "a part of the attempt to preserve the authority of a political system framed by the polite to protect their interests" (1983, 175). Johnson is complicit in this move when urging that the same care be shown for language as was shown for the constitution: "Life may be lengthened by care, though death cannot be ultimately defeated: tongues like governments, have a natural tendency to degeneration; we have long preserved our constitution, let us make the same struggles for our language" (1963, 27). The rules of good English go hand in hand with the laws of England. A healthy language inflects a healthy (and effective) ideological state apparatus, while social anarchy entails a similar lawlessness in the language. The *Dictionary*'s subtext is clear: how to control the turbulent tension between a printed, fixed writing and a fluid, incommensurate orality—an opposition itself analogous to the social one of polite-ancestral and banausic-mutative.

The law-language analogy has direct relevance to Johnson's deployment of the signed passages.[49] In sharp contrast to his philosophical belief in general nature and general truth, the *Dictionary* endorses the democratic right of singularities—of both the single word and the single passage. The binary nature of the book also repeats in the sphere of language what Burke speaks of as the cornerstone of the British constitution: the 1688 Declaration of Rights, which both settled regal succession and declared the rights and liberties of subjects (Burke 1993, 100). By analogy Johnson proposes meaning be settled for succeeding usage, endorsing the liberty of independent passages to move freely within that kingdom which is English letters.[50]

There is also a genuine conspiracy between the proper-name effect and legal power. Indeed, by decentering authority, and with analogical support, Johnson insinuates a different language-game: that of law in its specific manifestation as paternity. What the signatures guarantee is a collective filiation and the legal inflection of the latter should be specified. Being the process whereby a bastard child gains legitimation by identifying her or him as the child of a particular father, filiation serves as a governing force in establishing the arborescence of kinship and the Law-Name of the Father. This law of filiation connects, too, with the other law of ownership, mortmain, that ascribes property to "the dead hand" and through which inalienable ownership and posthumous control is guaranteed. Although avoiding univocal authority, Johnson can nonetheless inscribe—and with the support of constitutional law—the paternal gesture via his named citations.[51]

Any accurate assessment of Johnson's lexicographic achievement, like Bentley's editorial procedures, must link it both to its own times and to modernity—the work demands that double articulation. I hope I have shown that the *Dictionary* is a book that rewards scrutiny and encounter through current conceptual apparatuses, but that I have also indicated its sober aspects as a document of eighteenth-century Tory ideology. While grasping the essential turbulence and metamorphosis of living utterance, Johnson refuses to see the inherent shiftiness and intractability of quotations. Like footnotes and marginalia, quotations are by their very nature capricious objects of transfer—clinamens effecting dialogue and alterity. Yet Johnson's dream is to assemble these instable fragments as a reservoir of absolute exemplarity. As a result, the *Dictionary* registers as the convulsive confrontation of a lexical list by an anthology of cultural fragments.

Nonetheless, Johnson certainly deserves credit. He arrives at a pragmatic and contextual method of semantic explanation nearly two hundred years before Wittgenstein. Writing prior to the advent of modern linguistics and philosophy his prefiguration of a use theory of language is remarkable. "The true state of every nation is the state of common life" (S. Johnson 1971, 22). One might be tempted to argue that this social proposition is applicable to Johnson's ideas on language and meaning, but in reality he is too committed to the ideology of his day to embrace and consecrate the mutations of a living language in the state of common life. For Wittgenstein, whenever language changes, language lives; for Johnson, whatever moves in language is a threat to it. The challenge to Johnson was to read a book into existence.[52] He rose to this challenge with complex consequences less to the history of semantics than to the codificatory and normalizing demands of the typo-imperial ideology and coterie interest for whom (wittingly or unwittingly) he served.[53]

Like Kant before him, Wittgenstein thinks "the time is diseased by language" (quoted in Lyotard 1993a, 20). We can add Johnson's name to this short list of luminaries who diagnose the inevitable degeneration of language under the combined forces of orality, traffic, and demotic reconfigurations. For Wittgenstein the sickness locates in the ambient and constricting power of a technoscience that announces "the beginning of the end of humanity" (1980, 56e). In Wittgenstein, too, we can detect a clinamen in hope and credence. His early aspirations were not dissimilar to Johnson's. Similarly aware of the vagaries of natural language, Wittgenstein aspires to create in the *Tractatus* a language of perfect propositional univocity. As Bacon in prior times, the early Wittgenstein dreamed of an omnisolutional scientific language. The early dream of this perfect language dropped away in the *Investigations,* to be replaced by a Heraclitan-Lucretian narrative of flux and pragma. In Wittgenstein's post-tractarian thinking, words acquire meaning only in the stream of life. A meaningful language can only be a living language. More than anything else in the *Investigations,* I want to stress Wittgenstein's profound subscription to the truth of this statement.

Both Wittgenstein's and Johnson's thinking is insufficient on the question of language and the social bond. Johnson wishes to define and consecrate a cultural moment as the semantic and stylistic blueprint for all language to come. The heteroglossia of the mid-eighteenth century is ignored in favor of selected samplings from an elite bibliography. This vitiated corpus is then offered as authoritative. Johnson's authorial gatherings complete and authenticate an arboreal model of language, a language expunged of its diachronic instabilities and its oral, minoritarian, rhizomatic complexities. The picture emerges of an ideal tree of language: a ready-made phenomenon of linguistically stable units, curated and handed down from one generation to another as a patrilineal property, concealing the truth that language does not descend but is endured as a "continuous process of becoming" (Voloshinov 1986, 81).[54]

Such presumption to power is absent in Wittgenstein, and the classlessness of his ordinary language paradigms retains its force as the *Investiga-*

tions' instant, if evanescent, attraction. In reality, Wittgenstein remains captive to naive instances, failing to carry through a fully social articulation of those ideas and theories instantiated in his banal, interpersonal examples. As a consequence, no insights are offered into language's noninstrumental workings and effects. For Wittgenstein it is unproblematic to assert that "people use language" and inconceivable that language might be thought of as using people. He is to be thanked for returning philosophical discourse from metaphysics and ontology back to ordinary human phrases, but the question needs to be posed—what follows from this success? The task now is to overcome the humanism that Wittgenstein sanctifies and which Johnson decants and guards. These final words of Lyotard's thus seem an apt response to both the analysts and the guardians of a language: "Humanity is not the user of language, nor even its guardian; there is no more one subject than there is one language. Phrases situate names and pronouns (or their equivalent) in the universe they present. Philosophy is a discourse in which phrases thus try themselves out without rules and link themselves guided only by amazement at the fact that everything has not been said, that a new phrase occurs, that it is not the case that nothing happens" (1993a, 21).

"A dictionary begins," advises Bataille, "once it gives, not the meaning, but the task of words."[55]

Appendix to Chapter 6

Early English Lexicography

Dictionaries have a complex evolution as ideological commodities. The earliest prototypes, so far recorded, are bilingual word lists from West Asia dating back to the second millennium B.C.E. Sumero-Akkadian word lists excluded adjectives and verbs, itemizing exclusively nominal forms (Martin 1994, 88). The first European dictionaries were similarly bilingual word lists designed to explicate difficult Latin words. Typical of such dictionaries is Galfridus Grammaticus's *Promptorium parvulorum sive clericorum* (Storehouse for little ones, or clerics) of 1440. The absence of English dictionaries through the sixteenth century forced Tudor lexicographers such as John Baret, in his 1573 *Alvearie or triple Dictionarie in Englishe, Latin and French*, to base their definitions upon Latin equivalents. In 1580 William Bullokar, in his *Booke at large for the Amendment of Orthographie for English speech*, strongly urged the compilation of an exclusively English dictionary as a means to ensure and perpetuate both semantic and orthographic regularity, sentiments emphasized and adumbrated upon two years later by Richard Mulcaster in his *Elementerie*. Mulcaster's stridently nationalist and poly-discursive agenda is clearly evident in the following passage:

> It were a thing verie praiseworthie in my opinion, and no lesse profit-able then praise worthie, if som one well learned and as laborious a man, wold gather all the words which we vse in our English tung, whether naturall or in-corporate, out of all professions, as well learned as not, into one dictionarie, and besides the right writing, which is incident to the Alphabete, wold open vnto vs therein, both their naturall force, and their proper vse: that by his honest trauell we might be as able to iudge of our own tung, which we haue by rote, as we ar of others, which we learn by rule. The want whereof, is the onlie cause why, that verie manie men, being excellentlie well learned in foren speeche, can hardlie discern what theie haue at home, still shooting fair, but oft missing far, hard censors ouer other, ill executors themselues. (1925, 187)

For both Mulcaster and Bullokar, a dictionary's primary value is legislative and codificatory—a concise embodiment of the proper rules of a language. Richard Snell, writing in 1640, is convinced that the combined instrumentality of a dictionary and grammar will be sufficient to counter the natural tendency to volatile change in language, guaranteeing that desirable quality of immutability displayed by Latin. "The language of our Land," he writes, "thus brought to a fixed and immutable state, it will not as in former ages, so alter out of date and knowledge, but that posteritie may bee abel to read and understand, what was written by their Elders, that lived five hundred years before. . . . Wee shall reap all the same profits and advantages, that wee see the glorious *Romans* have gotten, by the means aforementioned" (quoted in Jones 1953, 296). The first English dictionary proper was Robert Cawdrey's *A Table Alphabeticall of Hard Usual English Words,* a 1604 volume containing fewer than three thousand listings. It was followed in 1616 by John Bullokar's *English Expositor* and in 1623 by Henry Cockerham's *English Dictionaire.* The latter introduced an encyclopedic dimension into English lexicography by presenting detailed descriptions of living creatures.

The authoritative account of early English lexicography remains Starnes and Noyes 1946. Cawdrey's *A Table Alphabeticall,* though apparently surviving in a unique copy now in the Bodleian, is generally available in a facsimile reprint (Cawdrey [1604] 1966).

7. Between Verbi Voco and Visual, Some Precursors of Grammatology

Scriptio Continua, Mercurius van Helmont,
Joshua Steele, Peter Walkden Fogg, and That
Precarious Binary of Speech/Writing

Backtracking rather than star trekking, this chapter traces filiations and descents, its impetus springing from the brief passage in *Of Grammatology* where Derrida cites Pound and Fenollosa as inaugural energies in the epistemic break with logocentrism. "This is the meaning of the work of Fenellosa [*sic*] whose influence upon Ezra Pound and his poetics is well-known: this irreducibly graphic poetics was, with that of Mallarmé, the first break in the most entrenched Western tradition. The fascination that the Chinese ideogram exercised on Pound's writing may thus be given all its historical significance" (Derrida 1976, 92). But why and how are Pound and Fenollosa inaugural? Derrida's "Chinese turn" in his theory of logocentrism is not without its problems. Both the irreducibly graphic status of the ideogram and the cogency of Fenollosa's theory have been seriously questioned by recent Chinese scholarship (cf. Zhang 1985). The fact, too, is that Pound, while including ideograms throughout his *Cantos* (see illustration 1), frequently affixes to them both their Western phonetic equivalent and the Western system of numerical superscripts to indicate the ideogram's spoken, tonal range, thereby linking explicitly the written sign to its utter-

義　　i⁴

Without historic black-out
　　　　they cannot maintain perpetual wars.
Taney ('34) showed an increase
　　　　　　in all branches of revenue
Benton b. 1782, d. 1858.
"How often had they been told trade was paralyzed
　　　　　　& ships idle?
"Hid the books but cd/ not hide weekly statements."
"In specie and without interest.
Against which such a bank is a nuisance."
16 to 1 for above 300 years in the Spanish dominions.
Against Biddle one million and some chicken feed
　　　　for which no vouchers are found.
Levari facias. Louis Philippe suggested that
　　　　　　Jackson stand firm
and not sugar his language.
　　　　　　Public debt was extinguished.　　　1834.

何　　ho²

必　　pi⁴⁻⁵

曰　　yüeh⁴⁻⁵

利　　li⁴

55

Figure 1. Ezra Pound, from "Canto 89," showing western system of numerical
superscripts

ance—in a manner vaguely reminiscent of Steele's earlier rational prosody, to be examined later in this chapter.

Despite Derrida's avowal that *Of Grammatology* "is a historical book through and through" (1992, 54), it fails to supply even an adequate ancestral series back to Plato. The history of logocentrism is portrayed as basically three leaps: from Plato and Aristotle through Rousseau to Saussure and Lévi-Strauss (cf. Derrida 1981a, 110) an axis that's partial, to say the least. Where does the Middle Ages (a vast stretch of cultural time from the seventh to the fifteenth century) figure in Derrida's thinking? Apart from a few brief quotes from Ernst Curtius, it's egregiously absent from his argument. Grammatological evidence from this period seriously compromises Derrida's historic focal points of logocentrism, for the Middle Ages is essentially a memorial culture in which epistemic profit derives from a third modality distinct from speech and writing: that of memory. Writing throughout this time is valorized for its visuality and its optical power to trigger mental recall and meditative practice, not for its promise of reconversion into "full" speech.[1] Similarly Agamben, in his reenvisioning of grammatology as "fundamentology" (1991, 38–40) calls into doubt the metaphysics of presence, arguing that Greek metaphysics "thought of language from the outset from the point of view of the 'letter'" (1993b, 156). In the examples presented in this chapter, I hope to adumbrate this lineage and complicate any claims to a logocentric subservience of writing to speech in Western thinking, arguing that the science of grammatology—as it now stands—less represents than suppresses several earlier scriptive conjectures.

Derrida's legacy manifests in two precipitations, one a science of writing based on novel insights into the significance and effects of temporal difference, the other a critical-philosophical methodology. It's safe to claim that grammatology and deconstruction have enjoyed a linked but uneven development within cultural capitalism.[2] Largely ignored and undeveloped, grammatology's fate is to be left as the crippled sister huddled around the fireside in poststructuralism's institutional cottage. By contrast, deconstruction, as a fashionable metatextual practice, triumphantly entered the North American academy with a speed and insurmountability that might best be compared to Atilla the Hun's entry into Rome.[3] Bernasconi and Critchley, in their introduction to *Re-Reading Levinas,* delineate the formulaic and deterministic disposition at the root of deconstructive practice: "[W]hat distinguishes deconstruction as a textual practice lies in double reading, that is, a reading that interlaces at least two motifs, most often first by following or repeating the intention of a text, in the manner of a commentary, and second, within and through this repetition, leaving the order of commentary and opening up the blind spots or ellipses within the text's intentionality" (1991, xii).

The ecumenical range of deconstructive readings is daunting. To mention Herman Rapaport's analysis of Milton (1983), Leigh Deneef's of Thomas Traherne (1988), William Dowling's Derridean approach to Boswell's *Life of Johnson* (1981), and Steven Lynn's study of Johnson's *Rambler* (1992) touches merely the tip of an academic iceberg. When adding to this the plethora of deconstructive readings handed in each year as graduate papers, the fact still remains that deconstruction has restricted itself to — indeed, can only operate within — the confines of normative typography. Where, for instance, are the deconstructive readings of Marinetti's *parole in libertà,* Apollinaire's *calligrammes,* or Iliazd's *Easter Island*? The palpable blind spot in deconstruction is its inability to engage the visible materiality of textual formats owing to the temporal and semiotic basis of deconstruction's presidential concepts. Johanna Drucker perceptively comments on this ineluctable abdication of the material base of the signifying forms. A problematic hiatus in Derrida's position obtains, Drucker says, "because the concept of écriture, of writing as trace . . . does not contain a condition for the apprehension of materiality" (1994, 39). Indeed, the very ground of signification in Derrida's thinking is inveterately antagonistic to the grapheme's stubborn materiality. The Derridean concept of signification, understood as deferral and difference, "cancels the possibility of ever apprehending substance. The metaphysical basis for presuming the existence of material substance is dissolved, in Derrida's analysis, into the continual play of difference" (Drucker 1994, 39).

My intention is not to excavate this blind spot but rather suggest how some of the shortcomings in deconstruction can be rectified by a considered engagement with grammatological evidence (not supplied by Derrida) in emergent, dominant, and residual writing systems. I take two examples of differential play from paleography (the syntactic practice of *scriptio continua* and the spatial practice of *per cola et commata*) and three obscure contributions to grammatology: Mercurius van Helmont's 1667 *Alphabeti vere naturalis hebraici brevissima delineato,* Joshua Steele's 1775 *Prosodia Rationalis,* and Peter Walkden Fogg's *Elementa Anglicana* of 1792–96. These works might be thought of as representing grammatology's clinamens — those eventist swerves from the laminar, conventional flow that complicate both accuracy in nomenclature and periodicity in general. My hope in this chapter is to show this material as collectively supplying poststructuralism with its own precessional catastrophe.

Scriptio Continua

The ancient scribal form of *scriptio continua*, by which a text was copied without separating words or indicating pauses, was common scribal practice through ancient Greece, surviving until the fourth century, at which time the use of punctuation to indicate pauses had been sufficiently adopted so as to generate a new scriptoral category: the *codices distincti* (Parkes 1993, 13).[4] In Rome, however, interpunctual writing was replaced by the earlier Greek model of *scriptio continua*, which became established as standard practice among Roman scribes by the end of the first century (Parkes 1993, 10). The method continued until the late seventh century, when Irish scribes began to separate words in both Latin and vernacular texts. Like Joyce's famous one-hundred-letter thunderclap words in *Finnegans Wake* and Kenneth Patchen's multiverbal compactions in *Sleepers Awake,* the deliberate absence of verbal distinctness requires detailed punctuational preparation by the reader.[5] "Rendering a text in *scriptio continua* proceeded from identification of the different elements—letters, syllables, words—through further stages to comprehension of the whole work" (Parkes 1993, 10). A major consequence of this initial lack of separation is a shift in bias from author to reader around the key issue of semantic determination. "The merit of the *scriptio continua* was that it presented the reader with a neutral text. To introduce graded pauses while reading involved an interpretation of the text, an activity requiring literary judgement and therefore one properly reserved for the reader" (Parkes 1993, 11). Writing in *continua,* then, required a supplemental intervention to create through spacing morphological distinctions.

There are several historical examples illustrating the psychological effects of reading *continua.* Quintilian, for example, stressed the need to divide attention " 'so that the eyes are occupied in one way and the voice another.' . . . The eyes had to be kept on what followed while the voice read out . . . what preceded" (in Parkes 1993, 10). A frequent issue was homophonic ambiguity. The fourth-century grammarian Servius censors Donatus for reading Virgil's "*exilio*" (exile) as "*ex Ilio*" (out of Troy). Pompeius, in the fifth century, mentions a similar ambiguity in book 8 of the *Aeneid,* "where the words can be separated either as *consipit ursus* ('a bear espies') or *conspicutur sus* ('a sow is espied') (in Parkes 1993, 10). "The marking of pauses in a copy of a text was normally left to the initiative of the individual reader who would insert them or not according to the degree of difficulty presented by the text, or the extent of his comprehension" (11).

The centrality of the homophone to Roussel's narrative method, Brisset's myth of the origin of man from frogs, and Bentley's editorial method have already been discussed in chapters 2 and 6. Suffice to add that Joyce, the exemplary homophonist of modernism, seemingly refers to *scriptio continua* in the mamafesto section of *Finnegans Wake:* "The original document was in what is known as Hanno O'Nonhanno's unbrookable script, that is to say, it showed no signs of punctuation of any sort" (1950, 123). *Scriptio continua* puts language into both graphic and semantic indeterminancy, resolved only by a reader's active intervention as the producer of periodicity and differentiation. A *censura caesura,* or prohibition upon pause, takes effect in which particles in void transform into a plenum. Language tropes itself as a sheet folded into nonarticulation.[6]

By confusing secondary articulation, and thus rendering the discretions of the very articuli indeterminate, *scriptio continua* creates a syrrhesitic movement of the text—a flowing together of verbal discretions precipitating a more intense, libidinal encounter with the written. In passing, one might note that Lecercle demonstrates how logophiliac *délire*—that confluence of language, nonsense, and desire—is experienced as a kind of *scriptio continua;* as a process not of separation but of segmentive erasure (1985, 16, 164–65). Because semantic clarity is dissolved, words in *continua* are initially encountered as letters-becoming-words, presignificatory instabilities and uncertainties in a protosemantic continuum. Punctuation and spacing—as well as its complicated conceptual incarnation as Derridean *differance*—can be thought of as severing activities that slice a continuum into culturally recognizable sequences but may also be seen as clinamens.

Now experience the foregoing paragraph in *scriptio continua.* It's a settled, entropic, undifferentiated unit—a text in equilibrium.

Byconfusingsecondaryarticulationandthusrenderingthediscretionsofthe
veryarticuliindeterminatescriptiocontinuacreatesasyrrhesiticmovement
ofthetextaflowingtogetherofverbaldiscretionsprecipitatingamoreintense
libidinalencounterwiththewrittenInpassingonemightnotethat
Lecercledemonstrateshowlogophiliacdélirethatconfluenceoflanguage
nonsenseanddesireisexperiencedasakindofscriptiocontinuaasaprocess
notofseparationbutofsegmentiveerasure(1985161646 5)Becausesemantic
clarityisdissolvedwordsincontinuaareinitiallyencounteredasletters-

becoming-wordspresignificatoryinstabilitiesanduncertaintiesinaproto-
semanticcontinuumPunctuationandspacingaswellasitscomplicated
conceptualincarnationasDerrideanddifferancecanbethoughtofasstereo
tomicactivitiesthatseveracontinuumintorecognizablesequencesbutmay
alsobeseenasclinamens.

"Articulated languages are parasited breaths" (Serres 1982a, 189). And it's
useful to regard punctuation as a "phrasal parasite" that produces equilibrium in message. By the routine clinamens of spacing, a turbulence and
discontinuity is introduced into the writing and from this flux another textual equilibrium emerges. To read the current of the prototext divides a
laminar flow into smaller particles. From the continuum emerges distinction, clarity, and thereby words. A Lucretius versed in French might name
this movement the "breeze" of reading, remarking both the sonic and etymological connection of "breeze" to *briser* (the French verb "to break").

Although *scriptio continua* is an ignored item in grammatology's archive,
the hortation to readerly production and its profound implications on the
sociology of readership—most especially the radical empowering of the
traditionally inferior term in the writer-reader binary—has witnessed important revivification in recent decades. If projective verse offered a poetics
of parousial impact grounded in the transit of the syllable-as-energy, then
Language writing responded with a disjunctive poetics anchored in the preeminence of readerly semantic production. If a slogan can encapsulate the
spirit of Language writing in its formative years (1975–86), it would read
ALL POWER TO THE READER. Antony Easthope describes succinctly this
"socialism of the text" which by "asking the reader to work through linguistic details that give the text its effect it has aimed to expropriate the poem
from its supposed 'owner,' the represented speaker or narrator, and put it
back into the hands of the reader who produces it" (1983, 162).

The application of this sociological clinamen in agency reappears, of
course, in reader response theory. Iser's own phenomenology of reader perception makes use of a virtual work, marked by gaps and indeterminacies,
and an ideal reader whose function is to fill in these aporia (cf. Iser 1978).
In granting to the reader central semantic productivity reader response
theory, Language writing and *scriptio continua* run in concerted opposition
to Deleuze's categorical assertion that "there's never anything like enough
consumption" (1995, 20). Earlier, in chapter 4, I presented evidence to historically relativize the novelty of Olson's indisputably important notions
about breath, syllable, and energy. A similar point is offered here, for in

its least impact, an awareness of *scriptio continua* and its productive assignments to the reader-function seriously challenges the way the psychology of classical reading has been bracketed out of consideration. An evolutionary narrative from primitive to civilized is seen to be untenable as an argument for change, for *scriptio continua* was established as common scribal practice from the first century throughout the Roman Empire as a system derived from earlier Greek practice and actually used to replace interpunctual writing.[7]

Per Cola et Commata

In its simplest description, *per cola et commata* is a system of line breaks installed into prose. The practice involves laying out each constituent element of a period on a separate line, flush left to the margin. This line then accommodates a complete unit of sense, and any such unit running over a line length is indented. The Amiatino manuscript, a vulgate Bible now in the Bibiloteca Medicea Laurenziana but copied by scribes at Wearmouth Jarrow in Northumbria no later than 716 C.E. uses this method. The following translation of fol. 349 (a part of one of the Psalms) preserves the *cola* and *commata* format.

> Blessed is the man who hath not walked in
>   the counsel of the ungodly
> and hath stood in the way of sinners
> and hath not sat in the seat of the scornful
> But his will is in the law of the Lord
> and in His law shall he meditate
>   day and night
> And he shall be like a tree transplanted
>   close by the streams of water
> that will bring forth its fruit
>   in due season

Saint Jerome encountered the system in copies of speeches by Demosthenes and Cicero (Parkes 1993, 179; Martin 1994, 57) and uses it in his own translations of Isaiah and Ezekiel. It was subsequently adopted by other scribes between the fifth and ninth centuries for copying biblical books and passages. Jerome locates the value of the system in its punctuational clarity by visual separation and spacing rather than graphic marking. In his prologue to Ezekiel, he refers to the method as a "new kind of writing [explaining] that which is written *per cola et commata* conveys more obvious sense to the reader" (in Parkes 1993, 15). This particular form of transcription—in broken phrases that nonetheless contain a complete idea—facilitates instant optic comprehension and thereby effective retention in the memory.[8] It's to such mnemonic ends that Quintilian recommends that *colas* be *"numeris conclusis,"* that is, rhythmically complete (quoted in Carruthers 1990, 112). Although its purpose is to visually isolate a complete unit of sense and to render such units as single lines, this early scribal practice is clearly an important, unacknowledged precursor of free verse. It does not attain, however, the quintessential balance of blank space and isolated word that is associated with the heirs of Mallarmé. Indeed, the word-free spaces left by the system are frequently filled with decorative motifs, a horror of vacuum—perhaps symptomatic of a desire for a lost continuum—that resurfaces in Blake's illuminated prophecies.

Nonetheless, in the light of *per cola et commata,* it seems impossible to base any definitive distinction between prose and poetry on a motivated deployment of line breaks. To merely admit that early Bibles take on the appearance of free verse effects relativizes any late-nineteenth-century claims to origin. This fundamental inapplicability of the binary of prose and verse at this period once more anticipates the more recent attempts by Ron Silliman (in his *Ketjak* and *Tjanting,* for instance) to inscribe a poetics within a prosaics by way of the new sentence (see chapter 9). Or should due credit for the invention of free verse be given through the words of Saint Jerome to Demosthenes?

Mercurius van Helmont

> Ask yourself: "What would it be like if human beings never found the word
> that was on the tip of their tongue?"
> —Wittgenstein, *Philosophical Investigations,* 219e

Mercurius van Helmont designed his *Alphabete vere naturalis hebraici brevissima delineato* (1667) as a practical and easy method by which deaf-mutes might learn to speak. Helmont arrives at the Hebrew alphabet through a sort of back-formation from the initial premise that there must be a primitive language that is easy to learn. Concluding that Hebrew is such a language, he proceeds to demonstrate that the sounds of Hebrew characters are the most easily pronounced owing to the supposed fact that these characters mimic the shape of the vocal organs. It's a curious, Baroque cur-

Figure 2. Mercurius van Helmont, *Alphabete vere naturalis hebraici brevissima delineato,* pronunciation plates of Hebrew characters

vature back from speech through the written to the body, supplemented in the book with pronunciation plates depicting a dissected mouth and throat in utterance. (See illustration 2.) These diagrams supplement an amazing claim: that the holy script of Hebrew actually graphs the shape and movement of the vocal organs in utterance.

Gérard Genette places Helmont's "true natural Hebrew alphabet" in the class of graphical cratylism as a "mimetic interpretation of existing writing systems" (1995, 54). Helmont hoped to prove the originary status of Hebrew as the true language of Adam, and both writing and speech as gifts of divine revelation. And while this mystical speculation can now be written off as whimsical nonsense, the actual system holds a contemporary attraction through its remarkable anticipation of biopoesis.[9] If nothing else, Helmont's theory profoundly unsettles the relationship of body coordinates advanced in Derrida's tenet that "[t]he history of writing is erected on the base of the history of the grammè as an adventure of relationships between the face and the hand" (1976, 84). Helmont's alphabet documents a profound instability in the frontiers between speech and writing. Is the letter presented as a latent force awaiting written activation in speech? Or does writing record in its tracings of letters the ephemeral movements of the tongue, throat, and larynx? For Helmont, these questions are shibboleths obfuscating a conspiratorial entanglement of speech and writing. In fact, he conflates the two, assigning priority to neither, situating the origins of both speech and writing in a mutual mimology through which the contortions of the human mouth in phonation actually "write" a letter as well as "voice" a sound. The Hebrew grapheme is simultaneously written and carnalized; its inscription does not record a speaking but exists as an invisible production folded *within* that speaking. Figured as fundamentally somatic, the ono-matopoeic template of a momentary musculature; the Hebrew letter is a natural, corporeal, and performative hieroglyph.

Ferenczi speaks of amphimixis—that interplay or commingling of or-gans, producing in language the pun, deployed so effectively by Brisset and Roussel and appearing in Joyce as the portmanteau word. In Helmont it manifests as a fold of utterance into the written. Resisting any logocentric reduction of voice to itself in a phonetism, Helmont's system causes voice to repeat a writing in a style of proprioceptive dictation. In a thorough re-pudiation of the Aristotelian legacy, Helmont offers an image of speech as being itself a system of writing. If we recall Olson's famous pronouncement on the physiological source of the poem as "down through the workings of [the poet's] throat to that place where breath comes from, where breath has its beginnings, where drama has to come from, where the coincidence is, all act springs" (see chapter 4), then it clearly emerges how Helmont's "true alphabet," transfixing, as it does, the configured movements of chords and muscles in action, both supplements and departs from Olson's biopoetics.[10]

It's hard not to recall Barthes's rhapsodies on the paralinguistic effects of the grain of the voice—an amorous entwining of timbre and language whose aim "is not the clarity of messages, [but a blissful search for] pul-sional incidents, the language lined with flesh, a text where we can hear the grain of the throat, the patina of consonants, the voluptuousness of vow-els, a whole carnal stereophony: the articulation of the body, of the tongue, not that of meaning, of language" (1975, 66–67). Despite the unmistak-able echoes of Helmont, there is no evidence that Barthes knew of his work when consecrating the body inside the written. "Writing is not speech . . . but neither is writing the written . . . to write is not to transcribe. In writ-ing, what is *too* present in speech . . . and *too* absent from transcription, namely the body, returns . . . through pleasure and not through the Imagi-nary (the image)" (Barthes 1985, 7). It's hard to deny also that Helmont's conclusion—that phonic utterance already arrives sedimented by a writing—is remarkably close to Derrida's own concept of a basal archewriting, preceding both speech and writing as such.

Drucker detects in Helmont's speculations a "profound belief that a close relation between written form and physiology would result in a more perfect alphabet" (1995, 213). And certainly physiology and grammatology implode in a manner that Derrida fails to address—an implosion carrying the ideological assumption that the human anatomy is inherently perfect. Helmont's theory is less a search for the origin of writing than a proof of anatomical perfection through the profound conspiracy of the written mark and an oral assemblage in motion. In such systems, Drucker comments, "The body carried no association of carnal impurity . . . but was a natural fact, and therefore, could be the basis of a neutral or even positive image. The social order was not in conflict with this natural image, but a logical—or even . . . *reasonable*—extension of its character" (213). But not to dwell on these obsolete, ideological shortcomings. Helmont's current value to poetics lies in the clinamen effect of deviating the focus of the poetic unit from word or line back to letters, and suggesting along the way how writing is always at play underneath—and despite of—any physiological labor of utterance.

Joshua Steele

Benjamin's remark that "written language grows out of music and not directly from the sounds of the spoken word" (1977, 214) bears directly on any candid assessment of Steele's vertiginous system of prosodic scoring outlined in his *Prosodia Rationalis* of 1775. (See illustrations 3 and 4.) Its accomplishment—nothing less than "the most precise and meticulous attempt to recreate the aural poem in visual form" (Bradford 1989, 15)—historically fulfills that need for emotive markers first called for in the eighteenth century by Duclos: "In writing we mark interrogation and surprise; but how many movements of the soul, and consequently how many oratorical inflections, do we possess, that have no written signs, and that only intelligence and sentiment may make us grasp! Such are the inflections that mark anger, scorn, irony, etc., etc." (quoted in Derrida 1976, 347 n.46).

Steele's complex and detailed system of super- and subsegmental markers effectively demolishes any linear negotiation of a text, answering Derrida's call for the full-scale desedimentation of four millennia of linear writing almost two centuries before that question is posed (1976, 86). Con-

remainder with all the marks of expreſſion, but without accents.

Figure 3. Joshua Steele, *Prosodia Rationalis*,
prosodic notation of part of Hamlet's soliloquy

sidered strictly as a notator, Steele might be thought to indulge the copyist's temptation "to add *supplementary* signs to improve the restitution of the original" (Derrida 1976, 227), supplementing, in other words, the normative poetic line with a complex chordal notation around a single word or syllable, providing simultaneous acoustic instructions as regards to intonation, accent, quantity, pause, and volume. It's inaccurate, however, to regard the system as merely an auxiliary notation of secondary features to an existing phonetic system, for in reality Steele offers a radically different treatment of language: an acute visual registration of locutionary variations.

Between Verbi Voco and Visual, Some Precursors of Grammatology 117

shall be nearly divided under the several degrees of emphasis of
heavy (△), light (∴), and lightest (..); as thus,

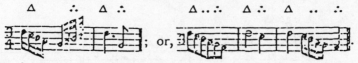

Having premised so much, I will now give a general precept
and example in the following sentence:

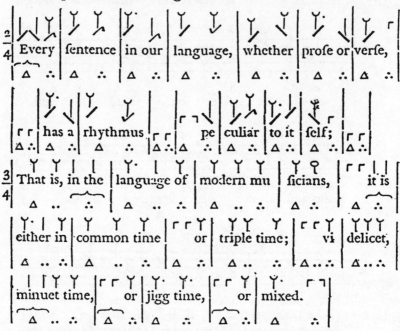

To the first member of the above sentence (which I have
written in common time, as marked by ⅔), I have noted the
accents, the *quantity* and *cadence*; to the latter member, which
is in triple measure, I have only marked *quantity* and *cadence*,
together with the proper *rests* or *pauses* throughout the whole.

Figure 4. Joshua Steele, *Prosodia Rationalis*, notation of silence in final bar

Paradoxically, rational prosody discerns the indiscernible, bringing to light those limitrophic zones of speech resistant to standardizing categories.

Michel Serres speculates on the grammatological origin of geometry as in part a transportation of certain Egyptian hieroglyphic characters into the alphabetic system of Greek. "Are the square, the triangle, the circle, and the other figures all that remains of hieroglyphics in Greece? As far as I know, they are ideograms" (1982b, 128). Steele's rational prosody is similarly an intricate interrelation of two systems of writing, the end product of which is an ideogrammic intertwining of various (and sometimes competing) linguistic impulses—phonetic and pictographic—purporting to support and supplement a normative phonocentricity. It's perhaps ironic to mention that Steele's notation of multiple stress offers a practical and more efficient system for scoring high energy transference demanded in projective verse than Olson does himself—especially so with Steele's ample accommodation of volume and pause.

Guattari warns of a "generalized suppression of . . . the semiotic components of expression"—a ban guaranteeing that the rules of speech will depend upon a law of writing" (1996b, 15). Steele, however, interrupts this law and shatters the feasibility of a speech/writing dyadic opposition. Paradoxically, his writing system unsettles the historical status of the written. Logos, word, imprint, call it whatever—that incised trace defined by Aristotle as the graphic sign of voice—is deprived of any settled logocentric itinerary. In its place is the apex of a curvature back—beyond speech—to the proprioceptive ephemera of vocality. By way of its ability to notate these somatic microcomponents of utterance, rational prosody threatens the logocentric status of the written as an image of the spoken, not by disproof or rebuttal, but in its hypercertification. Steele's writing, in its optimum efficiency, returns "speech" less to voice than to its source in bodies, musculatures, and vocal timbres. The capacity to record not a mind expressing its thoughts through lips but the physical evanescence of that expression's corporeal jetsam.

José Gil points to certain entropic forces whenever two disparate signifying systems meet: "There is an entropy proper to sign systems that diminishes their capacity to signify. When two opposed forces enter into relation, the force that takes the upper hand in the combat leaves a remainder. This remainder, which measures the relation between the forces, or the gap between them, is also a measure of the power one force has over the other" (*Métamorphoses du corps* 20, quoted in Massumi 1992, 149).

A thanatopractic effect obtains in Steele's own systemic remainder. There is an effective smothering of voice beneath graphic appurtenances transforming the linear text of Hamlet's soliloquy into a musical score. (See illustration 3.) "The oriental corpse is in the book," comments Derrida in an effervescent paraphrase of Rousseau. "Ours is already in our speech. Our language, even if we are pleased to speak it, has already substituted too many articulations for too many accents, it has lost life and warmth, it is already eaten by writing" (1976, 226). Assessing in 1928 the then recent technology developments, Adorno concludes that "the possibility of inscribing music without it ever having sounded has simultaneously reified it in an even more inhuman manner and also brought it mysteriously closer to the character of writing and language" (1990, 60)—comments certainly applicable to Steele's own musical prosody.

Despite Benjamin's assurance that the true genesis of writing is in music, not speech, it remains a moot point whether Steele adds life to the written or guarantees the triumph of graphism over the incommensurate accidents of utterance. Faced with its dazzling excess, it's tempting to accept rational prosody less as a writing than as a semiotic bombardment of one's cerebral circuitries. Rousseau no doubt would have considered this pluridimensional writing with its complicated system of supplementary markers the odious symptom of the miserable decay that any system of writing precipitates. Clearly as prosodic scoring Steele's method provides neither the visual mimography nor the logoclastic delight of Marinetti's *parole in libertà* or Dadaist Raoul Hausmann's optophonetic notation (see chapter 10). The demands of sound become a parasitic surplus on the dissipative system of writing, pushing it to a point of overdetermination. A practice of appurtenance frequently argues against a theory of ascesis, and doubtless the proliferation of these graphic attachments to the written results in a pictographic excess. But more important, by incorporating such visual minutiae Steele opens up a tacit misconception: that the transit between a written poem and its reading is neutral and unproblematic. In reality, during that passage, a vast gamut of intonational shifts and timbres are lost by going unrecorded. Steele tries to expand the potential of writing sufficiently to annotate both the instabilities and singularities of utterance. (Like Alexander Bell's later non-Romanic alphabetic system of *Visible Speech* [see illustration 5], it allows the precise recording of dialects.)

But beyond its form and system, rational prosody harnesses a delicate interplay of forces, those microphysical ephemeralities that constitute the vocal instant. Moreover, Steele discloses a teasing paradox of his time: that only through print logic can a poem's complex intonation and volume be

Consonants.   **Vowels.**

	Organic Name	Mixed	Divided	Mixed Divided	Shut	Nasal		Back	Back Wide	Mixed	Mixed Wide	Front	Front Wide
Aspirate,	O						High,						
Throat,					X		Mid,						
Throat Voice,							Low,						
Back,	C						High Round,						
Back Voice,							Mid Round,						
Front,							Low Round,						
Front Voice,													
Point,													
Point Voice,													
Lip,													
Lip Voice,													

Glides.

Modifiers and Tones.

Nasal.	Trilled.	Suction Stopped.	Abrupt.	Level Tone.
Nasal Mixed.	Divided.	Emission Stopped.	Hiatus.	Rising Tone.
Inner.	Inverted [To Back.]	Link.	Whistle.	Falling Tone.
Outer.	Protruded [To Lip.]	Accent.	Voiced Whistle.	Compound Rise.
Close.	Stopped.	Emphasis.	High Key.	Compound Fall.
Open.	Suction.	Holder.	Low Key.	

Figure 5. Alexander Melville Bell, *Visible Speech*, table of non-Romanic characters with corresponding spoken sounds

adequately recorded for reproduction. Boswell, acutely aware of the potential of Steele's system as an audiographic resource, laments the fact that Johnson's anecdotes had not been preserved by this method. The Doctor's "mode of speaking was indeed very impressive; and I wish it could be preserved as musick is written, according to the very ingenious method of Mr. Steele, who has shewn how the recitation of Mr. Garrick, and other eminent speakers, might be transmitted to posterity *in score*" (Boswell 1980, 599–600).

Steele reconfigures texts as repeatable acoustic-somatic performances, his system being a compensatory method for two unavailable—because uninvented—technologies: the record player and the tape recorder. (The application of the latter in contemporary sonopoetics is discussed in chapter 10.) Like Helmont, he demonstrates that writing never evacuates the body but rather repeats it in a graphic parody as both an incarnation through visible formats and as a transubstantiation. Steele, too, is the first ever to offer a system of notating textual silence. In a remarkable anticipation of John Cage and Jackson Mac Low, he scores the minute somatic activities and durations of silence in the space between, and at the end of, words. (See, e.g., the last bar in illustration 4.)

Peter Walkden Fogg

Fogg's *Elementa Anglicana* (1792–96) insists on a fundamental separation between a poem's meaning and the readerly pleasures derived from the material duration of its visual form. (See illustration 6.) He refers to this aesthetic potential as "wordless music," which in Fogg's own rendition presents one of the most remarkable rewritings of a linear text. Reflecting on the mental pleasures a reader derives from the discontinuities and harmonies of rhythmic poetry, Fogg offers an early version of reader response theory: "The traces of these delightful movements frequently remain in the mind, and serve as a kind of inspiration, allowing them no rest till they have filled up the craving void of these blanks of harmony with compositions of their own. The varied and yet regular maze affords numberless objects of comparison, which to perceive is unspeakably pleasant, though to point them out might seem tedious. Nay, as was before remarked on the *melody* of pauses, pleasure may be derived from a view of straight lines in the same variety and proportion" (1792–96, 2:198). These literal lines present a remarkable reworking of six lines from a poem by Blake's patron William Hayley and are designed to reproduce the pausal melody, variety, and proportion of Hayley's text while at the same time erasing it. The effect of these motivated deletions is a radical reduction of language to the condition of a totally material, nonsemantic trace. Fogg's wordless music is also, as Richard Bradford points out, a remarkable anticipation of Man Ray's famous 1924 poem "Lautgedicht," of which this is the opening:

We find in both the same visible suggestion of a verse-presence in the disposition of lines and pauses obliging their readers "to admit that we understand aspects of poetic writing which are outside its meaning" (Bradford 1989, 18). (The tactical nature of Ronald Johnson's related practice of

Of humbler mien, but not of mortal race,
Ill-fated Dryden, with imperial grace,
Gives to th'obedient lyre his rapid laws;
Tones yet unheard, with touch divine, he draws,
The melting fall, the rising swell sublime,
And all the magic of melodious rhyme.
See with proud joy imagination spread
A wreath of honour round his aged head!
But two base spectres, though of different hue,
The bard unhappy in his march pursue;
Two vile disgraceful fiends of race accurst,
Conceiv'd by Spleen, by meagre Famine nurst;
Malignant Satire, mercenary Praise,
Shed their dark spots on his immortal bays.   *Hayley.*

Figure 6. Peter Walkden Fogg, *Elementa Anglicana: or,*
The Principles of English Grammar, wordless music and its verbal source

deletion and subtraction is considered in chapter I; that of Mac Low in
chapter II. The ethical nuance of such operations on preexistent material by
certain other twentieth-century writers—Cage, Burroughs, and Phillips—
forms the core of my final chapter.)

Language, utterly immersed in a relational system, secured by grammatical rules and semantic norms, does not assign significance to such sublexical
events. The word, not the letter, constitutes the minimal unit of attention,
and the creative norm is scaled to the expressive regularities of the community practicing a particular set of conventions. What Steele, Fogg, and
Helmont commonly scrutinize are the efficacious effects beneath and beside
the static lexeme. And if (with apologies to Levinas) the history of writing
is only a growing awareness of the difficulty of reading, then Steele's system
certainly compounds that difficulty. The view that the study of literature

may evolve into "a stance toward language" rather than the definition of an object is posited by William Paulson (1988, 25). His revisionary proposal forwards an unambiguous thesis: the investigation of language ventured by writers and implicit in literary works should be made explicit in literary scholarship—especially if, by "language," we mean the cognitive ground of subjectivity as well as the social texture of community. It's precisely because of this "stance toward language" that Fogg, Steele, and Helmont warrant serious discussion. Also, as precessional phenomena, their endeavors unwittingly endorse Deleuze and Guattari's noted dictum that writing "has nothing to do with signifying. It has to do with surveying, mapping, even realms that are yet to come" (1987, 4–5). "To be at the end of fact," Wallace Stevens reminds us, "is not to be at the beginning of imagination, but it is to be at the end of both." [11]

On the basis of my errors, I have established principles; since that time,
I have known felicity.
—D. A. F. de Sade

The essential being of language cannot be anything linguistic.
—Heidegger

8. Sade

Writing and Modernity

It is especially to the experience of Sade's writings as a practice of limit that modernity must address its case and status. The demand placed upon its readers is to take up the cosmological implications of both its semiology and its representations; a demand that we know him *truly,* at the same time realizing that Sade mocks all knowledge and every epistemological arrangement that has pretensions to anything more than an eruptive evanescence. In a general comment, Alphonso Lingis refers to Sade's writings as "a Leibnizian mathesis universalis of evil" (in Klossowski 1991, x). Yet in reality they warrant affirmation as a complicated itinerary of innovations. He is the first novelist of the unconscious, the first practitioner of the modern subject, the first thinker to propose a world picture predicated upon transcendental negativity, and, in Simone de Beauvoir's estimation, a great moralist (4). His writings anticipate the postromantic shift away from forms and structures toward the demonstration of forces and intensities confined tenuously within the novel's generic carapace.[1] Replacing the policy of decorous exposition is a mobilized strategy for writing conceived as a movement along vectors of disruption that break open the rigid, cultural constructs of the Enlightenment and leave to subjectivity an affirmative but intensely ambivalent space in which to destroy or constitute itself. Sade searches for an alternative to both literature and philosophy that would bring both together for the purpose of their mutual obliteration along the temporality of the writing plane.

Sade's theoretical achievements, however, must be measured against the historical and empirical circumstances of their composition and the known biographical data of their author. His philosophic motivation from the outset is an extreme self-interest and perhaps even an absolute egotism out of which comes the guiding caveat of each character to pursue one's pleasure regardless of the cost to others. Such a morality can only be predicated upon the primary fact of absolute self-difference. Thirty of Sade's seventy-four years were spent in confinement. He was imprisoned for eleven years between 1779 and 1790, first in Vincennes and then in the Bastille. Freed in 1790, he was imprisoned three years later for a year plus fifteen days. In 1800 he spent several months in the hospital at Versailles. He was arrested again in March 1801, supposedly for his plan to reprint *Juliette* and *Justine*. He remained incarcerated until his death in 1814 in Sainte-Pelagie, Bicetre, and finally Charenton, where he composed comedies and farces performed by the inmates.

Moreover, the threat of death and execution remained omnipresent. On the "29th brumaire, year III" (November 1794), Sade writes to his lawyer of his condition:

> I went through four prisons in ten months. In the first, I slept six months in filth. In the second, eight days with persons afflicted with malignant fever of whom two died next to me. In the third, I was in the midst of the counter revolution of Saint-Lazare, a noxious poison from which I protected myself only through unbelievable prudence. Finally my fourth was a terrestrial paradise—a beautiful house, superb garden, select society, amiable women, when suddenly the place of executions was put virtually beneath our windows and the cemetery of the guillotined right in the middle of our garden. We buried 1,800, my dear lawyer, in thirty-five days, of whom one-third were from our unfortunate house. Finally my name had just been put on the list and I was to be the eleventh when the day before, the sword of justice came down on the new Sylla of France. (Quoted in Berman 1971, 571)

Bataille presents a sympathetic, if disturbing, description of the consequences of this condition:

> In the solitude of his prison Sade was the first man to give a rational expression to those uncontrollable desires, on the negation of which consciousness has based the social structure and the very image of man. It was in order to do this that he had to question every value which had

hitherto been considered absolute. His books give us the feeling that, by an exasperated inversion, he wanted the impossible and the *reverse* of life. (1973, 98)[2]

"[T]he most profound solitude," advises Benjamin, "is that of the ideal man in relation to the Idea, which destroys his human characteristics. And this most profound solitude we can first expect from the true community" (*Briefe* 1:86–87, quoted in Wolin 1994, 6). From the enforced solitude and silence of this "true community" Sade inverts the values of occidental thought. His writings constitute one man's solitary expenditure, a vast verbal emission for the most part deprived of the normal channels of reification and transmission. (To a Jesuit critic like Pontanus, the carceral genesis of Sade's compositions alone is sufficient reason to rank them lowest on the scale of his achievements.)[3] Sade dies believing his masterwork *The One Hundred and Twenty Days of Sodom* perished in manuscript, and to his death denied authorship of both *Justine* and *Juliette*. Though ultimately unprovable, it appears that Sade obeyed a compulsive command to supply, without demand, a claustrological writing that would never open up an exchange with the outside.

Simone de Beauvoir moves toward the essential discrimination between Sade the sadist and Sade the writer when claiming that he "made of his eroticism the meaning and expression of his whole existence" (1966, 19) — an existence that was largely writing. Beauvoir elaborates: "It was not murder that fulfilled Sade's erotic nature: it was literature" (1966, 33). This is another way of saying Sade wrote to prevent himself from going mad. His prisons are not emblematic topoi, but the genuine spaces for a singular psychic, social, and political correlation. Removed from the social sphere, Sade is able to populate his cell with dreams, episodes, and bodies whose historical erasure seem guaranteed by the institutional space that held them. His was a solipsistic and sacrificial outlay, but nonetheless one in which a monumental contract was agreed upon. Sade loaned writing to desire. The implications of this loan are taken up by Bataille when arguing that the sacrificial is always grounded in "a fear of release expressed through release . . . a process by which the world of lucid activity (the profane world) liberates itself from a violence which might destroy it" (1973, 100). It was Sade's representations that finally saved him from the destruction implicit on the level of their practical realization. Some 138 years after this bizarre sequence of confinements that formed the matrix for a violent, imprisoned writing, Beauvoir detects a curious but profound ethic. Sade's chief interest, she writes, "lies not in his aberrations, but in the manner in which he assumed responsibility for them. He made his sexuality an ethic" and, it should be added, of his desires a writing. Beauvoir also cautions, "To sympathize with Sade too readily is to betray him" (1966, 61).

Annie Le Brun compares Sade's writing to the way "one might ride a horse to death" (1990, xvi), praising his "integral literalness" and the stark materiality of his language (134–35), assuring that whoever reads him "comes out of it with one of those huge bruises of the soul whose unexpected hues can cause the far horizon to turn pale" (1). It's vital also to bear in mind that Sade's major decision in the area of representation is "to think of and describe an act instead of committing it" (Klossowski 1991, 13), negating the erotic act by discursive strategies of thought and description. Such deviation from actual praxis renders meaning and expression alike "always charged with an ethical significance" (Beauvoir 1966, 28). But to engage the novels as a series of fictive representations, or as the episodic narrative tableaux that indisputably in part they are, avoids the works' intrinsic modernity. Sade investigates power and desire[4] as they are precisely mediated through sexuality and articulated onto pornography, on the one hand, and into a radical, transversal writing, on the other.[5]

Readerly revulsion at the acts narrated occurs only on the level of a monologic encounter with Sade's polylogic texts, an encounter in which reading remains isomorphic with the horizon of narrative representation, locked in a verbal television that preserves the fetishized relation to the texts as mimetic commodities of story whose vehicular form is a purely instrumental language. To restrict Sade's iconoclastic fictions solely to this level of plot and description suppresses the profound relativity of his representations. The novels are never truly convincing as stories, with their depicted victims remarkable as much for their rapid returns to normal health as for the hyperexcessive intensity of their tortures. Conforming to a cartoon semiotics, they inhabit a kind of Tom-and-Jerry ontology in which the movement from real to imaginary and vice versa ensues by way of an "illusory osmosis in which the imaginary not only turns into reality, but reality also tends to become imaginary" (Le Brun 1990, 75). These osmotic passages through real and imaginary states are perhaps Sade's most powerful constant, reaching their most vertiginous in the compact taxonomies and cumulative sketches that make up the second half of *The One Hundred and Twenty Days of Sodom*—Sade's most Leibnizian work, with its exhaustive catalogs, recombinants, and permutations.

He fucks a goat from behind while being flogged; the goat conceives and gives birth to a monster. Monster though it be, he embuggers it. (1966, 603)

He fucks the nostrils of a goat which meanwhile is licking his balls; and during this exercise, he is alternately flogged and has his asshole licked. (604)

Sade's narrative mode of repetition and monotony neither promotes ascesis nor mobilizes a principle of insufficiency but rather accumulates an excessive order, a perverted principle of luxury and surfeit.

Equally, many of the characters lack verisimilitude. The Herculean Minski is a fine example of Sade's propensity to gargantuan, ithyphallic caricature. He is depicted as sporting a permanently tumescent penis, reported to be "a sausage of about eighteen inches long and sixteen inches round, topped with a vermilion mushroom as wide as the crown of a hat" (quoted in Le Brun 1990, 183). The libertine Dolmancé emphasizes theatricality as the basic posture of sexual pedagogy: "I should like men, gathered in no matter what temple, to invoke the eternal who wears their image, to be seen as so many comics in a theatre, at whose antics everyone may go to laugh" (Sade 1965a, 308). Judged on logical grounds, both the characters and their interactions must be dismissed or embraced—in Flaubert's words—as "entertaining nonsense." Yet, articulated onto Sade's own moral philosophy and theory of nature, these same comic, theatrical elements gain a significant cosmological dimension.[6]

Sade's books are the product of an incestuous union of description and ratiocination. Between vast stretches of philosophization, brief episodes erupt of incomparable intensity that enact the implications and ultimatums of his philosophical thinking. The entire rhythm of libertinal instruction, outlined in *Philosophy in the Bedroom,* is an oscillation between pleasurable discharge and ratiocinative recovery. The Sadean gaze, as Susan Stewart points out, "remains caught between movement and action, never quite satisfied and never engaged" (1988, 166). In turn, Le Brun observes that Sade creates "a new erotic relationship with knowledge itself [one in which] pleasure both leads to and is increased by cognition" (1990, 60). Like the fibrillations induced by the Cartesian separation of cogito from extension, Sade interlaces two heterogeneous discourses, two seemingly aberrant codes, to fabricate a singular writing that Horkheimer and Adorno acknowledge as being "the intransigent critique of practical reason" (1972, 94).

Sade cannot leave theories alone, cannot remain a mere novelist of imaginative fictions. In his work "there are neither ideas without bodies nor bodies without ideas" (Le Brun 1990, 147).[7] Readers must enter his writings as into huge fabrications in which rational thinking and theory implode into passional enactments of a singular oscillating economy, whereby the forces of reason (reiterated obsessively throughout the works) unleash the most irrational powers as monstrous parodies and reversals of logical production. By refusing to grant preferential status to either mind or body, Sade establishes a narratological tension between instinct and intellect, on the one hand, and a constant interaction of thought and perversion, on the other.[8] His narrative structures are economies whose pattern can be perceived by anyone who takes the trouble to read through their prodigious graphic networks. *Justine* and *Juliette*—together with the unfinished scheme for *The One Hundred and Twenty Days of Sodom*—all utilize identical concatenations by which libertines enunciate ideas, ideas shape theories, and theoretical proposals provoke the enactment of expenditures. Out of this rhythm Sade fabricates the polymorphous, gynandrean bodies that maintain a curious relation to language and thought; bodies subordinated to a powerful demonstrative function in their discourse and that exist as the diagrammatic agencies of the acts and states their various speakings describe.

Philippe Sollers isolates two distinct operative codes in Sade's writing practice (1983, 45–62). Alongside a discursive language of logical productions, arguments, theories, rational constructs and syllogistic devices is a language of pleasure, desire, obsession, obscenity, blasphemy, and affect. Sollers situates the operation of these two codes on three discrete signifying levels. A narrative level links Sade's writings to such works as *The Decameron* and *The Canterbury Tales* and finds its best instantiation in the libertine "women chroniclers" of *The One Hundred and Twenty Days of Sodom*. Next a mimetic level of interactive dialogue serves to reproduce the practices narrated on the first level. A third, syllogistic level supports the two previous ones by providing, through logical arrangements, a philosophy and theory to justify the acts described and their mimological repercussions. One consequence of this trilateral arrangement is that the texts are protected from any absolute generic annexation. Neither pure imaginative fictions (the source of their attraction for Swinburne and Flaubert) nor pure philosophical expositions, the works hover in extreme ambivalence, calling for a reading along lines of transversality that cut across the vertical assemblage of the call to action—that is, Sade's work read as a republican manual for "perversion"—and the lateral, syntagmatic groupings of the narrated scenes—Sade's work read as a call to descriptive consumption. Beyond this important destabilization of genre is the effect of the trilateral arrangement upon the work's semantic order. Through its incessant mixtures, Sade's writing positions meaning at a conflictual apex that combines linguistic value and semantic closure with a nonlinguistic, pornopropulsive desire.

To appreciate the enormity of Sade's project one must first scrutinize his notions of the subject-object relation—upon which any positive operation of communication must be posited—and the problematic nature and siting of the self, which, in his fictional apparatuses, enter into and contaminate the subject and object terms. Sadean bodies function as the pretenses for various conceptual implosions: subject into object, cause into effect, and—in the special instance of blasphemy—signifier into signified.[9] Compared to Rousseau, Sade's conception of the self and its constitution appears strikingly modern. The self is not an essence, not even a thing, but an extended function of matter and impulse that enters life already culturally systematized, coded, and interpreted into a unitized, social space. Sade's capital insight is into the fact that individuality is a complex and evasive socioeconomic construction, effected through numerous institutional agendas, evaluations, judgments, stratifications, and exclusions, and orchestrated as a ratio of needs set against possibilities.

The codes of cultural domination ensure that the subject is inaugurated as an institution and placed under the jurisdiction of the signifiers of control and prohibition. Sade's scriptive campaign is designed to expose this false and repressive unity. Individuality is not an institutionalized hypostasis but a temporary binding of multitudinous impulses that exploit a provisional confluence—known as the self—as a vehicle for their release. Unlike in Rousseau, the Sadean self is not a subject primarily of perception, judgment, and consciousness, but one of drive. Where Rousseau grounds the self in epistemology, Sade locates it in an uncompromising material ontology—among the intractable rhizomes of repressed and gregarious desires. Sade's purpose is not to narrativize a socially scripted self but to cosmologize an uncensored body and show "the sperm behind the voice" (Le Brun 1990, 134). His narrative mechanisms are obscene but simple: the use of loci more so than characters laminated upon temporal plots marking the sites where libidinal, rational, and corporeal extremes meet in collision. It is a highly precarious, acausal economy, one in which powers refuse to remain invested in individual bodies—such stasis would facilitate coherent sovereignties—but move as liquidities through transitory investments.

The Sadean self then finds its textual condition as a striation of the subject-object relation. Furthermore, this relationship is based fundamentally and without compromise upon cruelty as the factor that differentiates the two terms. Unlike pity (crucial to Rousseau's understanding of the subject-object relation as that through which the self acknowledges another self within the Other), cruelty implements a violently disjunctive ontology that condemns the Other to its alterity. As Mercken-Spaas rightly points out, cruelty is "an ongoing effort to avoid identification" (1978, 73). Sade constructs upon these premises of cruelty a world of noncommunicative, self-different beings.[10]

Deleuze, for his part, isolates two macro features in Sade's language. One is a personal element, articulated through a demonstrative functioning of the language, that depersonalizes the body and its drives and links to an ideal notion of pure reason and evil. Supporting this transcendental imperative that pushes language, thinking, and character to their limits is an effective undermining of the relationship of self and character to fiction and event.[11] As mentioned earlier, Sade's characters are unconvincing as verisimilitudes precisely because the *real* order of the impulse operates upon a syntax of the unconscious that connects language through writing to desire. This linkage determines the status of the body and its culturalized selfhood as a trace structure, an ancillary and subsequent effect of irrational forces in dispersal. What remains of classic individualism after Sade's percolation is a sort of incidental consequence of nonlinguistic drives that manifest in phantoms staged inside scenarios based on bodies in quasimechanical assemblages.

Both *Juliette* and *The One Hundred and Twenty Days of Sodom* anticipate sex in the age of mechanical reproduction, and Sade simultaneously parodies and exploits the machine in the choreography of his modular, sexual assemblages.[12] The typical erotic episode describes a site of mechanosexual display that serves as a venue for a veritable *ars combinatoria* of erogeneity:

> At the second sitting while each of our tribades was rubbing a prick on our faces we were frigging another in each hand, and two ecclesiastics were tonguing us: we were in a crouching position, squarely above the nose of the man who was licking our asshole; between our legs, kneeling there, was he who was sucking our cunt; the seventh and eighth stood by, prick in hand, awaiting instructions, and they would encunt or embugger us when, properly aroused by the sucker or the licker, we gave the signal for introduction. (Sade 1968, 490).

Horkheimer and Adorno discern in these orgiastic "gymnastic pyramids" the precision and regularity of a sports team such that the dominant purpose is less pleasure than organization (1972, 88), while Le Brun draws attention to the innate theatricality of these ensembles (1990, 79–81).[13] As sexual configurations, the libertines and their victims invariably move into articular but depersonalized postures, creating a complex of interlocking surfaces that can't be exchanged, only reinstated (which helps explain the obsessive repetitions through the books). "The Sadian anatomy is less a gendered body than a division into front and back" (Stewart 1988, 172), a system of appendages and apertures whose surplus value is pleasure in discharge. The libertines' rhythm is that of assemblage and disassemblage, "their sole reason for becoming organized is to get disorganized again" (Le Brun 1990, 53). The movement from equilibrium through disequilibrium into further equilibrium is, of course, the pattern of Prigogine's "dissipative" structure. Noircueil depicts nature as a similarly libertinal rhythm and in remarkably Prigoginian terms:

> There is nothing real, therefore, about crime; there is no veritable crime, no real way in which to violate a nature which is always on the move. . . . Laws are maintained through an absolutely equal mixture of what we term "crime" and "virtue;" nature is reborn through destruction and sustains herself through crime; in a word, death keeps her alive. A totally virtuous universe could not survive for even a minute; but the wise hand of nature *creates order from disorder, and without disorder, would never accomplish anything:* such is the underlying equilibrium which maintains the stars in orbit, suspending them in vast areas of space, and causing them periodically to move. (Quoted in Le Brun 1990, 129; emphases added)

In his detailed itemizing, Barthes underscores the catalytic nature of these machinic assemblages as provisional, improvisatory, dissipative structures:

> [The Sadean machine] includes a substructure constructed around the basic patient . . . and saturated when all the body sites are occupied by different partners . . . from the basic architecture, defined by rules of catalysis, an open apparatus extends whose sites increase whenever a partner is added to the initial group; the machine will tolerate no one's being solitary, no one's remaining outside . . . the machine in toto is a well-balanced system.(1976, 152–53)

At times, as in Madame Clairwill's experience in Francavilla's palazzo, this rhythm reaches vertiginous proportions.

> Before our mouths, cunts and pricks and asses succeeded one another as swiftly as our desires; elsewhere, the engines we frigged had but to discharge and new ones materialized between our fingers; our clitoris-suckers rotated with the same speed, and our asses were never deserted; in less than three hours, during which we swam in unending delirium, we were ass-fucked one hundred times apiece, and polluted the whole time by the dildo constantly belaboring our cunt (Sade 1968, 975).

Sade's sexual assemblages inhabit an economy whose surplus value is the multiple profits gained from simultaneity. At one point in her exploits Madame de Saint-Ange calculates: "Behold, my love, behold all that I simultaneously do: scandal, seduction, bad example, incest, adultery, sodomy" (Sade 1965, 272). There is an unmistakable confluence of copulation, numerical profit motives, and the industrial assembly line, either signifying, as Barthes suggests, "the sublimated emblem of labor" (1976, 125) or else the perverse parody of emergent industrial capitalism reflected in the obsessive return to a Statistical Code in the notorious Libertine Accounting:

Total Account:	
Massacred before March 1 in the early orgies	10
Since March 1	20
Those returning	16
Total	46

(1966, 672)

(It's hard not to see in this marriage of mathesis and statistics which concludes *The One Hundred and Twenty Days* a parodic Sade at work—a burlesque allusion to those mortality statistics found in contemporary documents like Burke's *Annual Register*.)

Sade's project is to write desire in a highly specific sense. Desire is not to connect with lack or need, nor with any categories of the internal. It is to remain "strictly immanent to a plane which it does not pre-exist, to a plane which must be constructed, where particles will emit themselves, where fluxes will combine" (Deleuze, quoted in Jardine 1985, 210). Unlike Kristevan *semiotike*, Sadean desire requires collective arrangements that reproduce orgasm and bliss; its mandate is to establish syntactic configurations that oppose the sovereign operation of interiority. As Barthes suggests, it is a practice of the sentence, not the word (cf. 1976, 157, 160).[14] To read the works in sequence from the 1782 *Dialogue between a Priest and a Dying Man* through the 1797 *Juliette* is to trace a path away from a concern with condensed individuation to an impersonal, unlimited, and undefined totality. This vector marks Sade's cosmological passage through Nature, and its constant, vehicular form is that of the libertine—Sade's epistemic contribution to the philosophy of singularity.

Libertines are neither types nor formulas yet equally neither subjects nor selves. The libertine is like that "fold of force" Deleuze detects in Foucault's thinking (Deleuze 1995, 92): a plication of turbulence and a transitory node knotting innumerable lines of flight. Deleuze might describe them accurately as intransitive bodies-in-becoming or as desiring machines opening flows and precipitating leaks from the social code. Brian Massumi describes such bodies-in-becoming:

> Becoming is an escape, but it is not for that reason negative or necessarily oppositional. The body-in-becoming does not simply react to a set of constraints. Instead, it develops a new sensitivity to them, one subtle enough to convert them into opportunities—and to translate the body into an autonomous zone effectively enveloping infinite degrees of freedom. The body is abstracted, not in the sense that it is made to coincide with a general idea, but in a way that makes it a singularity, so monstrously hyperdifferentiated that it holds within its virtual geography an entire population of a kind unknown in the actual world. (1992, 102)

The pantheon of these character-forces—Almani, Juliette, Clairwill, Norceuil, Saint Fond, Minski—never reduce to the one of identity but repeat themselves as a multiplicity of drives through the spaces of the fictions. As eroticized body-machines they are always in a state of motion toward motion, their passional telos never registering completion. A prime producer of their excessive affirmations is imagination, which, as "the stimulus of pleasures . . . governs and motivates everything [they] do" (in Le Brun 1990, 184). Belmor's confession to Juliette provides a practical case in point—effectively demonstrating the imagination as the esemplastic power Coleridge similarly proclaims. Belmor's imagination equally mimics, supplements, and challenges Nature in willful creation and recombinations but is also shown to exceed the possibility of natural combinants. As a libertine modality the imagination is both the gift and the perversion of Nature.

In truth, Juliette, I do not know whether reality is worth as much as chimeras, or if paroxysms from what one has not are worth a hundred times as much as those with what one has: behold your buttocks, Juliette, here before my very eyes; I find them beautiful but my imagination, which is always more brilliant and artful than nature, if I may say so, creates even finer ones. And is not the pleasure I derive from this allusion preferable to the peak I shall derive from truth? What you offer me is simply beautiful; what I am about to do with you is nothing more than anyone could do; and yet it seems that what I would do with the bum of my imagination, the gods themselves could not invent. (Quoted in Le Brun 1990, 198–99)

The libertine dynamic is phrasal, incomplete, and adds to a continuum of escaping singularities. Positioned at the syzygy of conscious and unconscious energies, it offers a concept of self as force that cannot assure the tractability of meaning.

The aggregate of thoughts and actions forming these "selves" should not be confined within a model of classical consciousness, nor should the libertine be considered as essentially gendered. One of Sade's lasting achievements is to take men and women out of opposition and to consider them impartially within a libidinal cosmology. There are—and can be—equally successful male and female libertines, a fact supporting, no doubt, Angela Carter's claim that Sade is responsible for putting "pornography in the service of women, or, perhaps, allowed it to be invaded by an ideology not inimical to women" (1978, 37).[15] Neither determine age nor sex but economic, monetary, and thereby ideological predications. Sade demands that successful entry into his counterdiscourse be gained through an expert integration into the dominant orders of the social code. Set apart from the ideological state apparatus—all of Sade's episodes are secretive and often staged within impregnable fortresses like Silling—the libertine is also a fundamental component of it.[16] Sadean econometrics require a successful straight who never manifests abnormality outside his or her clandestine and coded adventures.

Libertines, then, are far from socially dysfunctional perverts. Libertine ecclesiasts include the bishop of Grenoble and Pope Pius VI; Leopold is archduke of Tuscany, Borghese a princess, Ghigi a count, related to the pope and head of Rome's secret police, Saint-Fond a royal minister. Nonaristocratic libertines (Noircueil, Borchamps, and the Moscovite Minski) are all wealthy; and Juliette herself, the "ferocious little 'vulvovagant' dandy" of Le Brun (1990, 206) is the daughter of a wealthy Paris banker. All are powerful, wealthy, publicly legitimate, thoroughly versed in Machiavellian virtu, and mistresses and masters of controlling ideology. As such, the libertine registers as a witty transposition of Rousseau's noble savage into the savage noble.[17] Curiously Deleuze, in his monograph on sadomasochism (1971), fails to connect the libertine to his own concept of a "war machine" involving as its modus operandi "a certain type of space, a conjunction of very specific sorts of men with other technological and affective components [entering] history only indirectly by coming into sorts of different relations with state apparatuses" (1995, 30).

But to pursue the libertine strictly speaking as Sade's key concept in a philosophy of singularity leads to a perhaps surprising articulation. Indeed, Klossowski's integral monster, defined as the singular case that is separated from generic humanity, falls within the scope of the later heterological science of 'pataphysics discussed in chapter 2. Le Brun summarizes the qualities that connect Jarry and Sade in "the blackest and most brilliant vein of modern sensibility [in which] accumulation does not aim at mastery but leads to dizziness; systematization guarantees no equilibrium, but on the contrary, destabilizes; mechanical excess, instead, of returning to the laws of number, opens up onto the infinite possibility of lyrical excess" (1990, 187). (The final words in Le Brun's categories anticipate that ideology of excess detectable in Marinetti's words in freedom and his own pursuit of "lyric excess" noted in chapter 10.)[18] In both Sade's and Jarry's thinking, the general reveals itself as the sum total of particulars. When it's "to each her own clinamen," then the category of perversion of necessity reduces to the particulates of idiosyncrasy, which, when cathected, enter into glandular, muscular assemblage and there transmute into a desiring machine (it is idiosyncrasy, too, that survives the ephemerality of assemblage). Thus to invoke the general is in reality to petition instability. It's a characterizing nongenerality, too, that Deleuze ascribes as basic to the contemporary cinematic image: "a figure characterized not by any way it universally represents anything but by its internal singularities" (1995, 65).

The dynamic of the idiosyncratic is deviation from a norm, and the clinamen, as seen in the contexts of Lucretian particle theory and Jarry's 'pataphysics, formulates a profound connection between freedom and singularity. In Lucretian terms, the libertine is a social clinamen of sensual atoms, and deviation comprises a further passional clinamen. Libertinage deviates from the regulatory ethical norms of generic humanity, first and foremost shattering rationalism's fundamental premise that a rational being solely pursues rational ends. Moreover, in the pragmatics of libertinage,

Sade detaches eroticism from aesthetic matters to reposition it in a strategic zone of critique. By presenting crime and libertinage as the profit or surplus value of the dominant socioeconomic machine—in his own case, a fading aristocracy based on wealth and leisure—Sade provokes an enormous destabilization of his institutional referents.[19]

In the libertine a polymorphism links to totality and is thereby activated against functionalism in general. The confrontation, however, obtains only on the assumption that the repudiation of functionalism can be affirmed exclusively by those who can succeed in what they repudiate. Accordingly, the libertine effects subversion, not revolution. Moreover, he or she is never motivated in his or her criminality by revenge. This may explain Sade's paradoxical relation to his own historicality, for if, as Nietzsche claims, the essence of human history is revenge and reaction (*ressentiment*), then the libertine is free from historic essence, even though all life must be lived in the gestures of history.[20]

It's necessary to bear in mind, however, Sade's precise relation to republicanism. Sade introjects a historically specific revolution into the perpetual volatility of natural and libidinal phenomena. His dream is to libidinalize the Republic whose birth he witnessed, to capitalize upon the institutional breakdown and promote a passional political condition. His praxis is clandestine, his proposed model being the miniaturized institution in the form of a secret society whose cohesion obtains through a curious denial of the law. All Sadean criminality is covert and perpetrated within secret spaces, like the Gothic edifice of Silling, combining as they do the visionary, architectural monumentality of Ledoux's and Boullée's geometrical designs with the subterranean vaults of Piranesi and Desprez, which "speak of a blackness that takes on a new meaning through its contrast with the white light of the law of the day" (Starobinski 1988, 79).[21]

The subordination of insular libertinage to the secret institution marks Sade's unique and radical republicanism; a subordination that further registers his profound antilegality, for the Sodality of the Friends of Crime neither supports nor procreates laws.[22] Understood as an incorporation of separate libertine singularities, the secret society renders law unnecessary and presents itself as a free model for pure heterological pursuits. "Insurrection . . . is not at all a *moral* condition; however it has got to be a republic's permanent condition . . . for the state of a moral man is one of tranquillity and peace, the state of an *immoral* man is one of perpetual unrest" (Sade 1965a, 315).[23] Sade in effect commits the Republic to a vicious circle, condemning it to a permanent insurrection and thereby affirming that there can be no established and operative state apparatus. Anticipating later notions of desire, Sade's republic-in-motion is a drive without a goal beyond its own perpetual, intransitive manifestation. Universal transformation, as Vladislav Todorov recalls, is a basic trope of revolution (1995, 55) and one of the hidden inflections of German Romanticism via Goethe's botanical theories, which grant transformation priority over accomplished forms (see Goethe 1952).[24] Guattari glosses the revolutionary implication of Sade's sex-assemblages in his contention that the only potentially productive moment for revolution is at that point "where desire and machine become indistinguishable" (in Deleuze 1995, 20).

Noted already, libertines are, above all else, obsessed by reasoning and its use as a catalyst to their actions. In this respect the libertine can be seen as a late development of that Greek tradition, descending from Thales, of *physiologia* (reasoning about nature) whose intellectual program is precisely the one James H. Nichols ascribes to Lucretius and Epicurean teaching in general: to bridge the immense and troublesome gap between "the truth about nature and the best life consistent with that truth" (1976, 19). Indeed, instead of opposing Nature, Sade offers himself through his fictive interlocutors as its explicator. However, the libertine exists within this system of logic in order to subvert, and eventually to invert, its productions.

It would be fair to say that Sade successfully presents reason and dialectic as erotic forces in themselves. Put more bluntly, Sade sodomizes reason, exploiting its syllogistic cavities and conceptual protuberances to invent cultural and moral inversions that unsettle fixed relations and which redefine the so-called natural as an ideological construct. Yet a typological distinction between libertine agencies can still be drawn. Saint Fond, for example, invents a religion of evil by logical inversion. In his postulate of a Supreme God of Wickedness, libertine rationality does not decommission theism but maintains it in a negative relation. Other libertines reject this inverted theology, replacing deity with a philosophy of Nature based on unremitting movement.

In *Juliette*, through the mouthpiece of the pope, Sade outlines his famous materialist ecology based upon perpetual motion and annihilation:

Nothing is essentially born, nothing essentially perishes, all is but the action and reaction of matter; all is like the ocean billows which ever rise and fall, like the tides of the sea, ebbing and flowing endlessly, without there being either the loss or the gain of a drop in the volume of the waters; all this is a perpetual flux which ever was and shall always be, and whereof we become, though we know it not, the principle agents by reason of our vices and our virtues. All this is an infinite variation; a thousand thousand different portions of matter which appear under every form are shattered, are reconstituted to appear again under others, again to be undone and rearise. The principle of life is but the result of the four elements in combination; with death, the combination dissolves, each element returning entire into its own sphere, ready to enter new combinations when the laws of the kingdoms summon them forth; it is only the whole that changes form, the parts remain intact, and from these parts joined anew to the whole, new beings are forever being recomposed. . . . I serve Nature's laws in acting in consonance with the aims of perpetual destruction Nature announces, and whose purpose is to enable her to develop new castings, the faculty whereof is suspended in her owing to the continuing presence of what she has cast before. (1968, 772–73)[25]

Sade is not original in this return to macro concerns outside theology. His thinking, as I've suggested, draws heavily on the atheistic atomism of Epicurus and Lucretius. The theory furthermore emerges within a marked trend of the time toward atheistic theories of Nature, evident in the work of Helvétius and d'Holbach and the English deist John Toland.[26] Sade marks a significant departure from the optimism of the philosophes, however, for the replacement of a fixed, transcendental referent (the immobile God) by a concept of Nature, figured as perpetual motion, leads to ontic collapse and the dispersal of all referential certainties. The perpetual flux of Nature sentences the self to constant, unmotivated change under the presidential telos of a blind indifference.

At the instant we call *death,* everything seems to dissolve; we are led to think so by the excessive change that appears to have been brought about in this portion of matter which no longer seems to animate. But this death is only imaginary, it exists figuratively but in no other way. Matter deprived of the other portion of matter which communicated movement to it, is not destroyed for that; it merely abandons its form, it decays — and in decaying proves that it is not inert; it enriches the soil, fertilizes it, and serves in the regeneration of the other kingdoms as well as its own. (Sade 1968, 769–70)[27]

Sade's singularity lies less in a philosophization of Nature than in the specific redirection of his theory of Nature toward a liquidation of all moral categories and the sublimation of the consequent detritus into transcendental negativity. At a later point in the pope's speech, and in an earlier outburst by the chemist Almani, the self's impotence against the forces of nature gains compelling expression:

Regret nothing but that we are unable to do enough, lament nothing but the weakness of the faculties we have received for our share and whose ridiculous limitations so cramp our penchants. And far from thanking this illogical Nature for the slender freedom she allows us for accomplishing the desires she inspires in us, let us curse her from the bottom of our heart for so restricting the career which fulfills her aim; let us outrage her, let us abominate her for having left us so few wicked things to do, and then giving us such violent urges to commit crimes without measure or pause. (1968, 781–82)[28]

Almani projects the same impotent rage as does the speaker in Blake's "Infant Sorrow" expanded beyond the familial configuration. (Being virtually born into cruel feelings, Almani also anticipates Freud's theory of sexuality which ascribes libido to the child from birth.)

My mother groan'd! my father wept.
Into the dangerous world I leapt:
Helpless, naked, piping loud:
Like a fiend hid in a cloud.

Struggling in my father's hands,
Striving against my swadling bands,
Bound and weary I thought best
To sulk upon my mother's breast.
(Blake 1966, 217)

Sade, however, counters Blakean "sulkiness" with a paradoxical mimesis. In the desire to integrate cruelty into a cosmological system and to grant to passions a transcendental significance, both the pope and Almani, as most other of Sade's libertines, align themselves with nature as a reluctant, competing component. In libertinal apostrophes there is a kinship with the apophatic discourse of negative theology that takes the form of a negative response to the subject of God.[29] Paradoxically, libertine identification requires a basal revolt against the very bonding. In a movement similar to Hegel's *aufhebung,* the alienated, perverted self is rehabilitated in a nature that preserves the alienation. The desire is to *be* the system; the doom is to remain a subordinate part of it. In this libertine synecdoche Sade manages to implode the conceptual categories of self and other, reformulating the violent antagonism between terms as an internal dynamic of the singular, and in contrast to Levinas, he locates alterity not in a face but a force. (Worth nothing also is the similarity of this processual notion of the libertine as *dynamis* to Olson's sense of "man as object in a field of force declaring self as force because is force . . . as only force in field of force containing multiple other expressions" (1966, 111–12, 113). The libertine double agenda is clear: a desperate mimetic project by which to copy Nature's perpetual flux, and at the same time to redirect insular anger back at Nature for the latter's inflexible foreclosure of the human self. This is an agenda for incommensurate resemblance.

I detect two writings in the Sadean corpus, two modes of production governed by two different laws. One is based on the libertine pattern that generates a realist, representational practice that Sade frequently grounds in the historic turmoils of his times:

> Let us concur that this kind of fiction, whatever one may think of it, is assuredly not without merit: 'twas the inevitable result of the revolutionary shocks which all of Europe has suffered. For anyone familiar with the full range of misfortunes wherewith evildoers can beset mankind, the novel became as difficult to write as monotonous to read. There was not a man alive who had not experienced in the short span of four or five years more misfortunes than the most celebrated novelist could portray in a century. Thus, to compose works of interest, one had to call upon the aid of hell itself, and to find in the world of make-believe things wherewith one was fully familiar merely by delving into man's daily life in this age of iron. (1966, 109)

Sade refers here to the fashionable gothic fiction of Matthew "Monk" Lewis and Anne Radcliffe, drawing attention to the experiential intensity of their shared epoch. The imaginative force and violence of narrative fiction comes as an unavoidable consequence of an age of iron. There is a tangible relation to the sensations and data of everyday life, a condition of survival that Sade believes to be more novelistic than the novel itself. But he does not align writing, style, and form to revolution. Indeed, it is the nature of libertine writing to maintain complicit obedience to the status quo. Of the forty-five statutes defining Clairwill's Sodality of the Friends of Crime, the forty-third lists the following prohibition: "Under no circumstance does the Sodality intrude or interfere in government affairs, nor may any Member. Political speeches are expressly forbidden. The Sodality respects the regime in power; and if its attitude towards the law is disdainful, that is because it holds as a principle that man is incapable of making laws which obstruct or contradict those of Nature; but the disorders of its Members, transpiring privately, ought never to scandalize either the governed or their governors" (1968, 425).

This rule of the Sodality is likewise Sade's prescription for the written. Just as the libertine functions successfully within the ideological state apparatus (great wealth, as we have seen, is a prerequisite), so the imaginative transgressions of fiction must be represented through orthodox grammar and syntax. Sade purposefully does *not* invent a *zaum* language of blasphemy, nor implement neologistic vocabularies of pain and bliss, but rather insists upon a more complex causality between the ruling systems of domination and order (church, government, institutes of learning) and the clandestine criminality such systems produce. Despite the constant inversion of moral categories, the form of his writing is never oppositional nor its form particularly inventive. The representational paradigm of the ancien régime, embodied in its classical sentences, need not be toppled because of the inevitable presence of a clandestine "poetics" within and despite it. Sade's is not a semiotic of drive à la Kristeva, effected upon the sensuous materiality of the sign, but a controlled, classical unfolding of the monstrous as a content. This eschewal of formal innovation is a masterly fraud and one worthy of his libertine heroes, for by acquiescing to the established linguistic order, a normative contract with the reader is preserved then invested into a criminal incrimination. Sade, of course, is profoundly aware of the institutional nature of the reader function and of the ideological basis to style. The criminal implication is that of the vehicular neutrality of the language that demonstrates the same amoral, indifferent, and ultimately evil constitution as Nature itself. Through the innocuous transparency of classical language, the reader functions to reproduce — by consumption — Sade's primary, imaginary narrative and arguments.

Can language and style be so innocent in the face of such monstrosities? Sade's writerly strategy (and libertinal ruse) is to render the reader complicit in their production and thereby compromise all presiding morality by its destruction in the text. Barthes elucidates the historically apposite sentential base of this narrative style. The sentence "has [the] function of founding crime: the syntax, refined by centuries of culture, becomes an elegant (in the sense we use the word in mathematics, a solution is elegant) art; it collects crime with exactitude and address" (Barthes 1976, 157). The challenge in reading Sade, however, is to resist the "elegant" art; refuse the stable referential destinations of his sentences, and abrogate the Sade of novelistic simulacra and reassuring normative syntax in favor of his other writing, which develops from a connected but discreet model: the atomic motion and dissipative constitution he sees as Nature.

The theory of perpetual motion allows Sade to implode the sociohistoric system of writing, to fold that system back on itself and perpetuate its own production. Distinct from the libertine model of the clandestine is this natural model of the kinetic. Sade understood profoundly that the institution of value can be effected only at the expense of a permanent arrest of the linguistic sign. Long before Barthes's own brilliant elucidation, Sade provides the theoretical matrix that supports a processual system of intransitive writing.[30] Perversely recovered to mimesis, this other writing imitates, within a futile graphic context, the laws of Nature and its destructions.[31] In its sign economy there is no place for values and permanent meaning, only an indeterminate space for flows, intensities, and metamorphoses. At one extreme this liquidating writing would enact a sacrificial abolition of the fixed in a radically contentless system of perpetually overturning signs. At the other extreme it would be a system of kinesis whose constant flux and semantic replacements would open up the ideality and essence of the humanist sign to the spatiotemporal pluralities of writing.

For the most part, Sade holds latent this alterior writing—implicit in the nature of Nature but hinted at incessantly in the libertine set pieces of rhetorical persuasion. Sade's driving force is an ink-sperm equation that demands the sublimely futile effort to write what cannot be written. At one point in *Juliette,* occurs a comment on the crisis in contemporary (i.e., precinematic) representation: "Ah, if only an engraver could record for posterity this divine and voluptuous scene! But lust, which all too quickly crowns our actors, might not have allowed the artist time to portray them. It is not easy for art, which is motionless, to depict an activity *the essence of which is movement*" (quoted in Deleuze 1971, 61; emphasis added). One of Sade's great achievements is to preserve the linguistic stability of representation, but through the pervasive implication of this second order of writing to destroy all decisive links to cause and intention. He writes in a sense to tell us about language and the human relation to its categorical structures, reactionary formations, and conditioning.

Sade's comments on his 1810 manuscript *L'Union des arts ou les ruses de l'amour* suggest that he had an inkling that such a kinetically based writing was possible:

> What is particular about the play is that *it has no moments of rest and the action is continuous,* because after each episode the company is supposed to go back into the dressing-rooms to change costumes and rehearse the next episode; but these dressing-rooms are actually the stage . . . *the action thus* follows continuously, seeming to be interrupted for the different episodes, but actually continuing with subtlety, and starting again in a more exposed fashion in the dressing-rooms, so one can say it's *constantly in progress, without ever slowing down.* (Quoted in Le Brun 1990, 86; emphases added)

Le Brun cites this passage to draw attention to a novelty she detects in Sade's dramatic presentation via multiple viewpoints ("The multiplicity of points of view leads to a multiplication of the planes on which the action will unfold" [1990, 86]). What I wish to stress is what Le Brun ignores: the premonitory tremors in this passage of Sade's "other" writing. Continuous action, constant progress, incessance? Is this not the perpetuum mobile of Sadean Nature transposed to the specifics of dramaturgy's mise-en-scène?

Such a model of Sade is utterly at variance with the ones proposed by Le Brun, Blanchot, Bataille, Klossowski, and Barthes. Moreover, it foregrounds what Sade's procrustean, untransgressive narrative model itself suppresses: a virtual, passional stochastics. Klossowski's pious claims to graphic criminality aside, Sade's true literary crime is to betray writing to the space of the simulacra of speaking pictures, committing the reader to the role of a nonproductive, voyeuristic client. There are intimations of this graphic incessance in a comment of Blanchot's on Sade's rage to write: "Something more violent becomes clear in this rage to write; a violence which all the excesses of a proud or ferocious imagination can neither exhaust nor appease, although the imagination is always inferior to the transport of a language *which does not tolerate a halt, any more than it conceives of limitation*" (quoted in Le Brun 1990, 178; emphasis added). Le Brun herself hints at this inherent kinetics in Sade's writing, commenting on *The One Hundred and Twenty Days* as a text driven by the force of an internal motion and structured "like a petrified tornado. . . . A vertiginous sculpture depicting vertigo itself" (1990, 116).[32]

If Sade articulates not only a human monstrosity onto the natural state of perpetual motion but also the "natural" activity of the linguistic sign itself, then what is the fate of language under the full force of Sade? For one thing, meaning can no longer be envisioned through a Saussurean schema of differential opposition. The appropriate algorithm isn't "A is not B" but rather "becoming A becoming B," as in Prigogine's dissipative structures "a cat is not a dog" but rather "a cat becomes a dog" through indifferent recombinant motions. At one point in *Juliette,* the pope explains that "you can vary the forms, but you cannot annihilate them; you cannot absorb the elements of matter: and how could you destroy them, since they are eternal? You change their forms, and vary them; but this dissolution helps nature, since she reconstructs things from these destroyed parts" (quoted in Le Brun 1990, 192). This papal theory of recombinant, indestructible matter is a Lucretian inflection embodying an implicit poetics in which poems are to be understood as nonproductive organizations, returning the space of syntax to the time of writing. In addition, Sade's implicit semiology urges a profound rethinking of the pornographic outside of its normative, narrative panopticality and representations. Pornographic elements are justified in a carnal kinetics of writing, and the semantics of blasphemy can be reasserted in a festive expenditure and semiotic discharge. Hints of such a writing can be found in Pierre Guyotat's *Eden, Eden, Eden,* a work that exudes convulsive coagulations of body parts and fluids in a system of incessant phrasal becoming. Barthes alerts us to the fact that Guyotat's language does not serve sex in a representational bond—as a child, Guyotat masturbated constantly while writing (Guyotat 1981)—but unites with it in a sensuous-material venom (in Guyotat 1995, [ix]). I extract at random the following:

> boy sleeping on side ; tarantula crawling from sticky pubic hair, climbing up onto whore's swollen belly, distended abdomen dividing blood over chest ; body of whore shuddering, hands following steps of tarantula around right nipple : "..suck lower man.."; penis, tucked back into hollow of groin, hardening : tarantula brushing against tip of tongue poking between lips ; jissom slopping out of Wazzag's arse, pushed back, driven out along anal passage by date picker's member ; Wazzag stifling fit of laughter ; Khamssieh waking : tarantula, alarmed by twitching of muscles, crawling into nostril ; Khamssieh sniffing scent, stifling sneeze, pulling legs together, suppressing shivers of body smeared with cold sweat moistening dried blood, beads of sweat glistening in fresh blood over loins ; nostril swollen with jissom crushing spider ; Wazzag exploding into laughter ; tarantula stinging nostril : venom, flowing with

blood, veiling eyes of whore, softening eyelid ; Khamssieh's hand, weak, crushing tarantula in nostril : venom hardening forehead ; fingernails scraping cold blood around nipples ; pulling dead tarantula, pinching sticky legs, out of nostril, pushing crushed spider between buttocks ; exhausted elbows dropping onto heaps of floor-cloths : penis contracting into shrivelled scrotum ; odour of sodomy wafting through room ; rubbing of jeans, farts : regular in dawn silence. (1995, 29)

Ending this passage where I do lends a false sense of closure to the work. Indeed, to abstract from this book is to do it a great disservice, for its sustaining power lies in the incessant turmoil of part objects in constant movement, caught in phrasal brevities that simultaneously condense the representations and severely disorientate the reader's normal pornographic expectations. (The microdevice of spacing between punctuation marks serves to overcode the fragility and impermanence of these phrasal articulations.) The novel has its hero: Wazzag, an Algerian boy prostitute, but characters never emerge beyond a vague impression of sliding parts. Hardly libertinal but decidedly Lucretian, they populate a world of atomic volatility and writhing assemblage. Stephen Barber describes *Eden, Eden, Eden* as "a delirious and exhausting book to experience [propelling] its reader into itself with fury and adrenalized elation" (in Guyotat 1995, [vi]). Guyotat enters and occupies the phrase as a material unit of dynamic force, crippling pictorial mimesis under the weight of that metonymic, syntagmatic incessance and overturning promised by the "other" Sade.[33]

Sade's theory of writing as perpetual motion finds recent substantiation in the linguistic realm via Hjelmslev's theory of language as a system of continual flows of content and expression. Hjelmslev's theories have long suffered under the shadow of Saussure and Chomsky, especially the hegemonic status of the signifier in its structuralist manifestations—although Deleuze sees in Hjelmslev "a Spinozist theory of language" (1995, 21), an inversion of Saussure that returns primacy to utterance now envisioned as a content-expression in a kinetic and temporal *durée*.[34] Sade shows how in the condition of perpetual volatility Hjelmslev's plane of content-expression becomes a wave in turbulence. No thing or subject has being—only becoming. In his demonized cosmology crime and deviation are expressions of human nature following Nature. The libertine's actions are natural when Nature is understood as stochastic forces in perpetual movement. Morality must take its place inside—and be modified by—this ferocious ecology in which absolute death is impossible. Likewise, repentance is impossible in Sade's world, since the past can have no existence in cosmic, perpetual volatility. In the next chapter I examine the specific configurations of time and space as continuum that support a contemporary writing based similarly on a becoming-meaning.

Agreement cannot be satisfied by fragments.

—Friedrich Schiller

9. Temporality and the New Sentence

Phrase Propulsion in the Writing
of Karen Mac Cormack

Joyce ends *Ulysses* with a soliloquy, a woman's soliloquy unwinding in a forty-three-and-a-half-page rush of nonpunctuated phrases. Molly Bloom's famous monologue is an incessant becoming and passing of thought through language. A return to such phrasal propulsion has been a seminal factor in installing syntactic disjunction as a radical aspect of recent North American poetry, and Karen Mac Cormack's *Quirks & Quillets* is one of the vital poems to have emerged from this formative return. Most significantly, Mac Cormack shows how poems can be comprehended *kinetically,* exploiting the most radical implications of "the time of the sign" to demonstrate that words are not simply Saussure's diacritical oppositions in a syntagmatic chain, but that the chain itself is a verbal seriality of momentum—a *continuum,* rather than a *contiguum,* of textual time.

> Je suis comme une cascade dont chaque goutte aurait conscience de sa chute
> dans l'espace.
>
> —H. F. Amiel

> The only proper way to break an egg is from the inside.
>
> —Parva Gallina Rubra

Quirks & Quillets employs the deceptively simple format of forty single-sentence poems, set in large type and devoid of punctuation beyond a final period, with each poem occupying a single page. There are no deliberately calculated line breaks, and the poems are presented in the original edition with flush left and right margins. In its heavy kinetic stress and extreme disjunctions, the work seems propelled out of certain theoretical hesitations within the new sentence.[1] Ron Silliman's provocative theory for a prose poetry based on an innovative refusal to integrate its sentences either ignores or rejects the continuum—that condition obtained in writing when the velocity of signs through duration gains emphasis, and where meaning's certainty is risked by being subjected to the instability of spatiotemporal forces. This is not the occasion to enter into a detailed critique of Silliman's theory, which, as a platform for a new signifying activity within writing, remains productive. There are several aspects of his essay that need address, however.

Silliman (1987, 91) lists eight features that define the new sentence:

1. The paragraph organizes the sentence.
2. The paragraph is a unity of quantity, not logic or argument.
3. Sentence length is a unit of measure.
4. Sentence structure is altered for effects of torque, or increased polysemy/ambiguity.
5. Syllogistic movement is (a) limited and (b) controlled.
6. Primary syllogistic movement is between the preceding and following sentences.
7. Secondary syllogistic movement is toward the paragraph as a whole, or the total work.
8. By limiting syllogistic movement, the reader's attention is held close to the level of language, most often at the sentence level or below.

There are several points worth remarking. First, none of these qualities is exclusive to the new sentence. There are both historical precedents (e.g., Gertrude Stein) and near-contemporary writing (such as Stanley Berne and Arlene Zekowski's "neo-narrative") that satisfy one or several of these features. It seems, therefore, that the true novelty of the new sentence lies in the singularity of the amalgam of all eight features. Second, Silliman's theory provides little or no consideration of the tangible physics of language, nor the kinetics of linguistic signs. (This latter aspect might possibly be subsumed within the fourth quality Silliman describes, namely, the tactical alteration of the structure of a sentence; however, there is no clear suggestion that Silliman does so.) Third, Barthes's important contention that the sentence is in theory infinitely catalyzable seriously challenges the stability of these eight qualities. A sentence, Barthes argues, "is never saturable . . . it is catalyzable . . . by successive fillings according to a theoretically infinite process: the center is infinitely displaceable" (1985, 103). And again: "There is no obligation to end a sentence, it is infinitely 'catalyzable,' one can always add a little something to it" (Barthes 1985, 250). Barthes's argument casts serious doubt on Silliman's claim that "a clause is already partially a kind of sentence" (Silliman 1987, 86), facilitating the counterclaim that in theory a sentence can comprise an infinite linkage of phrases.[2] Fourth, syllogistic structure (figuring prominently in Silliman's discussion) requires a juxtaposition of discrete units.

Silliman offers for his example of the new sentence a single-paragraph poem by Carla Harryman, "For She."

> The back of the hand resting on the pillow was not wasted. We couldn't hear each other speak. The puddle in the bathroom, the sassy one. There were many years between us. I stared the stranger into facing up to Maxine, who had come out of the forest wet from bad nights. I came from an odd bed, a vermilion riot attracted to loud dogs. Nonetheless I could pay my rent and provide for him. On this occasion she apologized. An arrangement that did not provoke inspection. Outside on the stagnant water was a motto. He was more than I perhaps though younger. I sweat at amphibians, managed to get home. The sunlight from the window played up his golden curls and a fist screwed over one eye. Right to left and left to right until the sides of her body were circuits. While dazed and hidden in the room, he sang to himself, severe songs, from a history he knew nothing of. Or should I say malicious? Some rustic gravure, soppy but delicate at pause. I wavered, held her up. I tremble, jack him up. Matted wallowings, I couldn't organize the memory. Where does he find his friends? Maxine said to me "but it was just you again." In spite of the cars and the smoke and the many languages, the radio and the appliances, the flat broad buzz of the tracks, the anxiety with which the eyes move to meet the phone and all the arbitrary colors. I am just the same. Unplug the glass, face the docks. I might have been in a more simple schoolyard. (Harryman 1980, 57–58)

As a practice of the new sentence, Harryman's poem purposefully minimizes, or removes, the syllogistic integration of its sentences, favoring nonlogical, aesthetic, or "secondary syllogistic" connections. The infinite decentering of the single sentence of which Barthes speaks is rejected. Indeed, in requiring a closed multiplicity—and thereby juxtaposition—the new sentence surprisingly accords with Ruskin's caveat to "always stand by form against force." It is the *force* of language in its passage, the dynamics of the material sign through duration (understood as a *physis*) that eludes Silliman's scrutiny, anchoring new sentence productions such as Harryman's in structures and schema, *not* in changing ephemera sufficient to provoke in the reader the experience of a loss in meaning.[3] (It's thus telling when Silliman refers to Harryman's poem as "a contextual object"[1987, 92]).

I'm glad you came to punctuate my discourse.

—Coleridge

In a sentence a word can be felt as belonging first with one word and then with another.

—Wittgenstein

The following is typical of Mac Cormack's sentence poems:

Sawdust a partial stop to events childhood
sideways men of straw untwisted central
downmost isotherm undertow basement of
either attendance silt omission conjunction
of tangent facial grade antidote recursion
formula vendetta suspense applicable
street frequency over.

(Mac Cormack 1991, 43)

The poem presents a temporal without a logical sequence and a passage of semantic complexities that resist cognitive retention. As in all the poems in *Quirks & Quillets,* it's the passage *through* signs that is paramount. Indeed, a wholesale pluralization of the semantic order obtains, with an extremely localized distribution of meanings on levels prior to grammatical synthesis and paragraphic integration. The lack of grammatical constraint and the absence of integrating criteria (what links "sawdust" to "childhood" in the first line?) return meaning to the order of affect—as a reception/impact phenomenon like the clinamen—subordinating sign activity to dynamics and pulsation. Because the sign is committed to a phrasal propulsion—effecting turnings, deviations, rather than splittings—readerly attention is not called to any structural features; it is the passage of signs through time that dominates reading.[4]

One effect of the absence of punctuation is to undermine the equilibrium of syntactic units.[5] In places the propulsion creates a serial impact;

a torque of disconnected words ("tangent facial grade antidote") whose effect is complicated by an inherent provocation to develop single words into larger syntactic units via linkage (e.g., "facial" to "grade" to create an adjectival phrase). Progression in *Quirks & Quillets* is not additive but multiplicative; the latter is assured by nodes of ambiguity that dilate clear point into volume. The reader experiences in *Quirks & Quillets* what Barthes experienced when reading Tacitus: "the density of an acceleration" (1982, 162) in which the relation to meaning and reference is suspended and "thetic" naïveté removed so as to foreground the performity of signs (cf. Derrida 1992, 1–75). It's important to keep in mind that this is an articulated text, whose internal uncertainties come about through an active transgression of prescriptive grammar and punctuation. In the absence of these two stabilizing agents an unpredictable relationship emerges of unit (word) to totality (sentence). A complex overlapping of a meaning-in-being and a meaning-in-becoming occurs by way of a different overlapping of digital (discontinuous) and analog (continuous) communication.[6] ("Becoming," of course, is precisely what happens in the atom's clinamen, with its interaction between virtual and actual.) Through a complex indeterminacy in the relation of digital and analog, *Quirks & Quillets* attains a material movement and semantic complexity radically different from both syllabic, metric forms and the paratactic adjacencies of the new sentence.

On an ideological level—and in this respect like the new sentence—*Quirks & Quillets* actively confronts that power as transparent conduit historically enjoyed by prose. Kittay and Godzich offer a rewarding analysis of this prosaic world that establishes itself as matter and ground: "Prose is meant to have no place; prose does not happen. Prose is what assigns place" (1987, 197). More specifically, Mac Cormack confronts the lyric tradition of the "voiced" poem, which downplays the materiality of language to the adequate performativity of words in carrying ideal parcels of meaning without problem from one self-identical consciousness to another. This model of semantic transit links sound to vocality as an essential point outside the poem, at the same time repressing the necessary connection of sound to both morphemic pattern and phonetic occasion. This repudiation of voice, however, does not imply a rejection of linguistic sonority. Indeed, a profound compromise arises between its writer and her language, such that the latter speaks by virtue of the former's silence. Built on the fact that in speaking there are pragmatic linguistic occurrences but no sentences, Mac Cormack explores the temporality of linguistic movement and the attendant physical expenditures against which normative grammar always militates.

The book's radical gesture is to separate the event of language from its rules, restoring a material dimension to reading at a level of sensation and sensory impression upon which syntactic units are *experienced* more than understood.[7] Merleau-Ponty insists that "to understand a phrase is nothing else than to fully welcome it in its sonorous being" (1968, 155). Mac Cormack adds to this another welcoming: of the dynamics and palpable speed of phrases; their pulsation and evanescence through temporal passage. Whereas propositions are bound to both cognitive and rational orders, the phrase is eventistic, and "[c]onsidered as occurrence [the phrase] escapes the logical paradoxes that self-referential propositions give rise to" (Lyotard 1988a, 65). The absence of clearly recognizable syntactic units allows a new assertion of the temporal as a vector of sensuous events. The texts of *Quirks & Quillets* realize what Henri Meschonic terms "a meaning of time more than a meaning of words" (1988, 90). In sharp contrast to Heidegger's spatial model of the poem as a dwelling, Mac Cormack puts a rhetorical focus on motion, which, if as Hobbes argues, is nothing but change of place, forces reading to become the experience of passing through changes of semantic space. The words neither arrest attention nor inhabit time long enough to insist on comprehension, but rather fill out a space whose positionality or situation is measured as a temporal shift. Kineticized this way, meaning registers plurally as evaporative effects. By returning form to force in this manner and by positioning the bias of reading in favor of the experience of an irreversible dynamic, Mac Cormack commits writing to a general economic expenditure.

Quirks & Quillets neither defies nor provokes the rational, but resituates it in a *different* relation to writing practice: the precipitation of excess in a duration marked as impermanent and festive. Bataille argues that "by definition, excess occurs exterior to reason" and further reminds us that obscenity "is our name for the uneasiness which upsets the physical state associated with self-possession, with the possession of a recognized and stable individuality" (1962, 17). It is this precise sense of obscenity, with its extreme ontological implications, that *Quirks & Quillets* manages to enact.

> Men believe that their reason governs words. But it is also true that words,
> like the arrows from a Tartar bow, are shot back, and react on the mind.
> —Francis Bacon

The phrase—understood as an ephemeral production along the force of a continuum—is Mac Cormack's way of situating writing and reading in a base of temporality rather than semantics. Phrases evoke their own situations and call into play their own instances. Accordingly, a close nego-tiation of highly unstable instances of meaning is demanded, and in this one respect, the poetic effect is similar to the blocked integrations of the new sentence. However, a significant difference arises when considering the spatiotemporal notion of *linkage*. In the case of the phrase, linkage is always *through* the temporal and *not above it*. Utilizing the physics and tempo of metonymy, Mac Cormack's poem requires a reading that inhabits the dura-tion of the phrase without enjoying the residual profit of compound inte-gration. In Levinasian terms, the word becomes the moment that opens onto a nonappropriated, nonrecoverable otherness whose ethical stake is to risk the loss of meaning. The phrase links onto other phrases to produce a writing that distributes its linguistic parts along a space-time continuum in which transformations replace identities. This gives the phrase—in its condition of becoming-meaning—a triple status as an event, a trace struc-ture, and a displacement. The incessant movement and extradition of the phrase in *Quirks & Quillets* is thus similar to the status of Being as Lyotard describes it: "The gap separating one phrase from another is the 'condition' of both presentation and occurrences, but such a 'condition' remains un-graspable in itself by a new phrase, which in its turn presupposes the first phrase. This is something like the condition of Being, as it is always escaping determination and arriving both too soon and too late" (1988b, 32).

But *Quirks & Quillets* is writing and because words are involved consti-tutively, the reader never experiences pure or nonmediated data. A contes-tation is always present between a reference and a signification that pre-cludes the experience of this temporally charged-up "reading" from being just sensation. What the work demands for a minimum encounter is a double reading: both as an experience of delirium (the rapid passage of signs through time experienced syntagmatically) and as a construction from or recuperation of underdetermined significations. The model reader pre-sumed in this latter case is similar to that implicit in Kant's *Critique of Judge-ment*. The earlier *Critique of Pure Reason* elaborates a synthesizing power that Kant calls "transcendental apperception;" a power logically—if not empirically—necessary for successfully synthesizing heterogeneity within data. Kant allocates this power to unify and synthesize into Idea to the "I." In the *Critique of Judgement*, however, power shifts to the imagination. No longer staked within the synthesis, and not prescribed to reproduce—thereby rendering phenomena understandable—the imagination is free to engage in a productive play among the innumerable possible forms in which the data can be synthesized. Kantian imagination is a faculty of affection engaged among radically undetermined data. As offering a phenomenological encounter, a reader can engage each word of *Quirks & Quillets* as a "now-point" in a continuum. Borrowing terms from Husserl, we can speak of reading the work as an engagement with running-off phenomena (*ablaufs-phanomene*) experienced as modes of temporal orientation, complicated projectively by reference to protention and semantic labor that determines, or identifies, a certain phrase in time.

But doesn't the brevity of each poem argue against this insistence on a phrasal continuum? The book gathers together discrete poems that assume both iconic form and dimension—situated as units somewhere between a filmic frame and an ideogram. A threefold effect results from the shortness of the pieces. First, a repetitive punctuation is produced that emphasizes flows in their very arrestment. Second, the poems' brevity effectively parodies lyric formats. Third, the page-as-unit form calls attention to the parametric status of the sentence. It's precisely because the "beginnings" and "endings" of the poems appear arbitrary and unmotivated that the overall effect is one of switching on and off the phrasal continuum; an effect, that is, of interruption, not closure—and one, it might be added, closer to media circuitry than to the sign economy of the sentence.

Mac Cormack's poetic of phrase propulsion can be compared most profitably to the semiology, already found implicit in Sade (see the previous chapter) that commits writing to intransitivity, expenditure, and a physics of perpetual motion. The eighteenth-century deist John Toland anticipates this Sadean semiology:

> No Parts of Matter are ty'd to any one Figure or Form, losing and changing their Figures and Forms continually, that is, being in perpetual Motion, clipt, or worn, or ground to pieces, or disolv'd by other Parts, acquiring their Figures, and these theirs, and so on incessantly; Earth, Air, Fire, and Water, Iron, Wood, and Marble, Plants and Animals, being rarefy'd or condens'd, or liquify'd or congeal'd or dissolv'd or coagulated, or any other way resolv'd into one another. (Toland 1964, 189)

Mac Cormack similarly mobilizes words and phrases as material atomic parts in a continually overturning and semantically self-liquidating writing. Caroline Bergvall misses the point when referring to *Quirks & Quillets* as a "closed circuit of . . . textuality [in which] difference becomes the leitmotiv" of the writing. Rather than a radical metonymic organization "through chains of associations and contiguity" that take the reader for "a 'crabwalk' along an oblique chain of associations" (1993, 98–99), *Quirks & Quillets* commits meaning to Sadean semiological expenditure. Whereas its method can be described correctly as metonymic, the dynamic and pulsation to which that method is subjected is decidedly nonmetonymical. Instead of a leitmotif of difference, the work provides a force of radical indifference (not unlike the impact of Mac Low's systematic-chance generated texts discussed in chapter 11), an indifference encountered as the preferential power of becoming over meaning. Moreover, being experienced not as a process of separation but as one of segmentive disappearance—the disappearance of difference and the erasure of grammatical frontiers—*Quirks & Quillets* stages a delirious textuality. In Mac Cormack's inventive experiences, both within language and along it, we witness the analogous consequence to poetic discourse that Deleuze sees in Nietzsche's effect on philosophical discourse: the "toppling into a crystalline system, substituting the power of becoming for the model of truth" (Deleuze 1995, 67).

Mac Cormack has so far resisted theorizing her work as either feminist or postcolonial, although its strategic availability to both is obvious, being unquestionably engaged in that challenge to authenticity and essence proposed as characteristic of postcolonial writing by both Dennis Lee (1973) and Robert Kroetsch (1983, see esp. 11–21, 33–45, 69–80), and consistently questioning the hegemony of standard, grammatically normative English. Although the vocabulary of dominant, standard English provides its basic language, *Quirks & Quillets* successfully assaults the prelexical rules of colonial verbal ordering. The book is also consistent with Bickerton's postcolonial metatheory "which takes linguistic variation as the substance rather than the periphery of language study" (1973, 643). Most important, *Quirks & Quillets* articulates the political ramifications of linguistic eccentricity; its transgressions of grammatical norm and conventional rhetorical protocol cast doubt on the total system of cultural assumptions and philosophical categories on which colonial ideology and late capitalism depend: binary structuration, a transmission theory of communication, narrative and representational mimesis. It proves useful to apply Gregory Shaw's comments on the Caribbean writer Wilson Harris's use of linguistic disruption in his novel *Ascent to Omai* to Mac Cormack's phrasal productions. Shaw describes the condition of the word in Harris as " 'liberated,' hollowed out, emptied, through a dialectical process of paired contradictions. . . . Images crumble, shift, dissolve and coalesce in strange combinations or, to use Harris's own term, 'paradoxical juxtapositions,' reflecting a universe in the process of becoming. . . . Harris's works constitute a program for the dismantling of myth, a dismantling of history and society, of the object and even the word."[8] Similarly, Mac Cormack's preference for metonymic over metaphoric structuration finds parallels in postcolonial linguistic strategies. A metaphoric interpretation involves a universalist reading that fails to take into account the cultural specificities of texts that a metonymic reading can illuminate (cf. Bhabha 1984). But beyond these transparent affinities, Mac Cormack's writing adopts a more radical, linguistic stance and her categorical dissociation of the linguistic sign from corporeal origin (though not corporeal destination) would appear to be heterological to postcolonial praxis. The complex relationship of postcolonial usage to standard English is both agonistic and insinuational, disrupting "the privileged centrality of 'English' by using language to signify difference while employing a sameness which allows it to be understood" (Ashcroft, Griffiths, and Tiffin 1989, 51). But what this sentence masks is the fact that the "sameness" employed is in actuality a perpetuation of two fundamental colonial paradigms: narrative and representation.

Likewise, Mac Cormack's problematic positioning in regard to contemporary Canadian feminist practice needs to be mentioned. An affinity to Cixous's insurgent, counterrational *écriture feminine,* fueled by the "prodigious economy" of female drives and destined to unwrite phallocentric history, can certainly be argued (cf. Cixous 1987, 579.) Similarly, a moot but tenable argument can be made that the breakdown of grammatical pattern and consequential liberation of writing into an undifferentiated, genotextual flow suggests a menstrual model as the base of Mac Cormack's writing.[9] There are certainly stylistic similarities between *Quirks & Quillets* and some of the work of Canadian poet Daphne Marlatt, but these affinities are superficial. In her feminist writing, Marlatt maintains the body as a highly gendered and essential, prelinguistic site of its own manifestation in both linguistic cathexis and analogy. In a text from the mid-1980s Marlatt compares language to the maternal body in a manner curiously evocative of Heidegger's famous dictum that *die Sprache spricht:* "Like the mother's body, language is larger than us and carries us along with it. it bears us, births us, insofar as we bear with. if we are poets we spend our lives discovering not just what *we* have to say but what language is saying as it carries us with it" (Marlatt 1984, 46–47). This supports a view of language similar to Mac Cormack's in its stress on linguistic forces, flows, and excesses, though incontrovertibly dissimilar by way of its appeal to maternal simile.

A more explicit statement of Marlatt's lesbian erotics occurs later in the same text: "I feel language is incredibly sensual. The more musically we move into language, the more sensual it is, I suppose, because . . . it's the closest we get to that early sensual experience of fusion with the mother's body. And lesbian eroticism involves this incredible fusion, this merging of boundaries, because our bodies are so similar in their way of touching, of sensing each other, so I'm always wanting my language to somehow bring that into itself, that opulence of two incredibly sensual bodies moving together. I want that movement there in the way the words move" (1984, 51).

Unlike Mac Cormack's, Marlatt's agrammaticalities return language to a corporeal placement in the gendered, part oedipalized, body of the writer. In its organic base and expressionistic presuppositions, Marlatt's writing practice and recent lesbian encodings reveal their roots to be in proprioception and projective verse and remain expressive of a subject, no matter how much that subject is in process. By contrast, *Quirks & Quillets* upholds the primacy of the linguistic sign in a radical economy of expenditure beyond any gendered investment. Yet from this acorporeal notion of writing the work arrives at a biological relation to its reader. Rather than projecting a desiring body in the rhythms and sonorities of language, phrase propulsion opens up noncortical dimensions and implications involved in the act of reading. Inverting proprioception, it resituates agency in the empirical body of its model reader—a sociosomatic implication to which Christian Bök is alert: "Mac Cormack uses unpunctuated prose to transcribe the very impossibility of transcribing the proprioceptive experience of the author: the absence of the linebreak. . . . [Frustrating] any attempt to recuperate the originary processes of another body prior to the text even as the absence of the linebreak encourages the reader to explore the supplementary processes of their own body within the text" (1994, 27).

Equally unrewarding is to harness this work to some kind of enigmatic essentialness of self or psyche en route to positing that *Quirks & Quillets* adopts an antisocial stance, confronting its reader with an opaque system of private or cryptic allusion. Indeed, Mac Cormack's phrasal method is redolent with clarity. Lyotard reminds that "[a] phrase is not mysterious, it is clear. It says what it means to say. No 'subject' receives it, in order to interpret it. Just as no 'subject' makes it (in order to say something). It calls forth its addressor and addressee" (1988a, 67). In other words, a certain "death of the subject" is interlaced with a certain invocation of one.

Thus, to point to the poems' transgressions of the cognitive-rational regimen as faults or infelicities is precisely to miss the point and force of their phrasal consequence. To argue either that this work doesn't make sense or yields productively to semantic construction on the reader's part are ultimately and equally inappropriate responses. Indeed, *Quirks & Quillets* is best encountered—can truly only be encountered—through the impact of its numerous negativities: its referential instability and thwarted univocity, the resultant cognitive dissonance in its reception, and the serial dispersion of meaning—all of which ensure that this writing registers as the impact of untheorizable, protosemantic events.

Up to this point, Mac Cormack's work has attracted little critical attention.[10] The emerging Canadian canon has utilized a familiar spatial template to arbitrate its inclusions and exclusions. The model of the center relating to a periphery has positioned successfully both feminist and postcolonial writing practices as marginal *and therefore worthy of* critical attention. In so doing, Canadian criticism seems to be evading at least one critical implication: that, as the sentence is infinitely catalyzable, so, too, are the canon's own model margins.

There is no such thing as a neutral voice, a voice without desire, a voice
that does not desire me. If there was, it would be an experience of
absolute terror.
　　—Régis Durand

The rigor of performance [is] engaged with what memory wants to forget.
　　—Herbert Blau

10. Voice in Extremis

The ear, observes Certeau, "is the delicate skin caressed or irritated by
sound: an erogenous zone, exacerbated, so to speak, by the interdictions
which banish from language and good manners, coarseness, vulgarity and
finally passions" (quoted in Ahearne 1995, 140). How, then, to define the
ear's most intimate lover—the voice? Régis Durand (1977) demonstrates
the volatility of voice as a cultural and psychoanalytic concept positioned
between reality and representation and functioning as both a metaphorical
support of pure time and a physical production. Writing comes into being
through the midwifery of fingers and a competence with encoded incisions.
But in order to reach Certeau's erogenous zone, human sound, like human
birth, must pass from a cavity through a hole dilated under pressure. Indeed, "voice" seems inadequate to describe the full workings of this organ-
concept, and Certeau's definition of it as "a sign of the body that comes and
speaks," by factoring out the complex buccal and respiratory labor essential
to its functioning, proves insufficient (1988, 341). Voice is a polis of mouth,
lips, teeth, tongue, tonsils, palate, breath, rhythm, timbre, and sound; less a
component than a production of a materiopneumatic assemblage of inter-
acting bone, liquid, cartilage, and tissue. Enjoying such complexity, even
a single voice resonates as a simultaneity of corporeal, acoustic events; the
consequence of energy and respiratory force in flight through fixed cavities
and adjustable tensors.

　　The twentieth century presents two distinct scenarios for the voice in
poetry. One is a primal identity, culturally empowered to define the property of person. This is a phenomenological voice that serves in its self-

evidence as the unquestionable guarantee of presence. When heard and understood through its communication of intelligible sounds, this voice is named conscience.[1] The other scenario—renegade and heterological—requires the voice's primary drive to be persistently away from presence. This second is a thanatic voice triply destined to lines of flight and escape, to the expenditure of pulsional intensities, and to its own dispersal in sounds between body and language. Aspects of this second scenario are traced in this chapter as the *adventure* of voice, from the rebellious and jubilant pyrotechnics of early modernism, through its bigamous encounter with two graphisms, to its failure in the 1970s to establish the poem as community.

Barthes is responsible for introducing into theories of the voice the concept of granularity. Rhapsodizing on the paralinguistic effects of that vocal modification, as an amorous entwining of timbre and language whose aim, we are assured, "is not the clarity of messages," but the blissful search for "pulsional incidents, the language lined with flesh, a text where we can hear the grain of the throat, the patina of consonants, the voluptuousness of vowels, a whole carnal stereophony: the articulation of the body, of the tongue, not that of meaning, of language" (1975, 66–67). Notwithstanding Barthes's consummate rhetoric, this attempt to emancipate voice from code succeeds no further than a repositioning of the existing relationship. Language, signification, and code are certainly corporealized—Barthes is emphatic in this claim—yet voice, empowered by this embodiment, is still not freed from language. A voice outside of language? Blanchot offers a tremulous hint of such a siting in what he terms the "neutral" voice; a voice in intransigent nonidentification with a self.[2] Let me trace a similar dynamic in that protracted cultural irregularity, the twentieth-century sound poem, emerging in the late nineteenth and early twentieth centuries as an uncompromising effort at abstraction, its primary goal being the liberation and promotion of the phonetic and subphonetic features of language to the state of a *materia prima* for creative, subversive endeavors.[3] Mike Weaver describes the modus operandi of this poetry as that of "the figure (sound) [rising] off the ground (silence) producing a configuration of filled time against emptied time" (1966, 101). This key issue of the sound poem's temporality, had already been insisted on by the Dada poet Raoul Hausmann when claiming his own "optophonetic" poetry to be "an act consisting of respiratory and auditive combinations, firmly tied to a unit of duration" (quoted in Richter 1965, 121).

The 1950s saw the development of what might be termed a third phase in Western sound poetry. Prior to this time, in a period roughly stretching from 1875 to 1928, sound poetry's second phase was manifested in several diverse and revolutionary investigations into the nonsemantic, acoustic properties of language. In the work of the Russian futurists Khlebnikov and Kruchenykh, the intermedia activities of Kandinsky, the *bruitist* poems of the Dadaists—such as Ball, Schwitters, Arp, Hausmann, and Tzara—and the *parole in libertà* of the Italian futurist F. T. Marinetti, the *phonematic* aspect of language finally became isolated and explored for its own sake. Previous sporadic pioneering attempts had been made by several writers, including Aristophanes, Rabelais, the seventeenth-century Silesian mystic Quirinus Khulman, Molière, Petrus Borel (around 1820), Lewis Carroll ("Jabberwocky" appeared in 1855), Christian Morgenstern (in his *Galgenlieder* of 1875), and August Stramm (ca. 1912). This second phase is convincing proof of the continuous presence of a sound-poetry tradition throughout the history of Western literature. The first phase, perhaps better termed the *paleotechnic era* of sound poetry, is the vast, intractable territory of archaic and primitive poetries, the many instances of chant structures and incantation, of syllabic mouthings and deliberate lexical distortions still evident among many North American, African, Asian, and Oceanic peoples. One should bear in mind also the strong, persistent, folkloric strata manifesting in the world's many language games: the nonsense syllabary of nursery rhymes, mnemonic counting aids, whisper games, skipping chants, mouth music and folk song refrains, that serve as important compositional elements in work as chronologically separate as Kruchenykh's *zaum* poems, starting about 1913, and Bengt af Klintberg's use of cusha calls and incantations in 1965. Among the Russian futurists, both Khlebnikov and Kruchenykh openly acknowledge their debt to these populist forms.

F. T. Marinetti (1876–1944), the core architect of the Italian Futurist movement, launched his *parole in libertà* (words in freedom) in 1912 as an attempt at a radical syntactic explosion, the liberation of the word from all linear bondage and a consequent revision of the page as a dynamic field of typographic and by implication sonographic forces. In place of the ruling psychological paradigm, Marinetti substitutes "the lyric obsession with matter" (1971, 87). His list of abolitions includes syntax, all adjectives and adverbs, conjunctions, and punctuation (1971, 84–85). In performance Marinetti laid heavy stress upon onomatopoeic structures arrived at by the deliberate distortion of words. "[L]yrical intoxication allows us, or rather forces us, to deform and reshape words; to lengthen and shorten them; to reinforce their center or their extremities by increasing or diminishing the number of vowels and consonants" (quoted in Clough 1971, 50). Less interesting morphologically than the work of Kruchenykh—for in *parole in libertà* sound is still anchored in a representationality—Marinetti's work attempts to find a more basic connection between an object and its verbal sign than Saussure's oppositive, arbitrary relation; a connection predicated upon the efficacy of the sonic as a direct, unmediated vector.

The most significant effect of *parole in libertà* was less its sonological emancipations than its enduring impact on the possibilities of the poem's extended visual notation. Indeed, the futurist revolution in typography is one of its indisputably enduring achievements. Marinetti himself claimed that futurist typography allowed him "to treat words like torpedoes and to hurl them forth at all speeds: at the velocity of stars, clouds, aeroplanes, trains, waves, explosives, molecules, atoms" (quoted in Clough 1971, 52). His famous "Bombardamento di Adrianapoli" (The bombing of Adrianapoli) is a stunning typographic text of great visual excitement, employing different letter sizes in linear, diagonal, and vertical presentations to create a nongravitational text available for vocal realization. It marks one of the earliest successful, conscious attempts to structure a visual code for free, kinetic, and voco-phonetic interpretation. Moreover, Marinetti's typo-acoustic alliance is not an isolated case. Francesco Canguillo's "Piedigrotta" (Tiptoe-cavern) and "Caffè concerto, alfabeto a sorpresa" (Coffee concerto, alphabet to surprise) are similarly stupendous, unprecedented typographic tours de force.

Writing in 1920, Ardengo Soffici describes the purported qualities of futurist lettering. "The letters themselves are beautiful; in fact their beauty as an ideographic sign remains after it has become stereotyped in the alphabetic series. They have an extraordinary power of suggestion; they evoke past civilizations, dead languages. Their beauty may be enhanced by pictorial practices which, however, do not go beyond the means and instruments of the type-setter. Changes in size, arrangement, and colour give the requisite movement to a page which may, with justification, be called a work of art" (quoted in Clough 1961, 52). Graphic and sonic innovation thus go hand in hand in futurist practice. Yet despite its verbal deformations, *parole in libertà* still commits the performing voice to a textual dependency—a confinement clearly hinted at in Marinetti's comments on his own poem "Zang-tumb-tumb," where "the strident onomatopoeia *ssiii*, which reproduces the whistle of a tugboat on the Meuse, is followed by the muffled *fiiii fiiii* coming from the other bank. These two onomatopoeias have enabled me to dispense with a description of the breadth of the river which is thus measured by contrasting the consonants *s* and *f*'" (quoted in Clough

1961, 50). In its dominant goal—a mimophonic representation of ambient technology and powers by means of predominantly martial and industrial onomatopoeia—the most lasting accomplishment of *parole in libertà* is a graphic system of notation for sonic rhythms and forces: in other words, an efficient score for voice.[4]

Dada poet Hugo Ball (1886–1926) claims to have invented *verse ohne worte* (poetry without words), also termed *lautgedicht,* or sound poem. In a diary entry for June 23, 1916, Ball describes the compositional basis for his new poetry: "the balance of vowels is weighed and distributed solely according to the values of the beginning sequence" (Ball 1974, 70). In another entry (just above a quotation from Novalis: "Linguistic theory is the dynamic of the spiritual world"), Ball elaborates the performative implications of his poetry.

> Nowhere are the weaknesses of a poem revealed as much as in a public reading. One thing is certain: art is joyful only as long as it has richness and life. Reciting aloud has become the touchstone of the quality of the poem for me, and I have learned (from the stage) to what extent today's literature is worked out as a problem at a desk and is made for the spectacles of the collector instead of for the ears of living human beings (1974, 54).

The mantic base of the *lautgedicht* and its sacerdotal—even shamanistic—underpinnings are clearly evident in the program notes accompanying Ball's first sound-poetry performance at Zurich's Cabaret Voltaire: "In these phonetic poems we totally renounce the language that journalism has abused and corrupted. We must return to the innermost alchemy of the word, we must even give up the word too, to keep poetry for its last and holiest refuge" (Ball 1974, 71).[5] (I will show in the final chapter the way Levinas identifies a language without words as a pure communication.) Ball celebrates the realization of his aspirations in a journal entry for June 18, 1916: "We have now driven the plasticity of the word to the point where it can scarcely be equalled. We achieved this at the expense of the rational, logically constructed sentence. . . . We have loaded the word with strengths and energies that helped us to rediscover the evangelical concept of the 'word' (logos) as a magical complex image" (1974, 68).

To say the least, these desires are paradoxical: a quest through a "poetry *without* words" in order to obtain the word's innermost alchemy? Ball's problematic conjunction of religious utterance and linguistic innovation doesn't pass without comments by his contemporaries. Eugene Jolas insists that "[l]anguage must become vertical. The character of conjuration implied in the mystic faculty must be established by the poet who attempts to give voice to the superconscious. Mystics often invented their own secret language. But the new religious poetry cannot use a language the psychopathology of which is obvious. Words of the ecclesiastical tradition fail to impinge on the modern consciousness" (1941, 94). Jolas goes on to suggest the potentially positive contribution of technological vocabulary to revolutionizing sacred language. "Mystic language must be revolutionized. It may be possible that the much insulted vocabulary of technology may furnish us new symbols. Aeronautics, which is one element of ascension, should be able to renew the vertical speech. The vast changes in our conception of the universe made by modern physics will doubtless help to metamorphose the sacred language" (95).[6] In actual fact, the form of Ball's poems is not markedly different from earlier attempts at the end of the nineteenth century by such poets as Christian Morgenstern ("Kroklokwafzi" appeared in 1905) and Paul Scheerbart (whose "Kikakoku" appeared as early as 1897). The poems commonly present a morphological experience together with an absent, yet potential, "meaning" and can be accurately described as specimens of virtual semantics. To substantiate this claim, here are excerpts of both Ball's and Scheerbart's poems for comparison.

> Kikakoku!
> Ekoralaps!
>
> Wiso kollipanda opolosa.
> Ipasatta ih fuo.
> Kikakoku proklinthe peteh.
> Nikifili mopa Lexio intipaschi benakaffro—proposa
> pi! propsa pi!
> Jasollu nosaressa flipsei.
> Aukarotto passakrussar Kikakoku.
> Nupsa pusch?
> Kikakoku buluru?
> Futupukke—propsa pi!
> Jaollu . . . .
>   (Scheerbart, in Rasula and McCaffery 1998, 104)
>
> gadji beri bimba
> glandridi lauli lonni cadori
> gadjama bim beri glassala

glandridi glassala tuffm i zimbrabim
blassa galassasa tuffm i zimbrabim . . .
(Ball 1974, 70)

Is this any more than the "stupid incantations in a fake lingua franca, good for summoning dead men" that Artaud (1995, 85) finally saw his own wordless poetry to be? My own answer is yes. There are grammatical indicators in both pieces, while in Scheerbart interrogative and exclamatory markers function alongside capitalized "words" providing guides to emphases and intonational changes—two prerequisites of virtual semantics. Readers are deprived of semantic but not grammatical access. Similarly, despite the fact that the interior verbal transmutations of "Karawane" do approximate those undertakings of linguistic delirium noted by Foucault in Brisset— "to restore words to the noises that gave birth to words, and to reanimate the gestures, assaults and violences of which words stand as the now silent blazons" (quoted in Deleuze 1988b, 149 n.40)—the poem's structural and syntactic repetitions suggest a presidential grammar in operation.

The treatment of the sound poem as a text in another language formed the basis of the material used in the several "African Nights" presented at the Cabaret Voltaire and further developed by fellow Dadaist Tristan Tzara in a pseudo ethnopoetry realized most successfully in his *Poèmes Negres:* loose and often false translations from the African, which Tzara then used for sound scores.[7] The collective activities of Janco, Ball, Huelsenbeck, Tzara, and Arp at Zurich's Cabaret Voltaire culminated in the simultaneist poem: a high-energy, performance-oriented cacophony of whistling, singing, grunting, coughing, and speaking. Partly based on the earlier work of Henri Barzun and Fernand Divoire (Ball 1974, 57), the simultaneous poem stands as an early example of intermedia.[8]

Defying accurate categorization as either theater, music, or poetry, the Dada simultaneities emphasize the improvisatory and aleatoric possibilities of multivocal expression. Ball theorizes on the first presentation of the *poème simultane* on March 29, 1916, allegorizing both voice and noise: "The 'simultaneous poem' has to do with the value of the voice. The human organ represents the soul, the individuality in its wanderings with its demonic companions. The noises represent the background—the inarticulate, the disastrous, the decisive. The poem tries to elucidate the fact that man is swallowed up in the mechanistic process. In a typically compressed way it shows the conflict of the *vox humana* [human voice] with a world that threatens, ensnares, and destroys it, a world whose rhythm and noise are ineluctable" (Ball 1974). Despite Ball's conflictual narrative of human versus machinic, the prime acoustic effect of the simultaneity is to break down language into vocal, predenotational texture, arriving at effects strikingly similar to the later electro-acoustic manipulations of Henri Chopin (to be considered later in this chapter).

Raoul Hausmann is perhaps the most historically significant of Dada sonosophers because of his significant advances in the techniques of notation. In 1918 Hausmann developed his "optophonetics" utilizing typographic variations in size to indicate proportionate variations in pitch and volume. Writing in the *Courrier Dada,* Hausmann argues, "The poem is an act consisting of respiratory and auditive combinations, firmly tied to a unit of duration. . . . In order to express these elements typographically . . . I had used letters of varying sizes and thicknesses which thus took on the character of musical notation. Thus the optophonetic poem was born. The optophonetic and the phonetic poem are the first step towards totally non-representational, abstract poetry" (quoted in Richter 1965, 121). It's important to appreciate the technological contingency of this development. Like Marinetti's *parole in libertà,* optophonetic poetry draws directly on the advanced possibilities made available by early twentieth-century type design and display type.[9]

Moholy Nagy draws attention to this collusion between aesthetic and commercial criteria in 1947.

> Fortunately, the tremendous demands of business advertising have forced the typographer as well as the commercial artist to some imaginative solutions which can be understood as a successful preparation for the complex task of the new communication. . . . Catalogs of merchandise, illustrated advertising, posters on billboards, front pages of tabloid newspapers move towards inventive visual articulation. . . . Apollinaire's ideograms and Marinetti's poems served, perhaps, not so much as models, but as tradition-breakers which freed experimenters to create a quick, simultaneous communication of several messages. (Quoted in Kostelanetz 1982, 95)[10]

In their experimental *zaum,* or "transrational language," the Russian futurists Khlebnikov and Kruchenykh grant a similar autonomous value to sound—an independence endorsed and scientifically scrutinized by the Russian formalists. Yet even a cursory glance at their theoretical statements and manifestos makes clear that the voice's emancipation is at most a coincidental achievement and not *zaum*'s central concern. Kruchenykh describes his own *protozaum* texts as verbal constructs whose words "do not have a definite meaning" (quoted in Markov 1969, 44). The target of Kruchenykh's attack is not the word as such but the word's semantic and grammatical subordination to meaning.[11] Much *zaum* is Babelian rather than transrational, written consciously to imitate the sounds of foreign languages (cf. Markov 1969, 20)—an estrangement, to be sure, but hardly a shattering of the word as such. In his famous contention that the breadth of the word surpasses its meaning, Kruchenykh aims to uncouple the binding relation of signifier to signified but also strives to expand the word rather than effect its demolition. For Kruchenykh poetry is the conscious attempt to return language to its arational ground, involving the open sacrifice of meaning as a constituent of the poem (or rather meaning in its restricted, semantic sense) and the deployment of various paraverbal "poetic irregularities" such as clipped words, lexical hybrids, neologisms, and fragmentations.

Kruchenykh wrote his first *zaum* poem ("Dyr bul shchyl") in December 1912, three months before his definition of the form appeared in the manifesto *Declaration of the Word as Such*. He traces the genealogy of *zaum* back to religious glossolalia—the speaking in tongues practiced by religious mystics such as Sishkov of the Khlysty sect of flagellants (Markov 1969, 202).[12] Kruchenykh's ultimate attachment to the word (as a flexible organization of phonematic material capable of translogical, but nonetheless emotional, communication) is evident in several places. In his article "Novye puti slova" (The new ways of the word), Kruchenykh claims that "[o]ne can read a word backward, and *then one gets a deeper meaning*" (quoted in Markov 1969, 128; emphasis added). Earlier in the same article occurs the following call to battle: "One should write in a new way, and the more disorder we bring to the composition of sentences, the better" (128). The implication is clearly that a lateral disorganization of the word and sentence is preferable to their complete abandonment.

In similar spirit, Khlebnikov speaks of new meanings attained through bypassing older semantic forms to obtain meanings "rescued" by "estrangement." In his article "Vremya mera mira" (Time is a measure of the world), Khlebnikov endorses the aesthetic value of the word against its depreciating epistemic value: "[T]he word, though it is no tool for thinking anymore, will remain [as a medium] for art" (quoted in Markov 1969, 301). Against the contemporary claims of Baudoin de Courtenay that *zaum* is not language but a species of "phonetic excrement," the evidence presented suggests that in both Kruchenykh's and Khlebnikov's writings there persists an attraction to the word—as a teleological aura—in the condition of the semanteme's own, near excommunication.[13]

For all their subversive accomplishments, Dada and futurist sound poems fail to escape an ultimate organization by the signifier. Ball's verse without words, for instance, testifies to the omnipresent possibility in cacophony and gibberish of language returning either in recognizable words or in a comprehensible "syntax" suggestive of an unknown language. Certeau describes the experience of such heteroglossia as that of "voices" haunting a plurality of boundaries and interstices. "The voice moves, in effect, in a space between the body and language, but only in a moment of passage from one to the other and as if in their weakest difference. . . . The body, which is a thickening and an obfuscation of phonemes, is not yet the death of language. The articulation of signifiers is stirred up and effaced; there remains nonetheless the vocal modulation, almost lost but not absorbed in the tremors of the body; a strange interval, where the voice emits a speech lacking 'truths,' and where proximity is a presence without possession" (1988, 230).[14] The xenoglossic evocations in Ball's and Kruchenykh's poems conjure up a sense of texts whose meanings are inherent but defy comprehension. Voice retains its quality as ontologic presence with the mandate to communicate at least a semantic suggestion. Indeed, their poems inspire that amorous yearning to experience incomprehensible speech that St. Augustine notes in his description of the effect of hearing a dead word (*vocabulum emortuum*) as that of stirring in the soul a love of the will to know.[15] To link *zaum* and Ball's poetry without words to cross-cultural glossolalia or to the Jewish automatic speech known as "maggidism" is thus a natural temptation. For speaking in tongues, *zaum* and the Dada *lautgedicht* commonly retain the simulacra of a semiosis.

Despite their celebration of nonsense and attendant consecration of orality, Dada and futurism did not provoke a disavowal of the written. On the contrary, the legacy left by both is one of conspiratorial innovations realized through a bigamous relation with both sound and the written mark— its heritage, a condition of voice that can best be described (to borrow a category from Gertrude Stein) as a "dependent independence." One of the undeniable achievements of both Dada and futurist poetics is a decisive advance in the form of poetry's graphic notation. Ball's frequently reprinted "Karawana" employs a variety of typefaces in its first printed form, and Hausmann's optophonetic poetry achieves a notational precision that he himself likens to musical notation—a score for repeating the poem's vocalized entailments of intonation, volume, and pitch. Language, be it sonor-ized, pulverized, deracinated, plasticized, lacerated, or transrationalized by this collective avant-garde still resists an ultimate demolition. Voice, as a consequence, remains subordinated to the dictates of a graphism, the re-sultant poetry remaining an *ars dictandi*—that learned Scholastic expertise in the speaking of a written text.

Prior to the developments of the 1940s, sound poetry was still largely a word-bound practice, for while the work of the Dadaists and futurists served to free the word from semantic mandates, redirecting a sensed energy from themes and "message" into matter and force, their work nevertheless preserved a morphological patterning that still upheld the aural presence of the word. It could be said that what sound poetry achieved, up to the era of the tape recorder, was a full-scale revisioning of the word as a desired destination when purified of its cultural bondage to meaning. As part of this complex transformation of the semantic paradigm, the materiality of the sign emerged as a central, almost primitivistic, preoccupation.[16] This transcendental lamination of value onto the materiality of the verbal sign specifies the limits of sound investigation up to the 1940s, when the break with the word was finally accomplished.

Adopting a platform broadly similar to Van Doesburg's "phono-gymnas-tics" of the 1920s, the Lettriste poets of the 1940s offered a full-scale lexi-cal revolution based on parallel alphabetic revitalizations.[17] Isadore Isou and Maurice Lemaitre, founders of the group, opted for the letter over the word as the basic unit of their poetic composition. Celebrating the lettris-tic impulse among the debris of the word, they developed both visual and auditory innovations which, when realized in performance, enacted that "theatre of energies" called for by Lyotard (see Lyotard 1977). Isou's "New Letteric Alphabet" ascribes to alphabetic characters nonphonetic values and paralinguistic features to be employed in vocal performance: A = hard in-halation; B = exhalation; O = coughing, clearing the throat; P = a clicking of the tongue. Isou and Lemaitre further introduced scriptural systems (meta-graphics, or postwriting, and hypergraphy, respectively) that fetishize the graphic as irreducible to vocalization. The component characters in these scripts were a mixture of elements from non-Romanic alphabets, invented and imaginary signs and ideograms.[18]

The decisive move away from the written to a full orality begins in the early 1950s with four young French writers: François Dufrêne, the situa-tionist Gil J. Wolman, Jean-Louis Brau, and Henri Chopin—collectively known as the Ultralettristes. Dufrêne's *cri-rythmes,* Wolman's *mégapneumes,* and the *instrumentations verbales* of Brau are all morphological transformations in extremis. Less texts than sonic performances, the ultralettristic poems comprise a high-energy expulsion of inarticulate sounds, cries, and grunts. In linguistic parlance, ultralettristic performance emancipates non- and subphonomatic material from the necessity of primary articulation, and as a category of sound poetry it explores—at its maximum level of intensity—the area of human expression David Crystal terms paralanguage, "a kind of bridge between non-linguistic forms of communicative behaviour and the traditionally central areas of 'verbal' linguistic study—grammar, . . . vocabulary, and pronunciation" (1975, 162).

Jakobson supports phonemic hegemony in contending that significatory desire is the fundamental force behind the move from free sound production to the sign (1968, see esp. 42). Voice for him is preoriginary to speech, the protoplasmic paraphernalia out of which speech emerges via sonic selection and gained only at the price of substantial vocal impoverishment (cf. 1968, 27). Dufrêne's special achievement is to have renounced entirely the aura of the spoken and the regime of the phoneme, pushing the centripetal limits of the poetic and extending his investigations of the microparticulars of morphology into the full expressive range of predenotative human sonorities: grunts, howls, shrieks, and hisses—a truly profound disturbance of language "by the mad poetics of the scream" (Lecercle 1985, 66). For Dufrêne it is energy, not meaning, that constitutes the essence of communicated data. The *cri-rhythmes* are, first and foremost, conscious deformations of linguistic form beyond the phonemic boundaries of the Dadaists. Moreover, they eschew entirely the alphabetic mediation that characterizes Lettriste poetics, emerging instead from an intensely somatic base in subphonemic and graphically unnotatable units.

The complexities of Dufrêne's total poetic should be enumerated. Posited a priori within bodily performance as physical expenditure, his poetry appears to be incontrovertibly predicated on a biological paradigm and thus becomes unavoidably entangled in a metaphysics of presence. Additionally, there's the severe problem of the limitation of his art to the idiosyncratic athleticisms of the individual body. Aren't these performative demands a perverse resurgence of that romanticism which linked lyric extremity to power?[19] (Fellow sound poet Henri Chopin foregrounds this problem when declaring of himself "*le poème c'est moi.*") However, Dufrêne's *cri-rhythmes* further invite a crucial question: does the human cry mark an unmediated presence or trace a physiological outlay? Undoubtedly, Dufrêne's investigation of human sound in isolation, liberated from both phonematic structures and recognizable sign functions, together with his revisioning of the poem *as the practice of an outlay* mark important stages in establishing the agencies for a general libidinal emancipation through human voice. Yet equally the *cri-rhythme* opens to breath's other possibility. "What death transfigured, my sorrow reached like a cry" (Bataille 1991, 63). Cries are nonsemantic physical expenditures, the waste products of an anguish. Conceived as a dyadic covenant of inspiration and respiration, breath can be fissured in accordance with an ambiguity implicit in its own constitution. On the one hand, breath is life-giving, an inspiration, productive of a presence at once physical and metaphysical. However (as was seen in Olson's case in chapter 4), breath's other law involves the negative economy of involuntary expenditure. Dufrêne's work, then, involves a gestural poetics of severe ontological ambivalence: assertive, parousial, and romantic, but at the same time fragile, interstitial, and wasteful. As a new way to blow out old candles, *cri-rhythmes* expose an additionally economic peril, namely, the risk to self when the latter is committed to an unavoidable expenditure. (I'm here in disagreement with Guattari's contention that sound poetry is "the attempt to re-individualize subjectivity and creativity" [1996a, 116].) Dufrêne's poetry entails that general economy of inescapable discharge specified by Bataille.[20] Unlike Ball, who in his pursuit of the "innermost alchemy of the word" opts for the mystical, Dufrêne installs his poetic of the cry within the nonlogical emissions of the sacrificial. Regardless of these complexities, the *cri-rhythme* certainly satisfies that criterion set down by Kristeva for an authentic literary practice as "the exploration and discovery of the possibilities of language as an activity which frees man [*sic*] from given linguistic networks" and accordingly takes its place in the larger cultural struggle against all forms of preconditioning (1984).

Breton distinguishes the work of art as a "happening" from the work of art as a "ribbon" of repetitions, preconceptions, and anticipations (1993, 199). It's Apollinaire, however, in "The New Spirit and the Poets," who reminds us that poetry's greatest resource is surprise. The Ultralettriste performance is such a surprise happening. Neither a preconception nor a reified product, it registers, like pleasure, as a pure affect, reconfiguring performance not as a validation of authorial presence (there is no author) but as a profoundly destabilizing force, removing the poem from familiar semantic and orthographic certainties.[21] Poet Bob Cobbing describes the *cri-rhythmes* as utilizing "the utmost variety of utterances, extended cries, shrieks, ululations, purrs, yaups and cluckings; the apparently uncontrollable controlled into a spontaneously shaped performance" (in Kostelanetz 1980, 20). Be-

cause all normative meaning in this poetry is abolished, the distance between poet-performer and audience is radically altered from its standard
configurations. The functional separation deriving from a traditional transit
model of communication (with a message sent across a textual or auditory
space to a receiver) no longer obtains. Rather than validating their creators'
presence as an immediate emotional truth, ultralettristic performances de-
stabilize all ontological grounding, freeing the productions from both semantic and orthographic controls.[22]

The auditory reception of these performances, first presented in 1950
under the category of "Prelinguism," is described colorfully by Lora-Totino.
The sonic expulsions "strike the ear as brutally as a material in the pure
state of incandescence, a brute, heavy, physical substance still fresh from
the flesh that has expelled it, impregnated with the weight and the elec-
tricity of the tissue of the cells that has created it, a torrid place of existential
incubation" (1978, 33). Prelinguism carries no metaphor of primordiality (it
does not aspire to the status of an *ursprach* à la Schwitters) but shatters "the
totalizing and totalitarian phonemic control over voice" (Appelbaum 1990,
99). The sense evoked is of Barthes's vocal granulation pushed beyond all
connection to language, as vocal emissions without meaning whose closest
proximity is to a "death of language."[23]

Silence staked outside the political economy of the whisper, brain carved
by anonymous murmurs and then meticulously polished into aphonia.
Such is the voice without phonemic regulation, a becoming animal again,
a willful en-fans, an enveloping in animal of *homo loquens.* There's a profound and obvious commitment in Ultralettriste improvisation to releasing
primary instinctual processes and drives via spontaneous voicing. Writing
in 1963, Raoul Vaneigem extolls the revolutionary potential of spontaneity as a vital component of radical subjectivity: "Spontaneity is the true
mode of being of individual creativity, creativity's initial, immaculate form,
unpolluted at the source and as yet unthreatened by the mechanisms of
co-optation" (1983, 149). It's tempting to regard this description of vocal
Evian water as an attractive agenda for poetic praxis, but what guarantees
the emergence of unconscious drives in automaticity or spontaneity?[24] If
Kristeva's formulations are correct and a semiotic interruption of instinctual drives is always present in the sociolectal, symbolic order, then the
loss of conscious control within the spontaneous act of voicing will always
emerge as symptomatic of a double disposition and cannot fail to index a
dialectic of drives.[25]

Barthes, however, cautions against such an optimistic determinism, alleging that automatism "is not rooted at all in the 'spontaneous,' the 'savage,' the 'pure,' the 'profound,' the 'subversive,' but originates on the contrary from the 'strictly coded' " (1985, 244). "The 'spontaneity' which people normally talk to us about is the height of convention. It is that reified language which we find ready-made within ourselves, immediately at our disposal, when we do in fact want to speak 'spontaneously' " (Barthes 1987, 55). Lora-Totino shares similar misgivings about Ultralettriste performances, concluding that "divorced from the common language, repetition rapidly and inevitably generated boredom, for, when it comes to the point, inarticulate expression, like sex, does not have an infinity of ways of conjugation, in fact it is extremely limited" (1978, 33–34). It is also worth recalling the sober warning offered by Althusser "that every 'spontaneous' language is an ideological language, the vehicle of an ideology" (1971, 207).

Whether from premonition of this subsequent criticism or developing their own misgivings, the Ultralettristes quickly modified their performances into multimedia events. Early in their history, a technological turn occurred toward the use of human sound as a primary material for technological modification. Lora-Totino describes these works as embroideries of "primitive and indistinct material with rhythm, superimpositions, accelerations . . . creating veritable ballets of expectoration, cascades of little noises and disagreeable noises" (1978, 34). Paralanguage in such manifestations merges with concrete music, a component in a complex instrumentation of speed, timbre, volume, and quantity. If Charles Olson saw advanced and untapped possibilities offered to poetic notation by the typewriter, then Wolman, Dufrêne, Brau, and Chopin find equally lucrative potential offered to prelinguism by the tape recorder.

It would be straining genealogy to argue that these later Ultralettriste tape recorder productions comprise merely an extension into acoustics of the treated text—indeed, the intransigent difference between media here is absolute.[26] Clearly they signal a return to a graphism, arrested and repeatable, but most crucially through their recovery of human expenditure as a new vocabulary for secondary orality, they signalize a revised poetical economy. The tape enhancements of the Ultralettristes are the culmination of the romantic subject in the unfolding (via technological prostheses) of its insular "lyric" interiority. Unquestionably the conceptual base of the spontaneous voice is radically altered. Impromptu ephemera become recoverable, redeployable as combinatorial and distortable material in a complex, textural composition. If the *cri-rhythme* and *megapneume* fall within the purlieu of Bataille's general economy as acts of expenditure, these later poems—the products of recovery, preservation, and modification—announce the extreme limit of the voice in a powerful alterity: a cacophonous amplification, pulverized into a microparticularized Other, the experience of which is more that of an extra than a paralinguistic phenomenon. If such is the fate of voice, it's the sound poem's ironic destiny not to escape repetition but to enter it and give itself over to the fixity of digital imprint. For, with the seductive advent of the tape recorder, technology offered prelinguism a secondary orality capable of transforming its acoustic ephemerality into the electro-acoustic data of the Foucauldian archive.

Tape provided the revolutionary capability to finally transcend the biological limits of human bodily expression. Considered as an extension of human vocality, the tape recorder permits the poet to move beyond her own physical limitations. With the body no longer an ultimate, inflexible parameter, voice becomes a point of departure, not a teleologically prescribed point of arrival. Similarly, as a secondary orality, the sound poem is finally liberated from the athletic sequentialities of the human body. Cutting, in effect, becomes the potential compositional basis in which vocal segments can be arranged and rearranged outside of the binding unidirectionality of real-time performance. The tape recorder also shares micro/macro/phonic qualities permitting a more detailed appreciation of the human vocal range. Technological time can be superadded to authentic body time to achieve an either accelerated or decelerated experience of vocal time. Both space and time are harnessed to become less the controlling than the manipulable factors of audiophony. There exists then, through recourse to the tape recorder as an active compositional tool, a possibility of "overtaking" speech by the machine. Electro-acoustic sound poetry mobilizes a technicism to further decompose the word, allowing through speed changes the granular structure of language to emerge and make itself evident.

The phonetic poem, from Aristophanes to Isou, despite its nonsemantic registrations of the voice, still accepted the physical limitations of the human speaker as its own governing parameters, thus being more limited in the scope of its negation. The tape recorder, however, allows voice—for the first time in its history—a physical and ideological separation from speech. Cobbing underlines the paradoxical potential of tape: "Strangely enough, the invention of the tape-recorder has given the poet back his voice. For, by listening to their voices on the tape-recorder, with its ability to amplify, slow down and speed up voice vibrations, poets have been able to analyse and then immensely improve their vocal resources. Where the tape-recorder leads the human voice can follow" (quoted in Kostelanetz 1982, 386). Cobbing's anticipations are significant, for by avoiding a negative stance toward technology, he is able to envision a positive feedback to a human, non-technological ground: a recuperation back into acoustic performance.[27]

The advantages of tape began to be fully realized in the late 1950s by Henri Chopin (born in 1922), who made a decisive break from phonetic regimen and began developing his self-styled *audio-poèmes,* utilizing microphones of high amplification to capture vocal sounds on the threshold of audition. The *audio-poème* constitutes a much more radical break with the tradition of Western poetics than anything before. Ball, Marinetti, Khlebnikov, and Isou all maintained a paradigmatic ne plus ultra at the thresholds of the vowel and consonant. Upon this extenuated tradition Chopin unleashed a Copernican revolution.

His early work, circa 1955, comprises a decomposition and recomposition of vowels and consonants. Words are slowed down and accelerated with multiple superimpositions, additional vocalic texture being provided by a variety of respiratory and buccal effects. Still adhering to verbal elements as their constituents, these poems can best be described as technological assaults on the word. (One work from this period, for example, is based upon the words "sol air" with additional nonsemantic sounds, such as buccal and breathing effects, all of which are superimposed up to fifty times.) Later, Chopin discovered and used the "micro-particle" as the compositional unit of his work, abandoning the word entirely. This marks the birth of *poésie sonore,* which Chopin categorically distinguishes from *poésie phonetique.* His first *audio-poème, Pêche de Nuit* (Night Fish), was created in 1957. Using a core verbal text made up of an onomatopoeic listing of fish names, Chopin destroys all semantic recognition by subjecting the verbal text to six speed changes and an additional forty-eight superimpositions of the initial reading of the text. According to Larry Wendt, "words were lost for the sound: the ballet of captured fish had inspired a dance of micro-vocalic particles and buccal instances. It had the sound of life squirming in all of its articulated movements" (1993, 2).

Because his "vocal micro-particulars" are realizable solely through the agency of contemporary tape technology, Chopin's art is the first-ever poetry to be entirely dependent on the tape recorder. "Without this machine," claims Chopin, "sound poetry would not exist." It is an irrevocable marriage to a technological determinism which, Chopin argues, guarantees a radically nonaesthetic grounding for his electro-acoustic poetry. The *audio-poème* finds "its sources in the very sources of language and, by the use of electro-magnetics, [owes] almost nothing to any aesthetic or historical system of poetry" (Chopin quoted in McCaffery and Nichol 1978, 48). Chopin locates his text-sound compositions in the technophysical tension between available microsonics (their amplification and exteriorization) and the heuristic desire to explore one vital question: what would constitute a body without writing?

The body has always been a lodestar for analogical operations, seducing models and metaphors into its blank, unanswering space. Bataille, for one, situates the body outside technology in a basal opposition to nihilism. "The fundamental right of man," he writes, "is to signify *nothing*" (quoted in Richman 1982, 138). Bataille suggests that totality is grasped in a gesture of the *non sens*. Chopin proposes a homologous notion to this unmeaning: *the body without signification*. For Bataille and Chopin alike, it's the sociocultural denial to the body of a blank, meaningless space that supports a nihilism, not vice versa. The body is *nothing* when trapped within its systems of representations but becomes everything when posited outside of meaning. For Chopin, technology is the primary instrument by which that nonrepresentational, nonsemantic state is realized. Chopin's theoretic body emerges at the point where discursive realization is either abrogated or else collapsed into the intractable anticoncept of a postlinguistic corporeality.

The skeleton was an object of intense fascination to the Renaissance, and its cultural emergence as doubly emblem and icon coincides with the scientific understanding of the human body's complex articulations. Donne's poem "A Valediction: of my Name in the Window" is a meditation upon the proposed analogy between graphic and skeletal articulation:

> Or if too hard and deepe
> This learning be, for a scratch'd name to teach,
> It, as a given deaths head keepe,
> Lovers mortalitie to preach,
> Or thinke this ragged body name to bee
> My ruinous Anatomie.
> (Donne 1952, 22)

In contrast, Chopin explores less the articular than the muscular and cavernous aspects of human anatomy—the rhythm of pulses and resonances of cavities—in a speleography of sound that refuses to accommodate the spatial paradigm of bones transfixed upon an ossiographic and Baroque template.[28] Subjected to Chopin's creativity, technology functions first and foremost as a heuristic, amplificatory prosthesis, supporting an exploratory poetry of interior intensities, an art that unfolds the romantic interior self,

at once demythologizing human interiority (as the *hegemonikon,* the scholastic site of the soul) and debunking traditional, anatomical prohibitions.[29]
Chopin works to detect and revitalize the fragmentary, discontinuous waste
products of both respiration and orality. It's the shit and farts of speech that
attract him, the ignored expenditures that physically vehiculate the logocentric amalgam. Paying attention to the body's heterological sonic phenomena—in sum, the body's noise—he transforms them into a powerful,
expressive vocabulary, manipulating tensions between the microsonic and
its amplified exteriorization, making manifest an art of the insensible made
sensible through the magnifying powers of the tape recorder.

Chopin's notorious splicings and layerings organize the temporal appearance of the sonic like a writing. It would be inaccurate, however, to represent him as an exponent of a strictly secondary orality. Admittedly, he has
recorded his works extensively and used technology to realize an impressive and definable audiographics. Such work bears all the characteristics of a
graphism: iterability, retrievability, and replication. Chopin's primary concern in his use of tape, however, is to extend the parameters of performance.
If the quotidian impact of audiotechnologies has been the permanent separation of speech from a present subject (via radio, the telephone, and the
gramophone), then we must credit Chopin for repossessing vocality as a
new nonsemantic lexicon, a material modified, purified of the Logos and
then returned to a performative, gestural poetics.

Chopin's *poésie sonore* involves two distinct dimensions of technological
manifestation. In the first the microphone is used as a physical insurgent,
an anatomical probe utilized as the sonic equivalent of fibre optics, as a
search tool of the inaudible. In the second the tape recorder is deployed in
a mise-en-scène, a theatrical setting in which to demonstrate its own capabilities of public occasion. Into this recontextualized technology (as performance) Chopin enters as conductor to demonstrate the mind's control
over processed human sounds, through an expert orchestration of tonali-
ties and volumes, returning sound as an audible writing, an audio-graphic
imprint capable of controlled appearance and sequencing. The method is
patently anatomical *and* theatrical. (Often the volume and speed controls
of his pieces are placed in a separate area of the auditorium, and Chopin will
send eccentric, gestural signals to the sound technician regarding volume,
pitch, and channel changes.) We are reminded first of Vesalius *and then* of
Jules Verne; the former's detailed surgical engravings that first revealed to
the Eurocentric imagination a body with organs; the latter's narratives of
inner, microscopic journeys.

Like no other poet before him, Chopin reclaims technology from its invisible circuitries to the visible in human performance. The implications of this appropriation need not be hyperbolized. There's no crisis of the audiated sign involved but rather a plasticity in potential sufficient to accommodate the paradox. Having freed those heterological aspects that are necessarily constituent to speaking (the sound of the lips, the teeth, glottal movements) and having liberated them from all semantic paradigms, effectively proposing the body's other sounds as worthy of audition, Chopin returns his repertoire of expenditures back to a public, performative domain. These are my sounds. Normally inaudible, now audible through electronic enhancement. Moreover, these sounds are not only what you hear but what you see. Me, Henri Chopin: *Le poème c'est moi;* returning this way to the rhetorical discourse of the Sun King minus both Versailles and Logocentricity.[30]

But this recuperation of a self does not involve a necessary aggrandizement of the force of the subject. On the contrary, because of the scope of Chopin's work, his commitment to both technographic and performative paradigms, the subject position is rendered, if not unstable, then optional. It can be argued that Chopin's art continues that line of subversive decontextualizing first announced in the twentieth century by Duchamp's Readymades, intervening—with technological assistance—into the hidden processes of bodily functions, to decontextualize their acoustic waste products and resituate them inside the spectacle of public performance. The transgression here connects to Bataille's important observation that our shit, when inside of us, is perfectly acceptable but becomes heterological when it makes its excremental appearance in the world. Chopin, like Bataille, argues against the body's own physical interdictions as a censorial barrier. His success comes as the result of his tenacious explorations of the virtual ratios of body to both technology and poetics. Whereas proprioception provides a theoretical direction toward a reader's relation to equally theorized organs, Chopin stages these organs performatively as the active agents of noise, tone, and rhythm, redirecting Olson's projective narrative of organ tissues out through voice. What in Olson remains a composition by field becomes in Chopin an actual journey through the body into an inner exploration of corporeal cavities and a nonjournalistic recording of detectable, sonic phenomena.

Larry Wendt aptly describes Chopin's practice as a "caveman technology in action" (1993, 3), a paleotechnic *détourne* of electro-acoustic apparatuses.[31] Chopin's relation to prescribed technological functions is one of abuse, of circumventing designated usage and exploring the possibilities of extended, "unofficial" functions. Wendt recounts that Chopin "found the sound of his own spoken declamation to be disappointing. However, by interfering with the recording head and tape path through which a recording of his own spoken words would pass, he found interesting timbres in his voice which he was unaware of before. On a little bit better quality tape recorder, he found that changing the tape speeds and performing simple techniques such as defeating the erase heads with match sticks for multiple superimpositions, [Chopin] could produce a whole orchestra of vocal effects" (1–2).

An obvious parallel here is John Cage's prepared piano, used in his *Sonatas and Interludes* of 1946–48. In a manner similar to Chopin's prepared recorder, Cage intervenes into the structure of the piano, inserting screws, metal bolts, plastic spoons, and rubber bands so as to alter the sound of the instrument. It's this same transgression of normative function that situates Chopin's art within the wider issues of the politics of poetic form and the sociocultural domain of tactics (discussed in chapter 1).[32] In addition, we're made aware that the very concept of "technology" is incommensurate to its applications. The technosciences affect the arts in multiple ways with technologies that impoverish and ones that fecundate. In hyperspatial technology, especially, the hegemony of the digital and binary comes close to eradicating the simple fact that the cognitive is contexualized within actual human bodies. Chopin insists, "Poetry is the 'physical word' . . . the word that is simply movement. . . . Get rid of all those bits of paper, whole, torn, folded, or not. It is man's body that is poetry, and the streets" (quoted in McCaffery and Nichol 1978, 48).

In the light of Chopin's audiography, I want to emphasize a less obviously civic placement and add an important supplement to his Heraclitan poetics. His radical achievement is to have rescued the mouth's acoustic possibilities from anatomic limitations and resituated them in a technological, prosthetic synthesis. Chopin rejects not only all graphic rules and economies, those "vague tonal notations of sighs and groans" but also the several sonic limitations imposed upon the human mouth. More dangerous than the ideality of meaning are the procrustean restrictions of the phoneme and syllable. "The mouth," he reminds us, "is a discerning resonator, capable of offering several sounds simultaneously as long as these sounds are not restricted by the letter, the phoneme, or by a precise or specific word" (quoted in McCaffery and Nichol 1978, 48). Chopin effectively exposes a covert ideological issue within sound and orality itself. The stale binary of sound and writing is shown to be far from basal, for sound per se is the complex target for variant and oppositive appropriations. Beyond the sonic complexities of his pieces we are led into questioning the cultural construct-edness of the phoneme and syllable themselves, leading us to interrogate their status as linguistically positive phenomena.[33] Chopin is rarely brought into theoretical contestation with Olson, but I might initiate a step in that direction by announcing a poetic itinerary that moves not with "the HEAD, by way of the EAR, to the SYLLABLE / the HEART, by way of the BREATH to the LINE" but with "the CAVITIES, by way of the THROAT, to the SOUND / the BODY, by way of TECHNOLOGICAL EXTENSION to the STREETS." [34]

In the 1970s the body reemerges as both a conceptual and an actual pre-occupation in art and performance. Among its memorable examples might be cited the Dionysian enactments of Herman Nitsch, complete with drip-ping animal carcasses and blood-splattered stage; the self-mutilations of the Vienna Aktion group that culminated in Swartzkogler's phoney self-castration; the extreme physical submissions of Gina Pane or Chris Bur-den; and Linda Montano's self-application of acupuncture needles to her face in "Mitchell's Death." It was also the time of the antipsychiatric move-ment—Basaglia, Szasz, Guattari, the Psichiatria Democratica, the Sozial-istiches Patientenkollectiv, Laing's Kingsley Hall project, La Borde—and its attendant state suppressions (the notorious Heidelberg affair and the im-prisonment of Hubert and his wife on trumped-up charges; the harassment and subsequent trial of Guattari for suspected militancy and pornogra-phy).[35] The ambient theories of the times were to be found in *Anti-Oedipus, Libidinal Economy,* and *Revolution in Poetic Language,* each offering libidi-nal templates by which to reformulate a theory of the body as process, or becoming.[36] Out of this convulsive context appeared a species of collec-tive, improvised sound performance that might be dubbed "paleotechnic," its practitioners largely Canadian—*The Four Horsemen* (Rafael Barreto-Rivera, Paul Dutton, Steve McCaffery, and bp Nichol)—and British—*Konkrete Canticle* (Bob Cobbing, Paula Claire, and Bill Griffiths) as well as *Jgjgjgjg* (Cris Cheek, Clive Fencott, and Lawrence Upton).[37] Via such en-sembles, sound poetry reappears as a practice of outlay and dispossession. In Canada especially, there was a wholesale rejection of technological enhance-ment and manipulation of the voice.[38] Inspired neither by a purism nor a primitivism, a collective human group emerged highly conscious of the pressures from both its ambient cultural theories and radical psychopoli-tics—schizoculture—to rethink the body, poem, and community through formulations of assemblage, movement, and intensities.[39] Consciously developing (in part) from Tzara's famous dictum that "thought is made in the mouth," the paleotechnic sound poetry of the 1970s formed around two primary desires: to create a poetry of spontaneous affect predicated on a paradigm of unrepeatablity (this was the antitechnological component) and to reformulate the "poem" as a manifestation of unpremeditated and ephemeral collectivity.[40] Conceptually speaking, these vocal performances pushed ontology toward polis, addressing the accidental configuration of two intermeshed ensembles—performers and audience—as an urgent issue of community.

There is a Greek term—*hyponoia* (the underneath sense)—that aptly describes the telos of those performances. Absorbed from Marx and Freud— as a minimum—was a belief in the fundamental illusion of appearances. Beneath the envisaged performance of sonic outlay a loss of self was required in the region of spontaneous enactment. We might figure here a body-beyond-self as the negative presence operative in the paleotechnic sound poem. Breton had spoken earlier of his own desire to experience what lay beneath appearances as an uninterrupted quest (106). Conceived as a function of movement and evanescence, these collective spontaneities claimed the status of phonocentrism's heterological dimension and dynamic. Neither indexing nor supplementing stability, they functioned, through overdeterminations of rhythm and energy, as the conduit for a loss. Falling under the primary conceptual governance of expenditure rather than orality, voice in these occasions—no longer a guarantee of a conscious self—precipitates a maximum rupture in any signifying system.[41]

Replacing the traditional author is a complex machinic assemblage generating performances that take the form of pulsional escapes from meaning and being, their release effected by a community of "agent/poets" functioning as a complex interrelation of transistors. An assemblage (whose sadoerotic utilization is discussed in chapter 8) is to be understood as an "increase in the dimensions of a multiplicity that necessarily changes in nature as it expands its connections" (Deleuze and Guattari 1987, 8). The variant machinic assemblage is bifocal. "One side . . . faces the strata, which doubtless makes it a kind of organism, or signifying totality, or determination attributable to a subject; it also has a side facing a body without organs, which is continually dismantling the organism, causing asignifying particles or pure intensities to pass or circulate" (4). Rather than existing in opposition to the human organism, the machinic homologizes its very rhythms: the regular repetition of pulse and heartbeat is repeated in the regulated movements of cogs. And sight should not be lost of the intense corporeality of this machinic assemblage which I've insisted on calling a community. But can such assemblage be reconciled to a concept of community? As a community-in-process, yes, it can be constantly positioned in that double estrangement between a signifying social organic called "the group" and that group's self-diremption in a performed expenditure by numerous bodies in occasion—a performance "without organs."

In the distinction offered by romanticism between *ergon* and *energeia*, paleotechnic sound poetry, like its Ultralettriste precursor, sided unequivocally with the latter term of being-in-action, and the unqualified valorization of energy clearly links the paleotechnic sound performance to Olsonian notions of projective verse. With their depreciation of textuality and a stress upon high-energy emission, the sound improvisations of the 1970s entailed a forceful decanting—though not a rejection—of Olson's basic theories. The poem's source in both cases is physiological "down through the workings of [the poet's] throat to that place where breath comes from, where breath has its beginnings, where drama has to come from, where the coincidence is, all act springs" (Olson quoted in Cobbing and Mayer 1978, 24). In "The Gate and the Center," published in 1952 and coincidentally at the height of French prelinguism, Olson grants energy a cosmologic status: "The proposition is a simple one (and the more easily understood now that we have been shocked at what we did not know nature's energies capable of, generally): energy is larger than man, but therefore, if he taps it as it is in himself, his uses of himself are EXTENSIBLE in human directions & degree not recently granted" (1965, 22). But a substantive difference in application must be remarked. In Olson's biopoetics, the imperative project is to embed energy in a sonographism by means of precisely written placements of that energy within the imprinted syllable. The syllable is to Olson what onomatopoiea is to Marinetti: a threshold in biomaterial language where the paralinguistic enters graphic stability. The significant disagreement between the paleotechnic sound poem and Olson's projective verse thus centers on the issue of how and where that energy manifests. In retention and recall through the binding fixity of a printed text? Or in the anasemantic expenditure of performance?

The fundamental break from the prelinguism of the Ultralettristes made by this paleotechnic assertion is in rethinking the poem as a spontaneous community—what Pierre Mabille might term an *egregore*—that " 'collective psychic being' driven by a life of its own" (Breton 1993, 29). Its basal renunciation was the antisocial lyricism of individual composition, replete, in the case of the later Chopin and Dufrêne, with its technologically generated autoaffective nuncupations. The paleotechnic poem was conceived as a communal performance at its outset. Such improvisational activities, involving simultaneity and a resultant indeterminate textuality in its realization, are complicated when manifesting in a group context. Herbert Blau illuminates a crucial consequence of improvisation when insisting on "a critical gap between repression and pretense, the construction of an appearance and, more or less overdetermined, the appearance of indeterminacy" (1992, 4). Opening up the poem to such overdeterminations and indeterminacies of performed community was paleotechnicism's prime commitment.

I've described the intense corporeality of sound performance as a machinic assemblage of body and voice in the transmission and retransmission of asignifying, nonrepeatable energies, in a collectivity without preparation or forethought.[42] But is such a poetry of pure outlay even thinkable? Jean Barrot claims that "all activity is symbolic," creating simultaneously a product and a vision of the world (1987, 11). If symbolic impedimenta are unavoidable, then how do we assess this species of performance? Theorized through Bataille, the sound poem takes on the defining dynamic of inevitable vocal excess spilling over from a libidinal, phonorhythmic dispositif of evanescent expenditures and meaningless outlays. If it does achieve such a sovereign negativity, then the sound poem is truly deserving of the title of literature's *part maudite*—the heterological expulsion from the scriptural regime of Logos. But can voice ever escape a minimum signification? Barrot evidently thinks not, and if Durand's claim is true that "[t]here is no such thing as a neutral voice, a voice without desire, a voice that does not desire me"(1977, 103), then a poetry of pure expenditure really is unachievable and we can look back wistfully at these attempts at libidinal assemblage—these struggles to emancipate a praxis of voice from the presidential mandate to mean—and acknowledge their failure in legacy. The poem as exemplary community—ephemeral and symbolic—whose manifestation might take the place of the conventional poetry reading and its attendant ideology of appearance was sought after and was unattained.[43] A community was aimed at that would take existence paradoxically outside of language. Perhaps the closest theoretic formulation of such a group is Agamben's concept of the "Coming Community"—a community that lays no claims to identity or belonging in which "the coming being is whatever being" (1993, 1). So perhaps the final designation of all this work is anthropological rather than art-categorical; less failed genres or nongenres than the fate of material humanity in its technohistorical passage. Yet Derrida identifies chaos with an open mouth (1995a, 84), and, if by nothing else, the prelingual and paleotechnic sound poem serve philosophy by shattering its logocentric binary of speech and writing with the eruptive presence of their own third term—organic resonance: voice.

Do we write off the paleotechnic as yet another failed utopia in poetry? The precise realization of a body-in-process unavoidably involves an absolute decommissioning of the body politic—and a scream can never be a social contract. In his discussions of the differences between interjectional and propositional speech functions, Ernst Cassirer maintains propositional speech is unique to humans, configuring the world for us in permanent, stable forms "with fixed and constant qualities" (1979, 150). As an interjectional poesis, the sound poem renounces this unique attribute. Breaking with Cassirer's "Propositional Man"—at the historic moment Foucault proclaims the death of man—this hesitant poetics of negative presence faltered at its inability to specify the exact purpose of its energetic expulsion. Was the performance of expenditure merely recovered into that spectacular society Debord isolated and analyzed in 1967? Or can it be explained through the patinated rhetoric of the 1960s as an aftereffect of Ultralettrisme, whose dubious accomplishment was a failed radicality of the subject? From the plethora of statements available, I choose the following to exemplify the domestication of heterology into a community of hope: "If thought is really to find a basis in lived experience, it has to be free. The way to achieve this is to think *other* in terms of *the same*. As you make yourself, imagine another self who will make you one day in its turn. Such is my conception of spontaneity: the highest possible self-consciousness which is still inseparable from the self and the world" (Vaneighem 1983 150).

The extreme mission for poetry from Artaud to the performative enactments of the 1970s was neither expenditure nor spontaneity per se but rather the killing of speech in its capitalist, propositional embodiments. This death of speech—it should be qualified—entailed a theft of silence within sound. To paraphrase a thought of Valéry's that captures with beauty and accuracy the circularity of this mission, a scream escapes from pain. Out of this accident a poem is made, with an explanation round about it. In this context the scream acquires a role, a function. As was the case with Pascal's Thought: "I had a thought. I have forgotten it. In its place I write that I've forgotten it." [44]

11. Jackson Mac Low

Samsara in Lagado

Ezra Pound speaks of a selfless discourse with words "like the locust-shells, moved by no inner being" (1970, 26). A mischievous zoomorphic trope, no doubt, but an enticing phrase by which to introduce a historic shift in poetry from the endless interiority of a lyric self to the hesitant emergence of a postontological poetics. I will examine this in the next two chapters, here focusing on the "selfless" productions of Jackson Mac Low and in the final chapter moving on to the ethical implications in this practice—implications that unfold in the light of Levinas's philosophy. I devote this chapter solely to Mac Low in order to preserve my early political, preethical thinking on his work but offer it here as both an introduction and a supplement to the final chapter.

Mac Low's systematic-chance-generated compositions impress most perhaps in their consistent emergence out of a variety of austere programs that emphasize the traditionally negative or countervalues in writing: semic dissonance, grammatical transgression, the elimination of a conscious intention, the removal of the writer as a centered subject responsible for the texts it "writes," a suspension of the word's instrumental functions, and a provoked absence of the subject from the productive aspect of semantic agency. A profound ascesis entails by the very nature of his programs—an ascesis both challenging and unsettling to habitual modes of reading.

[S]uch poems are not vehicles merely of the vision of the individual poet but constructions or event-series which allow each reader or hearer to be visionary himself rather than the passive receiver of the poet's vision. Confronted by this kind of poem, the sympathetic reader or hearer (& the poet himself as he watches the product of his chance-operational actions appear) addresses his attention primarily to each word or series of words as it happens, without attempting consciously to find meanings beyond those obviously belonging to the words themselves. (Jackson Mac Low, quoted in Rothenberg and Quasha 1974, 372)

This is a far cry from Olson's sense of open verse ("the trochee's heave" and "revolution of the ear") whose *stance toward reality* (his words) takes the metaphysical status of the Subject uncritically and endorsing implicitly the essential, utilitarian, and instrumental value of writing.

Mac Low's first compositions by chance generation (the "5 biblical poems") date from late December 1954. He cites a catena of influences that include the *I Ching,* Gershom Scholem's *Major Trends in Jewish Mysticism,* the choreography of Merce Cunningham, and the music of John Cage, Morton Feldman, Earl Brown, and Christian Wolff (Mac Low 1986, xv–xvi). Mac Low himself has frequently stated his reasons for composing by systems derived from Zen Buddhist practice. In a 1974 interview with Barry Alpert he says:

> Zen, of course, which I studied academically with Dr. D. T. Suzuki, during the years he taught at Columbia (late fifties), and Kegon Buddhism, which he also taught, have both greatly influenced my art, both directly and through John Cage and his music. They taught me to look at each phenomenon (e.g., each sound, word, or word string) as being worthy of full attention, and thus of being presented in such a way as to elicit the full attention of spectators, auditors, or readers, quite aside from its "expressing" the thoughts, feelings, sensations, or volitions of the artist. Any phenomenon, we are taught when given full attention, can reveal its Buddha nature. Thereby we can be brought to realize that Samsara *is* Nirvana—that the continually changing "world of becoming" is, when seen correctly, ultimate reality itself. All types of Buddhism teach the ultimate illusoriness of the ego, and Kegon emphasizes the mutual interrelatedness of all things and sentient beings. Zen taught me both to try to minimize the expression of the ego during the act of composition and to let each word, etc., "speak for itself." Kegon taught me to make manifest the mutual interpenetration of beings, especially in performance works. (Mac Low 1975, 32)

Mac Low commented as early as 1962 on the Taoist principles behind his method:

> Underlying chance compositions are the Taoist ideal of Wu-Wei (non-action, letting the Way do it); the Buddhist conception of egolessness; the Zen Buddhist conception of the No-mind, the Way subsisting as unconscious Mind, below both the individual ("Freudian") unconscious and (if it exists) the collective ("Jungian") unconscious, and producing all phenomena, subjective and/or objective; the Zen Buddhist realization that Nirvana (enlightenment) and Samsara (the ordinary round of birth, life, death and rebirth), the universal and the individual, the subjective and the objective, are not two, and that close attention to any phenomenon or experience can lead to the abrupt realisation of this not-twoness; the Kegon Buddhist realisation that all individuals unobstructedly interpenetrate and are interpenetrated by each other and the whole; and the I Ching's assumption of the significance underlying or embodied in any simultaneously occurring events (1962, 71).

In a subsequent response to questions posed by Charles Bernstein, Mac Low outlines the compositional benefits of these Zen principles:

> Yes the Zen Buddhist motive for use of chance (&c) means was to be able to generate a series of "dharmas" (phenomena/ events, e.g., sounds, words, colored shapes) relatively "uncontaminated" by the composer's "ego" (taste, constitutional predilections, opinions, current or chronic emotions) (1984, 26).[1]

One purpose of this short chapter is to expand the aforementioned line of influence into a more complex genealogy and show that Mac Low's "dharmas" need not be channeled into nonoccidental influences and practices (Zen or the cabala) but can be understood as a critical manifestation of Western writing's "other side": Bataille's *part maudite* with its links more to indifference, indeterminacy, and outlay than to the logic of instrumental accumulation that would harness writing to a use inside intention.

Let me take as a point of departure Gulliver's visit to the Grand Academy of Lagado. Entering that part of the institution devoted to speculative learning, Swift describes a machine designed "for improving speculative knowledge by practical and mechanical operations":

> It was twenty foot square, placed in the middle of the room. The superficies was composed of several bits of wood, about the bigness of a die, but

some larger than others. They were all linked together by slender wires. These bits of wood were covered on every square with paper pasted on them, and on these papers were written all the words of their language, in their several moods, tenses, and declensions, but without any order. The professor then desired me to observe, for he was going to set his engine at work. The pupils at his command took each of them hold of an iron handle, whereof there were forty fixed round the edges of the frame, and giving them a sudden turn, the whole disposition of the words were entirely changed. He then commanded six and thirty of the lads to read the several lines softly as they appeared upon the frame; and where they found three or four words together that might make part of a sentence, they dictated to the four remaining boys who were scribes. This work was repeated three or four times, and at every turn the engine was so contrived that the words shifted into new places, as the square bits of wood moved upside down.

Six hours a day the young students were employed in this labour, and the professor showed me several volumes in large folio already collected, of broken sentences, which he intended to piece together, and out of those rich materials to give the world a complete body of all arts and sciences. (Swift 1933, 218)

In *Spectator* 63 for Saturday, May 12, 1711, Addison cites numerous "performances" of false wit in his description of the Temple of Dullness:

The temple was filled with votaries, who applied themselves to different versions, as their fancies directed them. In one part of it I saw a regiment of anagrams, who were continually in motion, turning to the right or to the left, facing about, doubling their ranks, shifting their stations, and throwing themselves into all the figures and counter-marches of the most changeable and perplexed exercise. Not far from these was the body of acrostics, made up of very disproportioned persons. It was disposed into three columns. The officers were all of them at least six feet high, and made three rows of very proper men; but the common soldiers, who filled up the spaces between the officers, were such dwarfs, cripples, and scarecrows, that one could hardly look upon them without laughing. (1789, 1:369–70)

One should not be surprised by these uncanny anticipations of Mac Low's systematic-chance writings and such poem-performance-events as *The Pronouns*. The eighteenth century had long been aware of the possibilities of "objective" or "mechanical" composition through Addison's delineation of "false wit":

> As true wit generally consists in this resemblance and congruity of ideas, false wit chiefly consists in the resemblance and congruity sometimes of single letters, as in anagrams, chronograms, lipograms, and acrostics: sometimes by syllables, as in echoes and doggerel rhymes: sometimes of words, as in puns and quibbles, and sometimes of whole sentences or poems, cast into the figures of eggs, axes, or altars. (Addison 1789, 1:360)

The "truthful" version of wit—at least since Locke—had been an egocentric institution with its cognitive roots in the intellect. False wit, by contrast, is a comparatively egoless mechanical operation upon the material bodies and components of signs. In the majority of Mac Low's work, one can detect the operation of a kind of writing machine that opens up scriptive practice—through the infratextual and combinatory nature of words—to the question of its own potentially infinite semiosis.

If Swift's writing machine shows logical discourse to be derivative from a nondiscursive aleatoric system, and scientific truth fabricated as a by-product of Addisonian false wit, then Mac Low's own mechanical operation proposes a writing machine that violently displaces the very notion of *literature* from a creation to an indifferent production. In both Swift's and Mac Low's models there is a radical questioning of the position of the subject in a language considered to be sovereign and external. No longer present to the productive moment of meaning, the subject situates as a witness to—and experiencer of—a particular outcome of method. The economy thus established is dialogic, intertextual, and parasitic in exchanges; its historic moment is specifically the passing of writing from creation to production—a shift entailing a radical detachment of writing from its traditional involvement with unitary meanings and the realignment of the significatory space within a kind of theater of linguistic event predicated upon semantic provisionality, destiny, and dispensibility.

Mac Low's contestation of the normative notion of writing, as an originary production, offers expanded possibilities to the writer as a subject-beyond-expression. The writing orchestrates two divergent orders of meaning, one a conventionally articulated semantic order declaring itself through a syntactic chain of discrete, detectable units, and the other a saturated, cryptonymic meaning, transphenomenal in nature, and hidden as a latent signification within other word configurations—errant, evasive, and resistant to an *immediately* legible appropriation. This second order of meaning finds release through the implementation of specific reading-writing procedures that disengage language from its utilitarian mandates and writing from intentionalist imperatives. Here is Mac Low's own description of the systematic-chance method used to generate the *asymmetries,* which form a substantial part of his *Stanzas for Iris Lezak:* "The 'Asymmetry' method produces poems that are, in a sense, 'self-generating.' Beginning with the first or a chance-designated subsequent word in a source text, the first line of such a poem spells out this word; the second line spells out the second word of the first line; the third line, the third word, & so on" (1971, 409). Striking in this description is the way textual production gets grounded in a problematics of repetition. The asymmetries, in fact, approximate a *translational* procedure, an activity between texts endorsing language as both a sedimentary and a cryptic system. Through chance operations, verbal arrangements emerge that were present but eluded manifestation in their source texts. The *asymmetries* in this way are a highly selective reading of a preexistent writing comparable to collage, which, too, develops a potential to recycling and citation. Mac Low's insight—and in this he is remarkably similar to Wittgenstein—is that to shift a word from one set of surroundings necessarily provokes a change in verbal function in response to variations in the new context. This marks a radical departure from the textural use of quotation in Pound, Olson, and Ronald Johnson. Indeed, Mac Low's writing is singular not so much in staging as in destroying the difference of the discursive forms it annexes.

The systematic-chance methods are in themselves extremely versatile and varied, but all involve a common strategy of an intervention that interrupts the settled status of a source writing.[2] *Stanzas for Iris Lezak,* through all its diversities, implements a draw-off mechanism whose operation is predicated upon a parasitical logic and economy—a one-way movement that extracts nonreciprocally from a "host" text a *new* poem, disturbing profoundly the historical relation of writing to the logic of exchange and its equilibrium. Poems—as Mac Low's "false wit systems" generate them—are no longer transits of reference and representation but nondiscursive seepages or extractions:

> Law I knew every
> As
> Mighty as pouring
> Thing how every
> As ran crated as not as

Only forth
Thing how every
Unutterable not I vividness every ran saw every
Law as yearning
But as ran every
But every forth only ran every
Mighty every

(Mac Low 1980, 81)

Although the above passage is linear, the lines themselves are disengaged from any sequential or recognizable logic and exist to demonstrate—as events of spectacular repetition—a rule-governed production that is at once rational and paralogical. Mac Low uses an acrostic system to generate a non-discursive poem of extreme cognitive dissonance. Dispersing a prior unity (viz. the source text) into a seemingly stochastic fallout, the poem in actuality demonstrates the workings of a certain rule. An important yet often overlooked implication in Mac Low's programmatic writing is that rule is relativized by rule. The one rule that would command a transparent writing of semantic utility and transport gets interrupted by the legislation of a different rule, requiring the sacrifice of propositional meaning and instrumental functions to the dictates of a patterned and paralogical production. This dialogic aspect is crucial to Mac Low's project; it is what commits his writing to economy rather than aesthetics and what makes reading Mac Low a political as well as a literal act.

The following passage is typical of Mac Low's programmatic substitution of a patterned production for the augmentive, syllogistic ordering of grammatical meaning:

The O
the have explore,
priests of pocket. Earth

through have explore,
of
themselves. Has evil:
have are very earth
exterior

(1971, 341)

The concept of "poem" here functions as the scene for an encounter between two adversarial drives: (1) a receding, logical one, spectral in the above (as in most others in the book) that orders a linear stanzaic disposition of meaning, and (2) a paralogical drive within the rule determinants of the letter patterns, that settles meaning in highly local, self-referential *events*. This encounter produces a fissure in the logical ground on which grammatical meaning rests and calls attention to the localized effects of meanings emerging from relations fixed within the material bases of the signs. Touch, not sight is the dominant sensory modality—the reader experiences a "feel for" rather than an "understanding of" these poems. Writing like the above comes close to being an experience *in* language rather than a representation *through* it. Grammar, like perspective in painting, organizes language toward a vanishing point in the punctum of the "message" where local meanings aggregate to advance a total meaning outside of the poem. Mac Low's words, however, operate nongrammatically as competitive contiguities, maintaining a constantly circulating surface and a structured decentering of meaning. The language isn't directed to a point beyond itself and—free of the presidential logic of the referent—the words free-float in an undetermined code.

Admittedly, the use of systematic-chance procedures in part reduces the contingent manifestations to a subsidiary aspect of the rule's operation. Procedural method functions simultaneously as the occasion for and the restriction upon sign difference. Mac Low's use of programmatic methods approximates the application of a transcendental rule—like Deleuze and Guattari's definition of the state—that governs the dispersal of fragments, functioning as an ideal predetermination of sequence and settling temporality inside the writing it generates while remaining itself atemporal. Yet equally, the procedure provides the occasion for these contingencies to emerge and, though the texts must be considered the formulations of rule-governed modes of production, the significance of the textural "events" as the rule generates them should not be reduced to the mere instance of a law. Here, as in so many other issues that Mac Low's writing raises, we face a crucial impasse of contradictory forces, both a fission and a fusion. The asymmetry is of a radically double order—both a mode of production and of deletion, both a distributive force and a force of containment. And if the implied transcendental status of the method throws serious doubt on Mac Low's writings as deconstructive texts and further questions their depth as politicolinguistic critiques, the profound relativization of the forces with the resulting ambivalence between contingency and indeterminacy, on the one hand, and rule determination and patterned inevitability, on the other, does provoke a powerful dynamic guaranteeing the texts their dialogic character.³

Mac Low explains in great detail the mechanics of his methods in accompanying statements to the poems, seeing the methods themselves akin to concept art:

> [T]he methods by which they [the poems] were made are often the basic art works—the making of the processes is itself a kind of concept art action. The *methods* are what come by inspiration—like the first line of a lyric that leads to all the rest. The actual poems aren't *secondary,* but they certainly follow. . . . So the poem's first actualization might be the method; the second actualization, the particular poem; the third would be the performances, if any, including those by people reading privately. . . . So you get a whole series of potentiality-actuality situations. (1975, 14)

This not only sentences the poems to be empirical realizations of the method but effectively prohibits their fetishization as formal objects or commodities. We can always relate to the opacity of the effect and measure it against the utter transparency of its mechanical inducement. At the same time, Mac Low's notion of a multiple actualization and consequent dispersal of the poem between object and program—and hence a radical nonsiting of the writing—unsettles authorial stability. The methods are potentially reiterative, with the actualized texts themselves available as source texts for further stochastic intervention. What is the creative status of a reader who adopts one of Mac Low's rule procedures to generate her own text? Mac Low's own comments on this are not entirely satisfactory: "[O]nce the method is formulated—*written down,* . . . anyone could use it to make another realization of the method. People do this from time to time—use my methods on materials they choose—and it's always a question, then, whether the new matter they use makes the poem more 'theirs' than 'mine'" (1975, 14).

As I indicated earlier, there are suggestions that Mac Low regards the poem as a sign construction offered for a reader's free usage: "such poems are not vehicles merely of the vision of the individual poet but constructions or event-series which allow each reader or hearer to be visionary himself rather than the passive receiver of the poet's vision." The implications of Mac Low's direct assault on both egocentric and primary creation are clearly far-reaching and constitute one of the major extra-aesthetic issues of his work as social fact. But the mechanical operations have far-reaching implications beyond originary proprietorship. Systematic-chance generation is an *economic* reworking of writing that makes manifest a force within the written which undermines the very notion of a *settled* meaning. Moreover, the dialogic nature of this writing opens up the critical viewpoint *from the other text*. Recall that Mac Low's writings are produced only at the expense of *the loss of another text*. The chance programs are as much a way of losing writing as of gaining it and entail that economy of loss and suppression inscribed within the mechanism of all translational procedures. Petitioning less an exchange than a parasitic appropriation, the poems situate close to potlatch: that programmatic destruction, fragmentation, and dispersal of an existent semantic wealth.[4]

This sacrificial dimension should be specified as follows: a production through mechanical operation of word-events out of a violated discursive fabric. Isn't this the opposition of the instant to history? Mac Low brings us to the conclusion that writing's interior is neither ideal nor essential but rather the temporal unwindings of anterior, preexistent sites, the complications of their interstices and the suppressed patterns of those combinants and surfaces that connect writing to power, economy, and game. The texts are not simply self-referential events, as a formalist reading might uphold, but relate to an *impossible* deployment of energy within writing. They open onto the necessary loss of several layers of possible meaning, both intertextual (the loss of a source text) and infrastructural (the inevitable sacrifice of alternative—yet equally possible—phonetic combinations).

Saussure is generally recognized as the founder of modern linguistics, but his most controversial (and least understood) work is his extensive research into late Saturnian verse—research of high pertinence to Jackson Mac Low's own mechanical operations. The Swiss linguist compiled 139 notebooks on anagrammatic and other patterned embeds in Saturnian verse, Lucretius, Homer, Virgil, Seneca, Horace, Angelo Politian, and the Vedic Hymns. He detects in all these works a persistently recurring group of phonemes that combined to form echoes of important words. In the *De rerum natura* of Lucretius, Saussure found extended multiple anagrams of the name APHRODITE. Implicit in this research is the curious nonphenomenal status of the paragram, that virtuality of any letter or phoneme to form semantic aggregates inaccessible to normal habits of readings.[5] As discussed in chapters 1 and 2, it's the unavoidable presence of the paragram—as a protosemantic force in all writing—that contaminates the notion of an ideal, unitary meaning and thereby counters the supposition that words can fix or stabilize in closure. Stanley Cavell's version of the paragram is the "word imp" recurrently combinative and in the condition of "words, living lives of their own, staring back at us, calling upon one another, giving us away, alarming—because to note them is to see that they live in front of our eyes, within earshot, at every moment" (1988, 122–25).

Mac Low exploits the paragrammic word imp in such generative methods as the asymmetry and diastic, both of which are variants on the acrostic (itself paragrammic and cited in Addison's enumeration of false wit) that make manifest a latent, embedded sequence of letters not immediately apparent in a reading of the source text.[6] The writing in this way links to a reading in which the former serves to elucidate what's concealed but already there in the normal syntactic deployment of words. The asymmetry and diastic, as stanzaic-acrostic forms, are also the contexts of a reading redoubled through a writing. The texts are secretions from a prior text and become available to reading only when passed back through a further act of writing. In this way each poem appears as a *suppressed tendency* within another text coming into being as a kind of negentropic "recovery" of certain acrostic readings lost and hidden in the anagrammic randomness of the source writing. Mac Low's actualized texts are written-readings that drive the source text inside—and thus beyond—an aspect of itself in order to elevate a different formation. It's as if the words, as dissipative structures, insist on their own right to pursue a different necessity. Paragrammic programs necessarily manufacture bifurcation points within semantic economies, engendering meanings but at the same time turning unitary meaning against itself.

The path of the paragram is one determined by the local indications of a word's own spatiophonic connotations that produce a centrifuge in which the verbal center is scattered. Paragrams are the flow-producing agents within Mac Low's chance methods that inscribe themselves among the induced losses of a different text. I've already noted the dialogic nature of the compositions and insisted in chapter 1 on the paragram's status as a fundamental disposition in all combinatory systems of writing. They are paraverbal lines of flight inside of all discursive frameworks, guaranteeing to any alphabetic assemblage a transphenomenal character and further committing writing to an unavoidable surplus of unrecoverable meanings.[7]

Paragrams propose the paradox of an unpresentability that serves as a necessary condition of writing's capacity to present. Although assignable to a certain order of production, value, and meaning, the paragram does not derive necessarily from an intentionality and is an inevitable consequence of Western writing's alphabetic combinatory nature. Emerging from the multiple ruptures that alphabetic components bring to virtuality, paragrammic meaning takes on a critical, constitutional nonpresence as an intransigent expenditure. Not necessarily a latent content or hidden intention, the paragram is a subproductive sliding and slippage of meaning between the forces and intensities distributed throughout a text's syntactic entirety. It thus ensures a constant superfluity of signifiers, an unavoidable presence of words within words, a necessary waste and nonrecovery of meaning.

Saussure himself remained disturbed by his discoveries. In 1908 he writes to his pupil Leopold Gautier, "I make no secret of the fact that I myself am perplexed—about the most important point: that is, how one should judge the reality or phantasmagoria of the whole question" (in Starobinski 1979, 105–6). In other words, does this persistence of paragrams indicate a conscious creation, or could it be simply a retrospective "creation" evoked and projected by a reader? Saussure's intellectual is precisely Mac Low's mechanical dilemma, for if we admit that the paragram can be both fortuitous and intentional, a conscious creation and a transphenomenal infraproduction, then we must further admit to the infinite resourcefulness of language to produce itself aimlessly and to fulfill all of the features Bataille demands of a general economy: unmasterable excess, inevitable expenditure and escape, and a thoroughly nonutilitarian outlay. (Ultimately we return this way to logophilia, to Bentley, Brisset, Roussel, and general protosemantic delirium.)

Beyond the local appreciation of Mac Low's poems are the intertextual and transphenomenal implications that the entire systematic-chance method of composition carries—dilating the aleatoric programs into a methodological force propelling writing beyond its object-specific forms into a gesture of excess. Mac Low shows that there can be no true separation of language from the implications of its products and that any writing availing itself of an alphabetic combinatory system is problematized, contaminated at source by its self-proliferating tendencies. This, too, is a decidedly social act showing that texts, like the self, are never unitary messages but always overdetermined by their own positional illogicalities. Mac Low chooses as the compositional base of his work the locus of writing's productional contradictions—where meaning is both produced and lost through and beyond the sieve of its "ordering" subject. The asymmetries and diastics are essentially self-generative language events and their lasting potential is to elude all productive finality. Constituting a semantic margin where the system of meaning overflows the limits prescribed by any self-identical, intentional subject, they invalidate any purposeful boundaries that would struggle to determine where meaning in writing begins and where it ends.[8]

How, then, does one read Mac Low? As a critique of instrumentality, his writing necessarily involves a significant revision in the reader function. There is initially the disappearance of both writer and reader, to be replaced by a witness as a model subject of the text straddling both of the old categories and affirming the nonintentionality of the sign experience. Mac Low presents to his reader an opaque condition of writing in which the normative transmission theory of communication is forcibly repudiated. Transmission theory—exemplified, for instance, in the early writings of Roman Jakobson—grounds all communication in an ideological schema of need and exchange. According to this theory, communication consists of the shunting of a message from a source to a receptor across a space. The context of this communication Jakobson proposes is an exchange between producers and consumers, speakers and listeners, writers and readers. Hypostasizing both a subject and an object, the theory fixes both as isolated terms in an abstract formula. In that way a circular system of power is generated by a copula of need. The need is not a biological need but a masked social formation connecting subject and object terms for the preservation of the abstract structure. The ideological model this supports is that of an "informationally desirous" subject entering into the textual model with an anterior need to communicate, or be communicated to. In actuality, this need is *not* anterior to the specific act but inherent in the very structure of the communication as presented. Exchange in this way discloses itself as a structure in which each operating term is defined by the other (Hegel's master-slave relation). The link between this schema and the consumer nature of readership needs no comment.

As previously noted, the works Mac Low proposes through systematic-chance generation do not produce a message according to a logic of exchange. Offering themselves first and foremost as graphic entities—"events" —they command the textual space as a patterned system resistant to idealist transmission. Replacing the transmitting subject is a mechanical operation whose resultant texts are highly patterned yet disjunctive:

> Burroughs until regularly. Rest under grab he since
> used next to in legend.
> Realized existed give under *Lunch,* you
> remains eating Stein the
> orgone flights

until 1955–56 down existed rigorous
garden room. Another brewed.
Have emotional
sheet it night catch eating

unhappy. Sit endless drink
1953, each.

(Mac Low 1971, 340)

The systematic exclusion of a subject promotes an extremely paratactic text, and the harsh juxtaposition of independent meanings results in a poem that escapes the finality of logical value. Regardless of the systematic nature of its generation, the poem frees up words to dispose themselves as "real events" to which a reader is free to bring an autonomous attitude. A coherent, integrated message is absent, encouraging readers to enter the poem as a productive engagement with extremely local operations. A global meaning no longer looms as a promised treat at the conclusion of a reading, yet the poem returns a use-value by offering itself to a reader as unexchangeable and outside the logic of the commodity. Not since Gertrude Stein has the *event* of reading been such a primary issue. Replacing the notion of the recipient-reader is that of the reader in heuristic engagement with language as a first order and trenchantly unmimetic experience. Words function — or dissipate — as material, sensible signs offering an immanent experience *in* language.

Abraham Cowley in the seventeenth century evinces a prescient awareness of the productive potential within the reader function. In a footnote to his *Pindaric Ode on the Thirty-Fourth Chapter of Isaiah,* Cowley makes the significant distinction between an *enthymemic* and a *syllogistic* disposition within the reception of a verbal message:

> The manner of the *Prophets* writing, especially *Isaiah,* seems to me very like that of *Pindar;* they pass from one thing to another with almost *Invisible* connexions, and are full of words and expressions of the highest and boldest flights of *poetry* . . . in the text there be no transitions from the *subject* to the *similitude;* for the old fashion of writing, was like *Disputing in Enthymemes,* where half is left out to be supplied by the Hearer: ours is like Syllogisms, where all that is meant is exprest. (1684, 50)

In Cowley's "old fashion of writing" — as in Mac Low's asymmetries — meaning is never a received plenitude but completed from an initial lack by the reader's addition of an absent term. The alternative to such readerly semantic production would be a more radical engagement with the text's sovereign externality. A reader might admit that these texts *are unreadable* and resist entirely the semantic exchange. Reading in this case might consist in a symbolic affirmation of the writing's nihilistic implications, especially its loss of both reader and writer before the paralogics of the machine within sign effects that cannot be consumed, comprehended, or dismissed. If the latter promises the *jouissance* of loss and expenditure rather than the pleasure of retentive accumulation, then Mac Low offers his readers the rich alternative of a three-dimensional enactment. In this third possibility, it's not speech that's installed within the writing as that which the written supplements or figures, but rather performance that becomes available as a derived operation of the communal (or multiple) subject upon grids of simultaneity and polyvalent reading paths, lines of flight that break down the dominance of a single, panoptic reading.

Mac Low is singular among contemporary writers in providing precise details and instructions for the live realization of his texts. One example should suffice:

> Asymmetries may be performed either by a single person or by a group including any number of people. Each performer follows either a Basic Method or one of nine other performance methods, while realizing successively each Asymmetry in a randomly selected or individually chosen series of poems. The individual performers decide their own reading speeds and other performance parameters not specifically (or only partially) regulated by the methods followed. All individuals perform simultaneously. Performers must become acutely conscious of both the sounds they themselves are producing and those rising from other performers, the audience, and/or the environment. . . . What is asked for is concentrated attention to all sound perceptible to the individual and an attitude of receptivity and responsiveness such that "choices" are made spontaneously, often seeming to arise from the whole. Schematically, this "whole" can be represented by concentric spheres: the inmost is that of the individual performer; next, that of the whole performance group; next, that of the larger social group including audience as well as performers; next, that of the performance space, including room acoustics, electronics, etc.; and finally, the larger spaces within which the performance space is situated: the rest of the building, the surrounding streets, neighbourhood, city (or rural area), etc., all of which may affect signifi-

cantly the aggregate of sounds heard by each individual at each moment. The spheres are best conceived as transparent and interpenetrating—not static sheets but concentric ripples travelling simultaneously out from and in toward each center (1980, xii–iv).

Mac Low continues to enumerate nine other methods for performance: words only, silence only, words, tones, and silences, one and one only, tones and silence, words and tones, spoken and whispered words, phonic prolongations and repetitions, and finally, words and indeterminate silences. The emphasis on the relativizing of the individual (sound or subject) by mutual interpenetration reflects the influence on Mac Low of Kegon Buddhist beliefs, but it also stands favorable comparison with Bakhtin's notion of heteroglossia and the relational nature of essence, as well as finding sympathetic, if distant, echoes in Saussure's belief in the differential, oppositive nature of meaning. Importantly Mac Low's simultaneities don't legitimate a Dadaist anarchy. The model performer proposed is a variant of Mac Low's "witness"—a sensitive, social subject whose spontaneity is regulated by a responsive sense of high contextual awareness. In Mac Low's performances there is no logocentric subject. Even in a solo performance the individual is constrained to the awareness of the interplay of ambient sounds and spaces. Replacing the single focus of reading is a complex network of actiants, contingent in their interfaces. A persistent paradox, however—and one Mac Low finds difficult to resolve—is that the open nature of the simultaneities are predicated upon a foreclosed and elaborately predetermined performer. In a seeming contradiction, Mac Low proposes not only the unbinding of signs and referents from the forced consecutivity of conventional reading but also a closed model of the performer, predefined by the performative dispositions he is commanded to adopt.

This irresolution in the implications raised by Mac Low's systematic-chance methods can't be ignored. Though comprising a heretical model, their "liberation" of both meaning and reading is seriously limited by these contradictory pulls. Ultimately Mac Low's writing admits there can be no clear opposition by which to stage the intractable relations of power to writing. Mac Low himself has frequently argued an analogical relationship of his work to political anarchy:

An "anarchist" does not believe, as some wrongly have put it, in social chaos. He believes in a state of society wherein there is no frozen power structure, where all persons may make significant initiatory choices in regard to matters affecting their own lives. . . . How better to embody such ideas in microcosm than to create works wherein both human beings & their environments & the world "in general" . . . are all able to act within the general framework & set of "rules" given by the poet "the maker of plots or fables" as Aristotle insists—the poet is preeminently the maker of the plot, the framework—not necessarily of everything that takes place within that framework! (Quoted in Leary and Kelly 1965, 540)

After all of his significant cultural emancipation, Mac Low is left with one residual parasite: value. It may be a fitting irony to leave the final word on Jackson Mac Low to Aristotle. From anarchy to the Stagirite? Isn't that the patent drift in a suppressed genealogical passage describing the maker of plot reappearing as the maker of rules? But even comparison is contaminated by its own typographical contours, and analogy itself is far from a pure operation. The linguistic analogy to a political potential or state? Perhaps. But bear in mind that analogy is a continuous operation presupposing a continuity from one term to another by symmetrical or proportional means and across an unquestioned base. Analogy—in the final assessment—suppresses the heterogeneous, and it's to Mac Low's lasting value that he preserves heterogeneity by including a built-in critique of his models.

true as only fiction can be.

—Emmanuel Levinas

Ethics and aesthetics are one and the same.

—Ludwig Wittgenstein

As long as God exists, I am not alone. And couldn't the other suffer the fate of God? It strikes me that it was out of the terror of this possibility that Luther promoted the individual human voice in the religious life. I wish to understand how the other now bears the weight of God, shows me that I am not alone in the universe. This requires understanding the philosophical problem of the other as the trace or scar of the departure of God.

—Stanley Cavell

12. The Scandal of Sincerity

Toward a Levinasian Poetics

Levinas's Ethics

Commenting on the language of Chateaubriand, Barthes claims "it is language, as Kierkegaard saw, which, being the general, represents the category of the ethical, since to be absolutely individual, Abraham doing sacrifice must renounce language; he is condemned not to speak. The modern writer is and is not Abraham: he must at once be outside the ethical and within language; he must create the general with the irreducible, re-discover the amorality of his existence through the moral generality of language: it is this *hazardous* passage which is literature" (1980, 53). Let me dispute Barthes here and propose that the issue for today's writer is not to position herself outside the ethical but to negotiate, after Levinas, ethics' inescapability and to construct an answer to an urgent question. What constitutes an ethical poetics within the ontological adventure? Is such a poetics possible required, as it will be, to negotiate two vastly different theories of signification and the problematic articulation of the transcendental onto the practical?[1]

The lasting achievement of Levinas is to have fundamentally dislocated the philosophical centering of Being, replacing ontology by an ethics of radical alterity. Yet his work does not offer a practical ethics, but rather a heuristic scrutiny of the meaning of ethics. As such, any attempts to apply it to the theoretical discourse of poetry runs the risk of procrustean formulations, if not blatant misinflections and lacunae.[2] Levinas tells us that to write and to read is already to have entered into the ethical. But in what way if not practical? Miller's neo-Kantian ethics of reading (1987) proves inadequate, as Simon Critchley's luminous critique makes clear (1992). In addition, Gerald Bruns's Levinasian reading of John Cage's writing is partial at best (Bruns 1994). Critchley offers what to my mind are the necessary articulations of Levinas's singular ethics onto poetical economies: "How is the ethical relation to the other person to be inscribed in a book without betraying it immeasurably? How does the ethical relation to the Other enter into the textual economy of betrayal? And how is that text to be read so as to preserve its ethical Saying?" (1992, 48)[3] My own proposal is two virtual highways into a conjectural "Levinasian" poetics. One extends by way of an exploration of the transcendental ethical relation as it announces itself in the Same's encounter with the primordial alterity Levinas terms the Face. The other highway passes through consideration of Levinas's later thinking concerning the relation of the Saying to the Said—an interlacement of thinking and analysis fully developed in *Otherwise than Being*. I will attempt to address the feasibility of such a poetic from three distinct but related foci: writer, reader, and text, conjecturing in turn a writerly, readerly, and textual ethics. The questions inaugurating this departure will be three necessary interrogations of constitution and conditions: what is required of a writing to be ethical? what comprises the ethics of reading? and what constitutes the ethics of a text? But let me start with a succinct overview of Levinas's achievement and of the challenges his thinking makes to conceptions of poetics.

Consonant with trends in modern Jewish philosophy (in the thinking of Hermann Cohen, Martin Buber, and Franz Rosenzweig, especially), Levinas focuses on the paramount need for individual responsibility for the other person and on that other's unique status as a separate, nonassimilable selfhood. The Other is an event outside of being, which determines subjectivity offering a theory of the latter as "the other in the same" (OB 111). The foundational experience is the encounter with the other through which an "I" becomes myself in responsibility and care for what is not me. Such individuality is grounded in responsibility taken by a self for an other: "The tie with the Other is knotted only as responsibility" (EI 97). Like the relation to death, responsibility for the other is intrinsically singular, yet my burden, though falling to me, is not initiated by a subject but is "always already" established. Responsibility is always rooted in a past. The road to the "self" (if indeed a self can still be conceived) is through the other who exists as a radical, foundational alterity before the emergence of any I. The I gains definition—even generation—through this pure fact of the Other. Levinas effectively reverses the egocentric bias in Husserlian and Heideggerian phenomenology, substituting alterity for ego as the emanating, central concept. Rejecting the familiar philosophemes of choice, will, and action, Levinas proposes a nonpractical transcendental ethics, an ethics "for nothing" and without pretense of founding a morality. The purpose of this ethics is precisely to shatter autarky and put consciousness into question, and as such is rather an ethics of ethics, an inquiry into the meaning of ethics—an ethicity or ultraethics.

Levinasian ethics does not happen to a self. Indeed, his ethical relation is nontotalizable and irreducibly singular. The reciprocity of obligation (the Other as the Same to the Same as Other) is a secondary consideration to the primordial ethical stance of a unilateral encounter of face to face and the reception of a univocity without return. Moreover, the relation of Same and Other is understood as a formal correlation, not the result of actual encounter. It marks a historic break from participation and immediacy—a break from philosophy itself toward the ethical. In Husserlian and Heideggerian thinking, Emerson's dream of "the central man" is solidly entrenched within the project of philosophy, its entire discourse and protensions constituted around a self-sameness considered fundamental. Levinas argues for ethics nothing less than a protophilosophic status. Prior to all categories and actions of an ego and prior to all knowing is an ethical relation to an Other. In repudiating a practical ethics, however, Levinas positivizes the very fact of ethics' impossibility. We commence from impossibility, and this impossibility is what renders the face legible.

Levinas defines the ethical in a brief footnote in "Language and Proximity": "We call ethical a relationship between terms such as are united neither by a synthesis of the understanding nor by a relationship between subject and object, and yet where one weighs or concerns or is meaningful to the other, where they are bound by a plot which knowing can neither exhaust nor unravel" (CPP 116 fn.6). This definition establishes immediately an important proscription for poetics. The relation of reader to text cannot be construed as the relationship of a subject to an object. The poem, understood as one sense of the ontological plot Levinas describes, must convolve both writer and reader in a tangle beyond the potency of an epistemic unwinding.

It is through the face that the Other finds expression. Indeed, the face is a passport to ethicity, for it is as the face that the Other calls to me as protosemantic expression, first discourse and, as a concrete figure of alterity, both a visitation and a transcendence (TO 359).[4] The face is not another name for personality but rather the latter's combined externalization and reception in its "original frankness" (PN 95). Repudiating a clandestine relation, the face appears "in the full light of the public order" (TI 212). Registering as an imperative affect, its encounter precipitates a "pacific opposition." Naked and nonthematizable, it further registers an "essential poverty" (EI 86) and the expression of a need.[5] The face, too, is a temporal disjunction, being "the point at which an epiphany becomes a proximity" (CPP 121).[6] Jill Robbins emphasizes the plastic force of the facial encounter, the face's overflow that comprises "a shaking up of the mundane, a collision between two orders" (1995, 175). The face has the verbal force of a coming toward me whose effect is vocative, interpellative, and commanding.[7]

Derrida calls this primary alterity, which ruptures consciousness and fractures selfhood in the encounter with the face, the "unthinkable truth of living experience" and which remains uncontainable by philosophic discourse (1978, 90). More so, this experience of the other-as-face undermines the foundations of any formal logical categories. In its sovereign otherness, the face is both close and distant, present and nonpresent in what Derrida teasingly terms "a certain absence" (1978, 91) and which Levinas calls enigma.[8] The latter entails both appearance and nonappearance. Never entering into relationship, it installs a radical precessionality or dysrelationship—like "an echo preceding the sound of a voice" (PN 7) or "a history whose conclusion precedes its development" (NTR 45).[9] As enigma, the face is also a trace in its singular Levinasian reverberations. In its usual sense, "trace" refers to residual phenomena arranged in an order in the world (and such would be the ordinary sense of the text as a remnant of its writer's presence). In this ordinary reception, the trace is the mark of an absence previously present. Like the print of Empedocles' sandal at the rim of Aetna, it is a derivative presence in our world. By contrast, the Levinasian trace is not an empirical sign of absence in this manner—it is not a fading but itself a form of absence already inscribed in the present in such a way as to obscure its presence. Occurring outside the categories of being and phenomenology, it is a presence of what has never been there (TO 358), like the hand of the man "who left traces in wiping out his traces," which is not a sign of the past but the actual passing toward the past of the other. It is in this movement and at this inclination that Levinas locates the absolute past of eternity.

In his formulation of *differance,* Derrida offers a general alterity in which presence is remarked as nonoriginary difference and deferral, defined beneath an unalterable dependence on the intervalic. "[E]ach element appearing on the scene of presence, is related to something other than itself, thereby keeping within itself the mark of the past element, and already letting itself be vitiated by the mark of its relation to the future element, this trace being related no less to what is called the future than to what is called the past, and constituting what is called the present by means of this very relation to what it is not" (1982, 13). In this archeconcept of *differance*, described as both "the becoming-space of time" and "the becoming-time of space" (1982, 13), Derrida rewrites through grammatology both the split self (*spaltung*) of Freud and the conscious, thinking ego of ontological discourse. Levinas might be understood as narrowing the focus from this general alterity to a specific ethical otherness considered protophilosophic, speaking of the trace as "the insertion of space in time, [a time which marks] a withdrawal of the other" (TO 358). Ultimately the Other to whom I am responsible, like Derridean "presence," is not there.[10]

A key concept in Levinas's ethics is the third party (*le tiers*) that articulates the Other (*l'Autri*) onto others (*les autres*). It is the illeity of the third party that ensures that the ethical relation always occurs in a public context. Ethics is an optics in the precise sense that "[t]he third party looks at me in the eyes of the Other" (TI 19, 213). The third party thus assures ethics a basal political ground in a fundamentally doubled structure—"a commonality among equals which is at the same time based on the inegalitarian moment of the ethical relation" (Critchley 1992, 227).

Levinas's Theory of Language

Before speaking of texts proper, those woven linguistic threads that sometimes manifest as poems, it will be salient to encounter Levinas's own sense of language. We have seen how the face is both trace and expression. What needs to be added to this description is the claim that the face is already detached as a signifier. Levinas had arrived at the conclusion that the face is equated with expression as early as 1961 when, in a radical modification of Saussure's and Jakobson's model of communication, he argues, "Expression . . . is of itself presence of a face [and] expression does not manifest the presence of being by referring from the sign to the signified; it presents the signifier. The signifier, he who gives a sign, is not signified" (TI 181–82).[11] Effectively emancipating the signifier from the domain of epistemology, Levinas relocates it in an ethicolinguistic negative relation to both sign and signified. By eluding signification, the signifier attains primordial manifestation as the face—inseparable, we must add, from its own appearing (cf. CPP 112). In this way the face is equally "first discourse" (CPP 96) and the essence of language (TI 64).[12] In "Language and Proximity," Levinas elaborates this *ursprache,* a language prior to language identified as a relation of proximity: "This relationship of proximity, this contact unconvertible into a noetico-noematic structure, in which every transmission of messages, whatever be those messages, is already established, is the original language, a language without words or propositions, pure communication" (CPP 119). Such ultraintentional proximity, Levinas adds, "is the relationship with the neighbor in the moral sense of the term" (CPP 119).

"Language, source of all signification, is born in the vertigo of infinity, which takes hold before the straightforwardness of the face, making murder possible and impossible" (TI 262). Ethics and language are coeval in the immediate facticity of the facial encounter. "The immediacy of the sensible is an event of proximity and not of knowledge" (CPP 116). For Levinas primordial signification is radically nonepistemological; it is a preestablished sensible event of proximity. Proximity is the Language before language; a saying before speech that escapes the temporal destination in the said. The original communication is thus a protosemantic nonintentionality without message; both the original language and the origin of language; a language that is triply distance, proximity, and relation. What is this pure communication? Levinas suggests it is a restlessness, a passing of "something" from one to the other in mutuality. The "something" here is not of the status of a message, and nothing is said beyond the averbal announcement of contact—a contact that interlaces complicity and alliance. This is the proximity prior to meaning, which is first language and pure communication, pure because "antecedent to every convention, all understanding or misunderstanding, all frankness and all guile" (CPP 119, 121).[13]

How can such a theory of language as proximity relate to an ethically inflected poetics? An a priori requirement is a relationship of writer to reader as that of neighbor to neighbor. (So already we are beyond Eco's semiotic schematic of the model reader as a textualized impress.)[14] Levinas reminds, "Proximity, beyond intentionality, is the relationship with the neighbor in the moral sense of the term" (CPP 119). Prior to receiving the Said is this nonverbal primordial encounter common not only to poetic but to all communication. Moreover, to rethink the reader as neighbor is to rethink the poem as necessarily incorporating a temporal gesture of a signifying without signification. Such a poetics would necessarily bifurcate its texts into a presupposed, and into an empirical encounter—a relationship not un-like that of base to superstructure in classical historical materialism.[15] "The neighbor" (in our case the reader and writer) is precisely what has a meaning immediately, before one ascribes one to her. The text in turn inscribes the trace of the neighbor, and so the effacement of the effacement of the mark of what has meaning immediately prior to a meaning being prescribed. Levinas's term for this prelinguistic meeting of neighbors is the caress, described as "the unity of approach and proximity" in which "proximity is always also absence" (CPP 120). The caress is not the fusion and decomposition of *jouissance*. "In the caress proximity remains a proximity and does not become an intention of something" (CPP 118). Levinas speaks of the restlessness of this proximity. "Something passes from one to the other and from the other to the one." It is moreover a nonthematizable proximity in which nothing is exchanged "but the contact by the contact itself" (CPP 121). Levinas constantly escorts his readers to a language prior to language and to a proximity antecedent to all forms of social convention. It is tempting to figure the reader as a neighbor ordered to the writer's responsibility, with an obligation to read a text as if responding to a face—its nudity and obligation. Like the Same's encounter with the face, the initial relation of a reader to a text is one of proximity, not knowledge. In this light, Levinas's own description of the critic-reader can be seen to present interpretive response as an unethical violence of appropriation rather than the pacific economy of neighborliness.[16]

In *Otherwise than Being*, Levinas proposes a modified version of this protosemantic condition—one articulated upon a difference between the Saying and the Said. Although the Saying carries a Said, it is not exhausted in some temporal transit; its significance remains more than that of a simple vehiculation. Before any "saying, of a said," the Saying carries the burden of disclosure and response. Indeed, "the saying is the fact that before the face I do not simply remain there contemplating it, I respond to it" (EI 88). Beyond the pure kerygma of a content, the Saying greets the Other, and "to greet the Other is already to answer for him" (EI 88). A fundamental noncoincidence thus obtains between the Saying and the Said. The latter, as statement and constative proposition—of the formula X is Y—results from the former's initiative. Like the face, the Saying is "primordial exposure in its purest form" (OB 48) and thus already presupposes the prelingual language of a "me voici." Levinas describes Saying as a handing over of meaning to another, a meaning not of preexisting signs or contents—in other words, the delivering over of a said—but as the very condition of communication (OB 48). In Saying the subject does not deliver signs but rather becomes him- or herself a sign (OB 48–49). Saying is the subject as a pure signification. This difference between the Saying and the Said is a fundamental distinction, which Levinas complicates with a further requirement. Jean Greisch explains: "[T]he donation of the originary sign, the signifyingness of the saying, is not an immediate certitude conquered once and for all. On the contrary, the 'scandal of sincerity' is that it always yet remains to be said! How can it be said? Precisely in the register of the *unsaying*!" (quoted in Bernasconi and Critchley 1991, 70). Levinas specifies "a need to unsay all that comes after the nakedness of signs, to set aside all that is said in the pure saying proper to proximity" (OB 198).

To summarize, Levinasian language—as the lucid utterance of sincerity uniting obligation with immediacy—is not a system of signs. For Levinas, all semiotic systems are dependent and secondary. "One only enters into language as a system of signs out of an already spoken language, which in turn cannot consist in a system of signs. The system in which the significations are thematized has already come out of signification, the one-for-the-other, approach and sincerity" (OB 199). A discernment becomes necessary between practical language-as-such, and a language prior to language—what Greisch terms Levinas's "transcendental language-game" (in Bernasconi and Critchley 1991, 70). Before entering a systematic linguistic economy, a saying occurs that is protosemantic "testimony, Saying without a said, a sign given to the Other" (OB 150).

In proposing the interlacement of two theories of signification—a transcendental signification of sincerity, obligation, and immediacy to the Other carried by a language of the Saying, and a Saussurean-style system of differential and oppositive signs constituting a language of the Said—Levinas initiates the virtuality of two perplicated theories of writing. A language prior to language, as an ethical *ursprache,* summons the possibility of a return to a gestural or performative poetics grounded in silence and immediacy. Franz Rosenzweig, while ruminating upon a practice of silence based on illumination and community, offers insights germane to this possible poetics. What forms the community is its collective listening to the reading of a scriptural passage. Rosenzweig explains: "The unanimity hearing, that is nothing but hearing, the hearing in which a multitude is 'all ears,' is not due to the person of the speaker, but to the fact that the living speaking person recedes behind the reader of words, and not even behind the reader, but behind the words he reads" (1985, 309). The critical recessionality invoked in this passage is that of speech before a text, yet, as Robert Gibbs makes clear, "The distinctive performance made possible by what is written is not in the act of writing but in the act of reading" (1992, 96). Rosenzweig's community of auditors emphasize the written text as a constant producer not of critiques but of new speakings. This community of the Other and the others is not one of dialogue and interaction but one of solidarity gained precisely by taciturnity and prelingual receptivity. The sentiment is echoed in Gemma Fiumara's claim that "[p]erhaps the *genius loci* of a community or the *daimon* of the individual may fare better in a silence that allows for listening than in the centrifugal dynamic of discourses that face outwards in order to achieve territorial control of their physical or cultural spaces" (1990, 132). The secular articulation of these notions of a community of reception and listeners is clearly onto the potential of the spoken word in the poem located in a real-time, performative dimension (a dimension I shall soon explore in the talk-poems of David Antin).

Another ethical articulation remains to be investigated. As remarked earlier, Levinasian ethics comprises a radical break with immediacy in light of which the poem can be conceived as a mediation that declares proximity to the writer as absence, in this way delivering writing not as gift or production but as a spatial distancing that establishes a correlation between neighborly parties, separating writer from reader and equally bringing both into proximity. The poem as ethics resides paradoxically in a language before its own language—in a language of gesture and antecedence. The poem, it might be said, already exists before it is written in the ethical obligation of proximity. As such, this primordial language persists as the trace of the Other in all pragmatic "secondary" discourse. Writing both depends on and effaces this primordial, nonverbal language. We arrive this way at a theory of writing as a trace structuring of an archelanguage (both transcendental and prelingual) that is critically dissimilar to Derrida's, whose own concept of the trace is decidedly textual and the outcome of temporal (deferring) and spatial (differentiating) forces.

Levinas targets cognition (knowledge) as a specifically phenomenological inquiry whose focus is *ipseity*, or "selfhood." Offered against ipseity is the concept of *illeity*, the third party, the neighbor—a concept appearing insistently throughout Levinas's thinking, which can be read as gendered: "him-ness" or neutral "it-ness." [17] "All the concrete relations between human beings in the world get their character of *reality* from a third term" (EE 41). In the specific case of the written, both writer and reader acquire their reality through the text's intervention as a third term. This ethical relation is also a semiotic relation where agency between subjects manifests as a fulfilling of functions demanded by the text. (Wittgenstein might see this as a relation between two players in a language-game.) [18] This intervention also names an apophatic interruption in the ethical relation of same to alterity. Writing, like ethicity, is constituted in a radical disruption of immediacy. Subject to the rigorous logic of the trace, it is a re-presentation after the writer's departure. Accordingly, it is tempting to conceive the poem as an act of violence by which a writer can say of the reader "he belongs to me." [19] The poem binds the reader to the author as a species of functional, if ephemeral, property, while the reader belongs to the writer through the writer's text. In turn, the reader may respond with "Here I am," repeating the Mosaic and Abrahamic obligation to ontologically affirm a willing and ready presence.

Blanchot detects a fundamental aporia in all written communication. Between writing and written, reading and read, is a temporal delay that ensures the binding relation of writer and reader is one of enantiomorphic nonpresence. "The past was written, the future will be read. This could be expressed in this form: what was written in the past will be read in the future, without any relation of presence being able to establish itself *between* writing and reading" (Blanchot 1992, 30). The written inscribes itself in the ethical perspective as a phenomenon between presence and absence, a gift offered by an absent party to another absent party. The writer, like God, the Platonic notion of the Good-beyond-being and the One of Plotinus, is absent from the ontological encounter, already traced in a significatory system as a proper name. We might say that the written cuts "the threads of a context" (CPP 65) relating as a correlated passivity to the act of writing and partaking of the modality of the adieu. [20] Writing, as the guaranteed nonpresence of its writer, assures that the latter is attributed that precise quality of enigma Levinas specifies as the manner in which the other manifests without manifesting, "seeking my recognition while preserving his incognito" (CPP 66). Writing, then, is both trace structure and departure as gift; the writer leaving her writing to enter only figuratively—if at all—a thanatopractic economy of traces and supplementarity. The writer is abscondite at the very moment the writing passes over into the written. To have written is to have made oneself dispensable to the communicative act. As Jabès soliloquizes, "I am absent because I am the teller. Only the tale is real" (1976, 58).

Agamben warns of an overwhelming paradox in contemporary sociolectal practice. "What hampers communication is communicability itself; humans are separated by what unites them" (1993, 81). It is precisely the autonomy of language, the separation of communicativity into an autonomous sphere that guarantees to language a uselessness in human intercourse. But for Agamben this alienation of linguistic being offers for the first time the chance to experience it, not as a thematizable content or truth, but in the very fact that one speaks. One need only add here that "one speaks *to* another not *about* another" to interlace Agamben's thesis with one of the major issues addressed by Levinas: the foundational exteriority of being in responsibility for the other effected in the primordial mise-en-scène of the face that is the Other. To understand the written as a fundamental nonpresence, the sign of the departed Other carries important consequences for readership. In reading the written, a confrontation obtains not of an ontological order between two beings, but as an ontico-ontological encounter with a trace: the text, third party, illeity. Readers receive writers enigmatically as apparent nonappearances in the written. The writer is enigma, a stranger, "the one who has come, to be sure, but left *before* having come" (CPP 68), the player at cards who throws in his hand before the game begins. Alternatively, the text might be thought of as interruptive, enjoying the third-person pronominal status of the *es gibt* and additionally occupying the space of the hyphen in the Buberian I-Thou relation. As such, the text represents the entry of a third party that troubles and problematizes my responsibility for the Other (cf. OB 157).

Levinas and Poetry

Let me now present Levinas's own critical ideas on poetry and art, juxtaposing his claims and their implications against the evidence of four contemporary writers hitherto unclaimed as "ethical" practitioners. To do this involves me reading the "critical" Levinas against the "ethical" Levinas.

In an aphoristic outburst, Levinas declares, "The proximity of things is poetry" (CPP 118). Elsewhere, he acknowledges poetry's disruptive and disseminatory powers. "Poetry can be said to transform words, the tokens of a whole, the moments of a totality, into unfettered signs, breaking the walls of immanence, disrupting order" (LR 156). He defines disturbance as "a movement that does not propose any stable order in conflict or in accord with a given order; it is a movement that already carries away the signification it brought" (CPP 66). Such positive remarks are rare in Levinas's writing on poetry, and in general his comments are of a negative nature. Although recognizing in the sonorhythmic forces of poetry (i.e., in its non-ideal, material, and durational dimensions) "a sort of passage from oneself to anonymity" (CPP 4), Levinas believes these forces constitute a captivation, an enchantment, not a movement beyond being. This movement, caused by poetic forces, is specified significantly as a move from self to "anonymity," that is, to an unnamed Self, not a passage to the Other. In one of several bold claims made in "Reality and its Shadow" (a claim that strategically facilitates the prioritization of concept over affect), he insists, "Art does not know a particular type of reality; it contrasts with knowledge" (CPP 3). Denied to poetry—and art in general—is a place in both the order of revelation (i.e., disclosure) and of creation (CPP 3).

Despite a general claim that it is precisely through the craft of writing that a perfect harmony is achieved between the Saying and the Said, Levinas's remarks on poetry are frequently disparaging. As the counterepistemological product of a will to obscure, poetry registers as "a descent of the night, an invasion of shadow" (CPP 3). "The most lucid writer finds himself in the world bewitched by its images. He speaks in enigmas, by allusions, by suggestion, in equivocations, as though he moved in a world of shadows" (CPP 13). Essentially disengaged, art elevates "in a world of initiative and responsibility, a dimension of evasion" (CPP 12).[21] Such comments condemn art and poetry to the unethical sphere of irresponsibility awaiting the responsible act of critical legitimation and the integration of "the inhuman work of the artist into the human world" (CPP 12). John Cage, David Antin, William Burroughs, and Tom Phillips, however, offer work that interrupts and unsettles the complacence of these Levinasian proclamations. And by recalling Levinas's ethics, especially his definition of the ethics of reception in "The Trace of the Other," the relation of the Saying to the Said, the face and proximity, and the central notion of substitution, it becomes possible to argue a case for the essential ethicity of their writing.

The Text as Gift

Levinas unfolds his notion of the text, conceived as work and gift, as labor unconditionally proffered to an other, in "The Trace of the Other." The gift is to be understood as a structural relation to alterity in whose irreversible movement and nonreciprocality the Other's alterity remains preserved. In offering this notion of gift, as a movement without return, Levinas adopts the Greek term "liturgy," indicating "the exercise of an office that is not only completely gratuitous, but that requires, on the part of him that exercises it, a putting out of funds at a loss" (TO 349–50). The movement without return is likened to the story of Abraham, "who leaves his fatherland forever for a yet unknown land, and forbids his servant to even bring back his son to the point of departure" (TO 348).[22] Levinas contrasts the unidirectional journey of Abraham to the circular pattern underlying the narrative of Ulysses: the paradigm story of departure and return.[23] This "Greek" return to the same, this refusal to remain in the beyond, Levinas terms "satisfaction" (EE 44).[24] I'll note, in passing, that Derrida likens all texts as forces committed to an Abrahamic trajectory. "A text, I believe, does not come back. I have insisted a lot on this theme," but adds a qualification: "It's better to produce texts that leave and don't come back altogether, but that are not simply and totally alienated or foreign. . . . They take off on their own, and one then tries to get them to come back a little even as they remain outside, even as they remain the other's speech" (1985, 156–57). In light of these comments, such lifelong projects as Pound's *Cantos,* Blaser's *Holy Forest,* and bp Nichol's *Martyrology* emerge as writings haunted by an obsessive desire to return, the growing writing of an unmovable text that refuses to separate and go on.

To return to Levinas. The poem as gift or liturgy, as the Said of the Saying, goes to the other as a radical generosity without anticipated profit of return. As an ethical economy, this act of saying must be received by the other with ingratitude, a radical nonreciprocity whose necessity is explained by the fact that gratitude involves "the *return* of the movement to its origin" (TO 349). Such a work—which constitutes "ethics itself" (TO 350)—is "a relationship with the other who is reached without showing himself touched" (TO 349). Is such an "Abrahamic" reading or writing possible? A writing which, like the city of the Great Khan's dream, "knows only departures not returns?"[25] In certain works of two otherwise heterogeneous contemporary writers, the reader finds a concrete application of this Levinasian itinerary producing an ethics in a poetics of method.[26]

William Burroughs's Cut-Up

In comments on his work, Burroughs has stressed less a graphic praxis of alterity than an interior, psychic exploration. "In my writing I am acting as a map maker, an explorer of psychic areas . . . a cosmonaut of inner space, and I see no point in exploring areas that have already been thoroughly surveyed" (quoted in Mottram 1971, 9). Elsewhere Burroughs speaks of cut-up as a quotidian, peripheral experience open to anyone.

Cut-ups make explicit a psycho-sensory process that is going on all the time anyway. Somebody is reading a newspaper, and his eye follows the column in the proper Aristotelian manner, one idea and sentence at a time. But subliminally he is reading the columns on either side and is aware of the person sitting next to him. That's a cut-up. (Quoted in Miles 1993, 163)

But examination of this transgeneric cut-up method (used by Burroughs to construct his trilogy of novels *The Soft Machine, The Ticket that Exploded,* and *Nova Express*) reveals an operation of radical textual alterity. Developed earlier by poet-painter Brion Gysin from cubist-futurist collage technique and the cinematic montage pioneered by Abel Gance, cut-up involves a tactile intervention into two separate texts subsequently recombined in a new configuration. Burroughs and Gysin elucidate:

Cut right through the pages of any book or newsprint . . . lengthwise, for example, and shuffle the columns of text. Put them together at hazard and read the newly constituted message. Do it for yourself. Use any system which suggests itself to you. Take your own words or the words of others said to be "the very own words" of anyone else living or dead. You'll soon see that words don't belong to anyone. Words have a vitality of their own and you or anybody can make them gush into action. (1978, 34)

Like the crystalline systems that Deleuze discusses, Burroughs's texts are "based on irrational cuts with only relinkings, and substituting for the model of truth the power of falsity in becoming" (Deleuze 1995, 67). The process is described, inside the fictive framework of *The Ticket that Exploded,* as a writing machine that produces texts without human intervention:

A writing machine that shifts one half one text and half the other through a page frame on conveyor belts — (The proportion of half one text half the other is important corresponding as it does to the two halfs of the human organism) Shakespeare, Rimbaud, etc. permutating through page frames in constantly changing juxtaposition the machine spits out books and plays and poems. (Burroughs 1967, 65)

Described here is nothing less than a scheme to displace writing as a cognitive investment in self-disclosure and to fix it as a practical act predicated on indifference and chance. As such, it takes an honest place alongside not only the famous writing machines of Kafka and Swift, but also Tristan Tzara's aleatoric Dadaist texts, as a productive response to Lautréamont's democratic decree, "Poetry should be made by all. Not by one" (1977, 75). At the proximity of a seam, a radical alterity occurs. Two texts are yoked together as one without respect for their prior existence as separate contents. Renouncing the traditional egological function of the writer, Burroughs chooses instead to combine two heterogeneous "liturgies" whose reception does not meet with a return.

> We were of course over the ground many times in different Ones on the road I pass through into rocket.
> Chef cooking in desert Ten Age Future Time..Sun seen from The Brass. Cutting if European..To arrive in Die..His feet of void..End should he fail en route Dry Air..The well in the mouth and wines light on The Drop Of Swiss Lakes. (Burroughs and Gysin 1960, 38)

Writing like this might exemplify Levinas's "unfettered signs, breaking the walls of immanence, disrupting order," but what I wish to stress is its interlocutory implication. It doesn't register as produced from the interior economy of a Self or Ego—entirely absent is the feeling that some Subject is speaking or writing to me. Intersubjective address is replaced by the readerly awareness that language itself is speaking. By physically dichotomizing two texts and recombining their disparate parts, Burroughs produces a dissonant univocity that dislodges any language of the Said. His approach to language is clearly evident in the foregoing passage. Words are less the predetermined instruments of intentionality than volatile, autonomous projectiles. Burroughs presents a democratic mandate to liberate a language-at-hand from a self's own cognitive control. And through it alterity emerges not in the Other, as reader, but as the Other of language.[27]

The initial violence of the cut-up ordains departure into a "new" text without the causal intervention of a writing subject. Significant to a Levinasian reading is the fact that Burroughs installs himself within his textual production as a recipient reader, not a writer. The resultant writing is the product of a radical dissymmetry in the writer-reader relation, eschewing reciprocity, amortizement, and exchange. The new text is also the production of a loss of the source text's initial content. What remains are juxtaposed defacements, two fragments brought together by the indifferent force of a graft. It's worth remarking, in passing, that Burroughs's method relies on the two qualities that Levinas points to as essential ingredients in Michel Leiris's exposition of the process underlying the inception of thoughts: bifurcation and erasure (NP 149).

John Cage's Mesostics

In his mesostic (or medial acrostic) method of systematic-chance text generation, Cage offers a comparable intervention in, and disturbance of, a preexistent textuality.[28] Like cut-up, Cage's mesostics issue from an *écrit donné* transmuted by way of systematic erasures to yield different texts. Describing the mesostic of James Joyce's name that forms the spinal motif of his *Writing through Finnegans Wake,* Cage outlines the rule "of first finding a word with J that didn't have an A, and then a word with A that didn't have an M, and then an M that didn't have an E, etc." (1982a, 76). Cage speaks of his work as an attack on traditional syntax for the explicit purpose of de-militarizing language (1974, [x]) but the focus here will be on maintaining the ethical interruption as an essential component in how the mesostic is conceived.

To describe Cage's method of text generation as a "parasitography" might introduce an appropriate neologism. The mesostic is truly of the order of secondary discourse and utterly dependent for its existence—in fact and theory—on a host text. As a parasite, moreover, it does not speak to the other but inhabits it, consuming it as a source of nonreciprocal nourishment.[29] It's evident how Cage leaves the vestige of Joyce's source text in the following short passage from the first three pages of *Finnegans Wake:*

> wrath with twone nathanJoe
> A
> Malt
> jhEm
> Shen
>
> pftJschute
> sOlid man
> that the humptY hillhead of humself
> is at the knoCk out
> in thE park
> (Cage 1979, 137)

Yet these lines are more than simply vestigial remnants. The mesostic obeys a syntactic rule which demands that each line appear in a severely verte-brated form. A flush left, normative linearity is denied the text through the rule of the mesostic spine that inscribes a capitalized overdetermination by its procedure, as well as manufacturing "verse" from a previous prose text. These are not the breath-lines suspending meaning in the charged white space of the page familiar from readings of Olson's or Creeley's poetry. A biopneumatic notation, requiring the line to end and start according to the laws and peculiarities of empirical human breathing, is not a factor here. The line and syntagmatic structure, being determined entirely by the decorative need and formal obligation to disclose a previously imperceptible phenomenon, advertise the covert presence of a name revealed when a formal rule is followed. Cage's mesostics are exemplary texts of disclosure by *mitzvot,* a speleography that draws out verbal threads from the cave of the given text under obligation to rigid constraints.

Bruns characterizes Cage's writing as a similar disclosure that puts at risk its ontological peculiarity, allowing "the world abide as what is alien to itself" (1994, 214). To accept alterity, preserve the integral otherness of the Other, is to inscribe Levinas's ethical obligation onto Cagean practice. And the abnegation of authorship in favor of textual generation by procedural constraint is precisely an ontological disturbance of place, a situating outside of knowledge and within proximity to the Other, already seen as a necessary condition of Levinasian ethics. Cage speaks of his desire "to let words exist" emancipated from human intentionality (1981, 151). And this refusal of a propositional, intentional language might be likened to a return of writing to a textual Saying. Generating a poem of disjunctive parts, the writing fails to gain the nature of a Said. By chance, nonintentionality, and subtraction, a disturbance is introduced that marks precisely the point of ontological, authorial retreat. Bruns likens this disturbance to Levinasian restlessness "in which the artist allows chance to recompose the order and fixity in which we otherwise frame things, not simply to undo this order, but to set free what it tries to contain (or, much to the same point, to let in what it tries to exclude). . . . The result of this disturbance is a text freed from the usual dialogue with a cognitive subject trained to reduce mere surface noise to underlying logical structures—a text freed from the old [read Buberian] I-Thou, which doubles as a freeing of the I, for one could just as well say in this event that the result (the outcome of Cage's art) is a disturbed subject, an I-think turned inside out by what is refractory, irreducible, uncontainable, anarchic. It would not be too much to speak of the Cagean I as the subject of the ethical" (1994, 216–17).

In addition to Bruns's sense of disturbance, Cage's work needs to be considered as an ethical itinerary whose nature is understood as fulfilling the Abrahamic paradigm in a gratuitous act that entails a putting out of funds at a loss. The Cagean mesostic is an oxymoronic construct, a production realized precisely by a loss, an inscription by mechanical and aleatoric era-sure. As a result, what Cage inscribes is not the cognitive invagination of his own subjectivity—an internal folding which still holds the subject to a knowledge, however skewed—but a departure from the Same without re-turn in a writing induced from a gift received without gratitude. It is the Abrahamic treatment of a source text, understood as gift, or liturgy, that guarantees this writing its "poethicality." [30]

Tom Phillips's *A Humument*

In *A Humument,* a treated text, excavated from the 1892 edition of W. H. Mallock's forgotten novel *A Human Document,* Phillips realizes his claim, "A good old text is a blank for new things." [31] Mobilizing an elaborate sys-tem of textual deletions, Phillips creates rivulets of text that open up a latent content (See illustration 7). Although chance operations were used to arrive at the treatment of page 99, Phillips in the main avoids the delib-erate aleatoricity noted in Burroughs and Cage and constructs a stunning hybrid work, part text, part pictorial transformation in pen and ink and acrylic gouache, arrived at through conscious deliberation. [32] Each page of Mallock's novel offers Phillips a reservoir of syntagmatic choices and plural combinations. A tactical opportunity for local improvisations within con-straint. As Phillips recollects, "some texts took years to reach a definitive state, usually because such a rich set of alternatives was present on a single page and only rarely because the page seemed quite intractable." [33] The mode of production suggests those "efficacious meanderings" of consumer practice described by Certeau (1984, xviii) and already examined in Ronald Johnson's *Radi os* (1977; see chapter 1). A similar concern is expressed with authorial voice and control that indirectly emerges in Phillips's careful de-ployment of his reading in pursuit of paragrammic threads and embedded textual possibilities. While a departure from the Same and certainly not the return as reciprocity that exegesis or critical commentary would sig-nify, Phillips's book has a different relation to alterity than the other works considered.

Significantly, the title of *A Humument* suggests to its author a process of exhumation rather than a birth from an other. [34] This colorful evocation aside, the exhumed text nonetheless inscribes a difference in sameness; an unfolding of the Same into a broader alterity. A more material difference is that the book retains the entirety of its original as a partial underprint, the

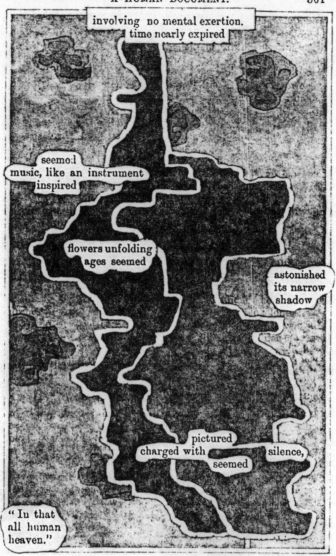

Figure 7. Tom Phillips, *A Humument,*
monochrome reproduction of original polychrome

entire work being a multimedia palimpsest. Levinas speaks of overprinting as the precise movement of the trace holding "the past of him who delivered the sign" (TO 357).

In a subsequent work, Phillips's translation and illustration of Dante's *Inferno,* fragments of *A Humument* are delivered as parallel commentaries to Dante. Phillips describes these pictoverbal glosses as "an alternative line of markers as the reader follows Dante's journey" (1985, 284). Clearly this is not the return of the Same to the Same evident in normative critical commentary but an additional itinerary in Mallock's departure from Mallock.

David Antin's Talk Poems

I wish to address David Antin's writing under governance of Levinas's formula of the Saying and the Said (whose perfected harmony, according to Levinas, is achieved in the craft of writing). Saying, as a precise mark of the Other, is both distinct from and dependent upon the Said. "For what escapes all that can be said is not only what must be said; it escapes only under the auspices of Saying and when kept back by the restraint that is Saying's alone" (Blanchot 1986, 114). Carried and deposited by Saying, the propositional economy of the Said holds this preoriginal Saying as a trace. As such the Said carries the mark of Saying. The urgent behest to separate the message of the Said from the temporal duration and proxemics of the Saying Levinas simply names "contact" (CPP 115), emphasizing the address to the other in the Same's moment of absolute disclosure. "Speaking is before anything else this way of coming from behind one's appearance, behind one's form, an openness in the openness" (CPP 96). Speech is born in the separation between feeling and felt, in that passive activity of time Levinas calls consciousness (CPP 114).

In the genre of the talk poem, Antin offers a practice of open address—a spontaneous, uninhibited outflow of speech toward the Other. Considered by William Spanos "as a kind of poetic anti-poetry" repositioned in the "peripatetic talk that is prior to print" (in Antin 1975a, 597–98), the talk poem offers, in Olson's words, "language as the act of the instant" (Antin 1975b, 4). (Despite being recorded for subsequent transcription and publication, the talks remain essentially the ephemeral orality of a speaking.) Antin speaks of his work in suggestively Abrahamic metaphors of protentive movement and travel. His rejection of Heideggerian ontology is tellingly phrased in the following response to Spanos: "Anyone who starts with 'Being' as a goal has already reduced the possibility of travelling" (1975a 623). The poem is "a way of getting somewhere" and the creative challenge is that of "steering" the poem "into open water" (1975b, 8, 30). What characterizes the talk poem, however, is its processual and improvisatory nature. (Antin distinguishes it from "prose," which carries "an image of the authority of 'right thinking.' " [35]) As in Barthes's diathetic model of the middle voice, the talk poem situates agency and act at their asymptosis, in the co-incidentality of action and affection; with the author situated interior rather than anterior to the moment of composition, present before a community of listeners with the work itself manifesting as "an inscription in being" (EE 27).[36]

Owing to its real-time and improvisatory nature, the talk poem enjoys the status of a Saying without a deposition in the Said—a true poetry of site-specific community that unfolds with parousial force as the approach to the Other. Its formal proposition, as explained by David Bromige, is "to go in the open, letting your face hang out, to trust to the luck of the mutuality of the occasion" (1975, 68).

> and you look over the boundary and you see him sitting there
> or standing   and hes painting a picture you see   you
> know hes painting a picture because this canvas is on an easel and the
> canvas is on a stretcher   anyway hes painting and you see that
> the way that hes painting seems strange   because hes got what
> appears to be a photograph   the photograph is in an opaque
> enlarger   and hes projecting the photograph onto the surface of
> the canvas and painting it on   now you say "hes got a photo-
> graph?   why does he have to paint it?
>
> (Antin 1976, 57)

The absence of punctuation and periods, together with the strategic trans-grammatic spacing, all help to notate a speaking voice inside the written. This return of the work back to speech names a gestural poetics whose base unit is a continuum of phrasal utterance. In its subsentential threading there is a movement neither to closure nor unity, but to a constant opening onto otherness along a nonreturning vector of digression.

Can Antin's talk poem—which opens up to an improvisatory, gestural poetics—be thought to evoke the proximity required by the Levinasian obligation? For Levinas interlocution is always preferable to description. One speaks *to*, not *about*, the other. To speak about opens up the violence of neutral discourse. The public basis of speaking is made clear by him: speech "in its original essence, is a commitment to a third party on behalf of our neighbor: the act *par excellence*, the institution of society" (NTR 21). As noted earlier, the original function of speech is not to designate an object in order to communicate with an other in some inconsequential game but rather "to assume toward someone a responsibility on behalf of someone else. To speak is to engage the interests of men. Responsibility would be the essence of language" (NTR 21).

Thus the communal nature of the talk poem is worth stressing. Antin talks to, not about, a collectivity of listeners, and delivers processual mentation not a predetermined content. Taking up Agamben's challenge to alienated linguistic being, Antin proffers a public experience of the very fact that he speaks. In foregrounding Saying, and not the Said, the talk poem makes intricate a passing of that restlessness assigned by Levinas to the averbal utterance of a contact. Prior to talk, and carried in the talking, is the tacit, prelingual space of a Self and others that ratifies and interlaces the efficacy of saying.[37]

I noted earlier how the Saying registers response before the Other, that beyond a talker's words the speaker's presence constitutes a greeting and a substitution. Already invoked in the talker's mere presence before an other, and beyond the sum of verbal content, is the nonthematizable proximity of talker and listener with nothing exchanged but the contact by the contact itself.

Antin, Cage, Burroughs, and Phillips alike offer a stark contrast to Edmond Jabès's profoundly egological notion of writing:

> He writes for the sake of his hand, his pen, to appease his eyes. For if he did not write, what would become of them? His pen would be unusable by now, choked with rust. His hand unreflected in any word, any letter. It would not have formed any image in ink. As for his eyes, they would have foundered on the page closed to them, uninvited at any moment of their passage. Only writing can keep the writer's eyes on the surface (1976, 53–54).

Admittedly, this is not the solipsistic reduction to an irreducible cogito but rather the exercise of the body's parts in a journey of both praxis and self-care. Yet a profound absence of an other marks Jabès's text. One writes for the sake of the goodness of a self in disregard of any other. In contrast, Cage, Burroughs, Phillips—we might also add Ronald Johnson and Mac Low— offer a practice of written-readings in which reading "is not writing the book again but causing the book to write itself or *be* written—this time without the writer as intermediary, without anyone writing it" (Blanchot 1981, 93). An innovative "lightness" obtains from this new authorless book, "a book without an author, without the seriousness, the labor, the heavy pangs, the weight of a whole life that has been poured into it" (Blanchot 1981, 93). It is precisely this lightness provoked by the departure of authorial weight that's evident in Burroughs's cut-ups and Cage's mesostics. As textual modifications and part erasures of received texts, they involve a structural nonreturn of a derivative writing to its origin, thus satisfying Levinas's ethical prescription of recipient ingratitude. Both writers practice a reading that might be likened to listening "to the song of the sirens [yet resisting] the return to its island" (NTR 33). From this resistance written-readings result, designed neither to master nor to reciprocate the gifts received in reading, but to liberate a new alterity via subtraction. By not giving a writing back to the given, the first gift becomes a source for further departures. Unlike Phillips and Antin, Burroughs and Cage offer largely egoless productions, ontologically dislocated in which the writer, as Same, is transferred to the position of witness, or first reader, of a language unfolding as an indeterminate alterity. Their "new" texts, the threads of preexistent writings, carry fragments of the Other's words but are no longer its kerygma.

But this recipient ingratitude, itself ethical, can be read as a different ethical act of substitution.[38] In his writings through Joyce and Thoreau, for instance, Cage's relationship as reader to the texts can be envisaged as an act of substitution where, at the precise moment of reading, a writer-as-reader enters to take the place of the writer-departed. Phrased in a similarly ethical manner, Phillips writes in Mallock's place and out of Mallock's gift to him as reader. It's tempting to compare Levinas's notion of "unsaying" with these two writers' "unreading" of their source texts. Cage's mesostics and Phillips's radically treated text involve an "unreading" of a previous work which, when proffered as gift, is neither returned, received, but unmade. Most so in Phillips's case whose ongoing project is to continuously revise *A Humument* to reach a point where there is a complete page by page replacement.[39] Levinas describes the relation of subjectivity to the Other as that of a "hostage" (OB 112), a term that captures precisely the obligatory captivity we feel in reading these radically alterior texts.

Levinas complicates the way a performative poetics must be formulated, and by approaching Antin's talk poetry through his thinking, by insisting on this presence of Levinas in his work, any mundane notion of presence and heterogeneity must be seriously rethought. Finally, it's the impossibility of escaping ethicity that urges us to examine the way in which it inheres in all poetic texts. In the cases of Burroughs, Cage, Phillips, and Antin, ethicity is not betrayed.

Not wishing to follow in the path of Ulysses, I open Agamben's *Idea of Prose* at "The Idea of Language" and depart with the following:

A beautiful face is perhaps the only place where there is truly silence. While character marks the face with unspoken words and with intentions that have remained unfulfilled, and while the face of the animal always seems to be on the verge of uttering words, human beauty opens the face to silence. But the silence then is not simply a suspension of discourse, but silence of the word itself, the becoming visible of the word: the idea of language. This is why in the silence of the face man is truly at home.

Appendix to Chapter 12

The Text as Written-Oral Law and Levinas's Talmudic Readings

I've noted that to conceive writing as presupposing reciprocality implicates the text in the nonethical, Ulyssean paradigm of a return from alterity to the same; of a writing back to the written. This was Derrida's own aporial predicament on being asked to write about Levinas, the response to which is the magisterial "At this very moment in this work here I am" (Bernasconi and Critchley 1991, 11–48). In her introduction to *Nine Talmudic Readings*, Annette Aronowicz announces the Talmud as "the center to which all the other expressions can be related" and describes this procedure as similar to Franz Rosenzweig's centripetal hortation. "We all know that in being Jews we must not give up anything, not renounce anything, but lead everything back to Judaism. From the periphery back to the center; from the outside in" (quoted in NTR xvii). But wouldn't such a movement involve the Ulyssean rather than Abrahamic itinerary evoked by Levinas: a return from the Other to the Same?

Might it then be claimed that Levinas's own Talmudic readings—in returning as commentary to the Same—fail to fulfill his own requirements for the ethical obligation? One of his own metaphoric (albeit fictive) descriptions of Talmudic exegesis suggests a primary agonistic stance before a semantically opaque text. "As if by chance, to rub in such a way that blood spurts out is perhaps the way one must 'rub' the text to make it spurt blood—I rise to the challenge! . . . [A reading] can only consist in this violence done to words to tear from them the secret that time and conventions have covered over with their sedimentations, a process begun as soon as these words appear in the open air of history. One must, by rubbing, remove this layer which corrodes them" (NTR 46–47). Apparently, then, Talmudic exegesis abrogates the ethical stance or, in Kierkegaard's terminology, requires a "teleological suspension of the ethical." Levinas suggests that the purpose of reading is to return the text-as-work (or liturgy) back to itself by an active desedimentation and grateful caring. A return to the same of the Same in a state of repair.[40] From the outside in. Ulysses. Not Abraham.

Are Levinas's own Talmudic readings then transgressions of his own ethical prescriptions outlined in "The Trace of the Other," which demand that to act ethically one must receive without gratitude and the gift must not be returned? Is Talmudic exegesis a response of gratitude and a giving back to the text by its reader? Levinas himself is suspicious of criticism's inherently parasitic constitution (a problematic constitution discussed in chapter 1). In literature, "[a] depth of reality inaccessible to conceptual intelligence becomes its prey. . . . Is not to interpret Mallarmé to betray him? Is not to interpret his work faithfully to suppress it?" (CPP 1). To answer the question affirmatively requires that the Torah be granted the status of a secular text and factor out its privileged nature as both prophetic and prescriptive. The socioreligious value of the Torah is its value as revelation and its cultural installation not as gift but Law. Levinas assures us (and in terms reminiscent of the ethical obligation toward the face) that "one accepts the Torah before one knows it" (NTR 42).[41] In turn, as a commentary on the Torah, the Talmud "governs the daily and ritual life, as well as the thought—including Scriptural exegesis—of Jews confessing Judaism" (NTR 3). The Talmudic texts known as Halakhah expound the economic, ritual, and social rules for proper living. The ones referred to as Aggadah comprise moral tales and counsel in which guise they address, if not philosophy per se, then "those experiences from which philosophies derive their nourishment" (NTR 3). Such exegesis and narrative properly situate not on the ethical plane of Levinas's discourse but on the juridical plane—in the active, disputative sphere of social interaction.

Levinas is unequivocal in his explanation of how a Talmudic text be read. Initially, it is to be read "in a way that respects its givens and its conventions, without mixing in the questions arising for a philologist or historian to the meaning that derives from its juxtapositions" (NTR 5). The subsequent task is to translate "the meaning suggested by [the text's] particulars into a modern language, that is, into the problems preoccupying a person schooled in spiritual sources other than those of Judaism and whose confluence constitutes our civilization" (NTR 5). The exegetic goal is not to return or reciprocate, but to liberate universal intentions from apparent singularities through a process of hermeneutic translation—a movement out of sameness into alterity. Instead of formulating commentary as a return of the Other to the Same—i.e., an act of gratitude offered to the Same—Levinas insists on the inseparability of the two. "The texts of the Oral Law that have been set into writing [i.e., the Talmud] should never be separated from their living commentary. When the voice of the exegetist no longer sounds—and who would dare believe it reverberates long in the ears of its listeners—the texts return to their immobility, becoming once again enigmatic, strange, sometimes even ridiculously archaic" (NTR 13–14). Exegesis as a form of interpretative resuscitation is clearly endorsed.[42]

For Levinas the Torah is the face, the Oral Demand. Less an anatomical phenomenon the face is a command, and Levinas assures that "commanding is speech, or that the true speech, speech in its essence, is commanding" (CPP 23). He offers the face as "a primordial desolation, a dereliction and a timidity" (CPP 65) and in its radical encounter with alterity the face is presignificatory, "the very emptiness of an irrecuperable absence" (CPP 65). In a passage that threads the trace with faciality and illeity, Levinas speaks of the face as "a trace, in which its visible invisibility is the face of the neighbor" (CPP 121). And isn't this the condition of all that's written? A trace structure bringing into visibility the distanced—because disposed—invisible writer? There's a sense in which all poems are offered as faces. Fundamentally, like the skin in Levinas's text, the poem "is nudity, presence abandoned by a departure [the writer's], exposed to everyone and then too profaned, persecuted, in fault and in distress" (CPP 121). Like the face, it "is an incision that does not bleed" (BPW 59). The poem abandoned, exposed to readerly scrutiny, persecution, the helpless victim of violent commentary or exegesis? To be placed as a reader before a text is to be in correlation with a face, situated "on the plane of a transitivity without violence which is that of creation" (CPP 22).[43] The Torah further provides Levinas with an *espace vital*—a living space which as subjects we enter. "It is through reading that references take on reality; through reading, in a way, we come to inhabit a place" (LR 192). Understood as dwelling, as the inhabitable, nourishing space of the written, the Torah commands a radically different behavior than one of ingratitude before a proffered writing.[44]

Notes

Chapter 1

1. Foucault 1976, 215–16.

2. This is, of course, a deliberately ungenerous description of theory's range and constitution. It would be utterly false to claim that theory relates to its object field solely by way of a unilateral empowerment. Cross-pollination is always possible, and a poetic procedure can equally appropriate a theoretical field. We might even argue for a sort of poetic "Darwinism" and urge that theory and literary criticism are less an appropriation than the poem's own method of ensuring its reproduction paragrammatically via discursive proliferation. My intention in this chapter is to maneuver into contention with critical stances and argue that appropriation is a sufficient, if not necessary, condition of the theoretical, and I do address a sedimentary aspect common to all theoretical practice. A more detailed study would take into account Althusser's important distinction between theoretical forces and theoretical relations, the latter including the social and ideological contexts in which theory is realized (academic papers, scholarly journals, university seminars) and its incorporation into individual and collective careerisms, party interests, and the incommensurable range of wills to power. Deliberately, this chapter concentrates upon the forces of the theoretical alone. Similarly, while arguing that the two works discussed are essentially nondiscursive, I acknowledge that a highly discursive context frames, and to a certain extent governs, their appearance. This discourse is the institution of Literature along with its constellation of procedures and implements: canonicity, the tradition, generic frame, marginal texts, and so on. Ultimately, it is impossible to separate either poem or theory from these complex networks of historical, economic, and institutional forces that govern and partake of their mutual production and reception.

3. The suppressed connection between structuralist method and le-Duc's architectural terms was first brought to light by Hubert Damisch. If only le-Duc's *Dictionnaire* were read, he contends, "with attention to the dialectic of the whole to its parts and the parts to the whole which is the avowed motivation for this 'descriptive' dictionary, it will inevitably seem to be the manifesto, or at least the oddly precocious, definite outline of the method and ideology of the sort of structural thought that is famous today in linguistics and anthropology" (introduction to *L'Architecture raisonnée, extracts from the Dictionnaire de l'architecture française of Viollet-le-Duc* [Paris: Herman, 1964], 14; quoted in Hollier 1989, 177).

4. A similar fate seems to have befallen Derrida with the forced migration of his thinking out of its historically specific and momentous force within the history of metaphysics into a kind of terminological adhesive for miscellaneous theories.

This applied and mediated "Derridanity" (if not Derrida himself) pushes literary theory perilously close to a one-dimensional phraseological consensus.

5. Kristeva distinguishes the *genotext* from the *phenotext,* a term she uses to denote "language that serves to communicate, which linguistics describes in terms of 'competence' and 'performance.'" The phenotext "is a structure" and "obeys rules of communication and presupposes a subject of enunciation and an addressee. The genotext, on the other hand, is a process; it moves through zones that have relative and transitory borders and constitutes a *path* that is not restricted to the two poles of univocal information between two full-fledged subjects" (1984, 87).

6. One of the more execrable instances of this Platonic silencing to appear in recent years is Easthope and Thompson 1991, comprising sixteen critical articles and marked by the utter absence of any dialogue between the two practices.

7. Bataille, equally alert to the threat of appropriation and the implications of transgression, provides a curious solution to the problem of critical annexation. In his book *On Nietzsche,* he demonstrates the proposition that to *not* betray an author, *one must not respect him.* "[I]t was only with my life that I wrote the Nietzsche book I had planned" (1994, xxv). Accordingly, Bataille writes an autobiography and thereby avoids reducing Nietzsche to an object of knowledge. Transgression of this kind exploits a practical, not a theoretical, modality and thus claims the rank of a *tactic.* The ethical implications of this form of "response by no response" are the subject of my final chapter.

8. In her complex theory of the unconscious, its drives, and their relation to language, Kristeva cites "modalities" and "articulations" that seem to mask an essential foundation. The most problematic concept is that of the *khora* (or *chora*), which Kristeva borrows from Plato's *Timaeus* and that describes a "nonexpressive totality formed by the drives and their stases in a motility that is as full of movement as it is regulated" (Kristeva 1984, 25). The *khora* purportedly precedes "evidence, verisimilitude, spatiality and temporality"; is subject to both "vocal and gestural organization"; underlies all figuration; and ranks as "a preverbal functional state" (26–27). The concept of the *khora* has been criticized by Derrida. In a footnote in *Positions,* he states, "Beside the reading of Benveniste's analyses that I cited in '*La double séance,*' the works and teachings of H. Wismann and J. Bollack also have guided me in this terrain. In the course of a seminar at the *Ecole normale* I attempted to investigate the text of the *Timaeus* from this point of view, especially the very problematic notion of the *chora*" (1981b, 106). Derrida's most complex discussion of the *chora* is "Khora" (1995b, 88–127).

9. Eco offers as an example of the political potential of a tactical, everyday reading Eugène Sue's *Les Mystères de Paris,* a novel generally considered to be a fashionable bourgeois consolatory fiction and ridiculed by Poe and Marx alike. The novel, however, gained unexpected popularity to such an extent that the book had a direct effect on the popular uprising of 1848. Details of this curious trajectory can be consulted in Bory 1963.

10. In his prefatory remarks Johnson writes of *Radi os,* "It is the book Blake gave me (as Milton entered Blake's left foot—the first foot, that is, to exit Eden) his eyes wide open through my hand. To etch is 'to cut away,' and each page, as in Blake's concept of a book, is a single picture." For an appreciation of *Radi os* as an apocalyptic text in the Blakean tradition and radically dissimilar to aleatoric productions such as Mac Low's and Cage's (considered in chapters 11 and 12, respectively) see Selinger 1992.

11. Underlying her theory, of course, is Freud's concept of the *spaltung,* the basal breach in subjectivity that holds configuratively and unpredictably a subject of desire and a subject of knowledge. I try to demonstrate in chapter 5 the fusion of delirium and interpretive closure in the editorial procedures of Richard Bentley.

Chapter 2

1. *De rerum natura* entered Renaissance culture after its discovery in 1417 by Poggio Bracciolini on an expedition during the Council of Constance. Bracciolini ordered a copy to be transcribed, and the poem was first printed in 1470, appearing again at Verona in 1486 and in the famous Aldine edition in 1500 (Singer 1950, 52). Lucretius, of course, is one of the great contemporary rediscoveries via Michel Serres, Ilya Prigogine, Jean-Luc Nancy, and Jeffrey Mehlman before the subsequent reappearance in Derrida's "My Chances/Mes Chances: A Rendezvous with Some Epicurean Stereophonies" (in Smith and Kerrigan 1988). Prior to this resurgence, Lucretius was a model for Pope's "Epistle on Man," and Lucretian philosophy permeates the *Dunciad.* Lucretius is central also to any serious consideration of Sade's thinking, especially his strategic notion of Nature as perpetual motion (on which see chapter 8). Thomas Creech's timely translation of *De rerum natura* in 1682 conveniently introduced entropy, atheism, and the second law of thermodynamics into post-Restoration politics and the bloodless revolution. Eighteenth-century experimental science (primarily in the work of Needham and Buffon) also verified the scientific theories outlined in Lucretius's poem. For the status and reception of Epicurean atomism in the eighteenth century, see Kroll 1991.

2. Joseph Glanville makes a curious appeal to atomistic explanation via the clinamen when describing the operation of fascination and imagination in witchcraft. "I am apt to think there be a *power* of *real fascination* in the *Witches eyes* and *imagination,* by which for the most part she acts upon *tender* bodies. *Nescio quis teneros oculus*—For the *pestilential spirits* being darted by a *spightful and vigorous imagination* from the *eye,* and meeting with *those* that are *weak* and *passive* in the bodies which they enter, will not fail to infect them with a *noxious quality* that makes *dangerous* and *strange alterations* in the person invaded by this *poisonous influence:* which way of acting by subtile and *invisible instruments,* is *ordinary* and *familiar* in all natural *efficiencies.* And 'tis now past question, that *nature* for

the most part acts by *subtile streams* and *apporrhoea's* of *minute particles,* which pass from one body to another" (1681, 23).

3. For his part, Derrida insists on a vital hedonistic implication in the clinamen that should be deviated into this present discussion of parapraxis and misprision: "The clinamen of the elementary principle—notably the atom, the law of the atom—would be the pleasure principle" (quoted in Smith and Kerrigan 1984, 8).

4. Deleuze is alert to the essential pertinence of both Roussel's method and Jarry's 'pataphysics to a complete understanding of Heideggerian ontology: "We could equally link Heidegger to Jarry to the extent that *pataphysics* presents itself precisely as a surpassing of metaphysics that is explicitly founded on the Being of the phenomenon. . . . We must not refuse to take Heidegger seriously, but we must rediscover the imperturbably serious side to Roussel (or Jarry). The serious ontological aspect needs a diabolical or phenomenological sense of humour" (1988b, 111).

Chapter 3

1. This paucity of critical attention has been somewhat rectified by Watts and Byrne 1999 which includes contributions by Charles Bernstein, Pauline Butling, Peter Quartermain, Clayton Eshleman, David Bromige, Thomas Marshall, Michele Leggott, Rachel Blau DuPlessis, Jed Rasula, Peter Middleton, Steve McCaffery, Michael Davidson, Nathaniel Tarn, and Andrew Schelling. In addition Ellingham and Killian 1997 (a biography of Jack Spicer) contains much biographical, bibliographical, and critical data on Blaser.

2. The monad is not entirely absent from *The Holy Forest*. Blaser refers to it in relationship to the music of Bach in the "Mappa Mundi" section (364). See note 16. Blaser's introduction to the philosophy of both Spinoza and Leibniz came through Jack Spicer as early as 1945. He also confesses to a familiarity with Leibniz's own description of the monad via Frances Yates's account in *The Art of Memory* (Blaser 1970, 20).

3. In addition to René Thom's authoritative account of catastrophe theory (1975), useful works include Casti 1979, Woodcock and Davis 1978, and Zeeman 1977. An insightful adaption of this theory to linguistic and rhetorical issues is Rice 1980. Purdy (1984) offers a textual entry into Pound's *Cantos* by means of catastrophe theory, and Herbert Smith (1994) a recent application of it to narrative interpretation.

4. Deleuze attributes this notion of the Self to Foucault (Deleuze 1995, 92).

5. Cf. Norman O. Brown's comments on ego-psychology: "The soul (self) we call our own is an illusion. The real psychoanalytic contribution to 'ego-psychology' is the revelation that the ego is a bit of the outside, swallowed, introjected; or rather

a bit of the outside world that we insist on pretending we have swallowed. The nucleus of one's own self is the incorporated other" (1966, 144). Purdy describes Pound's manner of descriptive accumulation in a way befitting of the Baroque fold. The images and descriptions in *The Cantos* "suddenly come together, a scene takes shape, and the edge of a fold in the manifold is reached" (1984, 45).

The fold, too, is an essential component in Foucault's description of *aemulatio* (the second figure of classical representation): "[E]mulation is a sort of natural twinship existing in things; *it arises from a fold in being*, the two sides of which stand immediately opposite to one another. Paracelsus compares this fundamental duplication of the world to the image of two twins 'who resemble one another completely, without its being possible for anyone to say which of them brought its similitude to the other' " (1970, 19–20). Foucault grants to emulation the power of potentially infinite plication, a potency in which "[l]ike envelops like, which in turn surrounds the other, perhaps to be enveloped once more in a duplication which can continue *ad infinitum*" (1970, 21, emphasis added). For a detailed discussion of the conceptual importance of the fold in Foucault's thinking, see Deleuze 1988b, 94–123. Deleuze 1995, 111–13 and 156–59 also provide useful comments on the fold. Needless to say this chapter is indebted throughout to Deleuze's book *The Fold*.

6. This notion of plication is consonant with Barthes's agenda for "disentanglement." See especially "The Death of the Author" in Barthes 1977, 142–48. The fold figures prominently in Derrida's deconstructive agenda of the 1970s. See, for instance, his extended meditation on Mallarmé in "The Double Session" where, among many references to plication, he describes rhyme as "the folding together of identity and difference" (Derrida 1981a, 277). Plication has been utilized at its most literal as a compositional method by William Burroughs and Brion Gysin in their cut-up and fold-in texts which arrive via acts of negative creativity at an insistently Baroque manifestation of heteroglossia. A description and consideration of cut-up can be found in the final chapter. Deleuze's related concept of perplication is explained in Deleuze 1994, 187, 201, 252, and 280–81).

7. Compare Heidegger:

What the Leibnizian proposition about the monads being without windows basically means can truly be made clear only by way of the basic constitution of the Dasein which we have—developed being-in-the-world, or transcendence. As a monad, the Dasein needs no window in order first of all to look out toward something outside itself, not because, as Leibniz thinks, all beings are already accessible within its capsule, so that the monad can quite well be closed off and encapsulated within itself, but because the monad, the Dasein, in its own being (transcendence) is already outside, among other beings, and this implies always with its own self. . . . In his monadological interpretation of substance, Leibniz doubtless had a genuine phenomenon in view in the windowlessness of the monads. It was only his orientation to the traditional concept of substance that prevented him from conceiving of the original ground of the windowlessness and thus from truly interpreting the phenomenon he saw. He was not able to see that the monad, because it is essentially representational, mirroring a world, is transcendence and not a substantival extant entity, a windowless capsule. (1982, 301)

Gerrit Lansing offers a windowless model for the relation of memory to events and Time: "The gates of memory & intuition, history & magic, open from a 'windowless' event into Time, the fateful Cross (crux) behind the shifting hexagrams" (1970, 83).

Certeau salvages a precious fragment from the works of the fourteenth-century mystic Hadewijch of Anvers describing the monadic interiority of the mystical itinerary: "They hasten, those who have glimpsed that truth, on the dark path. Untraced, unmarked, all inner" (quoted in 1992, 299). The enigmatic figures in Beckett's dance "Quad" are instantly evoked by this passage, but also anticipated is the windowless ontology of the monad. Certeau does not elucidate this affinity of mystic and monad. Indeed, the three references to Leibniz in his book refer to the *mathesis universalis* and to Leibniz's aspirations to encompass the regimes of infinite singularities.

Jean-Luc Nancy offers a Platonic version of the human corpus relevant to any reflection on monadic space and being: "The body was born in Plato's cave, or rather it was conceived and shaped in the form of the cave: as a prison or tomb for the soul, and the body first was thought *from the inside,* as buried darkness into which light only penetrates in the form of reflections, and reality only in the form of shadows. This body is seen from the inside, as in the common but anguishing fantasy of seeing the mother's body from the inside, as in the fantasy of inhabiting one's own belly, without father or mother, before all sex and all reproduction, and of getting hold of oneself there, as a nocturnal eye open to a world of chains and simulacra. This body is first an interiority dedicated to images, and to the knowledge of images; it is the 'inside' of representation, and at the same time the representation of that 'inside' " (1993, 191–92).

8. The monad is a concept fundamental to quantum mechanics. "In Niels Bohr's model of the atom each orbit is characterized by a well-determined energy level in which electrons are in steady, eternal, and invariable movement. The steady state of orbital electrons is the typical example of the monadic state. The orbits are defined as being without interaction with each other or with the world; it is as though they were isolated, alone in the world" (Prigogine and Stengers 1982, 146).

Duchamp's *Large Glass* is a modernist revision of the monad envisioned as a bachelor machine. Strikingly similar to Leibniz's model, this transparent work comprises an upper and lower chamber, the former being the "Bride's Domain," the latter containing the "Bachelor Apparatus." Duchamp names the floor dividing upper and lower levels the "Region of the Wilson-Lincoln effect." The *Large Glass* is reproduced and discussed in Harnoncourt and Kynaston 1973. Perspectives on Duchamp's piece in the context of similar celibate machinery can be found in Clair and Szeemann 1975, containing articles by Carrouges, Certeau, Lyotard, and Serres, among others. Blaser refers to the *Large Glass* in "Image-Nation 23" (1993, 328) but does not address its monadic affiliations. I might note here, parenthetically, that St. Teresa's own monad of the soul is architectural and crystalline: "[L]et us consider our soul as a castle, composed entirely of diamonds, or very clear crystal, in which there are many rooms" (1).

The monad finds a place in Giordano Bruno's cosmology, in which the world is constituted of "minima" or "monads," the infinite universe being regarded as a single continuum made from mobile, diverse, convergent parts and implying a universal scheme of symbiosis (Singer 1950, 73). "No being is lonesome in the universe, but every being is symbiotic" (Michel 1973, 255). In the *Lampas triginta statuarum* (*Op. lat.* III:63–68) Bruno portrays the monad as the figure of Apollo, which Yates renarrates:

> He stands in his chariot to signify the absolute one, he is naked to signify the one simplicity; the constancy and solidity of his rays signify the one pure truth. One crow flying before his face signifies unity by the negation of multitude. He denotes one genus because he illuminates all the stars; one species because he illuminates the twelve signs; one number through the lion his sign; one congregation through the chorus of the Muses over which he presides; one harmony or consonance, one sympathy of many voices, denoted by the lyre of Apollo which is called the spirit of the universe (1969, 310).

Bruno's works were suggested to Leibniz by the English Deist John Toland, who obtained a volume of Bruno's dialogues that had once belonged to Elizabeth I (Daniel 1984, 200). Sepharial draws attention to Bruno's influence on Leibniz in the following description of the latter's philosophical system:

> In [Leibniz's] system of thought we regard every part, every atom, as reflecting every other part of the body to which it belongs, and therefore every universe comes to be a reflex of the Divine, as if a light falling upon a crystal sphere should illuminate the entire sphere and therefore all of its parts or molecules, and thus there would be a myriad molecules, each consisting of millions of atoms, all illuminated from a single source of light; and, *mirabile dictu*, every atom is a sphere in itself (Sepharial 1974, 171).

Prior to Bruno, John Dee in the 1560s outlines his own geometrical model based on the *monas,* which, like the mystical letters of the Greeks and Hebrews, is generated from lines, a point, a circle, and semicircles. According to Dee, "the first and most simple manifestation" of things occurred by way of the line and circle. There is a geometric progression from the point to line, then circle—a circle being constructed by rotating a line around a point. In Dee's system, the monad equates with point and is the primal unit and source of number (Clulee 1988, 89–90). It should be remarked that Dee's *monas* is a portmanteau construction arrived at from a combination of the symbols for Mercury and Aries and apparently derived from postulates and diagrams in Geofroy Tory's 1529 alphabetic treatise *Champ Fleury*. (For more on this possibility, see Clulee 1988, 92.) The best detailed examination of Bruno's influence on Leibniz remains Brunnhofer 1890. For Leibniz's indebtedness to the hermetic tradition, see Yates 1969, 363–74. More recently, David Shapiro notes in John Ashbery's poetry the presence of an "essentially exquisite theatre of windowless monads" (1984, 164).

Ludwig Stein in his *Leibniz und Spinoza* informs that the term "Monad" was suggested to Leibniz by Francis Mercurius van Helmont (1618–1699)—a contemporary and an acquaintance (see Leibniz 1898, 34n). Helmont's *True and Natural Hebrew Alphabet* is considered in chapter 7. The word occurs earlier in Plato (*Philebus* 15b, and *Phaedo* 101e and 105c) as η μονασ with the precise meaning of numerical unit. For possible nonoccidental influences on Leibniz's concept of the monad—especially the neo-Confucian concept of *li*—see Mungello 1977, 79–86.

9. Cf. André Breton writing in 1952: "What the Surrealists in particular wanted was much less to create beauty than to express themselves freely, which meant expressing their inner *selves*. As such, taken together, they could not help expressing their times as well" (1993, 254). Such expressive interiorities clearly resemble both the perspective and the teleology of monads.

10. Problematic to Leibniz in the concept of the atom is its unavoidable status as an ultimate and indivisible unit. Whitehead is thus wrong to claim, "The monads of Leibniz constitute another version of an atomic doctrine of the universe" (1933, 168), an error Don Byrd repeats when describing the monad as "both an atomic entity and a cosmos" (1994, 269).

11. "And as the same town, looked at from various sides, appears quite different and becomes as it were numerous in aspects [*perspectivement*]; even so, as a result of the infinite number of simple substances, it is as if there were so many different universes, which, nevertheless are nothing but aspects [*perspectives*] of a single universe, according to the special point of view of each Monad" (Leibniz 1898, 248). What Leibniz conflates here is expression and essence.

12. Olson's preoccupation with place leads to focal points *without* paradox. Assisted by Leibniz, we arrive at Gloucester as a monad, understood precisely as the amplitude of a contraction. The residual question can be stated as follows: Is Gloucester an intense unicity or an aggregate of subdivisions?

13. In the specific case of Descartes, the material outside the cogito is mapped out and gridded along an axial of the thinking subject. In Leibniz's philosophy, sense perception does not involve a passive reception of data upon a tabula rasa, but performative endeavors on the monad's part to actively appropriate elements from the external world. As Deleuze reminds us, "what is expressed does not exist outside of its expressions" (1990, 112). Spinoza defines mode as "the Modifications

(*affectiones*) of a substance or that which is in something else through which it may be conceived" (*Ethics* I, def. 5). To this might be added Antonio Negri's observation that the mode partakes of a multiple existence as a whole made up of parts existing in a certain relationship of stasis and mobility. See Negri 1991.

14. In discussing the potentiality for new creation in the physical field, Whitehead outlines his own theory of monads: "The physical field . . . is atomized with definite divisions: it becomes a "nexus" of actualities. Such a quantum (i.e. each actual division) of the extensive continuum is the primary phase of a creature. The quantum is constituted by its totality of relationships and cannot move. Also the creature cannot have any external adventures, but only the internal adventure of becoming. Its birth is its end" (1969, 96).

Unlike Leibnizian monads, which change, Whitehead's are subject exclusively to a process of becoming. Whitehead's name for the monad is "actual entity," and it shares with Leibniz's category certain identical qualities. Both are mental and without substance, and both "mirror" the universe. The Leibnizian monad is alone, however, in partaking of that reality which underlies the physical.

Don Byrd identifies the monad with the statistical subject "able to define a local region clearly and distinctly, but with respect to the whole, its picture is necessarily fuzzy and its apprehension of itself is based on certain zones of statistically reliable frequencies" (1994, 269). It might be noted parenthetically that Herodotean historiography utilizes a monadic mode in which a discourse of evidence derives from active, personal living.

15. Heidegger is correct to point out that Leibniz's definition of the monad— as a unity of perception and appetition, of representation with struggle—commits it to being an operation of will.

16. On Diderot's use of the cataract, see Mehlman 1979.

17. In a suggestive passage, rich with deconstructive possibilities, Leibniz compares the mind to "a block of marble which has veins, rather than a block of marble wholly even, or of blank tablets, i.e. of what is called among philosophers a *tabula rasa*. For if the soul resembled these blank tablets, truths would be in us as the figure of Hercules in the marble, when the marble is wholly indifferent to the reception of this figure or some other. But if there were veins in the block which should indicate the figure of Hercules rather than other figures, this block would be more determined thereto, and Hercules would be in it as in some sense innate, although it would be needful to labour to discover these veins, to clear them by polishing, and by cutting away what prevents them from appearing" (1949, 45). There is an aesthetic parallel to this in William Morris's pithy insistence that there can be no beauty without material resistance, a pre-Raphaelist adage central to Jerome McGann's analysis of the irreducible materiality of certain modernist textual formats. See McGann 1991, 1992, 1993.

18. Elsewhere Blaser insists on the narrative nature of the serial poem, named the "serial narrative" that Robert Duncan, in 1962, dubbed "neo-narrative." "The

term serial was not adapted from serial music, but was intended to suggest the diremptions of belief, even in poetry, all around us" (Blaser 1970, 323). Serial poems "deconstruct meanings and compose a wildness of meaning in which the I of the poet is not the center but a returning and disappearing note" (Blaser 1979, 323). "The serial poem is not simply a sequence. It is meant to be a narrative that transfigures time, . . . it makes language direct and insistent without reference to a grid of meaning, which in our time has become intolerable, a-historical, a lie" (Blaser 1979, 324).

19. For the proposal of the scriptor, see "The Death of the Author" in Barthes 1977, 142–48.

20. "The most fertile methods today concerning the mythical text in general are regulated by an algebra and, more precisely, by a combinative algebra. There exists to begin with—or, better yet, it is possible to constitute—a set of discrete elements, of units. Out of this reservoir circulate combinative sequences that can be mastered. Hence the theory of musical forms that is certainly the most general available organon, both practical and constructible, for these operations. This algebraic method is, to my mind, a local realization three centuries later of the Leibnizian dream of an alphabet of human thoughts for which its author had forged an *ars combinatoria*—first invention, precisely, of combinative algebra as well as of a logic of the note, of any discrete note. From which Leibniz derived the idea that music was indeed the language closest to the universal language, or to the *mathesis universalis*. This was an idea to which philosophers turned a deaf ear, but which was heard by musicians, since at Johann Sebastian Bach's death, Leibniz's *De Arte Combinatoria* was discovered at the composer's bedside (which, in return, permits us to read several fugues)" (Serres 1982b, 45–46). Blaser was familiar with Serres's book quoting part of this passage, reflecting upon the Leibnizian aspect in Bach, and citing the conclusion of Deleuze's "startling book," that is, *The Fold* (Blaser 1995, 24–25).

21. Eco suggests three distinct types of labyrinth. The first classical, Minoan one of Crete, is fatalistically unidirectional and structured as a skein which on unwinding produces a continuous line. This type of labyrinth is intrinsically an Ariadne thread itself. The second is the maze presenting "choices between alternative paths, and some of the paths dead ends. . . . In this kind of labyrinth one does need an Ariadne thread." The third is a net, or rhizome, "a tangle of bulbs and tubers appearing like 'rats squirming one on top of the other' " (1986, 81).

22. Following Lucretius's comparison of atoms to letters (*De rerum natura* I:822–28, 905–12, II:688–99) the temptation arises to draw a similar analogy between the monad and the letter. Certainly, the alphabet provides a system of combinatorial "compossibles" that would have appealed to Leibniz. However, the analogy requires that we deny the letter its condition as a component or subset of the word and rethink it more along the Pythagorean lines applied to letters during the middle ages. As Dick Higgins explains, a "sacred power was attributed to letters, which

were not seen as mechanical components of the written word, but as essential and autonomous instruments expressing the process underlying them, analogous therefore to numbers and proportions. The process of forming words became, then, a very sacred one indeed, part of the divine game of realizing things out of their underlying numbers of letters" (1977, 8). The monadologist, of course, would emphasize here less the instrumental and more the expressive nature of the letter.

The book as monad is the Mallarméan seduction to which Deleuze himself proves susceptible—not to the spatial, minimalist economy of *un coup de dés,* but to the universal theater of the book outlined in *Le Livre.* The fold, not the projectile. The artefactual book envelops folds which subsequent acts of reading unfold. The page already emerges as a single fold as soon as its words are rethought as strata and appurtenance, not as lines. This is the geological implication of Mallarmé's "Book as Spiritual Instrument." Deleuze enumerates the monadic features of the book-machine or "the monad with multiple leaves." "Now it contains every fold, since the combinations of its pages are infinite; but it includes them in its closure, and all its actions are internal" (1993, 31).

23. The plenum is basic to methods of early Greek writing, which was organized according to a *scriptio continua* with no space provided between the letters. A full discussion of the readerly and semantic implications of this practice can be found in chapter 7.

24. In his 1676 *Pacidus Philalethi,* Leibniz outlines a theory of motion and change based on transcreation. "Motion cannot . . . be better explained than when we say that the body *E* is somehow extinguished and annihilated in [place] *B* and actually created anew and resuscitated in [place] *D,* which can be called, in new and most happy terminology, *transcreation"* (quoted in Rescher 1967, 101–2). Does this early theory of transcreational motion have direct bearing on the dynamics of quotation in general, and particularly on Blaser's use of collage throughout *The Holy Forest?* Understood "transcreationally," quotation results not in a simple decontextualization but rather an annihilation of the prior situation and a subsequent new resuscitation. The term "transcreation" is used by Fred Wah to describe his method of composing *Pictograms from the Interior of B.C.* (Vancouver: Talon Books, 1975). Wah makes no reference to Leibniz's transcreation, attributing the origin of the word to Coleridge.

25. I note in passing that the mathematical science of topology, or *analysis situs,* was invented by Leibniz. The topological nature of Leibnizian space is discussed by Rescher (1967, 100–1). Morrissette offers a succinct summary of the science: "Topology represents the primary intellectual operation capable of revealing the modalities of surfaces, volumes, boundaries, contiguities, holes, and above all the notions of inside and outside, with the attendant ideas of insertion, penetration, containment, emergence, and the like" (1972, 47).

26. But perhaps the basic constitution of the fold should be rethought. Rather than presenting either a material or an ideal hypothesis of substance, *The Monad-*

ology should be seen to offer an *imaginary* solution to the nature of the real. Considered this way, as a strictly hypothetical or "imaginary" explanation, Leibniz's theory unfolds as an exemplary document within the canon of 'pataphysics—Jarry's science of imaginary solutions discussed in chapter 2. Read as a 'pataphysical treatise, *The Monadology* emerges as a magnificent game in which "game" itself is redefined as "the perilous act."

27. For Leibniz's complex anticipation of the capitalist spirit, see Elster 1975.

Chapter 4

1. There are hints of proprioceptive awareness prior to Olson: in Diderot, for example, who writes in his *Letter to the Blind* of 1749, "I have never doubted that the state of our organs and senses greatly affects our metaphysics and our moral state, and that our most purely intellectual ideas, if I may thus express myself, correspond very closely to the structure of our bodies" (quoted in Le Brun 1990, 54). Proprioceptive concerns in art appear earlier in the century. Nikolai Evreinov's play *In the Stage-Wings of the Soul,* for example, is set inside a human body and depicts on stage enormous internal organs. The set, designed by M. P. Bobysov, also included a giant spinal column, kinetic lungs and heart, and mechanized intestines (Golub 1984, 42). Vladislav Todorov marks the proprioceptive pertinence of Evreinov's play, commenting that in it "the physiological transformation of the organisms preceded and determined any possible activity by the psyche" (108).

2. Cixous offers such proprioceptive exhortations as "Censor the body and you censor breath and speech at the same time. Write your self. Your body must be heard" (1987, 577) and "Inscribe the breath of the whole woman" (578). In her thought, woman enjoys a privileged proprioceptive relationship with the voice through maternal proximity. A woman, she insists, "is never far from 'mother'" (578).

3. In sharp contrast to James, Thomas Hobbes presents breathing as a physiological unfolding into uncertainty. In the respiratory act, atoms enter the body and find eventual passage into the vascular network. "By some of these small Bodies it is that we live; which being taken in with our breath, pass into our blood, and cause it (by their compounded Motion) to circulate through the Veins and Arteries; which the blood of itself (being a heavie Body) without it cannot do" (Hobbes 1678, 81). It should be remarked that Hobbes believes breathing to be a form of atomic infection, assigning to atoms a mediatory role between inside and outside. Descartes was convinced that atoms were "tiny flies" (Hobbes 1678, 81), and it was not until Lavoisier (1743–94) that an accurate account of the role of oxygen in respiration was advanced. Hobbes opposes breath to speech as vital to a voluntary motion (cf. *Leviathan* VI). The historical connection of breath to sexual tumescence goes back to Aristotle: "For sexual excitement is due to breath. The penis proves this as it

quickly increases from small to large because of the breath in it" (*Problems* 953b, quoted in Agamben 1993b, 16).

4. The function of syllables (specifically the *bija*) in Mantric formulas, along with the physiological basis of Sanskrit prosody, is discussed in Ginsberg 1972, 19–21. For a strikingly different use of the "syllable-king," see Kenneth Goldsmith's programmatic tour de force, *No. III 2.7.93–10.20.96* (1997). The text is constructed from the sum of phrases ending in sounds related to "R" collected by the author between February 7, 1993, and October 20, 1996. Phrases are arranged alphabetically by syllable-count, developing from a chapter of single-syllable entries ("A, a, aar, aas, aer," etc.) to a final 7,228-syllable entry. It goes without saying that Goldsmith has little interest in the biopoetic, proprioceptive potential of the syllable but rather its programmatic use in textual generative methods similar to the ones advanced by Lionnais, Harry Mathews, Queneau, and other members of Oulipo.

5. Olson's *Mayan Letters* first appeared in the Divers Press edition of 1953 and subsequently in *Selected Writings,* edited by Robert Creeley (Olson 1966).

6. Worth remarking is that while insisting on a Mayan worldview evident in the glyphs, Olson never extends his concerns beyond an anthropological response into the wider consideration of the sociopolitical conditions of the Maya that form the ground of their historical specificity. It is known that the glyphs functioned in a hieratic, not demotic, communication system. The glyphs were the property of a priest caste and were consciously maintained as a privileged—if not secret—script. Thomson informs that a knowledge of hieroglyphic writing, along with calendric computations, rituals, prophecy, and divination were taught by the high priest, or *ahau can mai,* to candidates for the priesthood (1970, 168). A similar protectionist measure was applied to scripture by the 1229 synodal decree of Toulouse, which decreed that "lay people shall not have books of scripture, except the psalter and divine office; and they shall not have these in the mother tongue" (quoted in Innis 1972, 131).

7. Olson is correct to repudiate the traditional binary coupling of a form with a content; however, his proposed alternative relation calls for comment. Olson reduces a binary system into a unitary term—A is subsumed in B to become an extension of the latter. Such a reduction-into-extension seems symptomatic of Olson's desire to establish a spontaneous, unmediated status for language as a direct physiological extension of the body. But given the fact that a text is articulated around numerous codes which it never exhausts, might it not be preferable to adopt Barthes's suggestion and treat the poem as comprising a multiplicity of forms without content, replacing the notion of a breath-line with that of a polyvocal volume?

8. The implications of the Viking Fund application's conjunction with Olson's statements on poetics written at the same time were first brought to my attention by Ron Silliman in a manuscript sent to me in 1977 and there called *The Horizon.* Silliman's significant insight is in several ways the ignition behind this chapter, and to him go my respect and gratitude. Curiously, neither the application nor the

Mayan Letters was reprinted in Don Allen and Ben Friedlander's collected edition of Olson's prose (Olson 1997).

9. In contrast, William Burroughs responds to the narrative potential that he finds in Mayan glyphs. The image of the centipede, for instance, haunting his writing from *Queer* onward, derives from a fragment of a Mayan codex depicting a man tied to a couch beneath a huge hovering centipede (Miles 1993, 99). Burroughs's own studies of the Maya centered on their calendar as a form of mind control. He went as far as developing his own version of the Mayan calendar, the "Dream Calendar," starting on December 23, 1969, and comprising eight separate months of twenty-three days each (Miles 1993, 175).

10. On Olson's spatial approach to page surface, cf. Christensen (1979, 83–87), who outlines his own—admittedly "speculative"—argument of a biaxial arrangement of Olson's poetic page. According to Christensen, an axis of event bisects an axis of thought down and across the center of the page. Each resulting quadrant is allocated responsibility for containing the transcription of various mentalities and dispositions—"tentative and initial, a lyric of emergent awareness . . . the reach toward the nameless and indefinable . . . the intervening stages of idea and argument . . . leap to final synthesis from the revelations of aroused subjectivity" (86). Christensen makes no comment on the possibility of a glyphic influence on Olson's page arrangement. Relevant passages in *Maximus*—relevant, that is, as poetic embodiments of Olson's theories of the glyph-block—include the sections "The Shoreman, Sunday Sep 10 1961" and " 'View': fr the Orontes" in *Maximus Poems IV, V, VI* (1970). Olson's more extreme departures from typographic linearity, such as pp. 120–21 in *Maximus Poems Volume Three* (1975a), seem less relevant to the present concern of Mayan glyph-blocks. A comparable division of page into tetrad forms as a hermeneutic device can be found in McLuhan and McLuhan 1988, 129–214.

Chapter 5

1. The Richardsons' work reaffirms the authenticity of Milton's expanded text of 1674, and their remarks on Bentley are predictably hostile. At one point Bentley is singled out as a linguistic felon, a semantic coin-clipper worthy of capital punishment. Defending the 1674 edition against Bentley's, they write, "We have Therefore Consider'd This Edition [of 1674] as bearing the Image and Superscription of *Milton:* and that to Mutilate or Alter anything in it (except the Error of the Printer, or Oversight is Apparent) is Clipping or Coining, and Capitally Criminal in the Republick of Letters" (J. and J. Richardson 1734, clxxi). The interlacing of monetary tropes and discourse with theories of language and government during Bentley's age is admirably discussed in Caffentzis 1989.

2. Among the many contemporary satires on Bentley are *Critical Remarks on*

Capt. Gulliver's Travels. By Doctor Bantley and *An Account of the State of Learning in the Empire of Lilliput; together with The History and Character of Bullum the Emperor's Library Keeper* (both attributed to John Arbuthnot); William King, *Dialogues of the Dead Relating to the Present Controversies Concerning the Epistles of Phalaris,* and Jonathan Swift, "A Discourse to prove the Antiquity of the English Tongue."

3. Bentley appears to have possessed a near libidinal attraction to textual controversy. William Whiston recounts an amusing anecdote in his *Memoirs* of Bentley's disagreement with his fiancée, Joanna Bernard, over a textual objection in the *Book of Daniel* that almost led to a termination of their engagement. The dispute, centering on the true size of the golden image of Nebuchadnezzar announced in *Daniel VI,* is described in detail in R. J. White 1965, 121. De Quincey offers a less captious portrait of Bentley, citing the latter's patient and charitable handling of the incivility shown him by Joshua Barnes (De Quincey 1871, 5:565.)

4. Bentley 1732. Bentley's preface is unpaginated. The rapidity (or otherwise) of Bentley's project remains moot. An entry in John Byrom's *Journal* for January 2, 1726, mentions having supper with Bentley and of the latter having said that "he made emendations upon Milton which he had given to Heylin" (Talon 1950, 79). This would suggest a relatively early start on the edition in 1725, lending credence to my claim that the project was more advanced than the merely "meditated notes" that Jebb argues was its status in 1726 (1882, 79n). This evidence would likewise run counter to Bentley's own statement in the preface of having put the notes to press "as soon as made." Internal evidence, however, strongly favors a rapid pace and an incomplete project. The work is a plethora of emendations and footnotes until the final two books, which are almost untouched and contain a minimum of editorial comment. This suggests that the project could not be completed to meet the opening of Parliament and throws doubt on the probity of Bentley's own reason: " 'Tis a pleasant Consideration to me, now weary and fatigu'd, to find that the Editor will seldom or never in this XII Book intermix his Pebblestones among the Author's Diamonds" (1732, 380). The phrase "now weary and fatigu'd" remains ambiguous, referring plausibly either to Bentley or to the phantom editor. Cohen and Bourdette (1980) provide a bibliography of studies on Bentley's edition.

5. De Quincey contends that Bentley's use of both an interpolator and an editor has a prophylactic purpose as regards the canon. "The reader must understand that Bentley, whilst retrenching many and long passages from the 'Paradise Lost,' on the pretense that they had been interpolated by some unknown person taking advantage of Milton's blindness, transforms this interpolator into a regular editor, though without a name, and in this way secures a subject for the volcanic torrent of his fury and disgust, without needing once to violate the majesty of the mighty poet" (1871, 5:578).

6. I am indebted to J. W. Mackail's excellent monograph *Bentley's Milton* (1924) for several of the subsequent examples.

7. In the *Cratylus,* Plato sets forth a view of language in which words are presented not as conventional and arbitrary signs (the nominalist view), but as "correct" and "true." According to this theory, the true word is attained through an etymologizing process by which a search through component parts leads to older, more authentic forms. In other words, meaning is proposed to be implicit in etymology.

8. Antin contends that the prosody of *Paradise Lost* is truly hendecasyllabic, a fact obfuscated by the visual unit of the line whose simulacrum is that of an "illusory blank verse metric." The blind do not think in lines of language. "The idea of a blind man composing poems in a purely page oriented syllabic measure is so unlikely that alternatives ought to be suggested. Either Milton's blindness was mythical (which doesn't seem likely), or he was not responsible for the final page arrangement of the poem he dictated, in which case the metric of *Paradise Lost* was largely due to the editors" (Antin 1968, 177). As early as 1680, George Delgarno likens the blind listening (with the proneness to acoustic confusion and the unidirectionality of utterance) to "the scribblings and blottings on the Table of the Blind man's memory" (1680, 16–17).

9. In his edition of Fulke Greville's *Remains,* Wilkes cites over two hundred instances of textual discrepancies between the manuscript and the printed edition of 1670. He divides these corruptions into numerous categories, including errors at source arising from a scribal misreading of the holograph copy being reproduced, and subsequent errors through misreadings by the compositor(s).

The majority of compositorial errors might be gathered under the general heading of textual clinamens or "parapraxes," analogous to slips of the tongue and forgetfulness in the psychopathology of everyday life. The most common would include errors of displaced letters ("firend" for "friend"); of fused letters ("insanity" for "in sanity") and of turned letters ("fiue" for "fine"). Similarly prevalent would be errors in typeface (e.g., failure to capitalize or italicize) and errors in punctuation. Unilateral decisions were frequently made by compositors regarding the expansion or contraction of words. The latter often occurred as an economic exigency due to the scarcity of a certain letter in a font or to avoid a wasteful line break and run-on. Expansions, too, might be erroneous, for instance, the ligatured contraction "coperative" might be expanded to "comperative" instead of the correct "cooperative." Where type was set from holograph copy (as in the *Remains*), innumerable instances of misreadings might arise from holographic ambiguities. Additional compositorial decisions might be made in cases where the setter was faced with an illegible passage due to ink blots or torn paper. Occasionally, a compositorial misreading of an initial scribal error can produce an accurate return to the ur copy. (Our author writes "fame," which the scribe misreads as "fime" but which our compositor alters back to "fame" by an independent judgment on his part.) Equally, the compositorial process can change an error into a different error. (In this case, our author writes "fame" again, which the scribe writes as "tame" and which our compositor alters to "time.") Other categories of errors listed by Wilkes are omissions of words and errors of attraction due to customary semantic integrations. ("Agrarian lands" instead of the correct "Agrarian lawes" is an error provoked by the mental association of a frequent predication.) Word omission, as well as incorrect word order, may also arise from the compositor's failure to memorize a stretch of copy in his head. This error of "overreach" would suggest a type-shop that did not use a caller of the text. Two further errors (those of regularization and of modernization) rank as nonauthorial, editorial interventions in order to remove the idiosyncrasies of an author's orthography and style.

It requires great temerity to defend all of Bentley's editorial hypotheses, yet a comparison of Wilkes's edition of Greville with Bentley's Milton will endorse, via precedent, the majority of textual cruxes and further lend support to many of Bentley's conjectural emendations. For additional details of this textual instability, see Wilkes 1965, 20–29.

10. Excellent discussions of the application of the compositor's rule (and other nonauthorial textual interventions) can be found in Masten 1997 and McKerrow 1927, 6–14. Dobson offers a brief and entertaining account of accusations against compositors (1954, 136).

11. This seasonal complication, however, did not pertain to the setting of *Paradise Lost*. Milton signed an agreement with his printer, Samuel Symons, on April 27, 1667, and the entry of publication in the register of Stationers' Hall is August 20. The book thus would have been typeset through the late spring or summer months before the end of August.

12. Christopher Hill is in partial agreement with Bentley on the spuriousness of this passage. Hill calls it "a poetic invention" and adds a footnote reading, "Not necessarily Milton's invention: there is something very similar in S. Pordage." (1979, 342). The book by Pordage referred to is the 1661 *Mundorum Explicatio*. Samuel Pordage [1633–91?] was a follower of the hermetic Familist Jacob Boehme, considered an influence on Milton's thinking.

13. Bentley's emendational practices are anticipated by John Taylor, the Water-Poet. In the 1630 folio edition of Taylor's *Works* is a twenty-six-line poetic errata in which Taylor cites several reasons for the inevitable presence of textual errors: his own sickness at the time of typesetting, the division of the book's production between four printers "dwelling farre and asunder," and inadequate proofreading. The pertinent lines of Taylor's Errata are the ones suggesting a readerly progress through the errors:

> Then in your reading mend each mis-plac'd letter,
> And by your judgement make bad words sound better.
> Where you may hurt, heale; where you can afflict,
> There helpe and cure, or else be not too strict.
> Looke through your fingers, wink, connive at mee,

And (as you meet with faults) see, and not see.
Thus must my faults escape, (or escape never,)
For which, good Readers, I am yours forever.

(J. Taylor 1630)

Taylor's democratic mandate for the reader is remarkably similar to Bentley's own method of conjectural emendation. He not only admits the inevitable inaccuracy of his text but encourages all readerly incursions into it to be of an emendational nature. Taylor, in fact, sanctions the reader as final authority on textual matters and in so doing volatizes the notions of both origin and intention. By refusing to specify the errors in a tabulate corrigenda, Taylor opens up his writing to a textual indeterminacy schematized along the following lines: "[T]his is not the book I wrote . . . this book is filled with errors and for good reason . . . I was sick at the time it was being set and the proof-readers were not too good . . . also, to make matters worse, the book had four different printers . . . so it's not surprising that it's inaccurate . . . but rather than point out all these mistakes, why don't you, the reader, make what changes you want." There is a comparable mandate to semantic determination in *scriptio continuum* considered in chapter 7.

14. Bentley's annotational procedure ran counter to the stylistic program of the Royal Society, which insisted as a provision within its Statutes that, not only in all reports "the matter of fact shall be barely stated, without any prefaces, apologies, or rhetorical flourishes," but also that all conjectural material "shall be done apart" (Williamson 1951, 282–83). Barney (1991) offers a rich and diverse range of viewpoints on footnotes, annotations, and marginalia.

15. Two notable passages curiously survived Bentley's rational surgery. He does not call attention to the famous passage, 9:515, which De Quincey cites as evidence of the use of laudanum in Paradise:

> So deep the power of these ingredients pierced,
> Even to the inmost seat of mental sight,
> That Adam, now enforced to close his eyes,
> Sank down, and all his spirits became entranced.
> But him the gentle angel by the hand
> Soon raised

The other is the short passage 3:260–61 problematizing the length of Christ's absence from heaven after the resurrection: "Then with the multitude of my redeemed / Shall enter heaven long absent[.]" "What was Christ doing," asks Christopher Hill, "between the Resurrection and the Last Judgement, here apparently conflated? Had he not ascended to heaven? Surely his soul did not sleep like those of his elect?" (1979, 392).

16. It may be useful to recall the contemporary status of *Paradise Lost* in 1732. The first edition of 1667 has eight variant title pages, suggesting the opposite of a

speedy sale and helping to advance the argument that the book was not immediately popular, was marketed cautiously and printed over a length of time to meet demand. It took two years to sell out of the entire edition of 1,300 copies. With the appearance of the second edition in 1674, the poem had undergone significant structural alterations, expanding from ten to twelve books. Significant paratextual additions are the commendatory verses by Andrew Marvell and Isaac Barrow, the latter claiming for Milton a status equivalent to both Homer and Virgil. These verses are retained in the third edition of 1677. In the same year, Dryden lavishes his own praises, claiming *Paradise Lost* to be "one of the greatest, most noble, and most sublime poems which either this age or nation has produced" (Mackail 1924, 10). Milton's reputation had advanced sufficiently for a sumptuous, illustrated folio to be published by Jacob Tonson in 1688, and it is to this edition that Dryden contributes his historic claim (beyond Barrow's) for the superiority of Milton over Homer and Virgil. Moore contains a full discussion of interpretations of *Paradise Lost* published between 1701 and 1734.

17. Compare. R. J. White 1965, 155–57.

18. The title of Bentley's collected lectures is *A Confutation of Atheism from the Origin and Frame of the World*. Prior to their publication, they were delivered as sermons. Kroll contends that Bentley's criticism of both Hobbes and Epicurus is superficial and selective, targeting for criticism "only those distinctly pagan and orthodox features of Epicurean thought which contradict the truths of the Christian faith" (1991, 150). Bentley reminds that "the Mechanical or Corpuscular Philosophy, though peradventure the oldest as well as the best in the world, had lain buried for many Ages in contempt and oblivion, recommending the Epicurean and Democritean Philosophy [as] providentially one of the best Antidotes against other impious Opinions: as the oil of the Scorpions is said to be against the poison of their stings" (quoted in Kroll 1991, 61).

19. The second and third parts of the *Lectures,* together with Newton's *Four Letters* to Bentley on the subject, are reprinted (in facsimile) in I. Cohen 1958, 279–394. Also included is an informative essay on Bentley and Newton by Perry Miller.

Bentley does, in fact, appeal to the atomic analogy in the *Boyle Lectures*. Writing derisively (and initially for oratorical delivery from the pulpit), he claims, "If a man should affirm that an ape, casually meeting with a pen, ink and paper, and falling to scribble, did happen to write exactly the *Leviathan* of Thomas Hobbes, would an atheist believe such a story?" (quoted in R. J. White 1965, 76). Beyond the logical confrontation of stochastics by a law of probability, there is the suppressed fact that such simian achievements remain theoretically possible due to the material nature of letters as atomic, mobile, and therefore infinitely recombinant particles. The purpose of this chapter is not to evaluate Bentley's refutation of atheism but rather to examine the Newtonian and atomistic background to his later editorial practices. Certainly the atomic status of letters and the nature of the literary text as material in motion proves a felicitous asset to Bentley's fastidious erudition.

20. Giordano Bruno, "De triplici minimo et mensura" in *Opera* I, iii. 119–361. Bruno's poem was first published by Johann Wechel and P. Fischer, Frankfurt, 1591.

21. I take the term "schismogenetic" from Bateson 1973.

22. For a detailed discussion of bifurcation theory, see Prigogine and Stengers 1984, 160ff. David Porush makes convincing use of bifurcation theory in his study of William Marshall's *Roadshow:* "Fictions as Dissipative Structures: Prigogine's Theory and Postmodernism's Roadshow" in Hayles 1991, 54–84.

23. The Soviet neuropsychologist A. R. Luria offers a fascinating example of the use of homophony to circumvent the problem of memorizing a text in an unknown language. Luria documents a long case study with a Russian journalist, Shereshevski (known as S.), of prodigious memory. When asked to memorize the first four lines of the *Inferno* and understanding no Italian, S. created in his mind tableaux constructed out of the Russian homophonic equivalents of Dante's words. Here is the system applied to the first line, *Nell mezzo del cammin di nostra vita:*

Nel—I was paying my membership dues when there, in the corridor, I caught sight of the ballerina, Nel'skaya.

mezzo—I myself am a violinist; what I do is to set up an image of a man who
    is playing the violin [Russ: *vmeste*], together with Nel'skaya.

del—There's a pack of Deli Cigarettes near them.

cammin—I set up an image of a fireplace [Russ: *kamin*] near them.

di—Then I see a hand pointing to a door [Russ: *dver*].

nostra—I see a nose [Russ: *nos*]; a man has tripped and, in falling gotten his nose
    pinched in the doorway [*tra*].

vita—He lifts his leg over the threshold, for a child is lying there, that is, a sign
    of life-vitalism.

(Luria 1968, 45–46)

A similar method of scenic placement for homophones is used for the next three lines. Luria reports that sixteen years later, on being asked without warning to repeat them, S. did so accurately and effortlessly. The system devised by S. naturally bears comparison to Roussel's exploitation of the homophone's potential for narrative generation discussed in chapter 2.

24. For McGann's boldly innovative theories of textual criticism, together with his contestation with Greg, Bowers, and Tanselle's theories, see McGann 1992. His related theory of textuality based in writing and production, as opposed to reading and interpretation, is presented in Mc Gann 1991.

25. A huge implication (not dealt with by Bentley) is the hypothetical corruptibility of other Miltonic texts. Although experiencing seriously weakened eyesight at the time of this appointment, Milton's official work was not reduced until 1655, after which time (with his salary commuted to a life pension) his work was limited to the translation of letters for Oliver and Richard Cromwell. A. E. Barker's assessment of the poet's achievement after blindness makes no hint of the un-

scrupulous transgressions that Bentley intimates: "His accomplishments after 1652 were courageously magnificent; but he was dependent for the materials of thought upon memory and the mechanical assistance of others" (Barker 1942, 234). *De Doctrina Christiana* was one important text composed under the limiting conditions of sightlessness.

The extant manuscript, now housed in the Record Office, indicates a hybrid script, posthumously recopied in part with numerous minor revisions in several hands. A detailed study of this manuscript can be found in Kelley 1941. Chapters 2 and 3 contain detailed analyses of the revisions Milton made in a version copied by an amanuensis between 1658 and 1661. Kelley argues that these revisions alter significantly Milton's original, dictated opinions. Milton himself first refers to the weakening condition of his eyesight in a letter to Leonard Philaris, dated September 28, 1654, as first occurring a decade earlier (Patterson 1931–38, 67). Barker argues, "In some degree at least, the obscurity of his political argument in the pamphlets written between 1649 and 1652 must be ascribed to this affliction" (1942, 136). Barker does not extend this thesis to Milton's later poetic productions.

26. Parkes is informative on the nature and extent of dictation and genuine authorial input prior to the sixth century.

> There is little evidence before the sixth century that guides to phrasing—punctuation—originated with the author. No manuscript containing a work in the author's own handwriting has survived from Antiquity; this absence of autograph material has been attributed to the practice of dictating one's own works, letters, and even one's own notes to amanuenses. . . . Even if we accept the tentative identifications of the handwriting of known authors in surviving manuscripts, these are either of brief corrections added to a completed manuscript of their own work, or of marginal comments added to copies of texts composed by others. If authors supplied punctuation to a text it was as readers not writers. Because the work of scribes or amanuenses was 'mechanical,' they confined themselves to reproducing as faithfully as possible what has been transmitted to them without further interpretation; hence they did not supply punctuation to a text. (1993, 9)

However, Parkes does not address the issue of errant transcription provoked by either malaudition or editorial interpolation.

Chapter 6

1. "I Gather the Limbs of Osiris" was the general name Pound gave to a series of articles published in *The New Age* between December 7, 1911, and February 15, 1912. All eleven are reprinted as Part 1 of Pound 1973, 19–44. Robert Bertholf describes Duncan's "grand collage" as "a collection and formation of visual and tex-

tual images from a vast diversity of sources within a new contextual complexity"
(Bertholf 1997, xii).

2. An inventory, Barthes recalls, "is never a neutral idea; to catalogue is not
merely to ascertain, as it appears at first glance, but also to appropriate . . . [which
is] to fragment the world, to divide it into finite objects subject to man in proportion to their very discontinuity: for we cannot separate without finally naming and
classifying, and at that moment, property is born" (1980, 26–27). Barthes traces
the genealogy of the encyclopedia back to Noah's ark and the ultimate antediluvian
gesture of naming and housing each kind of animal (27). The precise phenomenology of the *Dictionary* is, as I hope to show, both an alphabetic listing and a
weave of citations accumulating and conspiring into the dissemination of distinct
linguistic property.

3. S. Johnson 1963, 18.

4. Johnson refers to nonscientific vocabulary as "the popular part of the language" (1787, 10:187), a phrase evocative of Wittgenstein's "ordinary usage."

5. "I'm interested in the way a page of writing flies off in all directions and at the
same time closes right up on itself like an egg. And in the reticences, the resonances,
the lurches, and all the larvae you can find in a book" (Deleuze 1995, 14).

6. The structure of the *Dictionary,* too, might be described by another Situationist term as a vast *detournement* of preexisting elements by which such elements
are integrated "into a superior construction of a milieu" (Knabb 1981).

7. That the *Dictionary* offered itself to hedonistic readings is far from fanciful.
The fact is the monolithic and forbidding two-volume folio format was supplemented in the same same year as its first publication by a more encompassable
alternative of serialized parts. This serial version of the *Dictionary* was offered at
six pence per fascicle and intended to appear in 165 weekly installments. It was an-
swered by a serialized and revised version of Bailey's *A New Etymological Dictionary
of the English Language.* A new preface for the latter was supplied by Joseph Nichol
Scott. Although no doubt motivated by market considerations, such serialization
obviously facilitated a reader reception of the *Dictionary* as a series of part-objects
lending themselves to noninstrumental encounters. For a detailed study of the two
serializations, see Gove 1940.

8. "There are four ways of making a book. A man might write the work of
others, adding and changing nothing, in which case he is simply called a 'scribe'
(*scriptor*). Another writes the work of others with additions which are not his own;
and he is called a 'compiler' (*compilator*). Another writes both others' work and his
own, but with others' work in principal place, adding his own for purposes of explanation; and he is called a 'commentator' (*commentator*). . . . Another writes both
his own work and others' but with his own work in principal place adding others'
for purposes of confirmation; and such a man should be called an 'author' (*auctor*)"
(Saint Bonaventura, *In primum librum sententiarum,* proem, quest. 4. Printed in
Opera I, ed. Quaracchi, 1882, 14, col. 2. Quoted in Kittay and Godzich 1987, III.)

The preface consistently suppresses its true mode of production, which is team-work, specifically the transmission of material from a single reader-marker over to a team of copyists. Johnson publicly offers the work as a single man's toil, but when this humanist obfuscation is removed, the *Dictionary* can be seen to comply to the medieval theory of hierarchical text-production described in the foregoing quotation, descending from auctores through compilators down to actor or scribe. Peyton, the Macbean brothers, and Johnson's other shadowy amanuenses—those unsung heroes of the *Dictionary*—resurrect the lowly function of the scriptor. Certeau paints a positive portrait of the latter role, comparing the medieval copyist to the translator whose function is the production of otherness in a space where no authorial right can be claimed. In contrast, the copyist "transformed his body into the spoken word of the other," assimilating the verb into his own body but imitating and incarnating the text at hand "into a liturgy of reproduction" (1992, 119). I'll leave 'pataphysics to answer the question of whether Johnson's other six amanuenses experienced this same mystic state during their transcription of the quotations. For a detailed study of medieval theories of authorship, see Coleman 1981 and 1988. The same issues are also addressed in Hathaway 1989.

9. Johnson's parsimony can be gleaned from the following statistics relating to the items included in Bailey's last-minute additions to the *Dictionarium Brittanicum*. Of forty-two new listings found "in modern Authors, not occurring till the *Dictionary* was entirely printed," Johnson includes a mere thirteen. Notable omissions are "deputize," "reciprocality," "immurement," and, perhaps most surprising, "monotheism." Noah Webster's 1806 *A Comendious Dictionary of the English Language* fares quantitatively worse, however, containing a mere 37,000 word entries.

10. Earlier in the century, Alexander Pope had gathered numerous literary quotations intended to be incorporated as illustrations in a dictionary of the English language. Addison, too, made initial steps toward a similar compilation, and Ambrose Philips published his own "Proposals for Printing an English Dictionary in Two Volumes in Folio" including as part of its procedure supplementary quotations from written authorities. Such lexicographic plans were first realized in the *Vocabulario* prepared by the Florentine Accademia della Crusca, where extensive illustrative quotations appear, identified by source and page in the case of printed material and by the name of the owner when drawn from manuscript sources.

It should be pointed out that the *Dictionary* as published is a compromise formation containing only a sample of Johnson's vast illustrative gatherings. "To the weariness of copying," he laments, "I was condemned to add the vexation of expunging" (1963, 17). We might compare in passing Johnson's relationship to texts in his *Journey to the Western Isles* of 1775 where "it was his wish and endeavour not to make a single quotation" (1962, 2:368). Johnson himself had previously experimented with the interlacings of quotations and footnotes in his *Life of Richard Savage,* thereby introducing, in Richard Holmes' estimate, "a new biographical device" of authentic monolog (Holmes 1993, 46–47). The implications of resisting citation are summed up by Derrida: "To try and resist the removal of a textual member from its context is to want to remain protected against this writing poison. It is to want at all costs to maintain a boundary line between the inside and the outside of a context. It is to recognize the legitimacy of the relative specificity of each text, but it is also to believe that any system of writing exists *in itself,* as the relation of an inside to itself, particularly when it is 'true.' This amounts above all to an imposition of fundamentally classical limits upon generalized textuality. It is a kind of discontinuity prompted by resistance and protectionism" (1981, 316). This is not to claim poststructural potentials for the *Dictionary,* but rather to register the complex topological nature of its format. In the first publication of "Dissemination" in *Critique* 1969, 261–62, Barbara Johnson informs that Derrida provided a preliminary note claiming the work to be "but a tissue of 'quotations' " (Derrida 1981a, 287).

11. *Zettel,* German for "scraps of paper." I borrow the term from Richard Kuhns (1970, 219).

12. Wittgenstein 1953, v. In subsequent citations, the bracketed number following the quotation refers to the number of the proposition enumerated, not the page. Where page number alone is cited, it is followed by an "e."

13. A detailed analysis of the relation of dictionaries to encyclopedias can be found in Eco 1986, 46–86.

14. Bysshe hints at a more hedonistic reason for the brevity of the passages whose decentralized and nonnarrative nature "will divert and amuse [the reader] better; for here is no Thread of Story, nor Connexion of one Part with another, to keep his Mind intent, and constrain him to any Length of Reading" (Bysshe 1953, [iii]).

15. Johnson is known to have supplied the preface to Macbean's 1773 *Dictionary of Ancient Geography.*

16. Systems of taxonomy and indexing were first developed between the eleventh and thirteenth centuries, effecting a revolution in scholarly working method that Martin compares to the current revolutionary effects of electronic data banks (Martin 1994, 152). On the origins of referencing and indexing, see Rouse and Rouse (1982–86, 1:77–86).

17. For Wittgenstein, the nature of metaphorical meaning is derivative and secondary: "Could one speak here of a 'primary' and 'secondary' meaning of a word? — In both cases the explanation of the word is that of its primary meaning. It can only have a secondary meaning for someone if he knows its primary meaning. That is, the secondary use consists in applying the word with this primary use in new surroundings. To this extent one might want to call the secondary meaning 'metaphorical' " (1982, 102e).

18. Johnson's depreciation of etymology was detected and criticized by later thinkers. John Horne Tooke judged the *Dictionary* "to be the most imperfect and faulty, and the least valuable of any of his productions" (1860, 715), while Charles

Richardson accuses Johnson of abandoning his initial design in favor of an explanation through illustrated usage, concluding that Johnson's definitions are inauthentic because arrived at retrospectively to suit the individual citation. "What, then, shall we find in this Great Work;—A collection, I reply, of usages, quoted from (in general) our best English authors, and whose usages explained to suit the quotations; and those explanations including within them a portion of the sense pertaining to other words in the sentence" (C. Richardson 1838, 39).

19. Johnson's utilitarian paradigm stands in sharp contrast to the highly prescriptive logical grammars of his contemporaries Bishop Robert Lowth and Lindley Murray, both of whom emphasize "matters of correctness and precision, with only minor attention to merely utilitarian questions of clarity or force in the communication of ideas" (Leonard 1929, 231).

20. Underlying and presupposed in Johnson's procedure here, of course, are those time-honored Aristotelian categories of potential and act—the former a definitional essence, the latter an empirical realization in utterance.

21. Derrida (1985, 104) offers a useful neologism describing perfectly Johnson's method of construction. *Tranche-fert* means "piece," "slice," deriving from the verb *trancher:* to slice, separate, decide; and from the latter part of the word *transfert:* transference. Johnson's "tranche-ferts" are his citations—slices of text born of incision, cutting, and grafting.

22. The authors include Locke, Boyle, Swift, Dryden, and Hooker, and the samples drawn from dramatic, poetic, scientific, historical, and theological discourse. It is as if Johnson's inability to adequately define precipitates a collateral support from printed usage.

23. Detailed studies of the *Tractatus* are provided by Peterson (1990) and Finch (1971). Earlier, but still indispensable studies, include Anscombe 1963 and Black 1964. Finch offers a fascinating comparison of the *Tractatus* to Buddhist "four-fold logic" and a novel theory as to the book's perplexing structure. Kuhns (1970, 218) locates the *Tractatus* provocatively between the *Principia Mathematica* of Russell and Whithead and Eliot's *The Waste Land,* offering en route a suggestive comparison of the *Tractatus* to the poetry of Mallarmé, Valéry, and Pound.

24. In the *Course,* Saussure had already introduced the related distinction between *Langue* (the transcendental, abstract structure of rules) and *Parole* (the incommensurate eruptions of linguistic occurrences in utterance). Prior to Saussure, Marx and Engels had discussed language as practical consciousness and interactive social manifestation in *German Ideology.* "Language is as old as consciousness; language is practical consciousness, as it exists for other men, and for that reason is really beginning to exist for me personally as well; for language, like consciousness, arises only from the need, the necessity, of intercourse with other men" (quoted in Rossi-Landi 1983, 15). For a reasoned speculation on Marxist influences on Wittgenstein, especially the Italian Marxist economist Paolo Sraffi, see Rossi-Landi 1983, 1–34.

25. Evidence of Johnson's occasionally haphazard method of selection is provided in Reddick 1990, 36–37.

26. Hannah Arendt recalls Benjamin's similar passion for collecting quotations. "Nothing was more characteristic of him in the thirties than the little notebooks with black covers which he always carried with him and in which he tirelessly entered in the form of quotations what daily living and reading netted him in the way of 'pearls' and 'coral'" (in Benjamin 1969, 45). And according to Pierre Missac (1995, 144), Benjamin, from his work on the *Trauerspiel* to the final, unfinished *Passagen-Werk*, cherished the prospect "of producing a book composed principally, indeed, solely, of quotations."

27. Gove's own general and controversial editorial policies for the third edition of Webster's are discussed in Morton 1994.

28. On Johnson's oblique expression of his Jacobite sympathies in the *Dictionary*, see J. Clark 1994. A variant interpretation of Johnson's political agenda can be found in De Maria 1986. On the significance of Johnson's extensive revisions to the fourth edition of the *Dictionary* published in 1773, see Reddick 1990, 89–122. Kernan (1987, 181–203) offers an in-depth discussion of the *Dictionary* as a consequential product of print logic.

29. Ong points out the ideological commitment of print culture to reducing "restless, unpredictable, evanescent sound to the quiescent order of space" (1964, 108).

30. Johnson's culpability in this matter increases when we consider that word lists and glossaries of living speech were available to him. Francis Grose's *The Scoundrels Dictionary; or, an Explanation of the Cant Words used by Thieves, Housebreakers, Street Robbers, and Pickpockets about Town* appeared in 1754 and was itself an adumbration of the glossaries and word lists of slang to be found in Richard Head's 1665 *The English Rogue* and the earlier "Canters Dictionarie" included by Thomas Dekker in his 1609 *Lanthorne and Candel-light*.

31. In fairness to Johnson, it must be admitted that he frequently transgresses his own criterion of the preface, drawing examples from near-contemporary writers. Among many late seventeenth- and eighteenth-century authors included are Spratt, Atterbury, Bentley, Bramston, and Dryden. Johnson also inserts citations from his own "Vanity of Human Wishes" and his tragedy *Irene*. The lengthy definition of the word "loord" is signed "Macbean" (most likely Johnson's amanuensis Alexander Macbean). Commercial and mathematical terms are freely taken from Edmund Stone's *Mathematical Dictionary* and from the English translation of des Bruslons and Savary's *Universal Dictionary of Trade and Commerce*. The fact remains, however, that Johnson's personal inclinations are theorized and recommended in the preface. I am grateful to Courtney and Smith (1968) for much of this factual information.

32. Mention might be made of Noah Webster's own culpability in this regard, most prominently the geolectal parsimony in his illustrations, and his especial pre-

dilection for New England examples. Full details can be found in Krapp 1966, 363.

33. Apparently these views on the ephemerality of mercantile diction were soon revised. Two years after the publication of the *Dictionary*, Johnson, in his preface to Rolt's 1757 *Dictionary of Trade and Commerce,* upholds that book as one "which no condition of life can render useless, which may contribute to the advantage of all that make or receive laws, of all that buy and sell, of all that wish to keep or improve their possessions, of all that desire to be rich, and all who desire to be wise" (1787, 9:430).

34. Johnson offers three definitions of "barbarous" in the *Dictionary*, all equally disparaging: "1. Stranger to civility; savage; uncivilized. 2. Ignorant; unacquainted with arts. 3. Cruel; inhuman." His second definition of "barbarousness" reads "impurity of language."

35. Adam Smith (an early reviewer of the *Dictionary*) voices similar sentiments: "Our words must not only be English and agreeable to the custom of the country but likewise to the custom of some particular part of the nation. This part undoubtedly is formed of the men of rank and breeding" (1983, 4). Both Smith and Johnson follow the earlier recommendations of George Puttenham, who in 1589 urged that the standard of speech be set as "the usuall speach of the Court, and that of London and the shires lying about London within lx. myles, and not much above" (1904, 150).

36. Cf. Burke: "The best wisdom and first duty is to defend liberty not only from invasion, but from decay and corruption" (1993, 54). Like the Tory Johnson, the Whig Burke equates mutation and becoming with decay.

37. The same point is made humorously in the anonymous "Plan of an *English* Dictionary." Published in *The Gray's-Inn Journal,* no. 89, June 29, 1754, it proposes to index lexical mortality with a "weekly Bill of Words." In a more serious moment, the author confesses "I have ever looked upon the Permanency of our Language to be of greater Consequence than the Stocks, of whatever Denomination, and for that Reason, I should be glad that some Means were devised to hinder the Diction of our *Shakespear* and *Milton* from being obliterated" (233). The paper alludes, in passing, to Johnson's *Dictionary* as an erudite work in progress. Johnson's, Wittgenstein's, and these anonymous sentiments all derive ultimately from Horace: "As the forest changes its leaves at the decline of the year, so among words, the oldest die; and like all things young, the new ones grow and flourish. We and all that belongs to us, are destined for death" (Horace 1992, 69).

38. The agricultural evocation in the word "harness" here is not gratuitous. Lynn White informs of the drastic effects brought on by the introduction in the seventh century of the fixed-harness plow, which effectively converted the land — like printed literature — into an available space for incision, transforming the relation of man to nature from one of participation to one of exploitation. For a full discussion, see L. White 1967.

39. Philosophic and lexicographic methods are teleologically similar in their anti-Heraclitan motivation. For instance, Joseph Owens credits Aristotle in the *Metaphysics* with a similar purpose of "fighting against the flux" in the search for the principle that would ensure an entity to be a "definite abiding something" (1951, 376). Kant, too, seeks a resistant boundary to formlessness. The transcendental unity of apperception outlined in the *Critique of Judgement* conceptually supports a theory of synthetic unity in which the accidentality of empirical data and intuitions are held in a unity of consciousness. The similarity on this point to Aristotelian being-as-being was remarked upon in the late nineteenth century by Natorp (1888, 39) and later by Heidegger (1962, 9–22).

40. Johnson seems to conceive "authority" in a curiously medieval sense. As Mary Carruthers describes it, "both 'authority' and 'author' were thought of entirely in textual terms, for an 'auctor' is simply one whose writings are full of 'authorities.' And an 'author' acquires 'authority' only by virtue of having his works retained 'sententialiter' in the memories of subsequent generations" (1990, 190). This curious inflexion of a precapitalist notion of authority and text, however, does not alter Johnson's commitment to the print-based culture of his own day.

41. The phrase is immunologist Richard Gershon's, quoted in Haraway 1991, 206.

42. For instance, Johnson supplied anonymously the Parliamentary Debates that appeared in Edward Cave's *Gentleman's Magazine,* and *Rasselas* likewise first appeared anonymously as *The Prince of Abissinia: A Tale.* His essays were written under the personae of the Rambler and the Idler, and his multiplicity of ghost-writings include prefaces to Charlotte Lennox's *Shakespear Illustrated,* John Hoole's translation of Tasso's *Jerusalem Delivered,* and Alexander Macbean's *Dictionary of Ancient Geography.*

43. A radically different relationship to decentered authority lies at the heart of Madeline Gagnon's comments on woman's linguistic estrangement: "Taking over this language which, although it is mine, is foreign to me. Arranging it in my fashion and I don't translate. . . . I am a foreigner to myself in my own language and I translate myself by quoting all others" (quoted in Neuman and Wilson 1982, 156).

44. On the complex implications of the signature and "signature effects," see Derrida 1982, 327–30, and 1985. Compare also Father Breton's comments on the origins of authorship: "Everyone knows that in the Middle Ages, unlike today, scientific authorship was attributed to an individual such as Aristotle. Literary works, on the other hand, were not attributed. . . . But Breton discovered from a colleague of his, Father Chatillon, who was an extremely erudite medievalist, that in a violent controversy with the Averroists Saint Thomas [Aquinas] declared his opposition to the impersonality (in other words the 'anonymity') of the individual thinker, arguing very much as follows: all thought is impersonal since it is the product of the

intellect as agent. But since all impersonal thought must be thought by a 'thinking being,' it necessarily becomes the property of an individual. In law, it should therefore bear this person's name" (quoted in Althusser 1993, 209–10).

45. "Proper names belong properly to forces, events, motions and sources of movement, winds, typhoons, diseases, places and moments, rather than people" (Deleuze 1995, 34).

46. For Barthes, fragments are "*texts* without structure" that return language to a continuous fluidity (1980, 4). To Blanchot, "[t]he fragmentary promises not instability (the opposite of fixity) so much as disarray, confusion" (1986, 7). In turn, Baudrillard believes that a fragmentary style of writing "is non-dialectic, disruptive, indifferent to its origin and to its end, a literal transcription of objective irony that I believe I can read directly in the state of things itself. The fragment is like the nucleus of an ephemeral destiny of language, a fatal particle that shines an instant and then disappears. At the same time, it allows an instantaneous conversion of points of view, of humours and passions" (1993, 159). Johnson's myriad examples possess such disruptive powers, an omnipresent potential to insubordination, such that the coexistence between the *Dictionary*'s power and its encyclopedic force are precarious to say the least.

47. This aspect of the *Dictionary* is well documented by De Maria 1986.

48. See, for instance, the various lives of Johnson—a 1762 version by William Rider, a 1764 by David Erskine Baker, a 1774 by James Tytler [?], and a 1782 by William Cooke [?]—in Brack and Kelley 1974. An early and popular satiric attack on Johnson is Archibald Campbell's *Lexiphanes,* which ran through three editions between 1767 and 1783. Taking the form of a Lucianic dialog, it purports to restore the English tongue "to its ancient [i.e., pre-Johnsonian] purity." For the most part, it is a biting lampoon on Johnson's literary style. However, Campbell addresses the rationale of the *Dictionary* directly in his preface, alleging that Johnson's own corrupt style renders him incompetent as a lexicographer (F iv). The principle of constructing a lexicography from good authors for the purpose of creating further "good authors" strikes Campbell as a logical contradiction, since "good authors" are, by his own definition, nonderivative. Campbell additionally argues that a dictionary is shown to be unnecessary for good writing by the reservoir of prior achievements without one: "Homer and Virgil, Demosthenes and Cicero, Thucydides and Livy, all wrote without Grammar or Dictionary, and most of them without so much as knowing what they were. So have all the best writers of Italy, France and England" (1767, xxxiv). Campbell, in effect, accepts Johnson's standard of excellence but turns it against his lexical criterion. The "wells of English undefiled" is evidence that a dictionary is unnecessary. A rewarding analysis of Lucianic satire in its earlier form as practiced by Mennipus can be found in Kristeva 1980, 82–89, and Bakhtin 1968.

49. Martin, following Lévy-Bruhl, discriminates between juridical rules of cus-

tom and the law. The former "consists of the repeated use of a rule applied to a specific case [and] arises within the group without notice," appearing as the unmediated product of a collective consciousness (Martin 76). The law, in contrast, is authored, sealed, and promulgated via specific procedures (77). Johnson's use of a carefully chosen citational mechanism inflects the force of law by inclining away from collective customary usage.

50. Further applications of this analogy can be found in Barrell 1983, 110–75.

51. FILIATION. *n. f.* [from *filius,* Latin.] The relation of a son to a father; correlative to paternity. MORTMAIN. *n. f.* [*morte* and *main,* Fr.] Such a state of possession as makes it unalienable; whence it is said to be in a *dead hand,* in a hand that cannot shift away the property. Significantly, Johnson has entries in the *Dictionary* for both these words.

52. Johnson's projected epic-as-reading finds contemporary philosophical support. For instance, James Harris in his 1751 *Hermes, or a Philosophical Inquiry Concerning Universal Grammar,* forwards the revolutionary proposal that reading is caused by the written and that reading itself causes oral speech (Ong 1967, 65). Ong sees this appeal to the written, not the spoken, for both authority and evidence as symptomatic of the ascending tendency in the eighteenth century to regularize speech along the chirographic lines of learned Latin.

53. Bourdieu comments on how the dictionary as a codifiying and normalizing force "assembles by scholarly recording, the totality of the *linguistic resources* accumulated in the course of time and, in particular, all the possible uses of the same word (or all the possible expressions of the same sense), juxtaposing uses that are socially at odds, and even mutually exclusive. . . . It thereby gives a fairly exact image of language as Saussure understands it, 'the sum of treasuries of language,' which is predisposed to fulfill the function of a 'universal' code. The *normalized* language is capable of functioning outside the constraints and without the assistance of the situation, and is suitable for transmitting and decoding by any sender and receiver, who may know nothing of one another. Hence it concurs with the demands of bureaucratic predictability and calculability, which presuppose universal functionaries and clients, having no other qualities than those assigned to them by the administrative definition of their condition" (1991, 48).

54. The problems Johnson addresses are precisely the ones that engaged Voloshinov's attention in the 1920s, viz. the balancing of two antinominal trajectories: (1) the ideological investment in linguistically stable units (arrived at through the resources of a print-logic economy), and (2) the countertendency in language to uncontrollable evolution. Voloshinov also argues that the notion of language as a ready-made phenomenon handed down from one generation to another is a major feature of abstract objectivism, pointing out that language is not handed down but endured as a "continuous process of becoming" (1986, 77, 81). This helps specify the ideological issue of the *Dictionary* as a patrilineal descent of diachronically frozen linguistic usage.

55. Quoted in Barthes 1986, 248–49. The words open the entry on the term "Formless" in the *Critical Dictionary* to which Bataille contributed. See Brotchie 1995, 51–52 for the full listing. On the twentieth century phenomenon of mock dictionaries see Hollier 1989, 27–31.

Chapter 7

1. On the medieval connection between textual layout and memory, see Carruthers 1990.

2. Spivak mentions an earlier use of the term "grammatology" by I. J. Gelb in the 1952 volume *A Study of Writing: The Foundations of Grammatology.* There, however, it is used to designate specifically a modern science. "Grammatol" (meaning a smatterer) occurs in the Tudor poet John Skelton's "Speak Parrot" of 1529.

3. In claiming for grammatology the status of the Cinderella Derridean procedure, I stand in disagreement with Jeffrey Mehlman's assessment of 1986: "With the passage of time, Grammatology was to know its own bizarre destiny and emerge as the object of the literary adulation of a foreign intellectual community—our own—marginal to but very much part of the most powerful country in the world, perhaps. The most powerful foreign presence in France, to be sure" (1986, 8).

4. The modern system of punctuation (i.e., with the full point utilized to end sentences) dates back to around 615 C.E., arising as part of the calligraphic innovations initiated by the monk Agrestius at the abbey of Luxeuil (Morison 1972, 115). A contemporary development was a nonroman, Merovingian script from which the lowercase in printing took its rise. The Luxeuil script, in fact, inaugurates the optical unit of the sentence as we now know it. Puttenham discusses punctuation under the category of *cesure.* In his 1589 *Arte of English Poesie,* "three maner of pauses" are discussed, the shortest intermission being the comma ("as who would say a peece of speach cut of"). The second is the colon, which occupies "twise as much time as the comma." The third is the period that marks "a full pause" (Puttenham 1904, 2:77).

Ben Jonson, in his 1640 *The English Grammar,* emphasizes the biological exigencies: "For, whereas our breath is by nature so short, that we cannot continue without a stay to speak long together; it was thought necessary as well as for the speaker's ease, as for the plainer deliverance of the things spoken, to invent this means, whereby men pausing a pretty while, the whole speech might never the worse be understood" (Jonson 1875, 9:316). In his *Of the Orthographie and Congruitie of the Britan Tongue,* first published about 1617, Alexander Hume classifies punctuation under the category of "distinctiones" whereby sentences are distinguished in writing and reading in either a perfect or an imperfect form. His description of the comma is delightful: "The comma divydes the least partes of the period, and is pronounced in reading with a short sob" (Hume 1885, 34).

In Hume, Jonson, and Puttenham alike, the rationale for punctuation is based largely on residual orality. Distinctions are needed, not only to clarify sense, but also to allow the reader time to take a breath. This oral lamination onto reading links to the rhetorical, that is, pragmatic and performative, motives of sixteenth- and seventeenth-century writing. As early as the fifteenth century, however, punctuation is exploited for its capacity to obfuscate and to create deliberate ambiguity. This can be seen in the several "punctuation poems" whose pointing is such as to offer two opposite readings. Read one way there is a clear, unambiguous sense, but read in accordance to the other set of punctuation marks, the meaning is inverted. Examples can be found in Scattergood 1971, 227, 302.

5. One of the earliest examples of *scriptio continua* (ca. 400 B.C.E.) is the "Timotheus papyrus" written by Timotheus of Miletus and containing a work entitled "The Persians" designed to be sung to cithara accompaniment. For details, see Müller in Hussein 1975, 49–50, 68. The Hebrew Masoretic tradition, regulating the written transmission of the Bible, requires a similarly unpunctuated text. "[T]he inclusion of the punctuation elements necessary for the vocalization of the text (vowel points, end-stops, and chanting accents) was proscribed from being included in the scroll, since these elements were believed to be later human inventions rather than divinely decreed like the consonantal letters themselves" (Elsky 1989, 134).

6. Henri Marrou draws attention to the presence of student (rather than scribal) markings on early *scriptio continua* papyri serving to divide the text into words. To my mind such evidence runs counter to Martin's theory that the practice of *scriptio continua* was "connected with a concept of reading aimed primarily at the declamation of literary texts" (Martin 1994, 69).

7. This same demand on readerly production is noted by Masten, Stallybrass, and Vickers (1997, 5) in their introduction to *Language Machines: Technologies of Literary and Cultural Production*. This work came to my attention after completion of my own book.

8. In addition to Parkes and Martin, detailed discussions of the practice can be found in Wingo 1972, Moreau-Maréchal 1968, and Vezin 1985.

9. Helmont was a well-known cabalist whose work in this area attracted the attention of Lady Anne Conway and Lady Damarais Masham, the patronesses of Ralph Cudworth and John Locke, respectively. According to Webster, "Helmont became an important contact between the Cambridge Platonists More and Cudworth and their allies in the Low Countries. Given these affiliations in the close vicinity of Newton it is not surprising to find that Newton himself possessed a major edition [of his works]" (1982, 9). For more on Helmont, see Gottesman 1972 and 1976.

10. Olson's theories of pneumatic biopoesis, proprioception, and projective verse are readily available in Olson 1967.

11. Quoted in Lansing 1970, 83.

Chapter 8

1. For Sade's influence on nineteenth-century writers, see Praz 1970. A convenient summary of the extensive medical writing on Sade and sadism, together with a survey of the invaluable interpretations of Klossowski, Bataille, and Lacan, can be found in Dean 1992, 123–99.

2. On Bataille's lamination of his own erotic preoccupations onto those of Sade, see Le Brun 1990, 89–93.

3. Compare, for example, Pontanus's depreciation of Ovid's *Tristia* (1595, 41).

4. Foucault describes sadism as a "massive cultural fact," historically specifiable as the late eighteenth century and constituting "one of the greatest conversions of Western imagination: unreason transformed into delirium of the heart, madness of desire, the insane dialogue of love and death in the limitless presumption of appetite" (1973, 210). Sadism appears "at the very moment that unreason, confined for over a century and reduced to silence, reappears, no longer as an image of the world, no longer as a *figura* but as language and desire" (210). The intersection of interests in Foucault's notion of sadism and several recent feminist platforms vis-à-vis a discourse of woman and desire can only be hinted here.

5. Against my own belief that pornographic writing signifies a diminished sexuality (in that its drive is always transformative: the replacement of sex by language), I present the following comments by Deleuze, which insist on a necessarily transcendental and impersonal teleological destination for pornography. "Pornological [*sic*] literature is aimed above all at confronting language with its own, with what is in a sense 'nonlanguage' (violence that does not speak, eroticism that remains unspoken). However this task can only be accomplished by an internal splitting of language: the imperative and descriptive function must transcend itself toward a higher function, the personal element turning by reflection upon itself into the impersonal" (1971, 21–22). The question as to what form such a self-transcendental language might take according to Sade's own theories of perpetual motion is the subject of the rest of this chapter. On the issue of Sade and pornography and especially the parallels between Sade's approach and the Meese Commission's 1986 report on pornography, see Stewart 1988.

6. I concur with Le Brun in detecting an "existential humor" deriving "from the spectacle of life reasserting its rights over the illusion of ideas and feelings" (1990, 39). It's in this vein of humor that I can read the tragic irony of *Justine*.

7. Sade's own estimate of cognitive capital might be gleaned from the following passage in a letter to Gaufridy from May 1790: "beds, table, chairs and drawers can be replaced but not ideas" (1965b, 169).

8. In Lacan's estimation, this oscillation between active and ratiocinative states signals a compulsive return to reason as a law. Actions return for legitimation by reason—for Lacan (1989), this is the Kantian component in Sade, who Lacan argues remains ultimately submissive to the law of reason. The dialectic of Sadean

desire is enacted in the space of writing where disseminatory and confligatory forces enmesh within the territorializing reality of the law. It is the libidinal analogy to Johnson's lexicographic struggles to contain decentered and unpredictable speech acts and usage within the overdetermination of definition. (Sade and the Doctor would have offered a succulent dialogue in a damp chapter of Landor's *Imaginary Conversations*.) For a different reading of Sade's relation to law, see Le Brun, who claims Sade's tenet of the general (viz. the general is but the sum total of particulars) ultimately "utterly discredits the very idea of law" (1990, 62; see also 69–70). Horkheimer and Adorno insist that the Kantian categorical imperative and Sade's libertine volition alike "aim at independence from external powers" (1972, 114).

9. Blasphemies effect powerful moments in the breakdown (not reversal) of theological structures. Bataille explains that the "[p]erfect blasphemy negates nothingness (negates the power in nothingness)" (1994, 66). Sade, however, links blasphemy to orgasm as a fundamental discharge of both language and identity. Unlike orgasm, however, blasphemy takes place as an eruptive chiasmus in which expressive language implodes into itself, visceralizing and lacerating the referent while simultaneously inducing a utopian sign as its ultimate, total expenditure. Sade's blasphemies should be read as insurrections within the classical code and as transporting perversion (in a reduced and projected form) onto the order of the sentence.

10. This claim to a teleological suspension of communication as a reciprocity finds support in Sollers's claim that Sade's project is a "global formulation of the question of communication" (1983, 55) and in Bataille's observation that Sadean language is "a language which repudiates any relationship between speaker and audience" (in Deleuze, 1971, 18). Mercken-Spaas (1978) offers a brief, but useful, comparison of Sade's treatment of the self and Other with that of Rousseau's.

11. See Deleuze 1971, 15–116, which introduces McNeil's translation of Sacher-Masoch's *Venus in Furs*.

12. In his study of Sade and Fourier, Klossowski draws on the fact that the economic period of Sade's life was essentially one of manufacture and one in which "the suggestion and the living object of emotion are merged." After Sade came "the era of mechanical reproduction and industrial exploitation" (quoted in Hollier 1988, 219). I differ from Klossowski in my own belief that Sade occupies a more transitional phase that brings him closest to the exploitations of sexuality in an era of mechanical reproduction. To support this claim is the following list of inventions patented during Sade's lifetime (1740–1814): cast steel, iron wheels for coal cars, cement, air cylinders, the spinning jenny, steam carriages, caterpillar treads, the reverberatory furnace, the modern water closet, talking automatons, steamboats, the hot air balloon, power looms, chlorine, a steam-powered massager, soda, sewing machines, the gas engine, street lighting, the signal telegraph, food canning, lithography, toy helicopters, bleach, twin-screw propellers, the kymograph, power looms, and (the year of Sade's death) the steam printing press. (I am in-

debted to Lewis Mumford's *Technics and Civilization* for this information.) On the omnipresence of the machine in Sade's thinking and writing, see Le Brun 1990, 153–61.

13. Sade had a lifelong commitment to the theater. In addition to being the author of seventeen plays, he was employed as theater director at Evry in 1764; restored "at enormous cost" a theater room in his own castle at La Coste (where he staged several theatrical performances); and was placed in charge of entertainment at Charenton shortly before his death (Le Brun 1990, 79). Brochier in his preface to Sade's theater (Sade 1970) corroborates Le Brun's claim to the importance of the theater in Sade's life and argues that the system of narrative in the novels accurately fits into his system of theater. (See Le Brun 1990, 80).

14. Barthes's reading of Sade, while possessing the merit of opening up the texts to a productive scrutiny through semiotics (revealing this way numerous codes that constitute a language beneath the narrative level) tends to recover Sade for the cultural dominant. Barthes presents the substructures and infrastructures he detects as apologies for Sade's more "literal" (i.e., narrative) transgressions and perversions. Barthes, however, doesn't consider Sade's output as an inscribed ensemble of cultural, bodily, and graphic limits. Nor does he take adequate account of Sade's historical specificities and accidences (especially the crucial relation of his theory of Nature to his republicanism). Sadean extremities are filtered and watered down to a reflective surface of Barthes's own productive, but circumscribed, and ahistorical reading.

15. Timo Airaksinen makes the important observation that in Sade's fiction sexual climax is identical in men and women. Both are said to "discharge," precipitating a "detonation which destroys its own environment" (1995, 45). "Discharge" must be understood as a general economic expenditure in Bataille's sense of the term as unusable energy. But it's also the way that the cognitive order is suspended and the self returns to nature.

16. It's doubtful whether Sade's works can support a sympathetic feminist reading. Their common pattern shows a retreat of sexual difference into both codes of domination and the rhizomatic propensities of unconscious instincts and impulses. In the first case the woman succeeds by virtue of a strictly conditional mimesis. If she masters and adopts the mechanics and ideology of the patriarch, she will triumph. But even patriarchy takes second place to instinctual drives. Sadean force is both centrifugal and transcursive, requiring human conduction but not necessarily human organization. Sade constantly implodes the social production of the personal into its own blind impersonality such that sexual instincts tend to destroy gender categories along vectors of indifference. Moreover, the pleasure derived from pain marks the algorithm of only intermediate libertinage. The ultimate desire is directed to commit the imperfect, infinitely centrifugal crime, which obliterates both agency and known cause in transcendental negation. At one point Juliette delineates its form to Clairwill: "I should like . . . to find a crime with per-

petual repercussions, which would continue even after I had ceased to act, so there would not be a single instant of my life, not even when I was asleep, when I would not be causing some sort of disorder, a disorder so extensive as to involve general corruption, or so absolute a disturbance that its effect would be prolonged even when my life has ceased" (quoted in LeBrun 1990, 127).

The recognition of ambivalence is crucial to any reading of Sade; its practice is repeatedly linked to an active notion of the self. Ambivalence governs the intertextual relation between Sade's diptych of *Justine* and *Juliette*. The former relates the repetitive rape, torture, and brutalization of a virtuous girl whose virtue is rewarded solely with a sequence of atrocities. Justine survives them only to be struck down and killed by lightning. In contrast, *Juliette* recounts the progress of Justine's depraved sister, whose life of crime and profligacy is rewarded amply with pleasure and wealth. In both novels identical, or near identical, incidents occur to both heroines (whose histories in their essentials duplicate each other). *Juliette* differs from *Justine,* then, not in the experiences undergone but in the pleasure derived from them. Sade presses this reactive difference to identical acts (i.e., the principle of ambivalence) to demonstrate the inverted moral proposition that the elimination of virtue removes pain. Justine suffers from torture *because she is virtuous.* Juliette derives pleasure from the same torture because she is *depraved.* The removal of the moral category permits algorithmically the reversal of the actiants' reactions. I don't want to limit the intertextual implications here to irony but rather see the two works as an extended application of ambivalence, approaching in its subtextual proposals the perspectival notion of truth for which Nietzsche would become famous. The concept of ambivalence doesn't reach adequate theoretical coherence until the early twentieth century when Eugen Bleuler in his 1911 paper *Dementia praecox oder Gruppe der Schizophrenien* defines the term as a mental disposition within the schizophrenic that permits the simultaneous expression of two opposite psychic states. Ice is good for the skater but bad for the fisherman. Accordingly, if built on the notion of ambivalence, all theories of the mind resist categorical reduction and causal arrangement. By immediately bifurcating the subject, ambivalence problematizes identity as a unitary self-adequation and leads further to a rehabilitation of relativity into the process of thought itself. Sade, of course, doesn't annex ambivalence as a psychological, or even an epistemic category, but utilizes its potential to subvert the rational order of Enlightenment ideology, especially the unilateral, irreversible positioning of moral categories and the latter's repressive control over subjectivity and presidential conditioning of normal felicities. For a concrete example we might consider the point in *Juliette* where the libertine Dolmancé delivers a lengthy lecture on sexual pleasure. Dolmancé presents sex as a violent despotism guaranteed by inherent male superiority. But the overt sexism here can't be dismissed either categorically or simplistically. The fact is that Dolmancé delivers his lecture to an audience of women who themselves enjoy sexual supremacy. Sade's sexism here demolishes gender at the same time as it exploits its imbalance. This demonstrates a profound ambivalence that can be expressed syllogistically: "I am a woman punished by men. I punish men. I am not a woman." Carter offers a controversial study of Sade specifically from the relation of sexuality to power. (For a discussion of Sadean Nature as a phallic mother, see Gallop 1988, 61–66.) In conclusion let me offer the following perceptive and provocative comments from LeBrun: "If contemporary feminists had anything in view besides the promiscuity of womanhood, they might be able to perceive *Juliette* as a searching reflection on female freedom. Examining women both savagely and lucidly, Sade offers them no model, but suggests the one mode of functioning by which they might evade the traps of femininity. *At no time does Juliette react like a woman:* on the contrary, she constantly invents her freedom, abandoning with assiduity and the *brio* the ready-made behavior that is expected of her" (1990, 206–7).

17. On correlations in Sade's and Machiavelli's thinking, see Le Brun 1990, 140–53. On the similarities to Nietzsche's and Kant's thought, see Horkheimer and Adorno 1972.

18. It's highly probable that Jarry had Sade's libertine heroes in mind when conceiving his own supermale, André Marcueil, who achieves sensual excess through a steady diet of "Perpetual Motion Food" (see Jarry 1977).

19. Klossowski interprets Sade as a representative of an aristocratic individualism whose conceptual existence threatened the concentration of an absolute monarchic power and portrays Sade as unassimilable into the revolutionary values he had helped initiate (1988). Sade's fate is déchetism, a grand waste production in the process of decay between two regimes. For Byron's comparable unassimilability, see McGann 1990, 142.

20. Sade admits his own libertine nature in a confession interlaced with important disavowals. In a letter of February 20, 1781, he announces, "Yes, I admit, I am a libertine; I have imagined all that can be imagined in that domaine; but I have certainly not *done* all I have imagined, and certainly shall never do it all. I am a libertine, but I am neither a *criminal* nor a *murderer*" (quoted in Le Brun 1990, 73).

21. The work of Boullée and Ledoux is discussed with illustrations in both Rosenblum 1967 and Starobinski 1988. Of special relevance in this visionary architecture designed by Sade's contemporaries is Ledoux's *Oikema:* a penis-shaped building (with testicles) designed as a functioning brothel. An illustration of this perfect Sadean space can be found in Jenks and Silver 1972, 162. In notable contrast is Béatrice Didier's interpretation (1976), which likens Sade's edifices to Saint Teresa of Avila's interior castle.

22. Bataille, noting the links between the Third Reich and numerous decentralized fortress institutions, or *ordensburgs,* set up to prepare an elite of young and potential leaders, cites Alphonse de Chateaubriant's 1937 work *Le Gerbes des Forces,* which starts with a summary mention of "an institution that brings this initial institution i.e. the Teutonic Order to impressive perfection, and that can be called: 'The School for Führers'" (quoted in Hollier 1988, 216). I'll add to this J. M. S.

Tomkins's insight that, "It is from Germany also, refuge of Jesuits and stage of swarming societies of Freemasons, Illuminati, and Rosicrucians, that the thrilling theme of the vast secret society emerges, closely linked with that of alchemy and natural magic" (1969, 244). On the connection of Sade's Sodality to bourgeois freemasonry, see Horkheimer and Adorno 1972, 88.

23. Sade's own political stance is inconsistent. On December 5, 1791, he writes to his lawyer Gaufridy, "If I try to fathom this way of thinking, it is really for no party and is a composite of all. I am anti-jacobite, I hate them to death; I adore the king, but I detest the old abuses. I like a great many of the articles of the constitution, others revolt me. I want the lustre of the nobility to be returned because taking it away advances nothing. I want the king to be the leader of the nation. I don't want a National Assembly, but two chambers as in England, which gives the king mitigated authority, balanced by the co-operation of a nation divided into two orders. The third is useless, I don't want it. This is my profession of my faith" (*Correspondance inedité du Marquis de Sade, de ses proches et de ses familiers* [Paris: Librairie de France, 1929], 301–2; quoted in Berman 1971, 485). Sade states his modified preference for a limited and elected monarchy in *Les Ecrits Politiques suivis de Oxtiern* of 1791: "The French Empire can be governed only by a Monarch, but this Monarch must be elected by a free Nation and submit faithfully to the Law" (quoted in Berman 1971, 203). By April 11, 1794, however, he is writing in a strikingly different spirit: "I love the republic on principle and through gratitude and I shall shed my blood like you, when need be, to defend it" (quoted in Berman 1971, 570).

24. Goethe's ideas were reproduced in a series of epigraphs in Propp's study of the morphology of the fairy tale but are omitted in the English translation.

25. Hegel's early theological writings contain similar examples of this change in the nature of Nature: "The impression made on men's hearts by the flood in the time of Noah must have been a deep rending [*ein tiefes Zerreissen*] and it must have caused the monstrous disbelief in nature. Formerly friendly or tranquil, nature now abandoned the balance of her elements, now required the faith the human race had in her and with the most destructive, invincible, irresistible hostility; in her fury she spared nothing; she made none of the distinctions that love might have made but poured savage destruction over everything" (quoted in M. Taylor 1987, 5–6). This comparison of Hegel with Sade shouldn't be pushed too far. Hegel brackets and decommissions the aspect of a transcendental operation of judgment (viz. God's punishment sent to men) in order to place full emphasis on a radical change in the nature of Nature. He detheologizes the Flood, but at the same time resists an atheological position by preserving the framework of biblical narrative. That quality of destruction enters a plot, a line of events as a specific moment within the *history* of Nature. By contrast Sade stresses Nature's destructiveness as a permanent trait. It goes without saying that this description of Nature by the pope as an eternally

recombinant system describes exactly the nature and configuration of Sade's sexual groupings of shifting and interlocking ensembles.

26. As a changing openness, Epicurean nature shares affinities with Bergsonian time—a time that divides wholeness into an incessant journey of transformations. "Bergson's always saying that Time is the Open, is what changes—is constantly changing in nature—each moment. It's the whole, which isn't any set of things but the ceaseless passage from one set to another, the transformation of one set of things into another" (Deleuze 1995, 55). Bergsonian time thus conforms to the nature of Prigogine's dissipative structures.

27. Sade appears consistent in this belief, which figures prominently in his last will and testament: "My grave shall be dug in this thicket by the farmer of Malmaison under the inspection of Monsieur Lenormand, who shall not leave my body before it has been placed in the said grave. He can be accompanied during the ceremony, if he wishes, by those among my relatives or friends who without any show of mourning will want to give me this last sign of attachment. Once the grave has been filled in it shall be sown over with acorns so that afterwards the ground of the said grave having been replanted and the thicket being overgrown as it was before, the traces of my tomb will disappear from the surface of the earth, as I flatter myself that my memory will be effaced from the minds of men" (1953, 305). The will, as quoted here, perpetuates the notorious editorial intervention first insinuated in 1835 by Jules Janin. In the will proper the period does not end at "the minds of men" but continues, "except none-the-less from those of the small number of people who have been pleased to love me up to the last moment and of whom I carry into the grave a most tender recollection. Made at Charenton-Saint-Maurice when of sound mind and in good health, January 30th, 1806."

28. It's essential to acknowledge Sade's complex Oedipal configurations. He constructs androgynous beings whose victim is woman in her specific procreative role as mother. Behind all his cruelties is the ultimate desire for the total negation of the maternal. His own mother, Marie-Eleonore de Carman, was related to the House of Bourbon and for several years was lady-in-waiting to the Princess de Condé. Sade's mother-in-law was responsible for his arrest in 1772 and for his subsequent incarceration for five months in Miolans, Sardinia. In 1789 the chosen name for the new French Republic was *la mère-patrie,* or mother-fatherland. The effects on Sade of this symbolic prefixture of the mother to patriarchal authority must be left to speculation. What's certain is that the novels repeatedly stage obscene scenarios in which the daughter aligns with the father (often by an incestuous alliance) for the mutual destruction of the mother. Stewart astutely points out that the libertine's pleasure in large part derives from maternal duties—handling excrement, washing, feeding. She also draws attention to Sade's significant inversion of the relationship of intensities involved in childbirth: labor-pain-birth-pleasure become labor-pain-pleasure-death (1988, 189 fn. 33).

29. Coward and Foshay (1992) offer a diverse study of the tradition of apophatic thinking and its specific relation to the thought of Derrida.

30. On the nature and consequence of intransitive writing, see Barthes 1986, 11–21.

31. John Cage endorses this same natural paradigm in his claim that "Art = imitation of nature in her manner of operation" (1982b, [8]).

32. Le Brun takes issue with Blanchot on his sense of Sade's language as a deferred killing (1990, 178–79). My own focus here is less on writing as either homicide or thanatopraxis than on language theorized as a force of incessance. Wishing to emphasize the specificity of Sade's writing, Le Brun protects its singularity from those issues pertaining to language in general.

33. A similar effect of textual incessance obtains in Kenneth Goldsmith's *Fidget* (a conceptual text that transcribes the author's body movements and minute physical clinama during a thirteen-hour period on Bloomsday 1997): "eleven hours walking body moves arm contraunison leg movements deep breath inside salivation nine pm left finger index finger rubs eye counter clockwise . . ." (2000, 78).

34. See Hjelmslev 1969 and 1970 for a full delineation of these theories.

Chapter 9

1. Silliman 1987, 63–93. On this point I disagree with Christian Bök, who sees *Quirks & Quillets* as a version of the new sentence differing from it only in the range of its defamiliarizations. Whereas Silliman "defamiliarizes referential integration at the syllogistic level . . . Mac Cormack defamiliarizes referential integration at the grammatical level" (Bök 1994, 23). My own reading, by contrast, attempts to draw attention to the protosemantic force of the phrase continuum. Bök also presents a strong argument for a more feminist reading of the book. A recent study of Silliman's theory and its practical realization can be found in Perelman 1996. For a comparison of the new sentence to haiku-renga, see Motokiyu, Norinaga, and Kyojin 1991.

2. Interested readers might wish to compare Silliman's theory of the new sentence with the new sentence of Dadaist sound poet Hugo Ball. In a diary entry dated June 18, 1916, Ball compares his attempts at linguistic estrangement with those of the Italian futurist F. T. Marinetti:

> With the sentence having given way to the word, the circle around Marinetti began resolutely with "parole in libertà." They took the word out of the sentence frame (the world image) that had been thoughtlessly and automatically assigned to it, nourished the emaciated big-city vocables with light and air, and gave them back their warmth, emotion, and their original untroubled freedom. We others went a step further. We tried to give the isolated vocables the full-

ness of an oath, the glow of a star. And curiously enough the magically inspired vocables conceived and gave birth to a new sentence that was not limited and confined by any conventional meaning. Touching lightly on a hundred ideas at the same time without naming them, this sentence made it possible to hear the innately playful, but hidden, irrational character of the listener; it wakened and strengthened the lowest strata of memory. (Ball 1974, 68)

Ball's innovations go unrecorded in Silliman's historical overview of the sentence, and critics to date have failed to address the implications of Ball's theory to the historical status of the new sentence.

3. Contemporary examples of such catalysis include Philippe Sollers, *H;* Gabriel Garcia Marquez, *The Autumn of the Patriarch;* and Pierre Guyotat, *Eden, Eden, Eden.* A theory of grammarless writing and neonarrative as well as practical examples can be found in Berne and Zekowsky 1954 and Zekowsky 1969, 1976. Despite its relevance to a discussion of the new sentence, Silliman and Perelman seem unaware of Berne and Zekowsky's work.

4. My notion here of phrase propulsion is not unlike Charles Bernstein's description of the "imploded sentence" that refuses "the syntactic ideality of the complete sentence" in favor of a durational flow of meaning. "While in the complete/closed sentence, attention is deflected to an abstracted, or accompanying, 'meaning' that is being 'conveyed,' in the imploded sentence the reader stays plugged in to the wave-like pulse of the writing. In other words, you keep moving throughout the writing without having to come up for ideational air' the ideas are all inside the process" (Bernstein 1992, 60). Readers might productively compare Bernstein's imploded sentence with the theories of processuality outlined in Olson 1967.

5. Susan Stewart professes the absence of punctuation to be a deliberate "deficiency in communication [that creates] a false gestalt. . . . Another tactic that written discourse can take to play with a deficiency of signification is to present an ambiguity by an absence of punctuation, the words on the page form an undifferentiated mass" (1980, 104). Stewart's argument has direct relevance to any reading of *Quirks & Quillets,* although, as I argue, the deficiency in signification in Mac Cormack's book produces *ambivalence,* not *ambiguity.*

The inverse of Mac Cormack's method can be found in Carl Friedrik Reuterswärd's *Prix Nobel,* a text consisting entirely of punctuation marks without words. Reuterswärd explains his method. "The position or placing of a punctuation mark in the middle of a sentence does not decide its own meaning. (An exclamation mark in the middle of a sentence does not distort the mark itself but does distort the emphasis of the sentence.) Nor is there any mutual order of rank; a period is not superior to a parenthesis. It is in such neutral and equal linguistic attributes that I see an interesting alternative: not to ignore syntax but certainly to forego 'the preserved meanings of others.' The 'absence' that occurs is not mute. For want of 'governing concepts' punctuation marks lose their neutral value. They begin to speak an unuttered language out of that already expressed. This cannot help producing a 'colon concept' in you, a need of exclamation, of pauses, of periods, of parentheses. But a state that has come about at the expense of the noble prize: out of its own idea" (in Williams 1967, 257). Reutersward's premise seems to be that if a syntactic-spatial placement of punctuation marks is maintained, then a kind of ideogrammic value can be reached without the presence of words; the aura of the "concept" being something akin to a trace of the marks' usage in normative, written contexts. In the case of recent breath-based methods of notation, where orthodox punctuation is frequently avoided, pointing is supplied by the pauses indicated by white space. In *Quirks and Quillets* there is no spacing.

By contrast, an effective subversive deployment of overpunctuation occurs in V. S. Naipaul's novel *The Mystic Masseur,* where the future wife of Ganesh puts up a sign reading: NOTICE! NOTICE, IS. HEREBY; PROVIDED: THAT, SEATS! ARE, PROVIDED. FOR; FEMALE: SHOP, ASSISTANTS! According to Ashcroft, Griffiths, and Tiffin, Naipaul's use of punctuation here "is not merely idiosyncratic but directly synecdochic of the gaps, caesuras, and silences which exist between the language, which is the signifier of power, and the experience it is called upon to 'represent'" (1989, 55–56). A brief summary of the early history of punctuation can be found in chapter 7, footnote 4 of the present collection.

6. For a detailed discussion of analog and digital modes, see Wilden 1972, 155–201.

7. Compare Ricoeur's insistence that "an event is what happens only once" (Ricoeur 1984, 97). Also Derrida's comment, "The event remains at once *in* and *on* language" (1995b, 58).

8. Gregory Shaw, "Art and Dialectic in the Work of Wilson Harris," *New Left Review* 153 (September–October 1985): 125, 127; quoted in Ashcroft, Griffiths, and Tiffin 1989, 50.

9. For a cogent reading of Mac Cormack through Kristevan categories, see Bök 1994.

10. In addition to Bök's study is Derksen 1994, which calls for a feminist reading of the work. (As yet there has been no gendered reading of the book by a feminist critic.) A perceptive review is Glazier 1996. Mac Cormack's subsequent book *Marine Snow* has provoked a number of insightful reviews, including S. Pound 1996 and Joris 1997. The book has been the subject of a paper by Roberta Quance (1997) and is also discussed in Perloff 1998.

Chapter 10

1. "The voice is heard (understood)—that undoubtedly is what is called conscience—closest to the self as the absolute effacement of the signifier: pure auto-

affection that necessarily has the form of time and which does not borrow from outside of itself, in the world or in 'reality,' any accessory signifier, any substance of expression foreign to its own spontaneity" (Derrida 1976, 20).

2. For a full discussion of the "neutral" voice, see Blanchot 1969, esp. 564.

3. "Fascination with the abstract is an instance of *jouissance* proper. . . . The abstract does not act through a simulacrum-effect, but by means of the organization of its material alone. . . . [T]he libidinal dispostif is noticeable in every abstraction, and in particular of the theatrical kind, in that it thwarts the client's transference onto a simulated object, onto a reference" (Lyotard 1993b, 245–46). I note in passing that the futurist Depero named his version of onomatopoeic paroxysm *verbalizzazione astratta* (abstract verbalization).

4. Existing recordings of Marinetti's own readings of *parole in libertà* are convincing proof that in his enactments of voice he never aspired beyond a stentorian declamation. He can be heard reading "La Batagglia di Adrianopoli" on *Futurism and Dada Reviewed* (Marinetti 1988). This valuable CD also contains live performances by Cocteau, Schwitters, and Apollinaire.

5. It's tempting to identify Ball's creative motivations with those of fellow Dadaist Richard Huelsenbeck, to which Ball refers enthusiastically. "His [Huelsenbeck's] poetry is an attempt to capture in a clear melody the totality of this unutterable age, with all its cracks and fissures, with all its wicked and lunatic genialities, with all its noise and hollow din" (Ball 1974, 56).

6. Of interest in this respect is Gertrude Stein's first experience of flight that presented her with a view of the ground as a cubist painting. Significantly, Jolas commits himself solely to the lexemes and verbal imagery that constitute a technological discourse but does not engage the hypothetical strategies of vertical performance.

7. Tzara first expressed an interest in African art in a short article, "Note 6 sur l'art nègre," which first appeared in the magazine *Sic* (September–October 1917) and reappears with minor alterations in Tzara 1977, 57–58. The following short "Negerlieder," or Negro song, appeared in the 1920 *Dada Almanach*:

> Gesang beim Bauen
> a ee ea ee ea ee ee, ea ee, eaee, a ee
> ea ee ee, ea ee,
> ea, ee ee, ea ee ee,
> Stangen des Hofes wir bauen für de Häuptling
> wir bauen Für den Häuptling.
> (Huelsenbeck 1966, 141)

> Building Song
> a ee ea ee ea ee ee, ea ee, eaee, a ee
> ea ee ee, ea ee,

ea, ee ee, ea ee ee,
    Poles of the Court we're building for the chieftain
    we're building for the Chieftain.
                      (author's translation)

For a detailed discussion, see Paterson 1971, esp. 45–62.

8. Barzun's theory of simultaneity can be found in his "Voix, Rhythmes, et Chants Simultanés—Esthétique de la Poésie Dramatique," which appeared in issue 4 of *Poème et Drame* (May 1913). The poems were first performed in 1912. Pierre Albert-Birot's experiments in multivocity, published in *Sic* between 1916 and 1919, include "Blue Crayon" for four and three voices, respectively, and a "Promethean Poem." The work drew immediate objections from Apollinaire and led to controversy over "the visual and auditory claims to the term 'simultaneity.'" As Mike Weaver puts it, "[The] use of several voices in addition to the gramophone did not prevent Barzun's work from being a succession. Apollinaire put forward as a contrast his calligrammes 'in which simultaneity existed in the mind, even in the letter, since it is impossible to read them without immediately conceiving the simultaneity of what they express'" (1966, 107). For more on Barzun's theories, see Bergman 1962. Among the futurists, Giacomo Balla created an "onomatopoeic noise canzone for typewriter" scored for twelve simultaneous voices. Meltzer offers an informative and entertaining description of Dada performance. A more detailed, contextualized, and comparative discussion can be found in Matthews 1974. Though not listed in the *O.E.D.*, the first use of the term "intermedia" is credited to Samuel Taylor Coleridge by American Fluxus artist Dick Higgins. The term was reapplied by Higgins in 1965 "to describe art works which lie conceptually between two or more established media or traditional art disciplines" (quoted in McCaffery and Nichol 1978, 65). Examples of Higgins's own intermedia can be found in Higgins 1976.

9. Drucker 1994 provides an excellent analysis of twentieth-century typographic practice and its relation to the developments of modernism. Lacking the advanced capabilities of movable type in Russia, Kruchenykh achieves effects comparable to those of Hausmann and Marinetti by the manual use of rubber stamp letters. In the 1920s Hausmann invented the "optophone" described by Lucy Lippard as "a photo-electric machine for transmitting kaleidoscope forms into sound, a continuation of his new interests in electronic music and his early preoccupation with bruitist poetry, one of Dada's goals having been, as Hugo Ball put it, the 'devastation of language'" (1971, 57).

10. From Moholy Nagy's 1947 work *Vision in Motion,* quoted in Kostelanetz 1982, 95. Nagy is also the first critic to perceive an antecedent to Hausmann's optophonetic notation in Apollinaire's "Calligrammes." "The ideograms [*sic*] of Apollinaire were a logical answer to this dull typography, to the levelling effects of the gray, inarticulate machine typesetting. He not only printed the words, but *through*

the emphasis of position and size differerentiation of the letters, he tried to make them almost 'audible' " (quoted in Kostelanetz 1982, 95; emphasis added).

11. Although the invention of *zaum* (a contraction of the longer phrase *zaum-nyj jazyk,* meaning "transrational") is usually credited to Kruchenykh, Serge Fauchereau proposes Elena Guro (the pseudonym of Elena Von Notenberg [1877–1913]) as its inventor, citing the opening of her 1913 poem "Finland" as the primal *zaum* (Fauchereau 1988, 129). In his own more parsimonious assessment, Markov claims Guro's to be "a minor contribution" made "inconspicuously, subtly, and with feminine gentleness" [!] via a single neologism—*shuyat*—inserted in the same poem (Markov 1969, 19). Fauchereau, who attributes the invention to Guro's interest in children's language, counting-rhymes, and lullabies, doesn't cite Markov's example but quotes the poem in full with its arguably "transrational" opening: "Lula, lola, lala lu / Lisa, lola, lula-li." Guro was certainly a conspicuous presence among her contemporaries, and both her name and a passage from "Finland" appear in Khlebnikov's 1913 volume *The Word as Such.* For details on Guro's life and work, see Markov 1969, 14–23.

12. Markov alleges that the source of Kruchenykh's glossolalic theories is D. G. Konovalov's article "Religious Ecstasy in Russian Mystical Sectarianism," an "article he [Kruchenykh] never mentions" (Markov 1969, 202). Konovalov's work has also eluded the scrutiny of both Cutten 1927 and Goodman 1972 in their respective studies of glossolalia. A futurist book, *Zaumnaya gniga,* published in 1915, brought attention to a new *zaum* poet, called Alyagrov, known subsequently under his real name of Roman Jakobson (Markov 1969, 334).

13. In an article, appearing soon after the publication of Kruchenykh's *Declaration of the Word as Such,* de Courtenay claimed that *zaum* was "the result of a linguistic and an aesthetic chaos in [the] creators' heads." Stressing the need for words to be attached to referents, he argues that *zaum* "words" are neither words nor speech but "phonetic excrement." There is a detailed exposition of de Courtenay's argument in Markov 1969, 223. In contrast, Shklovsky argues that *zaum* is a personal and private, if not a transrational, language in which words lack definite meanings but nonetheless produce direct emotional affects (quoted in Markov 1969, 284).

14. Certeau's formulation of voice as the prime constituent of a breach in normal signification differs significantly from the one advanced by Derrida who—in the now famous critique of Rousseau's theory of speech—detects the marked privileging of speech over writing with the former authenticating presence and marking the closest proximity to the signified. (See Derrida 1976, 11.)

15. Augustine discusses this in *De Trinate.* I quote from the version that appears in Agamben 1999, 63–64: "The more the word is registered, without being fully so, the more the soul therefore desires to know that residue of knowledge. If it only knew the existence of this voice and not that it signified something, the soul would have nothing to search for once it had perceived the sensible sound as best

it could. But since the soul already knows that there is not only a voice but also a sign, it wants to have perfect knowledge of it. . . . Can it then be said that what he loves in them [i.e., the sound of the syllables in the dead word] is the knowledge that they signify something?"

16. Kornei Chukovsky first called attention to the primitive nature of *zaum* in 1914, claiming it to be of the nature of a protolanguage, hence not a language of the future. Having castigated the futurists as being in reality antifuturists, Chukovsky concludes that the genuine futurist of world literature is Walt Whitman! Full marks for Chukovsky and full details in Markov 1969, 220.

17. In 1921 Theo Van Doesburg, founder of de Stijl, published three "letter-sound images" with the following accompanying statement: "To take away its past it is necessary to renew the alphabet according to its abstract sound-values. This means at the same time the healing of our poetic auditory membranes, which are so weakened, that a long-term phono-gymnastics is necessary" (quoted in Jaffé 186). An example of Van Doesburg's poem can be consulted in Rasula and McCaffery 1998, 14.

18. Metagraphics is fully outlined in Isou 1964. The "New Letteric Alphabet" and the important "Manifesto of Lettriste Poetry" are contained in Isou 1947. The system of hypergraphy is outlined in Lemaitre 1956. A useful study of the latter is Drucker 1986. Lettrisme was quickly parodied as "bird-song" in an anonymous entry under "Expression" in the *Encyclopedia Da Costa,* published in the fall of 1947. This ephemeral publication is now generally available in Brotchie 1995, 107–56.

19. Arrigo Lora-Totino postulates a four-stage evolution in the movement of the written text into a full orality (1978, 8). First is the read text: "the poem is written, its author reading it aloud seeks to give it a different dimension (in this case the author's interpretation is just one of many that are possible, whether declaimed or merely recreated mentally)." Second is the spoken text, in which graphic and acoustic versions are of equal value, wherein "the sonic element may determine a different disposition of the written text, the declamation becomes an independent creation." Third is the spoken composition in which the written composition functions as a score initiating a declaimed event where "every sound of the mouth is admissible, rediscovery of onomatopoeia, creation of neologism, use of techniques of vocal instrumentation." The final stage is sonic composition: a free improvisation either in performance or directly onto recording equipment but without premeditation or revision and without the aid of written or visual texts. Lora-Totino claims as a precursor to the Ultralettristes the Italian futurist Canguillo, who performed an "Interventio di Pernacchie" (Intervention of Raspberries) at the Spovieri Gallery in 1914 (1978, 33).

20. "The general economy deals with the essential problem of the use of wealth. It underlies the fact that an excess is produced that, by definition, cannot be employed in a utilitarian manner. Excess energy can only be lost, without the least

concern for a goal or objective, and, therefore, without any meaning" (Bataille, quoted in Richman 1982, 70). This important theory of expenditure is outlined fully in Bataille 1988–91.

21. We owe to Levinas a primary insight into the ground of the groundlessness of pleasure. Pleasure is affect and as such derides the category being. John Llewelyn summarizes the nature of Levinasian pleasure as a pure dynamic of affect: "If pleasure is to augur escape from being then the categories of being cannot apply to it. It cannot be a state of being. This is why pleasure is an affect. It is affective rather than effective because affectivity is recalcitrant to the categories of activity or will and of being and of thought" (1995, 17).

22. If Robert Duncan's assessment is correct, there is a valid connection between prelingualism and the Joyce of *Finnegans Wake*. For Duncan, "*Finnegans Wake* returns (turns back) to the beginnings, not only in reference (intestinal alimentary mythic meaning levels) but in mimesis, as a thing done (the alimentary babbling of speech; the gobbling, the breaking down into). Here meanings are being churned up, digested back into the original chaos of noises, decomposed" (in Allen and Tallman 1973, 192).

23. The Ultralettriste performance is not without its Enlightenment precursors. As early as 1714 the Abbé Fénelon proposed a type of theater without language in section 6 of his *Lettre à l'Académie,* urging that language be replaced by gestures and predenotative cries. This occasioned a reply from du Bos focusing on the difficulty of tragic composition composed solely of cries. A detailed discussion can be found in Folkierski 1925, 175.

24. Guattari and Deleuze offer an innovative notion of the unconscious as a productive force, not—as in Freud's case—a primal scene of repeated complexual enactments. "The unconscious is not a theatre but a factory" (Guattari 1995, 75).

25. In an obvious updating of Nietzsche's famous agonistic binary of Apollo and Dionysus, Kristeva proposes a double disposition in all language toward two antinomial orders: symbolic and semiotic. The *symbolic* specifies that inclination within the linguistic subject toward naming, predication, order, and the communal linguistic apparatus of its sociolect. The *semiotic,* in contrast, is a disposition to asserting instinctual and prelinguistic drives as a propulsion *through* language. Interpreted through Kristeva's theory the sound poem, in so far as it abolishes the symbolic, involves a consequential privileging of the semiotic. The theory is outlined in detail in Kristeva 1984.

26. A prescient awareness of the possibility of sonic declamations for use in radio broadcast was a constant factor in the work of the futurist Fafa (Vittorio Osvaldo Tommasini), whose poetry Marinetti lauds in ebullient futurist terminology: "Sport is entering triumphantly into poetry, enhancing its elasticity, its heroic leaps, its tireless dynamism. We have finally emerged from the mephitic atmosphere of libraries. The muscular surge and the roar of engines impose new rhythmic laws and prepare us for the great aeropoetry." Among Fafa's deviant and

varied accomplishments, Marinetti lists, "Radio poems with transoceanic wave-jumps to revenge himself for his short-sightedness" (Marinetti quoted in [Lora-Totino] 1978, 16).

27. William Burroughs comments on the revolutionary potential of the tape recorder, referring to his own tactical use of it as "a cultural takeover, a way of altering the consciousness of people rather than a way of directly obtaining political control. . . . As soon as you start recording situations and playing them back on the street you are creating a new reality. When you play back a street recording, people think they're hearing real street sounds and they're not. You're tampering with their actual reality" (quoted in Miles 1993, 174). In passing, let me mention Laurie Anderson's altogether different alliance of electronic appurtenance and voice. In her performance "Americans on the Move," Anderson transgenders her own voice by processing it through a harmonizer. The effect of this is to drop her voice a full octave whereby it obtains a rich masculine quality—an effect Craig Owens terms "a kind of electronic transvestism" (1987, 587).

28. The skeleton, as well as infrastructural, is also the permanent part of the human body remaining after mortification and corruption, a value that did not pass unnoticed during the Renaissance.

29. O'Neill (1980) provides a fascinating discussion of the *hegemonikon,* together with its cardiac and thoracic sitings.

30. The only person to have traced the implications of Chopin's performance to a base in power is Italian sound poet Enzo Minarelli, who cites Walter Ong to support the thesis that "one cannot utter a sound without exercising a power." Both Minarelli and Ong locate power in the identical social vocality by which Althusser establishes the force of interpellation as constituting the self. Minarelli, however, lauds this embrace of power through sound, contextualizing it within the aesthetics (if not the politics) of Marinetti and the Italian futurists. In a passage in which it's impossible not to recall Luigi Russolo's art of noise, Minarelli writes of "that power which Henri Chopin always understood from his very first experiments, disregarding language as it is ordinarily understood, in order to liberate a meaningful art of noise—*un rumorismo significante*—skillfully combined with electronics, the other primary element in his sound poetry." Minarelli reaches the canny conclusion that Chopin realizes in his poetry both "a project and 'a power.'" (All quotations are from Zurbrugg and Hall 1992, 13).

31. *Détournement* is "the reuse of preexisting artistic elements in a new ensemble" whose "particular power [comes from] the double meaning, from the enrichment of most of the terms by the coexistence within them of their old senses and their new, immediate senses" (Debord 1981, 55). For examples of *détournement,* see Knabb 1981 and Sussman 1989. Debord's earlier association had been with the Lettriste International and Gils Wolman, who maintained early associations with the Situationist International in the late 1950s. There is, however, no record of Chopin's opinions on the SI.

32. A parallel effect can be traced in visual poetry in the systematic Xerox disintegration developed by bp Nichol and myself in the late 1960s. By the systematic reproduction of a copy, then a copy of that copy ad infinitum, there results a progressive distortion of textual clarity to a point where, if sufficient generations are produced, the initial text is unrecognizable. Like the audiopoem, systematic Xerox disintegrations foreground a paradox within a specific technological apparatus, inducing the paradoxical failure of the machine's designed function through a systematic, "proper" application of those same functions. The method is shown and discussed in McCaffery and Nichol 1992, 143–44.

33. The phoneme is defined by Mario Pei, citing Bloomfield, as the "minimal unit of distinctive sound-feature." The syllable is "a group of phonemes consisting of a vowel or continuant, alone or combined with a consonant or consonants, representing a complete articulation or complex of articulations, and constituting the unit of word formation." In addition the "PHONETIC syllable is identifiable with the CHEST PULSE," the latter being defined as a "sudden expiratory movement of the chest muscles, the outward impulse of breath so produced" (Pei 1966, 37, 200, 268–69).

34. Before leaving this discussion of the *audio-poème,* let me mention two other artists, younger than Chopin, both of whom situate their art in order to exploit, or complicate, this technological aporia. In his *Sound Poems for an Era of Reduced Expectations,* Larry Wendt (1981) employs voice, prerecorded tape, and cheap computers. It is a stunning amalgam of human voice and junk technology created from the insight that technological determinism leaks its own fecal residue in the form of obsolete equipment. The extinction of acoustic phenomena through development predicated on a performativity paradigm creates the fissures into which Wendt tactically intervenes. Quebec poet Pierre-André Arcand, in his "Livre Sonore," returns the scriptive gesture to purely sonic dimensions, profoundly questioning the role of the book as the center of all possibilities of writing. Arcand describes his "idiophonic" instrument as "a metal box, filled with fragmented words (book object). It sings, speaks, makes noises and rhythms when the microphone is rubbed on its open cover. The microphone is handled as if it were a pen. In order to create and record sounds" (in Richard and Robertson 1991, 209). Examples of the *livre sonore* can be heard on two compact discs by Arcand (1992, 1995). A related encounter of sound and the written is language-artist W. Mark Sutherland's "Scratch," a sound poem-object comprising a vinyl record on which is etched the single word "scratch." The recording contains no other sound than the polyrhythmic clicks occasioned by the needle passing over the scratched-on writing. Sutherland refers to his piece as an "isomerism whereby both the physical and aural experience/event are combined in one form and process" (author's liner notes accompanying the disk). The piece was self-published in 1998 in a limited edition of three hundred copies and first presented as a performance installation at the ACC Gallery, Weimar, Germany, April 3–19, 1998.

35. A concise and useful description of the antipsychiatric movement can be found in Genosko's introduction to Guattari 1996a.

36. Deleuze and Guattari 1977; Lyotard 1993b; Kristeva 1984. All three titles were originally published in 1974, and Lyotard's book is an acknowledged response to *Anti-Oedipus*.

37. It's frequently argued that twentieth-century sound poetry is a development of two opposing dispositions: the scientific and the primitive. Beneath this binary are two separate interests: one an embrace of technology as a positive alliance with the human voice, the other an eschewal of all forms of technological contact. Regarding the first interest, the voice is treated as a material point for departure; for the second, voice is a still not fully fathomed phenomenon in its basic libidinal-acoustic state. Ellen Zweig offers a peacefully coexistent version of this bifurcation: "Sound poetry explores the human voice as human. Sound poets take apart language to see how it works. . . . The poet becomes close to the animal, close to the child. Sound poetry explores the voice as other. Sound poets record and manipulate the voice. . . . They cut the voice into pieces, reverse it, change its speed, make it digital. The voice becomes electronic, a strange machine whining toward communication with other planets" (1981, 266).

38. For a rationale of this rejection, see Steve McCaffery, "Discussion . . . Genesis . . . Continuity: Some Reflections on the Current Work of the Four Horsemen" in Kostelanetz 1980, 277–80.

39. If we concur with Freud, however, that the unconscious is our oldest mental faculty, then we might confidently theorize improvisation as a species of primitivism—a sort of ur-performance.

40. René Viénet reproduces graffiti painted by the Marxist-Pessimist Youth during the French Student Occupation Movement of May 1968, which reads, "A bas le sommaire vive l'ephémère" (Down with abstraction, long live the ephemeral) (1992, 75). Viénet's book first appeared in French in 1968. I mention it to hint at the uneasy alliance across time between the abstractionist proclivities of Dada and the spontaneous ephemerality in which the group sound poem of the 1970s was figured.

41. Both Self and Identity, predicated upon static genesis, are strategic concepts in the arrest of becoming. Their ideological function is to halt or at least decelerate the flow of intensities producing, when successful, a mineralization of processual ontology.

42. An unacknowledged influence on the Canadian paleotechnic sound poem is Gertrude Stein's credo that there is no repetition, that each reiteration of an identical within a series registers with a slight variation in emotional insistence. Stein argues against the very notion of a neutral voice, an argument repeated in Durand 1977. There is a pertinence in Stein's assertion to Derrida's own metaconceptual notion of *differance* as difference and deferral—as if Stein anticipates this notion and transfers it from the grammatologic to the emotive plane.

43. The great disservice of the conventional poetry reading is surely to have fostered illusions of presence through a purportedly essential corporeal connection to a written text sufficient to restore the author to her work in a fetishized reunification. Celia Zukofsky records her husband's feelings around the otiosity of the poetry reading and its disagreeable requirement of authorial presence. "Why can't they read my poetry themselves? Why do I have to read it for them?" (1978, 372). Ron Sukenick advances his own misgivings, pointing to several negative implications. "A reading puts emphasis on the performance, not the poem. / Some good poets are bad readers. / Some bad poets are good readers. If the essence of poetry is its performance in public, why not hire trained actors for readings?" (in Vincent and Zweig 1981, 317). Both Zukofsky and Sukenick demonstrate a keen awareness of the threat to writing by a reading's demand for a necessary athleticism or elocutionary expertise. Their disagreements, however, refer to what might be roughly classified as "the spoken word" and fail to address that other confluence of the performative and poetic: the text-sound poem. Prior to both Sukenick and Zukofsky, Hugo Ball expressed his own disquietude around the shortcomings of poetry readings. (See Ball 1974, 236.) Ball's reservations, however, confess to a different motivation than Zukofsky's and Suckenick's. Indeed, they seem to spring from a strikingly polar conviction. Ball's implication is clear: the written poem alone is an inert configuration of signs requiring the corporeal supplement and oral vitality of the poet in real-time action to realize its destiny.

44. This final passage is a deliberate *détourne* of a beautiful thought of Valéry's: "A blob of ink falls from my pain. Out of this accident I make a face, with a drawing round about it. In this context the blot acquires a role, a function. As was the case with Pascal's Thought: I had a thought. I have forgotten it. In its place I write that I've forgotten it" (1980, 278).

Chapter 11

1. It would be misleading, however, to exclude ego-based composition from Mac Low's writing. In an interview with Barry Alpert, Mac Low speaks of the qualified reappearance of the ego in his work: "[A]fter 1961 I realized that one's own thoughts, feelings, sensations, and volitions are also worthy of the kind of dispassionate attention I'd been giving mainly to linguistic and aural phenomena through systematic-chance composition. Thus I came to mix personal elements with chance-generated ones, as well as to view my personal poetry, which I'd never stopped writing, as being also a vehicle through which one can see through the phenomena (in this case, feelings, etc.) to their Buddha nature. . . . I have come to realize two things: that each systematic-chance method is itself a product of the artist's ego and that the artist's "own" thoughts, feelings, sensations, and volitions can themselves be regarded as objective phenomena that arise of their own

accord and that can be contemplated and presented as such" (Mac Low 1975, 33). Mac Low's "composition by nuclei" that began in 1961, and by which some objective system determines and fixes a sequence of pivotal points between which the writer is free to compose, deliberately dialogizes the relation between ego-based and egoless writing. Examples can be found in the later *Light Poems*.

2. Of the numerous methods and forms that might be cited, the most prevalent are numbered asymmetries, diastics, matched asymmetries, music-notation translations, crossword gathas, mantram gathas, vocabularies, typewriter performances, repeating news-article poems, environmental asymmetries, and acrostic chance selection. Keep in mind, too, the breadth of Mac Low's career: his first poem "H U N G E R ST r i kE wh A t doe S lifemean" dates from the mid-1930s.

3. These comments are also relevant to much other procedural writing—the mesostics of John Cage, for instance, and Ron Silliman's *Ketjak* (1978), which utilizes the Fibonacci number series to structurally determine the work's paragraph accumulation.

4. An important exception to this pattern is Mac Low's "Vocabularies." He has termed these compositions from "limited letter populations" in which the text limits its productive possibilities to exhausting all the possible lexical constructions available from the combination and recombination of the letters comprising a single person's name. The vocabularies approximate an economic "thrift" being based on the parsimonious principle of a minimum of phonemic expenditure for the maximum of semantic gain. This is in stark contrast to the other methods here considered (asymmetries, diastics, etc.) in which—as noted—all "profit" involves a necessary "loss."

5. For a specific discussion of the paragram in operation, see "The Martyrology as Paragram" in McCaffery 1986, 58–76.

6. Mac Low himself defines the diastic as a coinage analogous to acrostic: "A diastic structure uses words or phrases with letters in places corresponding to those in the index word or phrase: e.g., 'Barry' could lead to: *B*ase b*a*ts lu*r*e sta*r*s earl*y*" (1975, 19). The diastic thus hybridizes the acrostic and the anagram, emancipating the former from an obvious patency (at the commencement of each of successive line, for instance) and permitting it, like the paragram, to saturate a text as a thoroughly internalized infrastructure.

7. For a detailed presentation of this figure, see Abraham 1979, 16–28.

8. There is a striking similarity between the structure of the asymmetries and Marx's analysis in *Das Kapital* of capitalist formation, where the latent contradictions inside capital accumulation—wage labor and surplus value—push the system beyond itself into a different mode of production. To treat the asymmetries as built-in critiques of their own sign-production—a critique in which the paragrammic disposition within the source texts push beyond themselves into another sign economy—is not only legitimate but crucial to a full appreciation of Mac Low's work as a critique of language under capitalism. The following is a succinct

paraphrase of the relevant section from *Das Kapital* to stress this linguistic analogy: the extraction of meaning (surplus value) from a text necessitates the suppression of polysemy, ambivalence, errant connotation, and undecidability (i.e., the semantic-paragrammic workforce) by means of the integrational forces and hierarchical constraints of grammar, in order that meaning does not proliferate beyond a bounded, intentional horizon (i.e., the surplus value is not eroded). It would be dangerous, of course (as my final comments in this chapter suggest), to push this analogy between paragrammic suppression and the class struggle too far, yet the parallel critiques offered, through *structural* rather than *intentional* relations, do hint at the relevance of Mac Low's work to Althusser's critique of Marxist humanism.

Chapter 12

References to Levinas's works in this chapter use the following letter abbreviations. In the text and notes, numerals following the letter abbreviations represent page numbers.

BPW   *Basic Philosophical Writings* (Levinas 1996a)
CPP   *Collected Philosophical Papers* (Levinas 1987)
EE   *Existence and Existents* (Levinas 1978)
EI   *Ethics and Infinity* (Levinas 1985)
LR   *The Levinas Reader* (Levinas 1989)
PN   *Proper Names* (Levinas 1996b)
NTR   *Nine Talmudic Readings* (Levinas 1994)
OB   *Otherwise than Being* (Levinas 1981)
TI   *Totality and Infinity* (Levinas 1969)
TO   "The Trace of the Other" (Levinas 1986)

1. Among several studies of the relation of ethics to literature and criticism, the following are recommended: Ziarek 1994, Miller 1987, Critchley 1992, and Wyschogrod 1995. A related book of interest is Siebers 1988. Specific writers addressed include Wallace Stevens and Paul Celan (Ziarek) and Eliot, Trollope, and Henry James (Miller).

2. At the outset, let me admit to certain culpabilities. A serious weakness is the fact that the issue of gender isn't addressed. Levinas's categories of Same and Other are presented in a way that unavoidably reduces gendered difference to a secondary issue. My intention, however, has been to subject the theoretical discourse of poetry to the ethical discourse of Emmanuel Levinas. In this intention I hope I've been consistent and sincere. I'm aware, too, that my choice of writers are all male and contemporary. This choice is due to the specific nature of my focus on the ethical inflection of counteregoic, procedural methods of composition, which ruled out consideration of groundbreaking writers such as Gertrude Stein, Susan Howe,

and Nicole Brossard and the remarkable writings of the Baroness Else von Freytag-Loringhoven. A cursory perusal of Ernst Curtius's monumental study *European Literature and the Latin Middle Ages,* with its abundant citations of procedural methods, and counteregoic writings produced by formal constraint should convince the most skeptical reader of Levinasian ethical applications outside of this century. My hope, of course, is that this chapter will serve as a point of departure for others into further periods, issues, instances, and encounters.

It would be excessive in this context to compare the ethics of Levinas with those of Lacan. Suffice to note that even a brief summary of the latter would raise important issues. For one thing, the Lacanian "Same" is a divided Subject and Other. The I = identity equation of "The Trace and the Other" is from the outset inapplicable, becoming problematic as unitary sense in a transcendental ethical obligation. Also, Levinas does not posit an ethical bond formed by transference (an egoic desire for alterity) as do both Freud and Lacan. Rajchman (1986) offers a provocative study of Lacanian ethics.

3. Critchley's book in large part outlines his own innovative "clôtural" readings of Derrida and Levinas. His approach bears the supplementary burden of carrying the argument for an ethical legitimation of deconstructive practice.

4. "Unlike the animal's face the human face is no mere continuation of the rest of the body. It has not come from below, finally reaching its destination on top of the body but has been, as it were, set down from above. The body comes to a full stop here, there can only be a completely new beginning. Language is the new beginning" (Picard 1963, 11). In turn Deleuze and Guattari announce, "The head is included in the body but the face is not. . . . The face is produced only when the head ceases to be part of the body, when it ceases to be coded by the body . . . when the body, head included, has been decoded and has to be *overcoded* by something we shall call the Face. This amounts to saying that the head, all the volume-cavity elements of the head have to be facialized. . . . Although the head, even the human head, is not necessarily a face, the face is produced in humanity" (1987, 170). The final sentence especially can be read as an endorsement to some extent of Levinas's appropriation of the face to function in the ethical encounter.

In Deleuze and Guattari's estimation, however, the face registers an initial inhumanity in human beings. The face is "by nature a close-up, with its inanimate white surfaces, its shining black holes, its emptiness and boredom. Bunker face. To the point that if human beings have a destiny it is to escape the face" (1987, 171). This view stands in stark opposition to Levinas's own version in "The Trace of the Other"—a difference explainable as a chiasmus in proxemics. For Levinas, face constitutes the primal discourse "and in its visitation it does not disclose a world but offers itself as abstract and naked" (TO 352). Moreover, the presence of the face, diremptive of the consciousness of the Same, evokes a basic ethical imperative: responsibility for the Other. Clearly the Levinasian face is framed in a distantiation, a proximity that is not the close-up manifestation of Deleuze and Guattari's white surface–black hole system.

Indirectly, Deleuze and Guattari open up an important matter not considered by Levinas: the speed and distance of the facial encounter. "The question of the body," they concur, "is not one of part-objects but of differential speeds." By factoring in a dromological dimension, the face takes on an agency quite alien to Levinas; it becomes a deterritorialization valued as "an absolute deterritorialization" removing "the head from the stratum of the organism" and connecting it to different strata (Deleuze and Guattari 1987, 172). This bunker face links instantly not to the responsibility of obligation but to an organization of power. "It is not the individuality of the face that counts but the efficacy of the ciphering it makes possible, and in what cases it makes it possible. This is an affair not of ideology but of economy and the organization of power" (175). The consequent conclusion is predictable: "face is a politics" (181).

5. It is of course a moot point whether or not the face's manifestation can escape the idea of a sign or transcend the semiosis of infinite play. At one point in *Of Grammatology*, Derrida aligns himself sensibly with Pierce: "There is . . . no phenomenality reducing the sign or the representer so that the thing signified may be allowed to glow finally in the luminosity of its presence. The so-called 'thing itself' is always already a *representamen* shielded from the simplicity of intuitive evidence" (Derrida 1976, 49).

6. Levinas's claim here is not without precedent. The thirteenth-century Provençal Hasid, Isaac the Blind, in his commentary on the *Sefer Yetsirah* (Book of Creation) speaks of face (*panim*) issuing from face and "of the 'faces above,' which the Creator made and which man finds in every direction as he immerses himself in higher things" (quoted in Scholem 1987, 282). Is it inaccurate to read this brief passage as arguing a transcendental placement of the face as a primordial or metaphysical encounter? A "panimistic" formulation similar to Levinas's own theory? Swedenborg, too, in his comments on angelic communication, foregrounds an elemental link between face and speech: "I have been informed by the angels that the very first speech in every earth was speech by the face, and from the two origins there, the lips and the eyes" (quoted in Yaguello 1991, 181).

The relation here of same to the Other that Levinas outlines also bears comparison to the similar relation of historical to messianic time that forms a constant theme of cabalistic messianic literature. Scholem describes the posthistorical moment as an encounter of historical time with a radical alterity. Rather than a steady transition between temporalities, a transcendence erupts "breaking in upon history, an intrusion in which history itself perishes, transformed in its ruin because it is struck by a beam of light" (1976, 10). One need only substitute the face of the other for the beam of light and the Same's consciousness for history to elucidate the similarity.

7. Compare Deleuze: "That the Other should not, properly speaking, be any-one, neither you nor I, signifies that it is a structure which is implemented only by variable terms in different perceptual worlds—me for you in yours, you for me in mine. It is not even enough to see in the Other a specific or particular structure of the perceptual world in general: in fact, it is a structure which grounds and ensures the overall functioning of this world as a whole" (1994, 281).

8. In one place Levinas links art via a similitude to enigma: "It is the essence of art to signify only between the lines—in the intervals of time, between times— like a footprint that would precede the step, or an echo preceding the sound of a voice" (PN 7).

9. I am grateful throughout this study for discussions with Jill Robbins on Levi-nas's concept of the face. Although I have attempted to remove all of her known phrases, a few recalcitrant ones may remain. Her recent study of Levinas, *Altered Reading: Levinas and Literature,* appeared in 1999.

10. There's a sedimented resonance in both Derrida's and Levinas's concept of the trace of Hegel's own version: "Wesen ist was gewesen ist" (Essence is what has been; quoted in Althusser 1993, 158).

11. It might be useful to interject Deleuze and Guattari's thinking on the face and its relation to the signifier:

Subjectification is never without a black hole in which it lodges its conscious-ness, passion, and redundancies. Since all semiotics are mixed and strata comes at least in twos, it should come as no surprise that a very special mechanism is situated at their intersections. Oddly enough it is a face: the *white wall/black hole* system. . . . The face is not an envelope exterior to the person who speaks, thinks or feels. The form of the signifier in language, even its units, would re-main indeterminate if the potential listener did not use the face of the speaker to guide his or her choices. . . . The face itself is redundancy. [It] constructs the wall that the subjectification needs in order to bounce off of; it constitutes the wall of the signifier, the frame or screen. The face digs the hole that subjectifica-tion needs in order to break through; it constitutes the black hole of subjectivity as consciousness or passion, the camera, the third eye. (1987, 167–68)

Elsewhere, in his analysis of Francis Bacon's paintings, Deleuze escorts us to an ontological brink where face in extremis becomes meat and where "[t]he head as meat is man becoming animal" (1985, 52).

I note in passing Levinas's disregard of the sort of possession by the face that occurs in seduction—described by Baudrillard as "the world's elementary dynamic" (1988, 59). Baudrillard's theory of seduction is outlined in chapter 1 as it pertains to the verbal sign and examined in chapter 4 in the light of Olson's Mayan project.

12. Critchley calls attention to an important grammatical articulation onto the ethical. The temporality of the future anterior tense eludes a location in the present, pointing simultaneously toward a past and a future. Evading a reduction to on-

tology, the future anterior registers "the temporality of the trace of Illeity, [and] is the time of ethics" (Bernasconi and Critchley 1991, 168).

13. To define language as contact, however, is to define language as parousial and hence subscribe to a pre-Derridean metaphysics of presence. For Blanchot, Levinas's definition has "grave consequences." As a mystical fusion, "Immediacy not only rules out all mediation; it is the infiniteness of a presence such that it can no longer be spoken of, for the relation itself, be it ethical or ontological, has burned up all at once in a night bereft of darkness. In this night there are no longer any terms, there is no longer a relation, no longer a beyond—in this night God himself has annulled himself" (1986, 24). Understood as contact, language precipitates a nihilism in which all terminology and communication is destroyed. Blanchot's answer to this problem is somehow "to understand the immediate in the past tense" (24). The contact named proximity—which Blanchot calls "an infinite affliction"—when understood as past links us to the "Others' affliction, and the other as affliction" (25).

14. Eco cleaves the ontological base with a foundational praxis, distinguishing a model from an empirical reader; the former implied by the complex interrelation of codes and vocabularies inherent in a text; the latter explicit, historically, and even quotidianly contingent—the human being who happens on a certain day to pick up a certain book and read.

The model reader has a theological resonance. Is not the model reader, like God, a transcendental absolute singularity, hidden and responsive in its nonresponse? And isn't it to this model reader that the empirical reader is obliged within an ethical relation that precedes all graphic praxis? And isn't the empirical reader's duty to this model—this implicit Other—unconditional and absolute? However, this absolute alterity is also an absolute interiority, a fold within a textual sameness. In reality the model reader is constructed as a compossibility within the text itself; a textual potential within a similarly virtual reading. "At the minimal level," Eco announces, "every type of text explicitly selects a very general model of possible reader through the choice (i) of a specific linguistic code, (ii) of a certain literary style, and (iii) of specific specialization-indices" (1984, 7). The model reader is projected, foreseen, and realized as a textual strategy. "Likewise the 'author' is nothing else but a textual strategy establishing semantic correlations and activating the Model Reader" (11). In light of this differential semantics, separating the anthropological from the structurally linguistic, Plato, Derrida, and Heidegger can each be referred to as a "philosophical style"—the model reader likewise appearing as a theoretical competence or expertise in negotiating and fully reactualizing those styles.

15. A major difference, however, is that while proximity is a fundamental requirement, it is not necessarily a determinant.

16. According to Levinas, the task of criticism is to integrate "the inhuman work of the artist into the human world. Criticism already detaches itself from its irresponsibility by envisaging its technique. It treats the artist as a man at work. Already

in inquiring after the influences he undergoes it links this disengaged and proud man to real history" (CPP 12). I discuss the somber consequences of this critical violence in chapter 1.

17. There is an irreducible ambiguity in the French term "il" when it occurs in isolation, a fact seemingly ignored by Critchley in his discussion of Derrida's reading of Levinas (Critchley 1992, 107–44) and somewhat circumvented in Derrida's own neologistic "elleity" (see Bernasconi and Critchley 1991, 3–48).

18. Illeity manifests grammatically in "is": the third-person present indicative of the verb "to be." On the complex resonances of "is" as copula, see Derrida 1982, 177–205 and Hollier 1989, 66–68.

19. This last phrase is taken from Gabriel Marcel's book *Creative Fidelity.*

20. On the theological resonance of the adieu, see Derrida 1995a.

21. It's important to remain alert to Levinas's photism as a metaphor that saturates his writings, organizing ethics, metaphysics, creativity, and epistemology as zones determined by an ultimately optical paradigmatic binary of night and light. With the strength of this metaphoric weapon, Levinas can claim that of itself "ethics is an optics" (TI 29). See, for instance, "Reality and Its Shadow" in CCP 1–13 and EE 46–51.

22. The trope of unidirectional departure without return first appears in 1941 in *Existence and Existents,* where Levinas chooses Baudelaire's "true travellers" as his exemplary case: "An evasion without an itinerary and without an end, it is not trying to come ashore somewhere. Like for Baudelaire's true travellers, it is a matter of parting for the sake of parting" (EE 25). Levinas might well have substituted for Ulysses a similar "Greek" paradigm of return announced by Parmenides: "It is decreed by divine law that Being shall not be without boundary. . . . There is a limit (*peiras*), it is complete on every side, like the mass of a well-rounded (*eukukleou*) sphere. It is all the same to me what point I begin, for I shall return again to this same point" (quoted in Critchley 1992, 59). It is of course a desire to break with Parmenides that motivates Levinas throughout *Totality and Infinity.* Levinas also offers an Abrahamic notion of time itself as "a dynamism which leads us elsewhere than toward the things we possess" (EI 61).

23. The mystic Angelus Silesius offers a similar (although more Jabèsian) itinerary of the beyond: "One must go beyond God . . . What should my quest be? I must go beyond God into a desert flee" (*The Cherubinic Wanderer* 2:117, quoted in Derrida 1995b, 53). Leibniz provides a further alternative, not considered by Levinas, but a favorite of Deleuze: "I thought I was coming into port, but when I started to meditate upon the union of the soul and the body, I was as it were thrown back upon the open sea" (in Deleuze 1995, 104). This passage (twice paraphrased and specifically indexed by Deleuze) speaks of that indeterminate clinamen known as the rebuffed return—a trajectory neither circular nor linear but entirely fractal in its virtualities. Prigogine and Stengers name this thrownness a bifurcation point— that crucial moment in the history of a dissipative structure when its highly dis-

equilibrial condition veers into either order or chaos (Prigogine and Stengers 1984, 14, 160–72). Ulysses is fractalized inside a turbulent narrative of return and re-projection. Like Olson's "figure outward," the same becomes projectile. An elaborate study of Ulyssean circularity, as it pertains via James Joyce to philosophy, can be found in "Ulysses Gramophone: Hear Say Yes in Joyce," trans. Tina Kendall and Shari Benstock, in Derrida 1992, 253–309.

24. On the intricate perplication of Greek and Judaic in Levinas's thinking, see Robbins 1991, esp. 100–32. Also "Violence and Metaphysics" in Derrida 1978, 79–153.

25. For the full context of this Abrahamic inflexion, see Calvino 1974, 55–56.

26. I discuss in chapter 11 the systematic-chance-generated poetry of Jackson Mac Low—in many ways the most exemplary of this conjecturally ethical writing.

27. Burroughs's related method of text-generation, the "fold-in," attains similar results through ingratitude. "A page of text, my own or someone else's, is folded down the middle and placed on another page, the composite text is then read across, half one text and half the other" (quoted in Mottram 1971, 25). In the fictive context of his narratives, Burroughs frequently employs cut-up to disrupt space-time continua. See, for example, the exploits of "Technical Tilly" in *Nova Express* and the alteration of time links to rid the world of nuclear weapons which forms the central theme of *Port of Saints*. The majority of Burroughs's theoretical writings are collected in Burroughs 1973. In the 1980s he extended the cut-up's randomizing potential into the painterly realm as "shotgun art," where paintings are produced aleatorically by paint sprayed onto a plywood panel by means of a shotgun blast exploding a pressurized paint can. Precursors of Burroughs's shotgun painting can be found in the work of both Niki de Sainte-Phalle and earlier in Duchamp. The latter information was related to Burroughs by Duchamp himself in 1958 (Miles 1993, 237).

28. The mesostic is not exclusive to Cage in contemporary writing and is used to intricate effect in Christine Brooke-Rose's novel *Thru* (1975). Her use of the device, however, does not involve application of systematic chance, nor is it employed on preexistent material.

29. In proposing the parasite as an example of the ethical ingratitude of nonre-turn, it's pertinent to mention Derrida's provoking conjecture that a logic of the parasite might constitute the law of all writing (cf. Derrida 1976, 54). An excellent and far-reaching study of the parasite as it pertains to anthropology, biology, and information theory is Serres, who offers, incidentally under the title "The Worst Definition," the following: "Ulysses won the contest, making a simple arrow, the relation, irreversible, with no possible return, through the lined-up axes, the iron that separates. End of the Odyssey, amidst the corpses" (1982a 252).

30. Bruns coins the term "poethics" admitting a Joycean inflection to the term (1994, 206). The same neologism also appears in the title of Joan Retallack's contribution in the same collection: "Poethics of a Complex Realism."

31. Phillips's words are taken from *A TV Dante* by Tom Phillips and Peter Green-away, commissioned for BBC 4 in the 1980s and broadcast July 1990 in eight ten-minute episodes. Commentary on this work can be found in Kinder 1997; Biga 1994, 167–71; and Vickers 1995.

32. Phillips, however, was aware and supportive of Burroughs's work. After reading an interview with Burroughs in the *Paris Review* (fall 1965), Phillips experimented with cut-up, developing his own version: the "column-edge poem." Admitting the inspiration of Burroughs's technique, he speaks of *A Humument* as an attempt to push such "semi-aleatoric devices into more ambitious service" (quoted in Daniel Traister, "Tom Phillips, and A Humument," available electronically on *Tom Phillips and A Humument*, Internet site http://www.wolfenet.com/ "duchamp/).

33. "Notes on *A Humument*" [unpaginated] in Phillips 1980. *A Humument* dates back to at least the autumn of 1970 when five pages of monochrome reproductions were published in *Collection Seven*, ed. Peter Riley (Department of English, Odense University, Odense, Denmark). In the same year appeared *In One Side & Out the Other* (London: The Ferry Press, 1970), by Andrew Crozier, John James, and Tom Phillips, a collaborative collection in which poems by Crozier and James are printed directly opposite the same poems subjected to Phillips's patterned erasures and treatments.

34. Phillips (1980) notes, "The title itself was arrived at by invited accident: folding one page over and flattening it on the page beneath makes the running title read A HUMUMENT, (i.e., A HUM(AN DOC)UMENT)."

35. From the dust jacket of Antin's *Talking at the Boundaries* (1976).

36. "[T]o write is today to make oneself the center of the action of speech, it is to effect writing by affecting oneself, to make action and affection coincide, to leave the *scriptor* inside the writing—not as a psychological subject, . . . but as agent of the action" (Barthes 1986, 18).

37. It's worth remarking that Antin's occasions of unmediated utterance don't obtain the quality of collective listening called for by Rosenzweig. In the latter's sociology of the multitude it's imperative that spontaneity does not occur—"Such words would serve only to dissolve the common attention of the hearers" (1985, 310). The unanimity of listening can be achieved only by the reading aloud of a preexisting text—both a scriptural passage and its exegesis.

38. The basis of Levinasian proximity is found in substitution (OB 19). I am responsible for the Other up to the point of taking her place (cf. OB 13). Levinas speaks, of course, of substitution as it governs the nature of subjectivity and obligation.

39. So far, there have been two revised editions published in 1987 and 1997 respectively. The first includes over fifty entirely reworked pages, and in the second a hundred pages are replaced by new versions. Needless to say, such a continu-

ous project of self-alteration takes a poetics of "recipient ingratitude" to a further registration.

40. But must we necessarily think of commentary as involving a return of alterity to the same? A giving back of the work to the work? Derrida opines that "the prosaic disembodiment into conceptual frameworks" constitutes "the first violence of all commentary"(1978, 312 n.7). If this assessment is correct, can we grant such violence the status of ingratitude? Derrida suggests that critical commentary effects a fundamental diremption of its source text. Less a loss *within* commentary than a conceptual abuse *by* it. Does critical labor elucidate and supplement a text, or does it violently co-opt it? For Derrida's own attempt to read Levinas ethically, see "At this very moment in this work here I am" (in Bernasconi and Critchley 1991, 11–48).

41. Critchley presents a Talmudic anecdote that ascribes to the text's status an almost human character: "The Torah is a body of writings which are given as much respect as the living body of a human being, and when that textual body is violated or fatally flawed it must be buried in accordance with the same ceremonies that accompany human burial. . . . The body of the faulty text is not censorially burnt and reduced to a pile of ashes, rather it is inhumed like a corpse where it is allowed slowly to decompose. The fault within the text slowly disappears as the text decomposes" (Bernasconi and Critchley 1991, 184). (Phillips's deployment of a similar trope of exhumation is certainly coincidental.)

42. Levinas describes the translational and rationalistic nature of his own personal brand of exegesis which "always consists in extricating from this theological language meanings addressing themselves to reason" (NTR 14).

43. John Llewelyn offers an adamant defense of artistic exegesis based on the trope of self-surrender: "Exegesis is the leading out, education, of the self from the ego, the turning of the named subject's will to mastery over itself and others into the other's educative mastery over the subject: the subjection of subjectivity to teaching, its destruction by instruction" (1995, 183).

44. On Levinas's notions of dwelling and habitation, see TI 152–74.

Works Cited

Aarsleff, Hans. 1982. *From Locke to Saussure: Essays on the Study of Language and Intellectual History.* Minneapolis: University of Minnesota Press.

Abraham, Nicholas. 1979. "The Shell and the Kernel," trans. Nicholas Rand. *Diacritics* 9, no. 1 (summer): 16–28.

Addison, Joseph. 1789. *The Spectator.* 8 vols. London. Printed by T. Wright for Payne, Rivington, Vadis, Longman, et. al.

Adorno, Theodor W. 1990. "Curves of the Needle." Trans. Thomas Y. Levin. *October* 55 (winter): 49–66.

Agamben, Giorgio. 1991. *Language and Death: The Place of Negativity.* Trans. Karen E. Pinkus with Michael Hardt. Minneapolis: University of Minnesota Press.

———. 1993a. *The Coming Community.* Trans. Michael Hardt. Minneapolis: University of Minnesota Press.

———. 1993b. *Stanzas: Word and Phantasm in Western Culture.* Trans. Ronald L. Martinez. Minneapolis: University of Minnesota Press.

———. 1995. *Idea of Prose.* Trans. Michael Sullivan and Sam Whitsitt. Albany: State University of New York Press.

———. 1999. *The End of the Poem. Studies in Poetics.* Trans. Daniel Heller-Roazen. Stanford, Calif.: Stanford University Press.

Ahearne, Jeremy. 1995. *Michel de Certeau: Interpretation and Its Other.* Stanford, Calif.: Stanford University Press.

Airaksinen, Timo. 1995. *The Philosophy of the Marquis de Sade.* London: Routledge.

Alexander, Jonathan J. G. 1992. *Medieval Illustrators and Their Methods of Work.* New Haven, Conn.: Yale University Press.

Allen, Donald M., ed. 1960. *The New American Poetry.* New York: Grove Press.

Allen, Donald, and Warren Tallman, eds. 1973. *The Poetics of the New American Poetry.* New York: Grove Press.

Althusser, Louis. 1971. *Lenin and Philosophy and Other Essays.* Trans. Ben Brewster. London: New Left Books.

———. 1993. *The Future Lasts a Long Time.* Trans. Richard Veasey. London: Chatto and Windus.

Altieri, Charles. 1979. *Enlarging the Temple: New Directions in American Poetry during the 1960s.* Lewisburg, Pa.: Bucknell University Press.

Angenet, Marc. 1984. "Structuralism and Syncretism: Institutional Distortions of Saussure." In *The Structural Allegory,* ed. John Fekete. Minneapolis: University of Minnesota Press.

Anscombe, G. E. M. 1963. *An Introduction to Wittgenstein's Tractatus.* 2d ed. London: Hutchinson.

Antin, David. 1968. "Notes for an Ultimate Prosody (Part One)." *Stony Brook* 1–2 (fall): 173–79.

———. 1975a. "David Antin: A Correspondence with the Editors, William V. Spanos and Robert Kroetsch." *Boundary* 2 (spring): 595–650.

———. 1975b. "An Interview Conducted by Barry Alpert." *Vort* 4:3–33.

———. 1976. *Talking at the Boundaries*. New York: New Directions.

Applebaum, David. 1990. *Voice*. Albany: State University of New York Press.

Arcand, Pierre-André. 1992. *ERES + 7*. Quebec: Obscure. Compact disc.

———. 1995. *ERES + 16*. Quebec: Obscure. Compact disc.

Artaud, Antonin. 1995. *Watchfiends and Rack Screams: Works from the Final Period by Antonin Artaud*. Trans. Clayton Eshleman with Bernard Bador. Boston: Exact Change.

Ashcroft, Bill, Gareth Griffiths, and Helen Tiffin. 1989. *The Empire Writes Back*. London: Routledge.

[Aubrey, John]. 1813. *Letters Written by Eminent Persons in the Seventeenth and Eighteenth Centuries: To Which are Added, Hearne's Journeys to Reading, and Lives of Eminent Men by John Aubrey, Esq.* 2 vols. London: Longman, Hurst, Rees, Orme, and Brown.

Bailey, Nathan. 1736. *Dictionarium Brittanicum*. London: T. Cox.

Baker, Houston A., Jr. 1984. *Blues, Ideology, and Afro-American Literature: A Vernacular Theory*. Chicago: University of Chicago Press.

Bakhtin, Mikhail. 1968. *Rabelais and His World*. Trans. Hélène Iswolsky. Cambridge, Mass.: MIT Press.

Ball, Hugo. 1974. *Flight Out of Time: A Dada Diary by Hugo Ball*. Trans. Ann Raimes. New York: Viking Press.

Barker, Arthur E. 1942. *Milton and the Puritan Dilemma, 1641–1660*. Toronto: University of Toronto Press.

Barney, Stephen A., ed. 1991. *Annotation and Its Texts*. Oxford: Oxford University Press.

Barrell, John. 1983. *English Literature in History, 1730–80*. New York: St. Martin's Press.

Barrot, Jean. 1987. *What Is Situationism? Critique of the Situationist International*. London: Unpopular Books.

Barthes, Roland. 1975. *The Pleasure of the Text*. Trans. Richard Miller. New York: Hill and Wang.

———. 1976. *Sade Fourier Loyola*. Trans. Richard Miller. New York: Hill and Wang.

———. 1977. *Image Music Text*. Trans. Stephen Heath. New York: Hill and Wang.

———. 1980. *New Critical Essays*. Trans. Richard Howard. New York: Hill and Wang.

————. 1982. *A Barthes Reader.* Ed. Susan Sontag. New York: Hill and Wang.

————. 1985a. *The Grain of the Voice: Interviews 1962–1980.* Trans. Linda Coverdale. New York: Hill and Wang.

————. 1985b. *The Responsibility of Forms.* Trans. Richard Howard. New York: Hill and Wang.

————. 1986. *The Rustle of Language.* Trans. Richard Howard. New York: Hill and Wang.

————. 1987. *Writer Sollers.* Trans. Philip Thody. Minneapolis: University of Minnesota Press.

Bataille, Georges. 1962. *Death and Sensuality: A Study of Eroticism and the Taboo.* New York: Walker and Co.

————. 1970. *Oeuvres Complètes.* Paris: Gallimard.

————. 1973. *Literature and Evil.* Trans. Alastair Hamilton. London: Calder and Boyars.

————. 1985. *Visions of Excess: Selected Writings, 1927–1939.* Trans. Allan Stoekl with C. R. Lovitt and D. M. Leslie Jr. Minneapolis: University of Minnesota Press.

————. 1988a. *Guilty.* Trans. Bruce Boone. Venice, Calif.: Lapis Press.

————. 1988b. *Inner Experience.* Trans. Leslie Anne Boldt. Albany: State University of New York Press.

————. 1988–91. *The Accursed Share.* 2 vols. Trans. Robert Hurley. New York: Zone Books.

————. 1991. *The Impossible.* Trans. Robert Hurley. San Francisco: City Lights.

————. 1994. *On Nietzsche.* Trans. Bruce Boone. New York: Paragon House.

Bateson, Gregory. 1973. *Steps to an Ecology of Mind.* London: Paladin.

Baudrillard, Jean. 1988. *The Ecstasy of Communication.* Trans. Bernard and Caroline Schutze. New York: Semiotext(e) Foreign Agent Series.

————. 1993. *Baudrillard Live: Selected Interviews.* Ed. Mike Gane. London: Routledge.

Beauvoir, Simone de. 1966. "Must We Burn Sade?" In Marquis de Sade, *The One Hundred and Twenty Days of Sodom and Other Writings,* trans. Richard Seaver and Austryn Wainhouse, 3–64. New York: Grove Press.

Bell, Alexander Melville. 1867. *Visible Speech.* London: Simpkin, Marshall and Co.

Benjamin, Walter. 1969. *Illuminations.* Ed. Hannah Arendt. Trans. Harry Zohn. New York: Schocken.

————. 1977. *The Origin of German Tragic Drama.* Trans. John Osborne. London: Verso.

Bentley, Richard. 1711. Q. *Horatius Flaccus ex recensione et cum notis R. Bentleii.* Cambridge.

————. 1732. *Milton's Paradise Lost. A New Edition.* London: Jacob Tonson.

———. 1958. *A Confutation of Atheism.* In *Isaac Newton's Papers and Letters on Natural Philosophy and Related Documents,* ed. I. Bernard Cohen, 313–94. Cambridge, Mass.: Harvard University Press.

Bergman, Par. 1962. *"Modernolatria" et "Simultaneità": Rescherches sur deux tendances dans l'avant-garde litteraire en Italie et un France à la veille de la première guerre mondiale.* Uppsala: Svenska bokforlaget/Bonniers.

Bergvall, Caroline. 1993. "No Margins to This Page: Female Experimental Poets and the Legacy of Modernism." *Fragmente* 5:30–38.

Berman, Lorna. 1971. *The Thought and Themes of the Marquis de Sade.* Kitchener, Ont.

Bernasconi, Robert, and Simon Critchley, eds. 1991. *Re-Reading Levinas.* Bloomington: Indiana University Press.

Berne, Stanley, and Arlene Zekowsky. 1954. *A First Book of Neo-narrative.* Stonington, Conn.: Métier Editions.

Bernstein, Charles. 1985. "Whole to Part: The Ends of Ideologies of the Long Poem." *Open Letter* 6, nos. 2–3 (summer–fall): 177–90.

———. 1992. *A Poetics.* Cambridge, Mass.: Harvard University Press.

Bertholf, Robert J. 1997. Introduction to *Robert Duncan Selected Poems,* xi–xiv. New York: New Directions.

Bhabha, Homi K. 1984. "Representation and the Colonial Text: A Critical Exploration of Some Forms of Mimeticism." In *The Theory of Reading,* ed. Frank Gloversmith. Brighton: Harvester.

Bickerton, Derek. 1973. "The Nature of a Creole Continuum." *Language* 49:3.

Biga, Tracy. 1994. "Cinema Bulimia: Peter Greenaway's Corpus of Excess." Ph.D. diss., University of Southern California.

Black, M. 1964. *A Companion to Wittgenstein's Tractatus.* Cambridge: Cambridge University Press.

Blake, William. 1966. *Complete Writings.* Ed. Geoffrey Keynes. Oxford: Oxford University Press.

Blanchot, Maurice. 1969. *L'entretien infini.* Paris: Gallimard.

———. 1981. *The Gaze of Orpheus.* Trans. Lydia Davis. Barrytown, N.Y.: Station Hill Press.

———. 1982. *The Space of Literature.* Trans. Ann Smock. Lincoln: University of Nebraska Press.

———. 1985. "Interruptions." In *The Sin of the Book: Edward Jabes,* trans. Rosmarie Waldrop and Paul Auster, 42–44. Lincoln: University of Nebraska Press.

———. 1986. *The Writing of the Disaster.* Trans. Ann Smock. Lincoln: University of Nebraska Press.

———. 1992. *The Step Not Beyond.* Trans. Lycette Nelson. Albany: State University of New York Press.

Blaser, Robin. 1970. "The Fire." *Caterpillar* 12 (July): 15–23.

———. 1979. "The Moth Poem" [statement by author]. In *The Long Poem Anthology*, ed. Michael Ondaatje, 323–25. Toronto: Coach House Press.

———. 1983. "The Violets: Charles Olson and Alfred North Whitehead." *Line* 2 (fall): 61–103.

———. 1993. *The Holy Forest*. Toronto: Coach House Press.

———. 1995. *Bach's Belief: A Curriculum of the Soul* 10. [Buffalo]: Institute of Further Studies.

Blau, Herbert. 1992. *To All Appearances: Ideology and Performance*. New York: Routledge.

Bloom, Harold. 1975. *A Map of Misreading*. Oxford: Oxford University Press.

Bogel, Fredric. 1987. "Johnson and the Role of Authority." In *The New Eighteenth Century*, ed. Felicity Nussbaum and Laura Brown, 189–209. London: Methuen.

Bök, Christian. 1994. "Q's, Queues, Cues: Quibbling with Sentences in *Quirks and Quillets* by Karen Mac Cormack." *Open Letter* 8, no. 8 (winter): 20–29.

Bory, Louis. 1963. "Presentation." In Eugène Sue's *Les Mystères de Paris*. Paris: Pauvert.

Boswell, James. 1980. *Life of Johnson*. Ed. R. W. Chapman. Oxford: Oxford University Press World's Classics.

Boundas, Constantin V., and Dorothea Olkowski, eds. 1994. *Gilles Deleuze and the Theatre of Philosophy*. New York: Routledge.

Bourdieu, Pierre. 1991. *Language and Symbolic Power*. Trans. Gino Raymond and Matthew Adamson. Cambridge, Mass.: Harvard University Press.

Brack, O. M., Jr., and Robert E. Kelley, eds. 1974. *The Early Biographies of Samuel Johnson*. Iowa City: University of Iowa Press.

Bradford, Richard. 1989. "The Visual Poem in the Eighteenth Century." *Visible Language* 23, no. 1: 9–27.

Breton, André. 1993. *Conversations: The Autobiography of Surrealism*. Trans. Mark Polizotti. New York: Paragon House.

Brewster, David, Sir. 1856. *Letters on Natural Magic, Addressed to Sir Walter Scott, Bart*. London: William Tegg.

Bromige, David. 1975. "Talking Antin as Writing." *Vort* 4:67–72.

Brooke-Rose, Christine. 1975. *Thru*. London: Hamish Hamilton.

Brotchie, Alastair, ed. 1995. *Encyclopaedia Acephalica*. London: Atlas Press.

Brown, Charles Brockden. 1926a. *Memoirs of Carwin the Biloquist*. Ed. Fred Lewis Patte. New York: Harcourt Brace.

———. 1926b. *Wieland; or the Transformation*. Ed. Fred Lewis Patte. New York: Harcourt Brace.

Brown, Norman O. 1966. *Love's Body*. New York: Vintage.

Brunnhofer, H. 1890. *Bruno's Lehre von Kleinsten als die Quelle der Prastäbilirten Harmonie von Leibnitz*. Leipzig.

Bruns, Gerald L. 1994. "Poethics: John Cage and Stanley Cavell at the

Crossroads of Ethical Theory." In *John Cage Composed in America,* ed. Marjorie Perloff and Charles Junkerman. Chicago: University of Chicago Press.

Bunting, Basil 1968. "A Statement." In Johathan Williams, *Descant on Rawthey's Madrigal Conversations with Basil Bunting by Johnathan Williams.* Lexington, Ky.: Gnomon Press.

Burke, Edmund. 1993. *Reflections on the Revolution in France.* Oxford: Oxford University Press World's Classics.

Burroughs, William S. 1964. *Nova Express.* New York: Grove Press.

———. 1967. *The Ticket that Exploded.* New York: Grove Press.

———. 1973. *The Job.* Rev. ed. New York: Grove Press.

———. 1980. *Port of Saints.* Berkeley, Calif.: Blue Wind.

Burroughs, William S., and Brion Gysin. 1967. *The Exterminator.* San Francisco: Auerhan Press.

———. 1978. *The Third Mind.* New York: Viking.

Byrd, Don. 1994. *The Poetics of the Common Knowledge.* Albany: State University of New York Press.

Bysshe, Edward. 1710. *The Art of English Poetry.* 4th ed. London: Samuel Buckley.

Caffentzis, Constantine George. 1989. *Clipped Coins, Abused Words, and Civil Government: John Locke's Philosophy of Money.* Brooklyn: Autonomedia.

Cage, John. 1974. *M: Writings '67–'72.* Middletown, Conn.: Wesleyan University Press.

———. 1979. *Empty Words: Writings '73–'78.* Middletown, Conn.: Wesleyan University Press.

———. 1981. *For the Birds: John Cage in Conversation with Daniel Charles.* London: Marion Boyars.

———. 1982a. "About Roaratorio: An Irish Circus on Finnegans Wake." In John Cage and Sorel Etrog, *Dream Chamber and About Roaratorio,* ed. Robert O'Driscoll. Toronto: Black Brick Press.

———. 1982b. *Themes and Variations.* Barrytown, N.Y.: Station Hill Press.

Calvino, Italo. 1974. *Invisible Cities.* Trans. William Weaver. New York: Harcourt Brace.

Campbell, Archibald. 1767. *Lexiphanes.* 2d ed. corrected. London: J. Knox.

Campion, Thomas. 1904. "Observations in the Art of English Poesie." In *Elizabethan Critical Essays,* 2 vols., ed. G. Gregory Smith, 2:327–55. Oxford: Oxford University Press.

Carruthers, Mary. 1990. *The Book of Memory: A Study of Memory in Medieval Culture.* Cambridge: Cambridge University Press.

Carson, Anne. 1985. *Eros the Bittersweet.* Princeton, N.J.: Princeton University Press.

Carter, Angela. 1978. *The Sadeian Woman and the Ideology of Pornography*. New York: Pantheon.

Cassirer, Ernst. 1979. *Symbol, Myth, and Culture: Essays and Lectures of Ernst Cassirer, 1935–1945*. Ed. Donald P. Verene. New Haven, Conn.: Yale University Press.

Casti, John. 1979. *Connectivity, Complexity, and Catastrophe in Large-Scale Systems*. New York: John Wiley.

Cavell, Stanley. 1988. *In Quest of the Ordinary: Lines of Skepticism and Romanticism*. Chicago: University of Chicago Press.

Cawdrey, Robert. [1604] 1966. *A Table Alphabeticall of Hard Usual English Words*. Reprint; Gainesville, Fla.: Scholars' Facsimilies and Reprints.

Certeau, Michel de. 1984. *The Practice of Everyday Life*. Trans. Steven Rendall. Berkeley: University of California Press.

———. 1988. *The Writing of History*. Trans. Tom Conley. New York: Columbia University Press.

———. 1992. *The Mystic Fable*. Vol. 1: *The Sixteenth and Seventeenth Centuries*. Trans. Michael B. Smith. Chicago: University of Chicago Press.

Christensen, Paul. 1979. *Charles Olson: Call Him Ishmael*. Austin: University of Texas Press.

Cixous, Hélène. 1987. "The Laugh of the Medusa." In *Art and Its Significance: An Anthology of Aesthetic Theory*, 2d ed., ed. Stephen David Ross, 573–89. Albany: State University of New York Press.

Clair, Jean, and Harald Szeemann. 1975. *Le Macchine Celibi/The Bachelor Machines*. New York: Rizzoli.

Clark, J. C. D. 1994. *Samuel Johnson*. Cambridge: Cambridge University Press.

Clark, Robert T. 1969. *Herder: His Life and Thought*. Berkeley: University of California Press.

Clark, Tom. 1991. *Charles Olson: The Allegory of a Poet's Life*. New York: Norton.

Clough, Rosa Trillo. 1961. *Futurism: The Story of a Modern Art Movement, A New Appraisal*. New York: Philosophical Library.

Clulee, Nicholas H. 1988. *John Dee's Natural Philosophy*. London: Routledge.

Cobbing, Bob, and Peter Mayer, eds. 1978. *Concerning Concrete Poetry*. London: Writers Forum.

Cohen, I. Bernard, ed. 1958. *Isaac Newton's Papers and Letters on Natural Philosophy*. Cambridge, Mass.: Harvard University Press.

Cohen, Keith. 1977. "The Delire of Translation." *Sub-Stance* 16:85–88.

Cohen, Michael M., and Robert E. Bourdette Jr. 1980. "Richard Bentley's Edition of *Paradise Lost* (1732): A Bibliography." *Milton Quarterly* 14:49–54.

Coleman, J. 1981. *English Literature in History, 1350–1400: Medieval Readers and Writers*. London: Hutchinson.

———. 1988. *Medieval Theories of Authorship*. Philadelphia.

Conte, Joseph M. 1991. *Unending Design: The Forms of Postmodern Poetry.* Ithaca, N.Y.: Cornell University Press.

Courtney, William P., and David Nichol Smith. 1968. *A Bibliography of Samuel Johnson.* Oxford: Oxford University Press.

Coward, Harold, and Toby Foshay, eds. 1992. *Derrida and Negative Theology.* Albany: State University of New York Press.

Cowley, Abraham. 1684. *Works.* 8th ed. London: Henry Herringman.

Critchley, Simon. 1992. *The Ethics of Deconstruction: Derrida and Levinas.* Oxford: Blackwell.

Croll, Morris W. 1969. *"Attic" and Baroque Prose Style.* Princeton, N.J.: Princeton University Press.

Crystal, David. 1975. "Paralinguistics." In *The Body as a Medium of Expression,* ed. Jonathan Benthall and Ted Polhemus. New York: E. P. Dutton.

Curtius, Ernst R. 1973. *European Literature and the Latin Middle Ages,* Trans. Willard R. Trask. Princeton, N.J.: Princeton University Press.

Cutten, George B. 1927. *Speaking with Tongues Historically and Psychologically Considered.* New Haven, Conn.: Yale University Press.

Daniel, Stephen H. 1984. *John Toland: His Methods, Manners, and Mind.* Montreal and Kingston: McGill-Queen's University Press.

Dean, Carolyn J. 1992. *The Self and Its Pleasures: Bataille, Lacan, and the History of the Decentered Subject.* Ithaca, N.Y.: Cornell University Press.

Debord, Guy. 1981. "Detournement as Negation and Prelude." In *Situationist International Anthology,* trans. Ken Knabb. Berkeley, Calif.: Bureau of Public Secrets.

———. 1983. *Society of the Spectacle.* Detroit: Black and Red Press.

Deleuze, Gilles. 1971. *Sacher-Masoch: An Interpretation.* Trans. Jean McNeil. London: Faber and Faber.

———. 1985. "Periods and Aspects of Bacon: A Summing Up." *FMR* 12 (June): 52–60.

———. 1988a. *Spinoza: Practical Philosophy.* Trans. Robert Hurley. San Francisco: City Lights.

———. 1988b. *Foucault.* Trans. Seán Hand. Minneapolis: University of Minnesota Press.

———. 1990. *The Logic of Sense.* Trans. Mark Lester. New York: Columbia University Press.

———. 1993. *The Fold: Leibniz and the Baroque.* Trans. Tom Conley. Minneapolis: University of Minnesota Press.

———. 1994. *Difference and Repetition.* Trans. Paul Patton. New York: Columbia University Press.

———. 1995. *Negotiations, 1972–1990.* Trans. Martin Joughin. New York: Columbia University Press.

Deleuze, Gilles, and Félix Guattari. 1977. *Anti-Oedipus: Capitalism and*

Schizophrenia. Vol. 1. Trans. Robert Hurley, Mark Seem, and Helen R. Lane. New York: Viking Press.

———. 1986. *Nomadology: The War Machine*. Trans. Brian Massumi. New York: Semiotext(e).

———. 1987. *A Thousand Plateaus: Capitalism and Schizophrenia*. Vol. 2. Trans. Brian Massumi. Minneapolis: University of Minnesota Press.

Delgarno, George. 1680. *Didascalocophus: Or, the Deaf and Dumb Mans Tutor*. London.

De Maria, Robert. 1986. *Johnson's Dictionary and the Language of Learning*. Chapel Hill: University of North Carolina Press.

Deneef, A. Leigh. 1988. *Traherne in Dialogue: Heidegger, Lacan, and Derrida*. Durham, N.C.: Duke University Press.

De Quincey, Thomas. 1871. *Works*. 11 vols. Boston: Houghton, Mifflin.

Derksen, Jeff. 1994. "Queued Up: Karen Mac Cormack's Quirks and Quillets," *Open Letter* 8, no. 9 (summer): 48–70.

Derrida, Jacques. 1969. "Dissemination." *Critique* (261–62).

———. 1976. *Of Grammatology*. Trans. Gayatri Chakravorty Spivak. Baltimore: Johns Hopkins University Press.

———. 1977. "Signature Event Context." Trans. Samuel Weber and Jeffrey Mehlman. In *Glyph 1*. Baltimore: Johns Hopkins University Press.

———. 1978. *Writing and Difference*. Trans. Alan Bass. Chicago: University of Chicago Press.

———. 1981a. *Dissemination*. Trans. Barbara Johnson. Chicago: University of Chicago Press.

———. 1981b. *Positions*. Trans. Alan Bass. Chicago: University of Chicago Press.

———. 1982. *Margins of Philosophy*. Trans. Alan Bass. Chicago: University of Chicago Press.

———. 1985. *The Ear of the Other: Otobiography, Transference, Translation*. Trans. Christie V. McDonald and Avital Ronell. New York: Schocken.

———. 1992. *Acts of Literature*. Ed. Derek Attridge. London: Routledge.

———. 1995a. *The Gift of Death*. Trans. David Wills. Chicago: University of Chicago Press.

———. 1995b. *On the Name*. Trans. David Wood, John P. Leavey Jr., and Ian McLeod. Stanford, Calif.: Stanford University Press.

D'Harnoncourt, Anne, and Kynaston McShine, eds. 1973. *Marcel Duchamp*. New York: Museum of Modern Art.

Dickinson, H. T., ed. 1974. *Politics and Literature in the Eighteenth Century*. London: J. M. Dent.

Didier, Béatrice. 1976. *Sade*. Paris: Denoël-Gonthier.

Dobson, E. J. 1954. *English Pronunciation, 1500–1700*. Oxford: Clarendon Press.

Donne, John, 1952. *The Complete Poems and Selected Prose*. Ed. Charles Coffin. New York: Random House.

Dowling, William C. 1981. *Language and Logos in Boswell's Life of Johnson.* Princeton, N.J.: Princeton University Press.

Drucker, Johanna. 1986. "Hypergraphy: A Note on Maurice Lemaitre's Roman Hypergaphique." *Poetics Journal* 6:109–16.

———. 1994. *The Visible World: Experimental Typography and Modern Art, 1909–1923.* Chicago: University of Chicago Press.

———. 1995. *The Alphabetic Labyrinth.* London: Thames and Hudson.

Durand, Régis. 1977. "The Disposition of the Voice." In *Performance in Postmodern Culture,* ed. Michel Benamou and Charles Caramello, 99–110. Madison, Wis.: Coda Press.

Easthope, Antony. 1983. *Poetry as Discourse.* London: Methuen.

Easthope, Antony, and John O. Thompson, eds. 1991. *Contemporary Poetry Meets Modern Theory.* Toronto: University of Toronto Press.

Eco, Umberto. 1984. *The Role of the Reader: Explorations in the Semiotics of Texts.* Bloomington: Indiana University Press.

———. 1986. *Semiotics and the Philosophy of Language.* Bloomington: Indiana University Press.

Elledge, Scott. 1967. "The Naked Science of Language, 1747–1786." In *Studies in Criticism and Aesthetics, 1660–1800: Essays in Honor of Samuel Holt Monk,* ed. Howard Anderson and John Shea. Minneapolis: University of Minnesota Press.

Ellingham, Lewis, and Kevin Killian. 1998. *Poet Be like God: Jack Spicer and the San Francisco Renaissance.* Hanover, N.H.: University Press of New England.

Elsky, Martin. 1989. *Authorizing Words: Speech, Writing, and Print in the English Renaissance.* Ithaca, N.Y.: Cornell University Press.

Elster, Jon. 1975. *Leibniz and the Development of Economic Rationalism.* Oslo.

Empson, William. 1950. *Some Versions of Pastoral.* London: Chatto and Windus.

Fauchereau, Serge. 1988. *Moscow, 1900–1930.* London: Alpine.

Finas, Lucette. 1972. *La Crue.* Paris: Gallimard.

Finch, Henry Le Roy. 1971. *Wittgenstein—the Early Philosophy: An Exposition of the Tractatus.* New York: Humanities Press.

Fiumara, Gemma Corradi. 1990. *The Other Side of Language. A Philosophy of Listening.* Trans. Charles Lambert. London: Routledge.

Fleeman, J. D. 1975. *The Sale Catalogue of Samuel Johnson's Library.* English Literary Studies Monograph Series, no. 2. Victoria, B.C.: University of Victoria.

Fogg, Peter Walkden. 1792–96. *Elementa Anglicana: or, The Principles of English Grammar.* Stockport, England.

Folkierski, Wladyslaw. 1925. *Entre le Classicisme et le Romantisme.* Paris.

Foucault, Michel. 1970. *The Order of Things: An Archaeology of the Human Sciences.* [No translator named.]. New York: Random House.

————. 1973. *Madness and Civilization.* Trans. Richard Howard. New York: Vintage.

————. 1976. "The Discourse on Language." Trans. Rupert Swyer. In *The Archaeology of Knowledge and the Discourse of Language,* trans. A. M. Sheridan Smith. New York: Harper and Row.

————. 1986. *Death and the Labyrinth: The World of Raymond Roussel.* Trans. Charles Ruas. New York: Doubleday.

Fussell, Paul. 1986. *Samuel Johnson and the Life of Writing.* New York: Norton.

Gadamer, Hans-Georg. 1997. *Gadamer on Celan.* Trans. Richard Heinemann and Bruce Krajewski with introduction by Gerald Bruns. Albany: State University of New York Press.

Gallop, Jane. 1988. *Thinking through the Body.* New York: Columbia University Press.

Garver, Newton, and Seung-Chong Lee. 1994. *Derrida and Wittgenstein.* Philadelphia: Temple University Press.

Genette, Gérard. 1995. *Mimologics.* Trans. Thaïs E. Morgan. Lincoln: University of Nebraska Press.

Gibbs, Robert. 1992. *Correlations in Rosenzweig and Levinas.* Princeton, N.J.: Princeton University Press.

Ginsberg, Allen. 1972. *Improvised Poetics.* San Francisco: Anonym.

Glanville, Joseph. 1681. *Saducismus Triumphatus.* London: J. Collins and S. Lownds.

Glazier, Loss Pequeño. 1996. "Quirks & Quillets." *Small Press Traffic Newsletter* 17 (spring).

Goethe, J. W. 1952. *Goethe's Botanical Writings.* Trans. B. Mueller. Honolulu: University of Hawaii Press.

Goldsmith, Kenneth. 1997. *No. 111 2.7.93–10.20.96.* Great Barrington, Mass.: The Figures.

————. 2000. *Fidget.* Toronto: Coach House Books.

Goldsmith, Steven. 1993. *Unbuilding Jerusalem: Apocalypse and Romantic Representation.* Ithaca, N.Y.: Cornell University Press.

Golub, Spencer. 1984. *Evreinov: The Theatre of Paradox and Transformation.* Ann Arbor: University of Michigan Press.

Goodman, Felicitas D. 1972. *Speaking in Tongues: A Cross-Cultural Study of Glossolalia.* Chicago: University of Chicago Press.

Gottesman, A. Coudert. 1972. "F. M. van Helmont: His Life and Thought." Ph.D. diss., University of London.

————. 1976. "A Quaker-Cabbalist Controversy." *Journal of the Warburg and Courtauld Institutes* 39:171–89.

Gove, Philip. 1940. "Notes on Serialization and Competitive Publishing: Johnson's and Bailey's Dictionaries, 1755." In *Oxford Bibliographical Society Proceedings and Papers,* vol. 5, 305–22.

————. 1967. "The Making of a Dictionary." In *Language Arts News* 31.

Grafton, Anthony. 1997. *The Footnote: A Curious History*. Cambridge, Mass.: Harvard University Press.

Guattari, Félix. 1995. *Chaosophy*. New York: Semiotext(e).

————. 1996a. *The Guattari Reader*. Ed. Gary Genosko. Oxford: Blackwell.

————. 1996b. *Soft Subversions*. Trans. David L. Sweet and Chet Weiner. New York: Semiotext(e).

Guyotat, Pierre. 1981. "Body of the Text." *Semiotext(e)* 4, no. 1: 14–21.

————. 1995. *Eden, Eden, Eden*. Trans. Graham Fox. London: Creation Books.

Hallett, Garth. 1967. *Wittgenstein's Definition of Meaning as Use*. New York: Fordham University Press.

Haraway, Donna J. 1991. *Simians, Cyborgs, and Women: The Reinvention of Nature*. New York: Routledge.

Harris, William V. 1989. *Ancient Literacy*. Cambridge, Mass.: Harvard University Press.

Harryman, Carla. 1980. *Under the Bridge*. Berkeley, Calif.: This Press.

Hathaway, N. 1989. "Compilatio: From Plagiarism to Compiling." *Viator* 20:19–42.

Hayles, N. Katherine, ed. 1991. *Chaos and Order: Complex Dynamics in Literature and Science*. Chicago: University of Chicago Press.

Heath, Stephen. 1972. *The Nouveau Roman: A Study in the Practice of Writing*. Philadelphia: Temple University Press.

Heidegger, Martin. 1962. *Kant and the Problem of Metaphysics*. Trans. James S. Churchill. Bloomington: Indiana University Press.

————. 1982. *The Basic Problems of Phenomenology*. Trans. Albert Hofstadter. Bloomington: Indiana University Press.

Helmont, Baron Franciscus Mercurius van. 1667. *Alphabeti vere naturalis hebraici brevissima delineato*. Sulzbach.

Higgins, Dick. 1976. *Some Poetry Intermedia*. Barrytown, N.Y.: Unpublished Editions.

————. 1977. *George Herbert's Pattern Poems in their Tradition*. West Glover, Vt.: Unpublished Editions.

Hill, Christopher. 1979. *Milton and the English Revolution*. Harmondsworth: Penguin.

Hjelmslev, Louis. 1969. *Prologomena to a Theory of Language*. Trans. Francis J. Whitfield. Madison: University of Wisconsin Press.

————. 1970. *Language: An Introduction*. Trans. Francis J. Whitfield. Madison: University of Wisconsin Press.

Hobbes, Thomas. 1678. *Decameron Physiologicum*. London: W. Crook.

Hollier, Denis. 1989. *Against Architecture*. Trans. Betsy Wing. Cambridge, Mass.: MIT Press.

————, ed. 1988. *The College of Sociology, 1937–39.* Trans. Betsy Wing. Minneapolis: University of Minnesota Press.

Holmes, Richard. 1993. *Dr. Johnson and Mr. Savage.* New York: Pantheon.

Horace (Quintus Horatius Flaccus). 1992. "Art of Poetry." In *Critical Theory Since Plato,* rev. ed., ed. Hazard Adams, 68–74. New York: Harcourt Brace Jovanovich.

Horkeimer, Max, and Theodor Adorno. 1972. *Dialectic of Enlightenment.* Trans. John Cumming. New York: Continuum.

Horne Tooke, John. 1860. "A Letter to Mr. Dunning." In *The Diversions of Purley.* London: William Tegg.

Huelsenbeck, Richard, ed. [1920] 1966. *Dada Almanach Im Auftrag des Zentralamts der Deutschen Dada-Bewegung.* Berlin: Erich Reiss Verlag. Reprint, New York: Something Else Press.

Huey, Edmund Burke. 1968. *The Psychology and Pedagogy of Reading.* Cambridge, Mass.: MIT Press.

Hume, Alexander. 1885. *Of the Orthographie and Congruitie of the Britan Tongue.* Ed. H. B. Wheatley. London: N. Trübner [Early English Text Society].

Hussein, Mohammed A., ed. 1975. *Les origines du livre. Du papyrus au codex.* French trans. Rodolphe Savoie. Leipzig: Edition Leipzig.

Innis, Harold A. 1972. *Empire and Communications.* Rev. ed. Ed. Mary Q. Innis. Toronto: University of Toronto Press.

Iser, Wolfgang. 1978. *The Act of Reading: A Theory of Aesthetic Response.* Baltimore: Johns Hopkins University Press.

Isou, Isadore. 1947. *Introduction à une Nouvelle Poésie et une Nouvelle Musique.* Paris: Gallimard.

————. 1964. *Les Champs de Force de la Peinture Lettriste.* Paris: Avant-Garde.

Jabès, Edmond. 1976. *The Book of Questions.* Trans. Rosmarie Waldrop. Middletown, Conn.: Wesleyan University Press.

Jaffé, Hans. 1967. *De Stijl.* Trans. R. R. Symonds and Mary Whitall. New York: Abrams.

Jakobson, Roman. 1968. *Child Language, Aphasis, and Phonological Universals.* The Hague: Mouton.

Jameson, Fredric. 1971. *Marxism and Form.* Princeton, N.J.: Princeton University Press.

Jardine, Alice. 1985. *Gynesis.* Ithaca, N.Y.: Cornell University Press.

Jarry, Alfred. 1965. *Selected Writings.* Trans. Roger Shattuck. New York: Grove Press.

————. 1977. *The Supermale.* Trans. Ralph Gladstone and Barbara Wright. New York: New Directions.

Jean, Georges. 1992. *Writing: The Story of Alphabets and Scripts.* Trans. Jenny Oates. London: Thames and Hudson.

Jebb, R. C. 1882. *Bentley*. London: Macmillan.

Jenks, Charles, and Nathan Silver. 1972. *Adhocism: The Case for Improvisation*. New York: Doubleday.

Johnson, Ronald. 1977. *Radi os*. Berkeley, Calif.: Sand Dollar.

Johnson, Samuel. 1787. *The Works*. 11 vols. Ed. Sir John Hawkins. London: J. Buckland, J. Rivington and Sons, T. Payne and Sons, L. Davis, et al.

———. 1962. *Johnsonian Miscellanies*. 2 vols. Ed. George Birbeck Hill. New York: Barnes and Noble.

———. 1963. Preface to the Dictionary. In *Johnson's Dictionary: A Modern Selection*, ed. E. L. McAdam and George Milne. New York: Random House.

———. 1968. *Johnson on Shakespeare*. Vols. 7 and 8 of *The Yale Edition of the Works of Samuel Johnson*. Ed. Arthur Sherbo. New Haven, Conn.: Yale University Press.

———. 1971. *A Journey to the Western Islands of Scotland*. Vol. 9 of *The Yale Edition of the Works of Samuel Johnson*. Ed. Mary Lascelles. New Haven, Conn.: Yale University Press.

Jolas, Eugène, ed. 1941. *Vertical: A Yearbook for Romantic-Mystic Ascensions*. New York: Gotham Bookmart Press.

Jones, Richard Foster. 1953. *The Triumphs of the English Language*. Stanford, Calif: Stanford University Press.

Jonson, Ben. 1875. *Works*. 9 vols. Ed. F. Cunningham. London: Bickers and Son.

Joris, Pierre. 1997."Revelry to Revery: A Review of Karen Mac Cormack's *Marine Snow*." *Sulfur* 40 (spring): 178–81.

Joyce, James. 1950. *Finnegans Wake*. London: Faber and Faber.

Kant, Immanuel 1952. *Kant's Critique of Judgement (1790)*. Trans. J. C. Meredith. Oxford: Clarendon Press.

Kelley, Maurice. 1941. *This Great Argument: A Study of Milton's De Doctrina Christiana as a Gloss upon Paradise Lost*. Princeton, N.J.: Princeton University Press.

Kernan, Alvin. 1987. *Samuel Johnson and the Impact of Print*. Princeton, N.J.: Princeton University Press.

Kerrigan, William. 1984. "Atoms Again: The Deaths of Individualism." In *Taking Chances: Derrida, Psychoanalysis, and Literature*, ed. Joseph H. Smith and William Kerrigan, 86–106. Baltimore: Johns Hopkins University Press.

Kinder, Marsha. 1997. "Screen Wars: Transmedia Appropriations from Eisenstein to a TV Dante and Carmen Santiago." In *Language Machines: Technologies of Literary and Cultural Production*, ed. Jeffrey Masten, Peter Stallybrass, and Nancy J. Vickers. New York: Routledge.

Kinder, Marsha, Peter Stallybrass, and Nancy J. Vickers. *Language Machines: Technologies of Literary and Cultural Production*. New York: Routledge.

Kittay, Jeffrey, and Wlad Godzich. 1987. *The Emergence of Prose: An Essay in Prosaics*. Minneapolis: University of Minnesota Press.

Kostelanetz, Richard, ed. 1980. *Text-Sound Texts*. New York: William Morrow.

————, ed. 1982. *The Avant-Garde Tradition in Literature*. Buffalo: Prometheus Books.

————. 1982. *The Avant-Garde Tradition in Literature*. Buffalo, N.Y.: Prometheus Books.

Klossowski, Pierre. 1988. "The Marquis de Sade and the Revolution." In *The College of Sociology, 1937–39*, ed. Denis Hollier, 218–32. Minneapolis: University of Minnesota Press.

————. 1991. *Sade My Neighbor*. Trans. Alphonso Lingis. Evanston, Ill.: Northwestern University Press.

Knabb, Ken, ed. 1981. *Situationist International Anthology*. Trans. Ken Knabb. Berkeley, Calif.: Bureau of Public Secrets.

Krapp, George Phillip. [1925] 1966. "American Dictionaries." In *The English Language in America*. Reprint, New York: Frederick Ungar.

Krieger, Murray. 1973. *Introduction to The Editor and Critic and The Critic as Editor*. Los Angeles: William Andrews Clark Memorial Library.

————. 1976. *Theory of Criticism*. Baltimore: Johns Hopkins University Press.

————. 1981. " 'A Waking Dream': The Symbolic Alternative to Allegory." In *Allegory, Myth, and Symbol*, ed. Morton W. Bloomfield. Cambridge, Mass.: Harvard University Press.

Kristeva, Julia. 1980. *Desire in Language*. Trans. Thomas Gora, Alice Jardine, and Leon S. Roudiez. New York: Columbia University Press.

————. 1984. *Revolution in Poetic Language*. Trans. Margaret Waller. New York: Columbia University Press.

————. 1986. *The Kristeva Reader*. Ed. Toril Moi. Oxford: Basil Blackwell.

————. 1989. *Language the Unknown*. Trans. Anne M. Menke. New York: Columbia University Press.

————. 1996. *Interviews*. Ed. Ross Mitchell Guberman. New York: Columbia University Press.

Kroetsch, Robert. 1983. "Essays." Ed. Frank Davey and bp Nichol. *Open Letter* 5, no. 4 (spring).

Kroll, Richard W. F. 1991. *The Material World: Literate Culture in the Restoration and Early Eighteenth Century*. Baltimore: Johns Hopkins University Press.

Kuhns, Richard. 1970. *Structures of Experience: Essays on the Affinity between Philosophy and Literature*. New York: Basic Books.

Kussel, Peter B. 1976. "From the Anus to the Mouth to the Eye." *Semiotext(e)* 2, no. 2: 105–19.

Lacan, Jacques. 1989. "Kant with Sade." Trans. James B. Swenson Jr. *October* 51 (winter): 55–75.

Lansing, Gerrit. 1970. "The Burden of Set # 1." *Caterpillar* 10 (January): 82–86.

————. 1983. *"Analytic Psychology," or, The Soluble is Swimming Across*. [Buffalo, N.Y.]: Institute of Further Studies.

Leary, Paris, and Robert Kelly, eds. 1965. *A Controversy of Poets.* New York: Doubleday.

Le Brun, Annie. 1990. *Sade: A Sudden Abyss.* Trans. Camille Naish. San Francisco: City Lights.

Lecercle, Jean-Jacques. 1985. *Philosophy through the Looking Glass.* La Salle, Ill.: Open Court.

———. 1990. *The Violence of Language.* London: Routledge.

Lee, Dennis. 1973. "Cadence, Country, Silence: Writing in Colonial Space." *Open Letter* 2, no. 6 (fall): 34–53.

Leibniz, Gottfried. 1898. *The Monadology and Other Philosophical Writings.* Trans. R. Latta. Oxford: Clarendon Press.

———. 1949. *New Essays Concerning Human Understanding.* Trans. A. G. Langley. LaSalle, Ill.: Open Court.

Leiris, Michel. 1991. *Rules of the Game I: Scratches.* Trans. Lydia Davis. New York: Paragon.

Lély, Gilbert. 1970. *The Marquis de Sade: A Biography.* Trans. Alec Brown. New York: Grove Press.

Lemaitre, Maurice. 1956. *La Plastique Lettriste et Hypergraphique.* Paris: Caracteres.

Leonard, Sterling. 1929. *The Doctrine of Correctness in English Usage, 1700–1800.* Madison: University of Wisconsin Press.

Levinas, Emmanuel. 1969. *Totality and Infinity.* Trans. Alphonso Lingis. Pittsburgh: Duquesne University Press.

———. 1978. *Existence and Existents.* Trans. Alphonso Lingis. The Hague: Martinus Nijhoff.

———. 1981. *Otherwise than Being, or Beyond Essence.* Trans. Alphonso Lingis. The Hague: Martinus Nijhoff.

———. 1985. *Ethics and Infinity: Conversations with Philippe Nemo.* Trans. Richard A. Cohen. Pittsburgh: Duquesne University Press.

———. 1986. "The Trace of the Other." Trans. Alphonso Lingis. In *Deconstruction in Context,* ed. Mark C. Taylor, 345–59. Chicago: University of Chicago Press.

———. 1987. *Collected Philosophical Papers.* Trans. Alphonso Lingis. The Hague: Martinus Nijhoff.

———. 1989. *The Levinas Reader.* Ed. Seán Hand. Oxford: Blackwell.

———. 1994. *Nine Talmudic Readings.* Trans. Annette Aronowicz. Bloomington: Indiana University Press.

———. 1996a. *Basic Philosophical Writings.* Ed. Adriaan Peperzak, Simon Critchley, and Robert Bernasconi. Bloomington: Indiana University Press.

———. 1996b. *Proper Names.* Trans. Michael B. Smith. Stanford, Calif.: Stanford University Press.

Lippard, Lucy, ed. 1971. *Dadas on Art.* Englewood Cliffs, N.J.: Prentice-Hall.

Llewelyn, John. 1995. *Emmanuel Levinas: The Genealogy of Ethics*. London: Routledge.

[Lora-Totino, Arrigo]. 1978. "What Is Sound Poetry?" In *Futura Poesia Sonora. Critical Historical Anthology of Sound Poetry,* ed. Arrigo Lora-Totino, 7–47. Milan: Memoria Spa.

Lucretius. 1995. *On the Nature of Things: De rerum natura*. Trans. and ed. Anthony M. Esolen. Baltimore: Johns Hopkins University Press.

Luria, A. R. 1968. *The Mind of a Mnemonist*. Trans. Lynn Solotareff. New York: Basic Books.

Lynn, Steven. 1992. *Samuel Johnson after Deconstruction: Rhetoric and the Rambler*. Carbondale: Southern Illinois University Press.

Lyotard, Jean-François. 1977. "The Tooth, the Palm." *Sub-Stance* 15:105–10.

———. 1988a. *The Differend: Phrases in Dispute*. Trans. George Van Den Abbeele. Minneapolis: University of Minnesota Press.

———. 1988b. *Peregrinations: Law, Form, Event*. New York: Columbia University Press.

———. 1993a. *Political Writings*. Trans. Bill Readings and Paul Geiman. Minneapolis: University of Minnesota Press.

———. 1993b. *Libidinal Economy*. Trans. Iain Hamilton Grant. Bloomington: Indiana University Press.

[Macbean, Alexander]. 1780. *Index to the English Poets*. 2 vols. London: C. Bathurst, J. Buckland, W. Strahan, J. Rivington and Sons, et al.

Mac Cormack, Karen. 1991. *Quirks & Quillets*. Tucson: Chax Press.

Mackail, J. W. 1924. *Bentley's Milton*. London: British Academy.

Mac Low, Jackson. 1962. "Poetry, Chance, Silence, Etc." *Nomad* (fall): 68–71.

———. 1971. *Stanzas for Iris Lezak*. Barton, Vt.: Something Else Press.

———. 1975. "Interview with Barry Alpert." *Vort* 3:3–33.

———. 1980. *Asymmetries 1–260*. New York: Printed Editions.

———. 1984. "Museletter." In *The L=A=N=G=U=A=G=E Book,* ed. Bruce Andrews and Charles Bernstein, 26–28. Carbondale: Southern Illinois University Press.

———. 1986. *Representative Works, 1938–1985*. New York: Roof Books.

Marinetti, Filippo Tommaso. 1971. *Selected Writings*. Ed. R. W. Flint. New York: Farrar, Straus and Giroux.

———. 1988. "La Bataglia di Adrianopoli." In *Futurism and Dada Reviewed*. Produced by James Neiss. Brussels: Sub Rosa. Compact disc.

Markov, Vladimir. 1969. *Russian Futurism*. London: MacGibbon and Kee.

Marlatt, Daphne. 1984. *Touch to My Tongue*. Edmonton: Longspoon.

Martin, Henri-Jean. 1994. *The History and Power of Writing*. Trans. Lydia G. Cochrane. Chicago: University of Chicago Press.

Massumi, Brian. 1992. *A User's Guide to Capitalism and Schizophrenia: Deviations from Deleuze and Guattari*. Cambridge, Mass.: MIT Press.

Masten, Jeffrey. 1997. "Pressing Subjects; Or, The Secret Lives of Shakespeare's Compositors." In *Language Machines: Technologies of Literary and Cultural Production,* ed. Jeffrey Masten, Peter Stallybrass, and Nancy Vickers, 75–107. London: Routledge.

Matthews, J. H. 1974. *Theatre in Dada and Surrealism.* Syracuse, N.Y.: Syracuse University Press.

Mauro, Tullio de. 1967. *Ludwig Wittgenstein: His Place in the Development of Semantics.* Dordrecht, Holland: D. Reidel.

McAdam, E. L., and George Milne, eds. 1963. *Johnson's Dictionary: A Modern Selection.* New York: Pantheon.

McCaffery, Steve. 1986. *North of Intention.* Toronto and New York: Roof Books.

McCaffery, Steve, and bp Nichol. 1992. *Rational Geomancy: The Kids of the Book-Machine. The Collected Research Reports of the Toronto Research Group, 1973–1982.* Ed. Steve McCaffery. Vancouver: Talonbooks.

———, eds. 1978. *Sound Poetry: A Catalogue.* Toronto: Underwhich Editions.

McColley, Grant. 1940. *Paradise Lost: An Account of Its Growth and Major Origins, with a Discussion of Milton's Use of Sources and Literary Patterns.* Chicago: Packard and Co.

McGann, Jerome J. 1990. "Private Poetry, Public Deception." In *The Politics of Poetic Form,* ed. Charles Bernstein, 119–47. New York: Roof Books.

———. 1991. *The Textual Condition.* Princeton, N.J.: Princeton University Press.

———. 1992. *A Critique of Modern Textual Criticism.* Charlottesville: University of Virginia Press.

———. 1993. *Black Riders: The Visible Language of Modernism.* Princeton, N.J.: Princeton University Press.

McKerrow, Ronald B. 1927. *An Introduction to Bibliography.* Oxford: Oxford University Press.

McLuhan, Marshall, and Eric McLuhan. 1988. *Laws of Media: The New Science.* Toronto: University of Toronto Press.

Mehlman, Jeffrey. 1979. *Cataract: A Study in Diderot.* Middletown, Conn.: Wesleyan University Press.

———. 1986. "Writing and Deference: The Politics of Literary Adulation." *Representations* 15 (summer): 1–14.

Meltzer, Annabelle Henkin. 1984. "The Dada Actor and Performance Theory." In *The Art of Performance: A Critical Anthology,* ed. Gregory Battock and Robert Nickas, 37–55. New York: E. P. Dutton.

Mercken-Spaas, Godelieve. 1978. "Some Aspects of the Self and the Other in Rousseau and Sade." *Sub-Stance* 20:71–77.

Merleau-Ponty, Maurice. 1964. *Signs.* Trans. R. C. McCleary. Evanston, Ill.: Northwestern University Press.

———. 1968. *The Visible and the Invisible.* Trans. Alphonso Lingis. Evanston, Ill.: Northwestern University Press.

Meschonic, Henri. 1988. "Rhyme and Life." *Critical Inquiry* 15, no. 1 (fall): 90–107.

Michel, Paul-Henri. 1973. *The Cosmology of Giordano Bruno*. Trans. R. E. W. Maddison. Ithaca, N.Y.: Cornell University Press.

Miles, Barry. 1993. *William Burroughs: El Hombre Invisible*. New York: Hyperion.

Miller, J. Hillis. 1987. *The Ethics of Reading*. New York: Columbia University Press.

Miller, Perry. 1958. "Bentley and Newton." In *Isaac Newton's Papers and Letters on Natural Philosophy*. Ed. I. Bernard Cohen. Cambridge, Mass.: Harvard University Press.

Missac, Pierre. 1995. *Walter Benjamin's Passages*. Trans. Shierry Weber Nicholson. Cambridge, Mass.: MIT Press.

Monk, Ray. 1990. *Ludwig Wittgenstein: The Duty of Genius*. New York: Free Press.

Moore, Leslie E. 1990. *Beautiful Sublime: The Making of Paradise Lost, 1701–1734*. Stanford, Calif.: Stanford University Press.

Moreau-Maréchal, J. 1968. "Researches sur la ponctuation," *Scriptorium* 22:56–66.

Morison, Stanley. 1972. *Politics and Script*. Oxford: Oxford University Press.

Morrissette, Bruce. 1972. "Topology and the French Nouveau Roman." *Boundary 2* 1, no. 1 (fall): 45–57.

Morton, Herbert C. 1994. *The Story of Webster's Third: Philip Gove's Controversial Dictionary and Its Critics*. Cambridge: Cambridge University Press.

Motokiyu, Tosa, Ojiu Norinaga, and Okura Kyojin. 1991. "Renga and the New Sentence." *Aerial* 6/7:52–59.

Mottram, Eric. 1971. *The Algebra of Need*. Buffalo: Beau Fleuve.

Mulcaster, Richard. 1925. *Mulcaster's Elementarie*. Ed. E. T. Campagnac. Oxford: Clarendon Press.

Mungello, David E. 1977. *Leibniz and Confucianism: The Search for Accord*. Honolulu: University of Hawaii Press.

Murdoch, Patrick, ed. 1762. *The Works of James Thomson*. London.

Murray, K. M. Elisabeth. 1977. *Caught in the Web of Words: James Murray and the Oxford English Dictionary*. New Haven, Conn.: Yale University Press.

Nancy, Jean-Luc. 1993. *The Birth to Presence*. Trans. Brian Holmes et al. Stanford, Calif.: Stanford University Press.

Natorp, Paul. 1888. "Thema und Disposition in der Aristotelischen Metaphysik." In *Philosophische Monatshefte* 24.

Negri, Antonio. 1991. *The Savage Anomaly: The Power of Spinoza's Metaphysic and Politics*. Trans. Michael Hardt. Minneapolis: University of Minnesota Press.

Neuman, Shirley, and Robert Wilson. 1982. *Labyrinths of the Voice: Conversations with Robert Kroetsch*. Edmonton, Alb.: NeWest Press.

Nichols, James H., Jr. 1976. *Epicurean Political Philosophy: The De rerum natura of Lucretius.* Ithaca, N.Y.: Cornell University Press.

Nichols, Miriam. 1996. "Robin Blaser." In *Dictionary of Literary Biography,* vol. 165: *American Poets since World War II,* 55–68. Detroit: Gale Research Inc.

Nietzsche, Friedrich. 1954. *The Portable Nietzsche.* Selected and trans. Walter Kaufman. New York: Viking.

———. 1968. *The Will to Power.* Trans. Walter Kaufman and R. J. Hollingdale. New York: Random House.

———. 1986. *Human, All Too Human.* Trans. R. J. Hollingdale. Cambridge: Cambridge University Press.

Olson, Charles. 1960. *The Maximus Poems.* New York: Jargon/Corinth Books.

———. 1966. "Mayan Letters." In *Selected Writings,* ed. Robert Creeley. New York: New Directions.

———. 1967. *Human Universe and Other Essays.* Ed. Don Allen. New York: Grove Press.

———. 1968. *Maximus Poems.* IV, V, VI. London: Cape Golliard.

———. 1973. "Project (1951): 'The Art of the Language of Mayan Glyphs.'" *Alcheringa* 5 (spring–summer): 94–100.

———. 1974. *Additional Prose.* Bolinas, Calif.: Four Seasons Foundation.

———. 1975a. *The Maximus Poems Volume Three.* Eds. Charles Boer and George Butterick. New York: Grossman.

———. 1975b. "Causal Mythology." In *Muthologos.* Vol. 1, 66–93. Ed. George Butterick. Bolinas, Calif.: Four Seasons Foundation.

———. 1997. *Collected Prose.* Ed. Donald Allen and Benjamin Friedlander. Berkeley: University of California Press.

Olson, Charles, and Ezra Pound. 1975. *Charles Olson and Ezra Pound: An Encounter at St. Elizabeth's.* Ed. Catherine Seelye. New York: Grossman Viking.

O'Neill, Ynez Violé. 1980. *Speech and Speech Disorders in Western Thought before 1600.* Westport, Conn.: Greenwood Press.

Ong, Walter. 1964. "Hostility, Literacy, and Webster III." In *College English* 26 (November): 106–11.

———. 1967. *The Presence of the Word.* New York: Simon and Schuster.

———. 1971. *Rhetoric, Romance, and Technology.* Ithaca, N.Y.: Cornell University Press.

Owens, Craig. 1987. "The Discourse of Others: Feminists and Postmodernism." In *Art and Its Significance: An Anthology of Aesthetic Theory,* ed. Stephen David Ross. Albany: State University of New York Press.

Owens, Joseph. 1951. *The Doctrine of Being in the Aristotelian Metaphysics.* Toronto: Pontifical Institute of Medieval Studies.

Parkes, Malcolm Beckwith. 1976. "The Influence of the Concepts of Ordinatio and Compilatio on the Development of the Book." In *Medieval Learning and Literature*, ed. J. J. G. Alexander and M. T. Gibson, 115–41. Oxford: Oxford University Press.

———. 1993. *Pause and Effect: Punctuation in the West*. Berkeley: University of California Press.

Parr, Samuel. 1828. *The Works of Samuel Parr, LL.D., with Memoirs of his Life and Writings, by John Johnstone, M.D.* 8 vols. London.

Patchen, Kenneth. 1946. *Sleepers Awake*. New York: Padell Book Co.

Paterson, Elmer. 1971. *Tristan Tzara Dada and Surrational Theorist*. New Brunswick, N.J.: Rutgers University Press.

Patterson, F. A., ed. 1931–38. *The Works of John Milton*. New York: Columbia University Press.

Paulson, William R. 1988. *The Noise of Culture: Literary Texts in a World of Information*. Ithaca, N.Y.: Cornell University Press.

Pei, Mario. 1966. *A Glossary of Linguistic Terms*. New York: Columbia University Press.

Peperzak, Adriaan. 1993. *To the Other: An Introduction to the Philosophy of Emmanuel Levinas*. West Lafayette, Ind.: Purdue University Press.

Perelman, Bob. 1996. *The Marginalization of Poetry: Language Writing and Literary History*. Princeton, N.J.: Princeton University Press.

Perloff, Marjorie. 1998. *Poetry On and Off the Page: Essays for Emergent Occasions*. Evanston, Ill.: Northwestern University Press.

Peterson, Donald. 1990. *Wittgenstein's Early Philosophy: Three Sides of the Mirror*. Toronto: University of Toronto Press.

Phillips, Tom. 1980. *A Humument: A Treated Victorian Novel*. London: Thames and Hudson.

———. 1985. *Dante's Inferno: The First Part of the Divine Comedy of Dante Alighieri Translated and Illustrated by Tom Phillips*. London: Thames and Hudson.

Picard, Max. 1963. *Man and Language*. Trans. Stanley Goodman. Chicago: Henry Regnery.

Pierssens, Michel. 1980. *The Power of Babel: A Study of Logophilia*. Trans. Carl R. Lovitt. London: Routledge and Kegan Paul.

Plato. 1961. *The Collected Dialogues*. Ed. Edith Hamilton and Huntington Cairns. New York: Bollingen Foundation.

Poole, Joshua. 1677. *The English Parnassus: Or a Help to English Poesie*. London: Henry Brome, Thomas Bassett and John Wright.

Pontanus. 1595. *Jacobi Pontani Societatis Iesu Poeticarum Institutionum libri III . . . edition Secundo emendatior*. Ingolstadii: ex typographia Adam Sartorius.

Pound, Ezra. 1970. *The Cantos of Ezra Pound*. New York: New Directions.

———. 1973. *Selected Prose, 1909–1965*. Ed. William Cookson. London: Faber and Faber.

Pound, Scott. 1996. "Making Poetry Happen." *American Book Review* 17, no. 5 (June–July): 25.

Praz, Mario. 1970. *The Romantic Agony.* Oxford: Oxford University Press.

Prigogine, Ilya, and Isabelle Stengers. 1980. *From Being to Becoming: Time and Complexity in the Physical Sciences.* San Francisco: W. H. Freeman.

———. 1982. "Postface: Dynamics from Leibniz to Lucretius." In Michel Serres, *Hermes: Literature, Science, Philosophy,* ed. Josué V. Harari and David F. Bell. Baltimore: Johns Hopkins University Press.

———. 1984. *Order out of Chaos.* New York: Bantam Books.

Purdy, Strother B. 1984. "Ezra Pound, René Thom and the Experience of Poetry." *Sub-Stance* 43:39–49.

Puttenham, George. 1904. "The Arte of English Poesie." In *Elizabethan Critical Essays,* 2 vols., ed. G. Gregory Smith, 2:1–193. Oxford: Clarendon Press.

Quance, Roberta. "Steinways: Karen Mac Cormack's *Marine Snow.*" Paper presented at First Symposium of Canadian Studies, November 1997, at Universidad Autonoma de Madrid.

Rajchman, John. 1986. "Lacan and the Ethics of Modernity." *Representations* 15 (summer): 42–56.

Rapaport, Herman. 1983. *Milton and the Postmodern.* Lincoln: University of Nebraska Press.

Rasula, Jed, and Steve McCaffery eds. 1998. *Imagining Language.* Cambridge, Mass.: MIT Press.

Rescher, Nicholas. 1967. *The Philosophy of Leibniz.* Englewood Cliffs, N.J.: Prentice-Hall.

Reddick, Allen. 1990. *The Making of Johnson's Dictionary 1746–1773.* Cambridge: Cambridge University Press.

Rice, Donald. 1980. "Catastrop(h)es: The Morphogenesis of Metaphor, Metonymy, Synechdoche and Irony." In *Sub-Stance* 26:3–18.

Richard, Alain-Martin, and Clive Robertson, eds. 1991. *Performance au•in Canada 1970–1990.* Quebec: Editions Intervention.

Richardson, Charles. 1838. Preface to *A New Dictionary of the English Language.* London.

Richardson, Jonathan the elder, and Jonathan Richardson the younger. 1734. *Explanatory Notes and Remarks on Milton's Paradise Lost.* London.

Richman, Michele H. 1982. *Reading Georges Bataille Beyond the Gift.* Baltimore: Johns Hopkins University Press.

Richter, Hans. 1965. *Dada Art and Anti-art.* New York: Abrams.

Ricoeur, Paul. 1984. *Time and Narrative.* Vol. 1. Trans. Kathleen McLaughlin and David Pellauer. Chicago: University of Chicago Press.

Riddel, Joseph. 1979. "Decentering the Image: The 'Project' of 'American' Poetics?" In *Textual Strategies: Perspectives in Post-Structuralist Criticism.* Ed. Josué V. Harari. Ithaca, N.Y.: Cornell University Press.

Robbins, Jill. 1991. *Prodigal Son/Elder Brother: Alterity and Interpretation in Augustine, Petrarch, Kafka, Levinas.* Chicago: University of Chicago Press.

———. 1995. "Tracing Responsibility in Levinas's Ethical Thought." In *Ethics as First Philosophy: The Significance of Emmanuel Levinas for Philosophy, Literature, and Religion,* ed. Adriaan Peperzak, 173–83. Bloomington: University of Indiana Press.

———. 1999. *Altered Reading: Levinas and Literature.* Chicago: University of Chicago Press.

Rosenblum, Robert. 1967. *Transformations in Late Eighteenth Century Art.* Princeton, N.J.: Princeton University Press.

Rosenzweig, Franz. 1985. *The Star of Redemption.* Trans. William W. Hallo. Notre Dame: University of Notre Dame Press.

Rossi-Landi, Feruccio. 1983. *Language as Work and Trade: A Semiotic Homology for Linguistics and Economics.* Trans. Martha Adams et al. South Hadley, Mass.: Bergin and Garvey.

Rothenberg, Jerome, and George Quasha, eds. 1974. *America: A Prophecy.* New York: Vintage.

Rouse, Richard H., and Mary A. Rouse. 1982–86. "La naissance des index." In *Histoire de l'édition française,* 4 vols., ed. Henri-Jean Martin and Roger Chartier. Paris: Promodis.

Sade, Marquis de. 1953. *Selected Writings of De Sade.* Trans. L. de Saint-Yves. London: Peter Owen.

———. 1965a. *The Complete Justine and Philosophy in the Bedroom and Other Writings.* Trans. Richard Seaver and Austryn Wainhouse. New York: Grove Press.

———. 1965b. *Selected Letters.* Ed. Margaret Crosland. Trans. W. J. Strachan. London: Peter Owen.

———. 1966. *The One Hundred and Twenty Days of Sodom and Other Writings.* Trans. Richard Seaver and Austryn Wainhouse. New York: Grove Press.

———. 1968. *Juliette.* Trans. Austryn Wainhouse. New York: Grove Press.

———. 1970. *Oeuvres Complètes.* Paris: Pauvert.

Scattergood, V. J. 1971. *Politics and Poetry in the Fifteenth Century.* London: Blandford Press.

Schlegel, Friedrich von. 1847. *The Philosophy of Life and Philosophy of Language.* Trans. A. J. W. Morrison. London: Henry G. Bohn.

Scholem, Gershom. 1987. *Origins of the Kaballah.* Trans. Allan Arkush. Philadelphia: Jewish Publication Society; Princeton, N.J.: Princeton University Press.

———. 1976. *The Messianic Idea in Judaism.* New York: Schocken.

Selinger, Eric. 1992. "'I Composed the Holes': Reading Ronald Johnson's *Radi os.*" *Contemporary Literature* 33, no. 1: 46–73.

Sepharial. 1974. *The Kabala of Numbers.* Hollywood, Calif.: Newcastle.

Serres, Michel. 1982a. *The Parasite.* Trans. Lawrence R. Schehr. Baltimore: Johns Hopkins University Press.

————. 1982b. *Hermes Literature, Science, Philosophy.* Baltimore: Johns Hopkins University Press.

Sewell, A. "Milton's De Doctrina Christiana." In *Essays and Studies by Members of the English Association,* 19:40–66.

Shapiro, David. 1984. "Poetry and Action: Performance in a Dark Time." In *The Art of Performance,* ed. Gregory Battock and Robert Nickas, 157–65. New York: E. P. Dutton.

Shattuck, Roger, ed. 1960. "What is ''Pataphysics'?" *Evergreen Review* 4, no. 13 (May–June).

Siebers, Tobin. 1988. *The Ethics of Criticism.* New York: Columbia University Press.

Silliman, Ron. 1978. *Ketjak.* San Francisco: This Books.

————. 1981. *Tjanting.* Berkeley, Calif.: Figures.

————. 1987. *The New Sentence.* New York: Roof.

Singer, Dorothea Waley. 1950. *Giordano Bruno: His Life and Thought.* New York: Henry Shuman.

Smith, Adam. 1983. *Lectures on Rhetoric and Belles Lettres.* Vol. 4 of the Glasgow Edition of the Works and Correspondence of Adam Smith. Ed. J. C. Bryce. Oxford: Oxford University Press.

Smith, Herbert F. 1994. *The Locus of Meaning: Six Hyperdimensional Fictions.* Toronto: University of Toronto Press.

Smith, Joseph H., and William Kerrigan, eds. 1988. *Taking Chances: Derrida, Psychoanalysis, and Literature.* Baltimore: Johns Hopkins University Press.

Sollers, Philippe. 1983. *Writing and the Experience of Limits.* Trans. P. Barnard and D. Hayman. New York: Columbia University Press.

Spicer, Jack. 1975. *The Collected Books of Jack Spicer.* Ed. Robin Blaser, with a commentary: "The Practice of Outside." Santa Barbara, Calif.: Black Sparrow Press.

Starnes, De Witt T., and Gertrude E. Noyes. 1946. *The English Dictionary from Cawdrey to Johnson.* Chapel Hill: University of North Carolina Press.

Starobinski, Jean. 1979. *Words upon Words.* Trans. Olivia Emmet. New Haven, Conn.: Yale University Press.

————. 1988. *1789: The Emblems of Reason.* Trans. Barbara Bray. Cambridge, Mass.: MIT Press.

Staten, Henry. 1984. *Wittgenstein and Derrida.* Lincoln: University of Nebraska Press.

Steele, Joshua. 1775. *Prosodia Rationalis: or An Essay Towards Establishing the Melody and Measure of Speech to be Expressed and Perpetuated by Peculiar Symbols.* London.

Steiner, Wendy. 1992. *The Colors of Rhetoric: Problems in the Relation between Modern Literature and Painting*. Chicago: University of Chicago Press.

Stewart, Susan. 1980. *Nonsense: Aspects of Intertexuality in Folklore and Literature*. Baltimore: Johns Hopkins University Press.

———. 1988. "The Marquis de Meese." *Critical Inquiry* 15, no. 1 (fall): 162–92.

Sussman, Elizabeth, ed. 1989. *On the Passage of a Few People through a Rather Brief Moment in Time: The Situationist International, 1957–1972*. Cambridge, Mass.: MIT Press.

Swift, Jonathan. 1933. *Gulliver's Travels*. Ed. W. A. Eddy. Oxford: Oxford University Press.

Talon, Henri, ed. 1950. *John Byrom: Selections from His Journals and Papers*. London: Rockcliff.

Taylor, John. 1630. *All the Workes of Iohn Taylor the Water-Poet*. London: James Boler.

Taylor, Mark C. 1987. *Alterity*. Chicago: University of Chicago Press.

Teresa of Avila, Saint. 1852. *The Interior Castle; or, the Mansions*. Trans. John Dalton. London: T. Jones.

Thom, René. 1975. *Structural Stability and Morphogenesis: An Outline of a General Theory of Models*. Trans. D. H. Fowler. Reading, Mass.: W. A. Benjamin.

Thomson, J. Eric S. 1970. *Maya History and Religion*. Norman: University of Oklahoma Press.

Todorov, Vladislav. 1995. *Red Square Black Square: Organon for Revolutionary Imagination*. Albany: State University of New York Press.

Toland, John. 1964. *Letters to Serena*. Ed. and with an introduction to the 1704 original by Günther Gawlick. Stuttgart: Friedrich Frommann.

Tomkins, J. M. S. 1969. *The Popular Novel in England, 1770–1800*. London: Methuen.

Tzara, Tristan. 1977. *Seven Dada Manifestos and Lampisteries*. Trans. Barbara Wright. London: John Calder.

Valéry, Paul. 1980. *Analects*. Trans. Stuart Gilbert. Bollingen Series, vol. 45, no. 14. Princeton, N.J.: Princeton University Press.

Vaneighem, Raoul. 1983. *The Revolution of Everyday Life*. Trans. Donald Nicholson-Smith. London: Left Bank Books.

Vezin, Jean. 1985. "La division en paragraphes dans les manuscrits de la basse antiquité et du Haut Moyen Age." In *La notion de paragraphe*, ed. Roger Laufer. Paris: Editions du CNRS.

Vickers, Nancy J. 1995. "Dante in the Video Decade." In *Dante Now: Current Trends in Dante Studies*, ed. Theodore Cachey Jr. Notre Dame, Ind.: University of Notre Dame Press.

Viénet, René. 1992. *Enragés and Situationists in the Occupation Movement, France, May '68*. New York: Autonomedia.

Vincent, Stephen, and Ellen Zweig. 1981. *The Poetry Reading: A Contemporary Compendium on Language and Performance.* San Francisco: Momo's Press.

Voloshinov, V. N. 1986. *Marxism and the Philosophy of Language.* Trans. Ladislav Matejka and I. R. Titunik. Cambridge, Mass.: Harvard University Press.

Watt, Ian. 1962. "Dr. Johnson and the Literature of Experience." In *Johnsonian Studies,* ed. Magdi Wahba, 15–22. Cairo: n.p.

Watten, Barrett. 1985. "Olson in Language: Part II." In *Writing/Talks.* Ed. Bob Perelman. Carbondale: Southern Illinois University Press, 157–63.

Watts, Charles, and Edward Byrne. 1999. *The Recovery of the Public World: Essays on Poetics in Honour of Robin Blaser.* Vancouver: Talonbooks.

Weaver, Mike. 1966. "Concrete Poetry." *Lugano Review* no. 5–6: 100–25.

Webster, Charles. 1982. *From Paracelsus to Newton: Magic and the Making of Modern Science.* Cambridge: Cambridge University Press.

Wendt, Larry. 1981. *Sound Poems for an Era of Reduced Expectations.* Toronto: Underwhich Editions.

———. 1993. "Henri Chopin and Sound Poetry." *Furnitures* 10:2.

White, Lynn, Jr. 1967. "The Historical Roots of Our Ecological Crisis." *Science* 155, no. 3767 (March 10): 1203–7.

White, R. J. 1965. *Dr. Bentley: A Study in Academic Scarlet.* London: Eyre and Spottiswoode.

Whitehead, Alfred North. 1933. *Adventures in Ideas.* New York: Macmillan.

———. 1968. *Modes of Thought.* New York: Macmillan.

———. 1969. *Process and Reality.* New York: Macmillan.

Wilden, Anthony. 1972. *System and Structure.* London: Tavistock.

Wilkes, G. A., ed. 1965. *Fulke Greville: The Remains.* Oxford: Oxford University Press.

Williams, Emmett, ed. 1967. *Anthology of Concrete Poetry.* New York: Something Else Press.

Williamson, George. 1951. *The Senecan Amble.* Chicago: University of Chicago Press.

Wimsatt, William K. 1948. *Philosophic Words.* New Haven, Conn.: Yale University Press.

———. 1959. "Johnson's Dictionary." In *New Light on Dr. Johnson,* ed. Frederick W. Hilles, 65–90. New Haven, Conn.: Yale University Press.

Wingo, E. Otha. 1972. *Latin Punctuation in the Classical Age.* Janua linguarum series practica, 133. The Hague: Mouton.

Wittgenstein, Ludwig. 1953. *Philosophical Investigations.* Trans. G. E .M. Anscombe. New York: Macmillan.

———. 1958 *The Blue and Brown Books.* Oxford: Basil Blackwell.

———. 1961. *Tractatus Logico-Philosophicus.* Trans. D. F. Pears and B. F. McGuiness. London: Routledge and Kegan Paul.

———. 1966. *Lectures and Conversations*. Ed. Cyril Barrett. Berkeley: University of California Press.

———. 1967. *Zettel*. Ed. G. E. M. Anscombe and G. H. von Wright. Oxford: Basil Blackwell.

———. 1978. *Philosophical Grammar*. Trans. Anthony Kenny. Berkeley: University of California Press.

———. 1980. *Culture and Value*. Trans Peter Winch. Chicago: University of Chicago Press.

———. 1982. *Last Writings on the Philosophy of Psychology*. Vol. 1. Ed. G. H. von Wright and Heikki Nyman. Trans. C. G. Luckhardt and Maximilian A. E. Aue. Oxford: Basil Blackwell.

Wolin, Richard. 1994. *Walter Benjamin: An Aesthetic of Redemption*. Rev. ed. Berkeley: University of California Press.

Wood, David, and Robert Bernasconi, eds. 1988. *Derrida and Difference*. Evanston, Ill.: Northwestern University Press.

Woodcock, Alexander, and Monte Davis. 1978. *Catastrophe Theory*. New York: E. P. Dutton.

Wyschogrod, Edith. 1995. "The Art in Ethics: Aesthetics, Objectivity, and Alterity in the Philosophy of Emmanuel Levinas." In *Ethics as First Philosophy,* ed. Adriaan Peperzak, 137–48. New York: Routledge.

Yaguello, Marina. 1991. *Lunatic Lovers of Language: Imaginary Languages and Their Inventors*. London: Athlone Press.

Yates, Frances A. 1969. *Giordano Bruno and the Hermetic Tradition*. New York: Vintage.

Zeeman, E. C. 1977. *Catastrophe Theory: Selected Papers, 1972–1977*. Reading, Mass.: Addison-Wesley.

Zekowsky, Arlene. 1969. *Seasons of the Mind with the Correspondence of Sir Herbert Read*. New York: George Wittenborn.

———. 1976. *Image Breaking Images: A New Mythology of Language*. New York: Horizon Press.

Zhang Longxi. 1985. "The *Tao* and the *Logos:* Notes on Derrida's Critique of Logocentrism." *Critical Inquiry* 11, no. 3 (March): 385–98.

Ziarek, Krzysztof. 1994. *Inflected Language: Toward a Hermeneutics of Nearness*. Albany: State University of New York Press.

Zukofsky, Celia. 1978. "1927–1972." *Paideuma* 7, no. 3: 371–72.

Zurbrugg, Nick, and Marlene Hall, eds. 1992. *Henri Chopin*. Queensland College of Art Gallery, Griffith University, Australia.

Zweig, Ellen. 1981. "Sound Poetry: An Introduction." In *The Poetry Reading,* ed. Stephen Vincent and Ellen Zweig. San Francisco: Momo's Press.

Index

Ferenczi, 115
Finas, Lucette, xvi
 La Crue, 10–12, 14
Fiumara, Gemma, 212
Flaubert, Gustave, 129, 130
Fogg, Peter Walkden, xvii, 107
 Elementa Anglicana, 108
 monad-fold in, xxi
 "wordless music," xvii
  described, 122–23
fold, xvii, xxi, 32, 235n5
 as *aemulatio,* 235n5
 defined, 33
 as invagination, 36
 as 'pataphysical, 241n26
footnotes, 66–67. *See also* Bentley,
 Richard
Foucault, Michel, 3, 95, 167, 186, 234n4
 on Sadism, 263n4
Four Horsemen, 182
Franz-Passow, 88
Freud, Sigmund, 141, 183, 233n11
Freytag-Loringhoven, Baroness Else
 von, 284n2
Fussell, Paul, 75

Gagnon, Madeline, 258n43
Gance, Abel, 217
Gassendi, Pierre, 69
Gautier, Leopold, 198
Gelb, I. J., *A Study of Writing: The
 Foundations of Grammatology,* 261n2
Genette, Gerard, 114
genotext. *See* Kristeva, Julia
Gibbs, Robert, 212
Gil, José, 119
Ginsburg, Allen, 243n4
Glanville, Joseph, 233n2
glyphs, Mayan, 53–57, 243n6, 244n10.
 See also Olson, Charles
G.O.D. ("Governor of Diversity"),
 Samuel Johnson as, 96

Godzich, Wlad. *See* Kittay, Jeffrey, and
 Wlad Godzich
Goethe, J. W. von, botanical theories,
 139
Goldsmith, Kenneth
 Fidget, 290n33
 No. 111 2.7.93–10.20.96, 243n4
Goldsmith, Steven, 58
Gove, Philip, 88–89, 90, 256n27
Grammaticus, Galfridus, *Promptorium
 parvulorum sive clericorum,* 103
grammatology, xxi–ii, 105–24
 and deconstruction, 107–8
 as "fundamentology," 107
Gray's-Inn Journal, "Plan of an English
 Dictionary," 257n37
Greisch, Jean, 211
Greville, Fulke, *Remains,* textual dis-
 crepancies in, 246n9
Griffiths, Bill, 182
Grose, Francis, *Scoundrel's Dictionary,*
 256n30
Guattari, Félix, 119, 139, 182, 277n24.
 See also Deleuze, Gilles, and Félix
 Guattari
 on sound poetry, 173
Guro, Elena, "Finland," 275n11
Guyotat, Pierre, *Eden, Eden, Eden,*
 146–47, 271n3
Gysin, Brion, 217, 218, 235n6

Hadewijch of Anvers, 236n7
Hallett, Garth, 83
Hanna, Ralph, 66
Harris, James, *Hermes,* 260n52
Harris, Wilson, *Ascent to Omai,* 157
Harryman, Carla, "For She," 151
Hausmann, Raoul, 120, 168, 170,
 274n9. *See also* optophonetic poem
Hayley, Wiliam, xvii, 122
Head, Richard, *English Rogue,* 256n29
Heath, Stephen, 72

and protosemantic, xx

Radi os, 10, 14

Johnson, Samuel, xvi, xx, 71, 76, 83, 101, 253n10

anonymous writings by, 258n42

on Bentley, 64

as decentered author, 96

Dictionary of the English Language, xvi, 58, 71–102

and Burke's *Reflections,* 91

citationality in 98–100

and clinamen, xx

contemporary writers in, 256n31

contending forces in, 94

dialects, 91–92

folding in, xxi

heteroglossia, 102

Jacobite sympathies shown in, 256n28

Richardson's opinions on, 255n18

satires on, 249n48

serialized version of, 252n7

Smith's review of, 257n35

Tooke's opinions on, 254n18

Johnson's Poets, aim of Index, 80

Journey to the Western Isles, 253n10

law-language analogy, 100–1

and lexicography, xx, 81

Life of Richard Savage, 253n10

Lives the Poets, 259n48

modernist subject, Johnson as, 94–95

"Plan," 81–82, 89

"Preface," 81, 89–90, 93–95, 98, 100

Rambler, 108

and Tory ideology, 101

Jolas, Eugene, 273n6

on poetic language, 165–66

Jonson, Ben, *English Grammar,* 261n4

Joyce, James, xxii, 6

Finnegans Wake, 110,

Cage's treatments of, 219–21

Duncan on, 277n22

and *scriptio continua,* 109–10

Ulysses, 149

Kafka, Franz, 217

Kandinsky, Wassily, 163

Kant, Immanuel, 35, 47, 55, 102

Critique of Judgement, 155, 258n39

Critique of Pure Reason, 155

transcendental apperception, 155–56

Khlebnikov, Velimir (Viktor), 163, 167–70, 177. *See also zaum*

"Vremya mera mira," 169.

Khulman, Quirinus, 163

Kierkegaard, Søren, 204, 228

Kircher, Athanasius, xxii

Kittay, Jeffrey, and Wlad Godzich, 153

Klintberg, Bengt af, 163

Klossowski, Pierre, 128, 137, 145, 267n19

Konkrete Canticle, 182

Konovalov, D. G., 275n12

Krieger, Murray, 7, 59

Kristeva, Julia, xv, 7, 9, 12, 21, 76, 143, 173, 174

genotext, xv, 5

khora, 232n8

phenotext distinguished from genotext, 232n5

"Psychoanalysis and the Polis," 12

Revolution in Poetic Language, 182

symbolic/semiotic relation, 277n25

textual practice, 6

theoretical subject described, 3

Kroetsch, Robert, 157

Kroll, R. W. F., 249n18

Kruchenykh, Aleksei, 163, 164, 168–70, 274n9, 275n11. *See also zaum*

"Declaration of the Word as Such," 169

"Dyr bul shchyl," 169, 275n13

"Novye puti slova," 169

labyrinth, 240n21
Lacan, Jacques, 5
    ethics, 78
Laing, R. D., Kingsley Hall Project,
    182
Language writing, 111
Lansing, Gerrit, 236n7
Lautréamont, Comte de (pseu. of
    Isadore Ducasse), 6, 217
Lavoisier, 242n3
law-language analogy, 100–1
Le Brun, Annie, 128, 129, 130, 131, 133,
    136, 137, 145, 263n6, 267n16, 270n32
Lecercle, Lean-Jacques, xix, 28, 29–30,
    74, 110, 172
Ledoux, Claude-Nicolas, 138
    Oikema brothel, 267n21
Lee, Dennis, 157
Leeuwenhoek, 43
Leggot, Michelle, 234n1
Leibniz, Gottfried, xv, xvii, xviii, 32,
    33, 34, 35, 36, 37, 40, 41, 43, 51,
    234n2, 235n6, 237n8, 238n9
    Arte Combinatoria, 240n20
    Letter to Ramond, 35
    Monadology, 32, 34, 242n26
    Pacidus Philalethi, 38, 241n24
    Response to Bayle, 34
    Theodicy, 41
Leiris, Michel, 218
letters, as atoms, xix. *See also* atoms
Lemaitre, Maurice, 171. *See also* Let-
    trisme; Ultralettrisme
Lettrisme, 171, 276n18
Levinas, Emmanuel, 6, 83, 142, 187,
    204–29, 277n21, 291n42
    Abraham compared to Ulysses, 216
    on criticism, 287–88n16
    ethics, 204–26, 283–85
        compared to Lacan's 284n2
        defined, 206
    Existence and Existents, 288n22

face, 206–7
illeity, 212, 288n18
"Language and Proximity," 206, 209
language, theory of, 208–14
Nine Talmudic Readings, 227–29
Otherwise than Being, 205, 210–11
    photism in, 288n21
    poetry, 214–15
    proximity, 290n36
    "Reality and its Shadow," 215,
        288n21
    speech, 223
    text, as gift, 215–16
        as Oral Law, 227–29
    Totality and Infinity, 288n22
    "Trace of the Other," 215, 228, 284n2
Lévi-Strauss, Claude, his logocentrism,
    107
Lewis, Matthew, "Monk," 142
lexicography, 75–104
    Adamic myth and, 77
    by Bysshe, 79–80
    early English, 103–4
    by Johnson, 81
    by Poole, 79–80
    Walpole's reservations on, 95
li, as monad, 238n8
libertine. *See* Sade, Marquis de
Lingis, Alphonso, 125
Lionnais, François Le, 243n4
Lippard, Lucy, 274n9
Llewelyn, John, 277n21, 291n43
Locke, John, 92, 191
Lombard, Peter, 77
Longinus, 43
Lora-Totino, Arigo, 175, 276n19
Lorca, Garcia, 31, 39
Lowth, Robert, 255n19
Lucretius, Titus Carus, xv, xviii, xix,
    xx, 18, 46, 137
    De rerum natura, xix, 17, 20–21, 69,
        70, 196, 240n22

early publication of, 233n1
and Sade, 139–40
Luria, A. R., 250n23
Lynn, Steven, on Johnson's *Rambler,*
108
Lyotard, Jean-François, xix, xx, 49, 75,
91, 103, 154, 155, 159, 273n3
Libidinal Economy, 182
Lyra, Nicolas de, 77

Mabille, Pierre, 184
MacBean, Alexander, 80
Dictionary of Ancient Geography,
254n15
Mac Cormack, Karen, 149–60
and Canadian feminism, 158
Mac Low and, 157
Marine Snow, 272n10
Marlatt and, 158–59
perpetual motion, 156
postcolonialism and, 157–58,
Quirks & Quillets, 149–50, 152–59,
271n5
Bök on, 270n1
and Husserl, 156
phrasal propulsion in, 152, 154–55,
165
Reutersward and, 271.n1
Mackail, J. W., *Bentley's Milton,* 245–
46n6
Mac Low, Jackson, xvi, 122–23, 187–
203, 281n1
anarchy and, 202–3
Aristotelean aspects of, 203
"asymmetries," 192
Bakhtin and, 202
clinamen and, xx
Cowley and, 200
diastics, defined, 282n6
compared to *Das Kapital,* 282n8
"false wit," 191–92, 197
"5 biblical poems," 188

methods of composition, 282n2
musical influences on, 188
as paragram, 196–98
performance, 201–2
Pronouns, 190
protosemantic in, xx
reading strategies, 199–201
Stanzas for Iris Lezak, 192–93
Swift's model of writing compared,
191
systematic-chance composition,
187–90
"Vocabularies," 282n4
Zen buddhist influences, 188–89,
202
Mallarmé, Stephane, 6, 100, 105, 113,
228, 253n6
Coup de dés, 241n22
Le Livre, 241n22
Mallet, David, *Of Verbal Criticism,* 58
Mallock, William H. *See* Phillips, Tom
Marcel, Gabriel, *Creative Fidelity,*
288n19
Marinetti, Filippo, Tommaso, 163, 177,
274n9, 277n26
"Batagglia di Adrianapoli," 273n4
"Bombardamento di Adrianapoli,"
164
onomatopoeia in, 164–65, 184
parole in libertà, 108, 137, 163–65,
273n4
typography, 164
Zang-tumb-tumb, 164
Markov, Vladimir, 275n11
Marlatt, Daphne, 158–59
Marquez, Gabriel Garcia, *Autumn of
the Patriarch,* 271n3
Marshall, Thomas, 234n1
Martin, Benjamin, 94
Martin, Henri-Jean, 50, 97, 260n49
Marvell, Andrew, 249n16
Marx, Karl, xviii, 183

clinamen, xviii
dissertation, 19
influence on Wittgenstein, 255n24
Das Kapital, 282n8
Marx, Karl, and Friedrich Engels,
German Ideology, 255n24
Masoudy, Hassan, 49–50
Massumi, Brian, 135
Mauro, Tullio de, 86
Mayali, Laurent, 66
McCaffery, Steve, 182, 234n1
"Discussion . . . Genesis . . . Conti-
nuity," 280n38
systematic Xerox disintegrations,
279n32
McGann, Jerome, 72
theory of textuality, 250n24
"meaning-in-becoming." *See* becoming
meaning
Mehlman, Jeffrey, 233n1, 261n3
Meillet, A., 60
Melville, Herman, *Pierre,* 77
Mercken-Spaas, Godelieve, 132
Merleau-Ponty, Maurice, 32, 39, 43,
154
Merton, Thomas, 31
Meschonic, Henri, 154
metalepsis, 18
Middleton, Peter, 234n1
Miller, J. Hillis, 205
Miller, Perry, 59
Milton, John, 59, 60–1. *See also* Bent-
ley, Richard; Johnson, Ronald
Paradise Lost, 58–74
Minarelli, Enzo, 278n30
Missac, Pierre, 256n26
Moholy Nagy, Laszlo, 168
Vision in Motion, 274n10
Molière, 163
monad, xvii, xviii, xxi, 13, 33, 34–41, 51,
237n8
atom and, 238n9

Baroque and, 32
book as, 241n22
Byrd on, 239n14
fold and, 32
as *li,* 238n8
nomadology and, 41
quantum mechanics and, 236n8
Whitehead on, 239n14
monad-fold, xv, xxi
Monk, Ray, 78–79
Montano, Linda, "Mitchell's Death,"
182
Morgenstern, Christian
Galgenlieder, 163
"Kroklokwafzi," 166
Morris, William, 239n17
Morrissette, Bruce, 241n25
Morton, Herbert C., 84
Mulcaster, Richard, *Elementarie,* 104
Mumford, Lewis, *Technics and Civili-
zation,* 265n12
Murdoch, Patrick, 74
Murray, Elisabeth, 88
Murray, Lindley, 255n19

Nacal, J., 38
Naipaul, V. S., *Mystic Masseur,* 272n5
Nancy, Jean-Luc, 51, 233n1, 236n7
Negro, Antonio, 239n13
"neo-narrative," 150, 239n18
New Sentence. *See* Silliman, Ron
Newton, Isaac, 60, 84
Four Lectures, 249n19
Principia, 69
transverse impulse, 69–70
Nichol, bp, 182
Martyrology, 216
systematic Xerox disintegrations,
279n32
Nichols, Miriam, 31, 40–42
Nietzsche, Friedrich, 16–30, 138,
266n16

Picard, Jeremie, 62
Picard, Max, 284n4
Pierssens, Michel, 13, 29
Piranesi, Giovani Battista, 138
Plato, 32
    Apology, 5–6
    Cratylus, 48, 246n7
    khora, 252n8
    logocentrism, 107
    Phaedo, 238n8
    Philebus, 238n8
    Republic, 5
    Timaeus, 90, 232n8
Politian, Angelo, 196
Pompius, 109
Pontanus, 127, 263n3
Poole, Joshua, English Parnassus, 79, 80
Pope, Alexander, 253n10
    Dunciad, 233n1
    "Epistle on Man," 233n1
Pordage, Samuel, *Mundorum Explicatio,* its influence on Milton, 247n12
pornography, Delueze on, 263n5
Porush, David, xxii
Pound, Ezra, xxii, 31, 75, 187
    Cantos, 19, 99, 106, 216, 234n3, 235n5
    Chinese ideograms, 105–6
    "I Gather the Limbs of Osiris," 251n1
    periplum, 19
Prelinguism, 174
Prigogine, Ilya, and Isabelle Stengers, xv, xviii, 13, 30, 43, 233n1, 236n8
    bifurcation theory, 250n22, 288n23
    dissipative structures, xv, xvii, xxiii, 14, 30, 133, 146, 269n26
    defined, xviii
    hypnon, xviii
print shop, 17th century English, 63

Prior, Matthew, 84
Projective Verse. *See* Olson, Charles
proper-name effect
    in Johnson's *Dictionary,* 96–98
    as Law-Name of Father, 101
proprioception, 119
    defined, 45
protosemantic, xv, xxiii, 198
    in Levinas, 211
protozaum. See zaum
Psichiatria Democratica, 182
punctuation
    history of, 261n4
    of poems, 262n4
Puttenham, George, *Arte of English Poesie,* 201n4

Quatermain, Peter, 234n1
Queneau, Raymond, 243n4
Quintilian, 109, 113

Rabelais, 163
Radcliffe, Anne, 142
Rajchman, John, 78, 284n2
Raleigh, Sir Walter, 90
Rapaport, Herman, on Milton, 108
Rasula, Jed, 234n1
Ray, Man, "Lautgedicht," 122
Rescher, Nicholas, 40
Reddick, Allen, 76, 98
Retallack, Joan, 289n30
Reutersward, Carl Friedrik, *Prix Nobel,* 271n5
Richardson, Charles, on Johnson's *Dictionary,* 255n18
Richardson, J. and J., 58, 244n1
Ricoeur, Paul, 272n7
Robbins, Jill, 207
    Altered Reading: Levinas and Literature, 286n9
Robinson, Kit, 72

Starnes, de Witt T., and Gertrude E. Noyes, 104
Starobinski, Jean, 138
Steele, Joshua, 51
  Boswell on, 121
  Prosodia Rationalis, 108, 116–22
  notation of *Hamlet* in, 117
  notation of silence in, 118
Stein, Gertrude, 31, 150, 170, 273n6, 283n2
  différance and, 280n42
Stein, Ludwig, *Leibniz und Spinoza,* 238n8
Stengers, Isabelle. *See* Prigogine, Ilya, and Isabelle Stengers
Stevens, Wallace, 124
Stewart, Susan, 78, 129, 133, 271n5
Stramm, August, 163
Sue, Eugène, *Mystères de Paris,* 232n9
Sukenick, Ron, 281n43
Sutherland, W. Mark, "Scratch," 279n34
Swartzkogler, 182
Swedenborg, Emanuel, 285n6
Sweet, Harry, *Primer in Phonetics,* 46–47
Swift, Jonathan, 217
  Battle of the Books, 60
  Gulliver's Travels, 189–90
Swinburne, Algernon Charles, 130
syzygy, xxi, 21, 136
  defined, 17, 29
Szasz, Thomas, 182

Tacitus, 153
Talmud, texts. *See also Torah*
  Aggadah, 228
  Halakhah, 228
Tarn, Nathaniel, 234n1
Taylor, John, *Works,* 247n13
Temple, Sir William, 60
Teresa of Avila, Saint, 237n8, 267n21

Textor, *Latin,* 80
  Thesaurus Poeticus, 80
Thales of Miletus, 139
Thom, René, xxi, 234n3
Thomson, J. Eric, 243n6
Todorov, Vladislav, 139, 242n1
Tommasini, Vittorio Osvaldo (Fafa), 277n26
Torah. See also Talmud
  Critchley on, 291n41
  as face, 229
  as revelation, 228
Toland, John, 140, 156, 237n8
Tomkins, J. M. S., 268n22
Tooke, John Horn, on Johnson's *Dictionary,* 254n18
Tory, Geofroy, *Champ Fleury,* 238n8
Tozzer, Alfred, *Maya Grammar,* 53
transcendental apperception, 155–56
"transcreation," 241n24
"transrational language." *See zaum*
Tzara, Tristan, 163, 167, 182, 217
  "Negerlieder," 273n7
  "Note 6 sur l'art nègre," 273n7
  Poèmes Negres, 167

Ultralettrisme, 171–75, 184, 186. *See also* Lettrisme
  Enlightenment precedents of, 277n23
Upton, Lawrence, 182

Valéry, Paul, 186, 281n43
Van Doesburg, Theo
  "letter sound images," 276n17
  "phono-gymnastics," 171
Vaneigem, Raoul, 174, 186
Van Helmont, Mercurius. *See* Helmont, Mercurius van
Vedic Hymns, 196
ventriloquism, 51
Verne, Jules, 179

Vesalius, Andreas, 179
Viénet, René, 280n40
Vienna Aktion group, 182
Viollet-le-Duc, *Dictionnaire de
l'architecture française*, 4, 231n3
Virgil, 196
voice, 161–85
Voloshinov, V. N., 102, 260n54

Wah, Fred, *Pictograms from the Interior
of B.C,* 241n24
Wallin, J. E. Wallace, 47
Walpole, Horace, 95
Warburton, Wiliam, xii, 16
Watt, Ian, 75
Watten, Barrett, 46
Watts, Isaac, 82
Weaver, Mike, 162, 274n8
Webster, Charles, 262n9
Webster, Noah, 256n32
*Commendious Dictionary of the
English Language,* 253n9
Wendt, Larry, 177, 180–81
*Sound Poems for an Era of Reduced
Expectation,* 279n34
Whiston, William, *Memoirs,* 245n3
Whitehead, Alfred North, 32, 34,
238n10
on monads, 239n14
White, Lynn, 257n38
Whitman, Walt, 31
and *zaum,* 276n16
Williams, William Carlos, 31
Wimsatt, William K., 88
Wittgenstein, Ludwig, 75, 79, 82, 84–
86, 88, 94–95, 102, 152, 204, 213,
254n14

meaning, concept of, 83
meaning, metaphorical, 254n17
names, 96
Philosophical Investigations, 76, 79,
82–88, 90–94, 102–3
pragmatic language, 84
Tractatus Logico Philosophicus, 85,
102, 255n23
Wörterbuch für Volkschulen, 78
Zettel, 79, 254n11
Wolman, Gil J., "mégapneumes," 171,
175
Wooton, William, 60
"word imp," 197
"wordless music." *See* Fogg, Peter
Walkden
"words in freedom," (*parole in libertà*).
See Marinetti, Filippo Tommaso

Yates, Frances, *Art of Memory,* 234n2

zaum, 143, 163, 168–70, 275n11, n12,
n13, 276n16
Courtenay on, 275n13
genealogy of, 169
invention of, 275n11
mysticism and, 169
protozaum, 169
Shklovsky on, 275n13
Zdanevich, Ilia. *See* Iliazd (pseu. of Ilia
Zdhanevich)
Zekowsky, Arlene. *See* Berne, Stanley,
and Arlene Zekowski
Zukofsky, Celia, 281n43
Zukofsky, Louis, 31
Zweig, Ellen, 280n37

Illustration Credits

Page 106. Ezra Pound. From "Canto 89." In *The Cantos(1–95)*. New Directions, 1956.

Page 114. Mercurius van Helmont. *Alphabete vere naturalis hebraici brevissima delineato*. 1667. Reproduced in Johanna Drucker. *The Alphabetic Labyrinth*. London: Thames and Hudson, 1995. Page 197.

Page 117. Joshua Steele. *Prosodia Rationalis*. London, 1775. Page 40.

Page 118. Joshua Steele. *Prosodia Rationalis*. Page 28.

Page 121. Alexander Melville Bell. *Visible Speech*. London: Simpkin, Marshall, 1867.

Page 123. Peter Walkden Fogg. *Elementa Anglicana: or, The Principles of English Grammar*. 2 vols. Stockport, 1792–96.

Page 222. Tom Phillips, *A Humument*. London: Thames and Hudson, 1980.